A Research Agenda for Public Diplomacy

Elgar Research Agendas outline the future of research in a given area. Leading scholars are given the space to explore their subject in provocative ways, and map out the potential directions of travel. They are relevant but also visionary.

Forward-looking and innovative, Elgar Research Agendas are an essential resource for PhD students, scholars and anybody who wants to be at the forefront of research.

For a full list of Edward Elgar published titles, including the titles in this series, visit our website at www.e-elgar.com.

A Research Agenda for Public Diplomacy

Edited by

EYTAN GILBOA

Professor of International Communication, School of Communication, Bar-Ilan University, Israel

Elgar Research Agendas

 Edward **Elgar**
PUBLISHING

Cheltenham, UK • Northampton, MA, USA

Published by
Edward Elgar Publishing Limited
The Lypiatts
15 Lansdown Road
Cheltenham
Glos GL50 2JA
UK

Edward Elgar Publishing, Inc.
William Pratt House
9 Dewey Court
Northampton
Massachusetts 01060
USA

A catalogue record for this book
is available from the British Library

Library of Congress Control Number: 2023935547

This book is available electronically in the **Elgar**online
Political Science and Public Policy subject collection
http://dx.doi.org/10.4337/9781802207323

Printed on elemental chlorine free (ECF)
recycled paper containing 30% Post-Consumer Waste

ISBN 978 1 80220 731 6 (cased)
ISBN 978 1 80220 732 3 (eBook)

Printed and bound in the USA

For Nicholas J. Cull

Contents

Contributors

Editor

Eytan Gilboa (PhD Harvard University) has been Professor of International Communication and founding and first Head of both the School of Communication and the Center for International Communication at Bar-Ilan University. He also teaches public diplomacy at the University of Southern California and was the founding Chair of the Israel Public Diplomacy Forum. He has been a visiting professor in many top universities in the USA and Europe, most recently at the University of Pennsylvania and the Vienna Diplomatic Academy. He has published 15 books including *Media and Conflict* (Brill, 2002); *US–Israel Relations since 9/11* (Routledge, 2009); and *The American Public and Israel in the Twenty First Century* (BESA, 2020). He has published more than 200 scholarly and professional articles in leading journals in communication and international relations. He has won several international awards including the 2001 Best Article Award from the International Communication Association and the 2023 Distinguished Scholar Award in International Communication from the International Studies Association. He has advised several governments and parliaments on public diplomacy and has been a popular op-ed writer and television commentator.

Contributors

Sohaela Amiri is Research Associate at the USC Center on Public Diplomacy (CPD). In this capacity, she works on CPD-initiated research and consulting projects that entail program evaluation, data analysis and program development. She also manages all research-related activities such as the CPD

Research Fellowship and Awards programs. Sohaela is a PhD Candidate at Pardee RAND Graduate School (PRGS) and a PRGS Fellow at the RAND Corporation. Her work tackles the concept and practice of City Diplomacy.

Simon Anholt has advised the Heads of State and Government of over 60 nations to help them improve their economic, political, and cultural engagements with the international community. His work covers economic development, public diplomacy, cultural policy and cultural relations, national identity and reputation, trade promotion, tourism, foreign direct investment, security and defence, immigration and sustainability, talent attraction and major events. Anholt is founder and publisher of the annuals *Anholt-Ipsos Nation Brands Index*, *City Brands Index*, and the *Good Country Index* (GCI). Professor Anholt was Vice-Chair of the UK Foreign Office's Public Diplomacy Board between 2000 and 2009. He was Founding Editor of the journal *Place Branding and Public Diplomacy*. His books include *Brand New Justice* (Macmillan, 2003); *Brand America* (Cyan Books, 2004, 2009); *Competitive Identity* (Palgrave Macmillan, 2007); *Places* (Palgrave Macmillan, 2010), and *The Good Country Equation* (Berrett-Koehler, 2020). Anholt has an MA degree from the University of Oxford and studied international relations and security studies at the Royal College of Defence Studies. He was appointed Honorary Professor in Political Science by the University of East Anglia in 2013.

Phillip Arceneaux (PhD University of Florida) is an Assistant Professor of Strategic Communication at Miami University. He researches political public relations and public diplomacy, with supplemental interests in law and public policy. His work merges a variety of disciplines to develop policy frameworks and solutions to issues posed by modern political and communication practices, ranging from disinformation to computational propaganda and influence operations. His work has been published in journals including *New Media & Society*, the *Journal of Public Diplomacy*, *Journal of Information Warfare*, and *Journal of Public Affairs*. He has also published book chapters, policy papers, and thought leadership pieces. Arceneaux has consulted with a variety of agencies across the US government, including the Department of State, Naval Academy, and Central Intelligence Agency. He has also served as a research consultant for the Carnegie Endowment for International Peace's Partnership for Countering Influence Operations.

Amelia Arsenault (PhD University of Southern California) is Director of the Public Diplomacy Research and Evaluation Unit (REU) in the office of the Under Secrètary for Public Diplomacy and Public Affairs at the US Department of State. She provides guidance and direction for research and evaluation strategy based on rigorous audience research and monitoring for US public diplomacy practitioners. She has an extensive record of academic and professional publications related to public diplomacy, global media ownership, network theory and new media. She was previously an Assistant Professor of Communication at Georgia State University, a non-resident fellow at the USC Center on Public Diplomacy, a resident fellow at the Center for Media, Data, and Society and the Institute for Advanced Studies at Central European University, and the Media and Democracy Research Fellow at the University of Pennsylvania Annenberg School. She holds a BA in Film and History from Dartmouth College, and an MSc in Global Media and Communication from the London School of Economics and Political Science.

Wilfried Bolewski (Dr. jur. Phillips-Universität Marburg) is Professor of International Law and Diplomacy at the Freie Universität Berlin. He has also been teaching at Hertie School of Governance, Berlin, the American University of Paris and Sciences Po Paris. Previously, he was a German Ambassador and Chief of Protocol to Chancellors Schröder and Angela Merkel when they were accompanied on diplomatic visits by global business leaders. As a career diplomat, he practiced bilateral diplomatic, consular, and multilateral missions on all continents, and had access to foreign policy decision-making in formal and informal meetings at the highest level. His recent publications include an article published in the *International Journal of Diplomacy and Economy* and a chapter published in the edited volume *Diplomacy, Organizations and Citizens: A European Communication Perspective* (Springer, 2022). He is also a Diplomatic Commentator at France 24 TV.

Caitlin Byrne (PhD Bond University) is Professor and Pro Vice Chancellor (Business), Griffith University. As Director of the Griffith Asia Institute, she previously led the University's research agenda focused on strategic developments in Asia and the Pacific. A former diplomat, Caitlin is recognized as one of Australia's leading academic practitioners with a special interest in Australian public diplomacy and soft power. Her work is widely published, and she is actively engaged in the delivery of diplomatic training in Australia and the Asia Pacific. Caitlin is a Faculty Fellow of the University of Southern California's Centre on Public Diplomacy (CPD) and Fellow of the Australian Institute for International Affairs (AIIA).

Nicholas J. Cull (PhD University of Leeds) is Professor of Public Diplomacy at the University of Southern California. He is a leading historian of the role of communication in foreign policy. His books include two volumes on the history of US public diplomacy and a volume on British propaganda in the Second World War. His conceptual introductory text: *Public Diplomacy: Foundations for Global Engagement in the Digital Age* (Polity, 2019) has become a standard point of entry into the field and has been published in Italian and is forthcoming in Spanish and Mandarin. He is co-editor of the second edition of the *Routledge Handbook of Public Diplomacy* (Routledge, 2020) and co-editor of *Canadian Public Diplomacy* (Palgrave Macmillan, 2021). He has worked closely with foreign ministries and diplomatic academies around the world including those of the USA, UK, Canada, South Korea, and Switzerland. He is the recipient of the 2023 Distinguished Scholar Award from the Diplomatic Studies Division of the International Studies Association.

Kathy R. Fitzpatrick (JD Southern Methodist University) is Professor and Director of the Zimmerman School of Advertising & Mass Communications at the University of South Florida (USF). She is a faculty fellow in the Center on Public Diplomacy at the University of Southern California. Prior to joining USF, she served as professor and senior associate dean in the School of Communication at American University. Fitzpatrick is the co-founder and senior editor of the Palgrave Macmillan Book Series on Global Public Diplomacy. She is the author of *The Future of US Public Diplomacy: An Uncertain Fate* (Brill Nijhoff, 2009); and co-editor of *Ethics in Public Relations: Responsible Advocacy* (Sage, 2006). Fitzpatrick received the 2021 Distinguished Scholar Award from the International Studies Association Diplomatic Studies Division and the 2020 AEJMC Research Prize for Professional Relevance from the Association for Education in Journalism and Mass Communication.

Alicia Fjällhed is a PhD candidate at the Department of Strategic Communication, Lund University. Her research focuses on communication ethics, disinformation, fake news, information influence, hybrid warfare, misinformation, foreign election interference, and psychological operations. She has an MA in Public Sector Communication from University of Gothenburg, a BS in Strategic Communication from Lund University and 10 years of experience working with PR, marketing, internal communication, crisis and political communication, place branding, and visual communication in public, private, and non-profit organizations. She is also a part of a team producing reports and handbooks, offering training and scenario exercises, as well as process and policy support for governments and international organizations to help strengthen society's resilience against disinformation. She has published works on disinformation and election interference in general and more specifically its relation to public diplomacy.

Natalia Grincheva (PhD Concordia University) is a Program Leader in Arts Management at LASALLE College of the Arts and an Honorary Research Fellow in the Digital Studio at the University of Melbourne. She is an expert in innovative forms and global trends in contemporary museology, digital diplomacy, and international cultural relations. She has received many prestigious international academic awards, including Fulbright (2007–09), Quebec Fund (2011–13), Australian Endeavour (2012–13) and SOROS research grant

(2013–14). In 2020, she was a visiting researcher at the Digital Diplomacy Research Center at the University of Oxford. Her most recent publications are *Museum Diplomacy in the Digital Age* (Routledge, 2020) and *Global Trends in Museum Diplomacy* (Routledge, 2019). Grincheva's professional engagements include dedicated work for the International Fund for Cultural Diversity at UNESCO (2011) and International Federation of Coalitions for Cultural Diversity (2011–15), as well as service for the international Cultural Research Network (CRN) (2018–20).

Craig Hayden (PhD University of Southern California) is Associate Professor of Strategic Studies at the Marine Corps University Command and Staff College. From 2015 to 2018, he served as Coordinator and Chair for the Diplomatic Mastery Program at the Department of State, Foreign Service Institute. Hayden also taught courses in international communication and international relations theory at the American University School of International Service. He has been a Research Fellow at the USC Center on Public Diplomacy and a member of the Public Diplomacy Council. He has served as the Division Chair for the International Communication section of the International Studies Association. He is the author of *The Rhetoric of Soft Power: Public Diplomacy in Global Contexts* (Lexington, 2011) and co-editor of the *Routledge Handbook of Soft Power* (Routledge, 2016). He has published articles in journals such as the *International Journal of Communication* and in edited volumes such as the *Handbook of Communication and Security* (Routledge, 2019).

Paul Lachelier (PhD University of Wisconsin-Madison) is a Political Sociologist, and Founder and Director of Learning Life, a non-profit lab devoted to innovating education and citizen engagement. He leads three programs – the Family Diplomacy Initiative, an International Mentoring Program, and Democracy Dinners – all designed to develop innovative learning communities that nurture more caring, capable and connected global citizens. In 2020, Paul initiated the Public Diplomacy Council's Citizen Diplomacy Research Group (CDRG), which gathers citizen diplomacy scholars, students, and practitioners worldwide to better understand and nurture the world's expanding citizen diplomacy sector. He taught at Stetson, Harvard, Tufts and the University of Wisconsin. His writing, research and programmatic work focus on the intersection of democracy, culture, and education. His recent writings on family diplomacy, the ethics of diplomacy, and democratizing diplomacy, have appeared in academic and professional journals as well as in popular media.

Ilan Manor (PhD University of Oxford) is a Senior Lecturer in Communication at Ben Gurion University in Israel and a member of Oxford University's Digital

Diplomacy Research Group. Manor is also a Visiting Fellow at the University of Southern California's Center on Public Diplomacy. His research focuses on the use of digital technologies during times of crises as well as their impact on the norms, values and working routines of diplomats. He is the author of *The Digitalization of Public Diplomacy* (Palgrave Macmillan, 2019) and co-editor of *Public Diplomacy and the Politics of Uncertainty* (Palgrave Macmillan, 2020). Manor has contributed to numerous publications including *Review of International Studies, Cambridge Review of International Affairs, Media, War & Conflict, Place Branding and Public Diplomacy, Global Policy* and *The Hague Journal of Diplomacy.*

Sherry Lee Mueller (PhD Tufts University) is Distinguished Practitioner in Residence at the School of International Service (SIS), American University, Washington, D.C. She served as President of Global Ties US from 1996 to 2011. Prior, she worked 18 years for the Institute of International Education (IIE) including as Director, Professional Exchange Programs. Sherry has served as President of the Public Diplomacy Council since 2019. She served on the founding Board of the Center for Citizen Diplomacy that merged with PYXERA Global in 2013. Sherry received an IIE Centennial Medal in 2019. In 2011, "One To World" presented her with the *Fulbright Award for Citizen Diplomacy* for "lifelong contributions to global understanding and cooperation, one handshake at a time, in the Fulbright tradition." She is co-author *of Working World: Careers in International Education, Exchange, and Development* (Georgetown University Press, 2014). She has also published works on citizen diplomacy in the *Foreign Service Journal* and the *Routledge Handbook of Public Diplomacy* (Routledge, 2020).

James Pamment (PhD Stockholm University) is Associate Professor of Strategic Communication and Director of the Lund University Psychological Defence Research Institute. He is also Editor-in-Chief of the journal *Place Branding and Public Diplomacy.* His main research interest is in the role of strategic communication in countering hostile foreign interference, such as information influence operations and hybrid threats. Publications include British Public Diplomacy & Soft Power: Diplomatic Influence & Digital Disruption (Palgrave, 2016), and New Public Diplomacy in the 21st Century (Routledge, 2013). The most recent edited book is Countering Online Propaganda and Violent Extremism (with Corneliu Bjola, Routledge, 2019). Previous affiliations include the Carnegie Endowment for International Peace, the Centre for Asymmetric Threats Studies at the Swedish Defence University, University of Texas at Austin, and the University of Oxford.

Steven L. Pike teaches Public Relations and Public Diplomacy at the Newhouse School at Syracuse University. He published a chapter in *Public Diplomacy in*

Times of Uncertainty (Palgrave Macmillan, 2020) and articles in *Place Branding and Public Diplomacy*. His current project is a textbook tentatively titled *Public Relations Case Studies and Critiques: An Ethical and Methodological Approach*. Prior to joining the Newhouse School, he spent 23 years with the US Department of State as a diplomat and foreign service officer. He served as director of policy for the Bureau of Educational and Cultural Affairs; public affairs counselor at the US Embassy in the United Arab Emirates; and spokesman and media director of the US Mission to Canada. He also served as a State Department Pearson Legislative Fellow in the office of Senator Joseph I. Lieberman. He holds a BA in Politics from Wesleyan University, an MS in Foreign Service from Georgetown University and an MA in National Security and Strategic Studies from the US Naval War College.

Shawn Powers (PhD University of Southern California) is the Chief Strategy Officer, U.S. Agency for Global Media. He leads its interagency engagement, strategic planning, strategic initiatives, and partnerships with key international stakeholders. He oversees the Agency's Office of Policy and Research (OPR), Office of Policy (VOA), and its Internet Freedom and circumvention programs, and has more than a decade of experience working at the nexus of public diplomacy, technology, and national security. Powers researches the geopolitics of information and technology and published the award-winning *The Real Cyber War: A Political Economy of Internet Freedom* (The University of Illinois Press, 2015). He has over 40 publications in academic and mainstream outlets. Previously Powers served as Executive Director of the United States Advisory Commission on Public Diplomacy. Before that, he was an Associate Professor at Georgia State University, where he launched and directed its Center for Global Information Studies.

Giles Scott-Smith (PhD Lancaster University) is Professor of Transnational Relations and New Diplomatic History at Leiden University, and Dean of Leiden University College. He is one of the organizers of the New Diplomatic History network and an editor of the network's publication *Diplomatica: A Journal of Diplomacy and Society* (Brill). He is co-editor for the Key Studies in Diplomacy book series with Manchester University Press and on the editorial board of *New Global Studies*. His research interests broadly cover the role of nonstate actors and public diplomacy in the maintenance of inter-state (particularly transatlantic) relations. Recent publications include *The Transatlantic Era in Documents and Speeches (1989–2020)* together with Bram Boxhoorn (Routledge, 2021) and "Some Notes on Mobility," *Diplomatic History*, 45, (2021), 604–10.

Efe Sevin (PhD American University) is an Assistant Professor of Public Relations at the Department of Mass Communication at Towson University.

His current research focuses on identifying and measuring the impacts of social networks on place branding and public diplomacy campaigns. Prior to joining Towson University, he worked at Reinhardt University (Georgia, USA), University of Fribourg (Switzerland), and Kadir Has University (Turkey). His works have been published in several academic journals and books including *American Behavioral Scientist, Public Relations Review* and *Cities*. His most recent co-edited volume is *City Diplomacy Current Trends and Future Prospects* (Palgrave MacMillan, 2020).

Jack Lipei Tang is a PhD candidate at the Annenberg School for Communication and Journalism at the University of Southern California. His research interests include digital activism, social networks, and computational social science. His work has been published in academic journals, including *International Journal of Communication, The Network Society,* and *Journal of Broadcasting & Electronic Media.*

Jian Wang (PhD University of Iowa) is an Associate Professor at the University of Southern California's Annenberg School for Communication and Journalism and Director of the USC Center on Public Diplomacy. He has published widely on the role of communication in the contemporary process of globalization. He is the author of Shaping China's Global Imagination: Nation Branding at the World Expo (Palgrave Macmillan, 2013); and co-editor of Debating Public Diplomacy: Now and Next (Brill, 2019). His research has been published in *Journal of Communication, Journal of Broadcasting & Electronic Media, Management, Communication Quarterly, Public Relations Review and Place Branding & Public Diplomacy.* He serves on the editorial board of the *International Journal of Communication.* His contributions to policy reports include "U.S. Public Diplomacy and National Security" (a CSIS–CPD report) and "Data-driven Public Diplomacy" (US Advisory Commission on Public Diplomacy). He previously worked for the international consulting firm McKinsey & Company.

Candace L. White (PhD University of Georgia) is a Professor Emerita in the Tombras School of Advertising and Public Relations, and a Global Security Emeritus Fellow of the Howard H. Baker, Jr. Center for Public Policy at the University of Tennessee. Her research interests include the role of global corporations as nonstate actors in public diplomacy, and how corporate social responsibility (CSR) and CSR communication affects the image and national reputation of the country with which a corporation is associated. She co-edited *Bridging Disciplinary Perspectives of Country Image, Reputation and Identity* (Routledge, 2018), and has numerous publications in the areas of public diplomacy, corporate social responsibility, and intercultural communication in journals that include *Place Branding and Public Diplomacy, International*

Journal of Strategic Communications, Corporate Social Responsibility and Environmental Management, Journal of Communication Management, and *Public Relations Review*. She is active in the Public Diplomacy Interest Group of the International Communication Association and on the advisory board of the Cultural and Public Diplomacy master's program at Università degli Studi di Siena, Italy. In 2010 she was a Fulbright Senior Specialist at the University of Salzburg, Austria.

R.S. Zaharna (EdD Columbia University) is a Professor of Communication at American University in Washington, D.C. and Faculty Fellow with the Center on Public Diplomacy at the University of Southern California. She received the 2018 Distinguished Scholar Award in International Communication by the International Studies Association. She is the author of *Battles to Bridges: US Strategic Communication and Public Diplomacy after 9/11* (Palgrave Macmillan, 2010, 2014); *The Cultural Awakening in Public Diplomacy* (Figueroa Press, 2012); and *Boundary Spanners of Humanity: Three Logics of Human Communication and Public Diplomacy for Global Collaboration* (Oxford University Press, 2021). She is also co-editor of *The Connective Mindshift: Relational, Networked and Collaborative Approaches to Public Diplomacy* (Routledge, 2013). She has testified before the US Congress on several occasions and has addressed diplomatic and academic forums on public diplomacy, including the Otago Foreign Policy School, Confucius Institute Global Conference, Royal United Services Institute for Defense and Security Studies (RUSI) and DERSAT (Bahrain), International Islamic University of Malaysia, and NATO Defense College.

Preface

Research, teaching, and practice in public diplomacy (PD) have significantly increased since the early 2000s and this is the right time to evaluate the progress the field has been making, which topics have been adequately researched, what are the main gaps and challenges, and what would be the best and the most promising ways to close them. This volume provides a research agenda for PD in the next decade and will help PD scholars, students, and practitioners to find a common language, comprehend the broad boundaries of the field, share ideas, and establish research priorities for the various subfields.

The volume includes 18 chapters, an introductory general survey of the entire field, and the rest equally divided among three categories: actors, disciplines, and instruments. The idea is to address actors that usually have been neglected or insufficiently researched, mostly nonstate actors. The first chapter explores research on PD contests among major powers in Asia: China, Japan, and Australia. The other chapters in Part I analyze nonstate actors: international organizations, corporations, cities, and citizens.

PD is a highly multidisciplinary field and therefore Part II suggests a research agenda for PD within disciplines including history, international relations, public relations, relational and collaborative approaches, disinformation, and management. Part III focuses on PD instruments including culture, branding, international broadcasting, international exchanges, digital diplomacy, and hybrid communication. Each chapter follows a similar structure: a survey of existing research, major deficiencies, challenges and gaps, and the most promising ways and methods to overcome them.

The authors are veteran and well-known scholars who have accumulated an impressive record of research and publications in PD as well as highly talented young researchers, who have already made significant contributions to the field, expanded its foundations and boundaries, and added scientific depth to analysis and interpretations of existing and new findings. They come from different countries and cultures around the world with diverse academic or practical training and experiences. Most contributors are scholars teaching PD and doing research at universities and research centers, but a few have been outstanding practitioners. They all share passion for building the field and make it more scientific, coherent, comprehensive, and useful for leaders and officials.

Structure

In Chapter 1, Gilboa discusses the current state of knowledge and research in PD and identifies needed changes, modifications, and adjustments for systematic expansion and development in the next decade. The chapter presents and applies to PD, criteria for defining a field of scholarship and practice. It critically analyzes definitions of PD, meta-analysis of research output, the road to scholarly independence, boundaries, methodologies, evaluation, and PD's potential contributions to combat global crises. Gilboa argues that much progress has been made but there is still a long way to go in building PD as an independent field of science.

Part I of the book explores actors: states, international organizations, corporations, cities, and citizens. Byrne contributes the first chapter in this part and explains the role of PD in contests for power and influence in Asia. She explores the challenges China presents and the responses of regional middle powers including Japan and Australia. Byrne argues that within the contests, the powers use competing platforms for a regional order. Against the backdrop of a transforming Asia, the chapter explores shifts in PD practice and scholarship through the lens of "strategic narrative," illuminating potential avenues for future research along the way.

States and nonstate actors use PD campaigns to influence the behavior and decisions of international organizations but also employ international organizations to achieve PD goals. International organizations also use PD to achieve their goals. In Chapter 3, Arceneaux analyzes uses of PD at organs of the UN including competitions for membership at the Security Council and the General Assembly. He also uncovers uses of PD by international organizations and provides examples from the International Court of Arbitration, the EU, the African Union's "African Renaissance" and cultural diplomacy of the Association of Southeast Asian Nations. The chapter also highlights the use of debt-trap diplomacy by the International Monetary Fund and the World Bank.

Governments use global corporations to achieve PD goals, but corporations use PD to achieve their own commercial goals. In Chapter 4, White and Bolewski identify key issues in research of corporate diplomacy including coordination between business and governments. They explain the differences in coordination among countries based on infrastructural variables including political, economic, and sociocultural structures. They suggest differentiating diplomatic activities benefiting only the corporation from benefits to broader social issues; using case studies on diplomatic outcomes rather than on analytical lines between governments and nonstate actors, generating empirical data from different regions to examine stakeholder expectations of corporate diplomatic activities, and examination of corporate involvement in sub-areas of PD such as "city diplomacy" and "cultural diplomacy."

Cities, not only the rich in affluent countries, conduct PD to attract tourists, investments, attractions, and international events of all kinds. In Chapter 5, Sevin and Amiri explain that city diplomacy at its core is about global engagement, people-to-people connections, international relationship building, and representations of policies, identities, and competence. They reveal important gaps in understanding of city diplomacy, including scholar–practitioner gap, local–national gap, and agent–agency gap. They suggest possible research questions for future research with an emphasis on interdisciplinary approaches, innovation, and system analysis.

Individuals also conduct PD. The digital revolution enables ordinary citizens to produce videos and pictures and organize networks of publics around the world around a cause. In the last chapter on actors, Lachelier and Mueller, two leading practitioners of citizen diplomacy, argue that this type of diplomacy is growing due to increasing education levels, internet access coupled with global problems that have spurred more connections and collaborations among ordinary citizens in different countries. Tracking this growing citizen diplomacy sector is vital to understanding the cutting edges of globalization, democracy, civil society, and global citizenship. Lachelier and Mueller first offer a conceptual framework for studying citizen diplomacy, defining it in relation to PD and identifying key categories of citizen diplomacy activity.

Part II of the volume explores the research agenda for PD within disciplines including history, international relations, public relations, relational and collaborative approaches, disinformation, and management. In the first chapter of this part, Cull, a noted historian of PD, looks at the value to the field of the systematic study of the past by historians. The chapter begins with an overview of how the historical study of PD has worked in the past, paying attention to its strong links to the state and its declassification processes. It continues with an exploration of key topics suggested by the path of scholarship and development of events including national and regional diversity, exploring the domestic dimension of PD, previous transitions to new technology, media literacy and peace building, study of nonstate actors and multi-stakeholder partnerships.

The "soft power" theory has provided the first intellectual foundation for the contemporary study and practice of PD. The theory is anchored in the study of power and influence in international relations. In Chapter 8, Craig Hayden critically examines the concept, exposes its weaknesses and proposes more useful ways to research its contributions to PD. The chapter begins with the attempt to understand the decline in American soft power and argues that it provides an opportunity to reconsider the theoretical assumptions and methods used to assess the role of soft power in foreign affairs. It argues that if soft power is largely contingent on the characteristics of the *relation* between the agent and the subject or target of soft power activity, then the conceptual framework should accommodate the diverse routes to influence, which can be advanced through outcomes-oriented study of PD programs and campaigns. Hayden also explores the growth of relationalism in soft power studies and dwells on linkages between soft power, reputation, and credibility.

Much has been written about the conceptual and practical connections between public relations and PD. In Chapter 9, Fitzpatrick, a well-known expert in public relations, explores opportunities for cross-fertilization between the two academic disciplines and professional fields by examining the applicability and potential value of public relations concepts and theories in under-researched areas in PD. The chapter discusses aspects of theory building related to relationships, power, publics, and ethics. It considers the developing domain of strategic communication and its possible impact on PD's development as a multidisciplinary enterprise. Fitzpatrick suggests new ways of thinking about and studying PD via insights from public relations that can help move PD forward.

Chapter 10 explores relational and collaborative approaches to PD. Zaharna and Arsenault explain that these approaches have meant promoting dialogue, forming partnerships, or building networks. The chapter expands the vision of PD relational approaches by introducing two distinct relational lenses: The "lens of separateness" assumes that PD actors are separate entities and work independently of other actors and publics. The chapter discusses illustrative examples of how individual PD actors try to create, manage, or strengthen relations with separate target publics. A second, emerging "lens of connectivity" assumes that PD actors are inherently connected directly or indirectly to other actors and publics. Relational PD initiatives viewed through the lens of connectivity are exposing new, unexplored relational functions of PD that focus on how PD actors and publics seek to mediate identities, respond to public emotions, or engage in problem-solving.

Chapter 11 discusses one of the greatest challenges of our time to society: fake news and disinformation. In the next decade, fighting disinformation may become a significant subfield of PD. Fjällhed and Pamment argue that disinformation comes with a set of opportunities for PD that open new perspectives to unresolved theoretical discussions, while at the same time challenging PD researchers to develop a strategic research agenda that accommodates for the volatile nature of the empirical phenomena. They tell PD scholars to begin from the transdisciplinary frontier of disinformation research spanning from philosophy to psychology and sociology. A new research agenda could be advanced by translating these insights into pre-existing PD frameworks and through continuous engagement with PD professionals.

The last chapter in Part II, Chapter 12, focuses on a highly neglected area in PD research: the management of PD as a profession. Pike, a former senior state department official turned scholar, asserts that policy implementation by various actors – e.g., foreign ministries or international organizations – requires an operationalization of theory, a professional sociology, and institutional mechanisms for strategic planning and resource management. Little formal research has been conducted on the institutional management of PD activities. This chapter adopts a widely accepted taxonomy within the management field (planning, decision-making, organizing, leading, controlling, and the strategic management process), and identifies potential units of analysis and initial questions that research into this area could profitably and productively address.

Part III of the book explores several classic and new instruments of PD including culture, branding, international broadcasting, international exchanges, digital diplomacy, and hybrid communication. The first chapter in this part examines cultural diplomacy, one of the classic and the most frequently used instrument of PD. Grincheva explains that cultural diplomacy is a dynamic practice that brings together artists, policymakers, governments, and civil society. The chapter conceptualizes transformations caused by the emergence of new technologies, artistic expressions, cultural trends, and arts practices. It demonstrates that while cultural diplomacy is dynamically changing to cope with the pace of all these new developments, there is a growing need to explore more closely new hybrid models and digitally mediated environments of international cultural communications which increasingly engage non-human actors.

Simon Anholt transferred the idea of branding to places: states, regions, and cities. He established the journal *Place Branding and Public Diplomacy* and has consulted many governments and organizations. His chapter contributes to clarify the "nation brand" concept. He argues that the field suffers from confusion over terminology, the absence of an underlying theory and a provable model of success, supported by properly measured case studies; the undemocratic approaches to the exercise on the part of many governments; the fact that practitioners and governments seldom bother to set targets, let alone report on whether they have been met. He further argues that countries simply are not in control of their images; yet the widespread assumption that the right kinds of communications and budgets will change public perceptions of countries is seldom challenged. However, the "Good Country" theory (that national image is strongly correlated with world-friendly, collaborative national behavior), leads to a set of principles which he refers to as "Place Branding 2.0."

Chapter 15 explores international broadcasting defined as state-sponsored or funded media aimed at foreign publics. Powers, a scholar turned policymaker, observers that scholarship on this topic lacks theoretical frameworks, particularly in light of structural changes in international communication, technological diffusion, and media complexity. He applies the two-level game metaphor of international bargaining to analyze state informational activities in a more complex media age. Using case studies, this chapter identifies the different stakeholders involved in sending and receiving information via international broadcasting. Broadcasting in the information age is better analogized as bargaining between domestic policymakers, mobilized issue publics, foreign governments, and target opinion leaders and groups in receiving states.

International exchanges – the organized cross-border movement of individuals or groups for the purposes of educational or professional training, teaching, research, or "cultural awareness" – have been a feature of international relations for well over a century. In Chapter 16, Giles Scott-Smith explains that social scientists have developed tools for assessing their effectiveness in changing attitudes and opinions, but gaps remain, due to a combination of limitations in measuring effectiveness and an ongoing reluctance to grant exchanges a too prominent role in social relations. Even in PD research there has been a tendency to shy away from studies of exchanges, due often to the requirements of a credible methodology. This leads to ongoing uncertainties as to what exchanges have achieved, and how one can argue for their continuing importance in an era of collapsed distance through digitalization. The chapter puts forward future avenues of enquiry that can further assist with integrating the role of exchanges in our understanding of international relations in general.

Since the early 2010s, digital PD has become a popular PD instrument. In Chapter 17, Manor defines it as the impact of digital technologies on the norms, values, and working procedures of diplomats. He points out three important gaps in current research. Scholars' emphasis on social media sites even though diplomats employ a host of other technologies in PD activities including WhatsApp groups, network analysis, big data analysis, and algorithms. Second, scholars must examine the growing use of digital technologies in diaspora outreach thus diversifying the research corpus that has examined Western PD. Finally, scholars have failed to examine whether social media sites, which are rich in cognitive and emotional stimuli, lead to priming effects which impact users' interpretation of diplomatic messaging. The chapter offers a comprehensive summary of existing research while articulating a new research agenda that may guide scholars.

In the last chapter of the book, Wang and Tang look at the future of PD via the lens of "hybrid communication." They argue that in a hybrid future, the various tools and platforms of PD will need to be overhauled to incorporate both live and digital elements in new and adaptive ways. This chapter seeks to explore the conceptual foundations for hybrid communication in the practice of PD. It examines the concept of hybridity in a range of disciplines and discusses their relevance and implications for the study and design of hybrid communication in terms of combining in-person and virtual communication in PD. The chapter captures the analytical threads in the studies of hybridity, examines the fundamental shifts in PD, and puts forth key issues and challenges in understanding hybridity in PD in its conceptual grounding as well as from an empirical standpoint.

Acknowledgments

I would like to thank all the contributors to the volume for taking the time to think and write about the highly needed new research agenda for PD in the next decade. Most of them have been colleagues but also friends who all share a passion for the advancement of both scholarship and practice in the field. I thank Bar-Ilan University, especially President Moshe Kaveh and several Rectors, for supporting the Center for International Communication which I established and directed for 15 years. I also thank the founder of the Center on Public Diplomacy (CPD) at the University of Southern California (USC), Geoffrey Cowan, and all the Center's directors for inviting me to teach and work at the Center since 2005. I thank many of my students at Bar-Ilan, USC and other universities in the USA and Europe for helping me to develop my ideas and thoughts about PD. I owe special thanks to my colleague and friend Nicholas J. Cull with whom I established the Summer Institute in Public Diplomacy at CPD. We have exchanged many thoughts about the history and theory of PD which can be seen across this volume. I dedicated this book to him. Finally, I thank the outstanding staff at Edward Elgar Publishing for producing this volume: Harry Fabian, Holly Doogood, Hannah Ross and Brian North.

Eytan Gilboa

1 Moving to a new phase in public diplomacy research

Eytan Gilboa

Introduction

Public diplomacy (PD) is a very young and developing field of study and practice and naturally struggles with critical questions of boundaries, theory, models, methodology, and practice. Many studies, primarily the epistemological ones, often begin with questions about the legitimacy of PD as an independent field of science. Several scholars have claimed that it may not be at all an independent field but rather a subfield of international relations or public relations (PR). Others, who believe it may be a field, argue that PD is still a fuzzy concept and lacks theoretical and methodological depth. The "legitimacy question" has been especially challenging to PD researchers because PD is the most multidisciplinary field in the social sciences, cutting across many disciplines in the humanities, social sciences, technology, and exact sciences. It is also playing run and catch with the rapidly developing and constantly changing landscapes of international relations, and the dramatic digital revolutions in communication.

PD became a substantial area during the Cold War, dominated by the delicate balance of nuclear weapons, and the global ideological battle for the hearts and minds of peoples around the world. It became again a critical element of foreign policy and national security, following the 9/11 terror attacks of al-Qaida on New York and Washington, D.C. and the emergence and domination of digital media. A new scholarly field is established when several conditions are met. It must be clearly distinguished from other scholarly fields; delineates several subfields, shares theories, models, and methodologies, has its own periodicals and sections or divisions in international scholarly association, establishes academic teaching programs and research centers and must win both internal and external recognition.

Fifteen years ago, I wrote an article about the state of art in PD research (Gilboa, 2008). I presented and critically evaluated attempts to theorize and

1

conceptualize PD. I also examined research methods used to investigate PD including models, case studies and comparative analysis. Although, the field has not yet developed a core theory or a major analytical model, much progress has been made in meeting all the other criteria of establishing a new scientific field. The progress can be best seen in several studies that examine patterns of research overtime in PD, in debates about the boundaries of the field, and in new frameworks for analysis and methodologies.

Due to space limitations, this chapter can only focus on selected major topics and issues and provide examples and illustrations that usually do not receive sufficient attention in existing research. If at all, it may only briefly touch upon topics that will be discussed in more detail in the following chapters. This chapter will explore definitions of PD, meta-analysis of research output, moving to scholarly independence, boundaries, models, case studies and comparative analysis, evaluation, and PD's potential contributions to combat global crises.

Definitions

The effort to find some order, direction, and research agenda in PD has been very frustrating because it has been marred by confusing terms, definitions, methodologies, and research questions. This is not unusual for a new multidisciplinary scientific field that must integrate theories, models, and ideas from several disciplines. But in PD this conceptual chaos seems to have been more severe and challenging then in the development of other disciplines or subdisciplines in the social sciences. Still, a definition of the core concept acceptable to most scholars in any scientific field is needed to advance both research and practice.

A few scholars of PD have been suggesting that PD is still a fussy concept that many actors use in very different ways for very different purposes and tasks. Almost every study of PD begins with a different definition of the phenomenon. It seems that 30 years ago, Signitzer and Coombs (1992), PR experts, probably offered the first modern definition of PD: it is "the way in which both government and private individuals and groups influence directly or indirectly those public attitudes and opinions which bear directly on another government's foreign policy decisions" (p. 138). This definition was innovative and important because it recognized actors other than states and more accurately described what they did. Fitzpatrick, Fullerton, and Kendrick (2013) also explored conceptual connections between PR and PD.

Several definitions have long been trying to encapsulate in one sentence all the main characteristics of PD. Sharp (2005) defined PD as "the process by which direct relations with people in a country are pursued to advance the interests and extend the values of those being represented" (p. 106). The next definition is often cited: PD "is used by states, associations of states, and nonstate actors to understand cultures, attitudes, and behavior; build and manage relationships; and influence opinions and actions to advance interests and values" (Gregory, 2008, p. 274). Cull (2019, p. 3) proposed a much shorter definition: PD "is one of the ways in which an international actor seeks to manage the international environment." Gregory's definition may be too long and Cull's wording too short. It seems that most PD scholars agree at least on the main characteristics of PD: actors, goals, and process. Gilboa (2016, p. 1297) attempted to propose such a formulation: "PD is a communication process states, nonstate actors, and organizations employ to influence the policies of a foreign government by influencing its citizens."

This formulation suggests a two-step influence process: first, an actor employs direct or indirect communication to create supportive public opinion in another state; and second, the informed foreign public influences its government to adopt a friendly policy towards that actor. PD is designed to bring about understanding for an actor's ideas and ideals, its institutions and culture, as well as its national goals and policies. In conflicts, PD is used to defend an actor's policies and attack those of the enemy or the other side (Wiseman, 2019). In other situations, the goal is to conduct a constructive dialogue, to build relationships, to understand the needs of the other side, to correct misperceptions and to jointly work for common causes. PD requires a capability to effectively use credible information to persuade different types of actors and audiences to understand, accept, and support policies and actions.

There is still much confusion in the literature about types of power and the relationship between PD and soft power. Wei (2020) suggested that the most important function of PD is to "transform a country's general assets into soft power resources." A different formulation would argue the opposite. Soft power provides resources that PD practitioners could use to achieve goals of foreign policy and national security. Power is the ability to influence others to obtain the outcomes one prefers (Nye, 2008, 2019). Today, there are five types of power in international relations: hard, soft, smart, collaborative, and sharp.

"Hard power" means obtaining outcomes by using or threatening to use force or sanctions or inducing compliance with rewards; "soft power" means obtaining outcomes by attracting and persuading peoples through values, policies, institutions, and culture; "smart power" refers to the combination of hard and soft power, where each reinforces the other; "collaborative power" denotes a bottom-up process of obtaining preferred outcomes by mobilizing and connecting global communities around a cause via digital media; and "sharp power" means utilization of distraction, "fake identity," "false information," and manipulation. It is the abuse of soft power through initiatives often pursued by authoritarian regimes such as Russia, China, North Korea, and Iran (Walker, 2018).

Cull (2019a) argued that soft power was useful for the study of powerful states but less relevant to vulnerable states and contemporary global crises. He suggested to reframe soft power as a new category of "reputational security" (RS). It refers to the ability of states to achieve legitimacy to their sovereignty over territory in international public perception. He thought that Ukraine lacked RS when in 2014 it lost Crimea with little resistance from the international community. RS demonstrates the difficulty of differentiating among goals, conditions, resources, and techniques in PD. The goal is to deter aggression against weak states or receive support when deterrence fails; RS is a strategic condition; soft power represents resources needed to achieve this condition; and there are specific soft power techniques states can use to acquire RS.

While soft power is relevant to states and nonstate actors, RS applies exclusively to states. It is also limited to rare threats against the territorial integrity of states. RS cannot replace soft power, but it has the potential to expand the applicability of soft power to conflicts and war. To a certain extent, smart power does this function. In 2022, Ukraine had gained RS. It didn't deter Vladimir Putin but was sufficient to trigger massive military and diplomatic aid. The war in Ukraine and violence in other parts of the world, showed that contrary to predictions made after the end of the Cold War, hard power and protracted full-scale wars have not become obsolete. PD scholars may have to think about ways to expand and better integrate concepts of power and RS.

Much of the PD research during the Cold War focused on the information battle between the United States (US) and the Soviet Union. The end of this war and the emergence of the "soft power" concept led scholars to focus on the role of PD in time of peace. In the world of practice, the US, the remaining sole superpower, dismantled the United States Information Agency (USIA) believing it had no role to play in the post-Cold War era (Cull, 2012). Due to the 9/11 terror attacks in New York and Washington, D.C. scholars returned to the use of PD in conflict situations. The Covid-19 pandemic and the war in Ukraine have also increased research on this type of PD. Still, much more attention to PD in conflict situations and global crises will have to increase in the next phase of research in PD.

The two main parent disciplines of PD are communication (public) and international relations (diplomacy). Both consider PD as a subfield of their respective disciplines. Sevin, Metzgar, and Hayden (2019, p. 4821) found that 15 of the 30 journals that since 1965 published the most work about PD, 11 percent of the articles they analyzed (n=234), were in international relations. Communication was ranked second with five journals accounting for 5.5 percent of the articles analyzed (n=124). Yet, Gilboa (2008, p. 74) identified no less than 13 disciplines or subdisciplines contributing knowledge to PD.

Meta-analysis

One sign of progress, reflection, and evaluation is the emergence of several meta-analysis studies of research and publications in PD overtime. For this important contribution, however, scholars defined somewhat different research purposes and employed different time frames, methodologies, and analytical categories. Still these studies have helped to develop better understanding of boundaries, major trends, and core issues.

Vanc and Fitzpatrick (2016) produced one of the first quantitative surveys of research in PD. It was limited, however, to the period between 1990 and 2014 and only to works published by PR scholars. During that period, they identified 120 works: journal articles (n=102, 85 percent), books (n=4, 3 percent), book chapters (n=12, 10 percent), and monographs (n=2, 2 percent). After 2003, they found a marked increase in interest in PD research among PR scholars (n=116, 97 percent), compared with only 4 works published during 1990–97 (n=4, 3 percent), and no works during 1998–2002. They analyzed the data by journals, authorship, topics, methodologies, and contributions to PD theory.

Sevin, Metzgar, and Hayden (2019) expanded the time frame (1965–2017), the relevant disciplines (social sciences), and the outlets (all journals). They assembled peer-reviewed articles published in English from various datasets and identified a total of 2,124 PD-focused articles. They analyzed the data by volume, journals, disciplines, topics, states, regions, and key words in topics. In terms of volume, they found that from 1965 to 2001, the annual overall output was in single digits and accounted for less than 4 percent (75 articles) of the entire dataset. But from 2001 to 2017, the number of articles published each year rose dramatically, and from 2008 to 2017 reached over 100 articles annually. In 2017, the number of published articles was more than seven times higher than the number in 2001. Ayhan (2019) adopted a narrower goal. He wanted to create a taxonomy of PD perspectives and for that purpose identified and analyzed 160 articles published between 1985 and 2017 with the term PD in their title. He identified five main perspectives divided mainly between state and nonstate actors (they will be discussed below).

To identify methodologies PD researchers have been using, Hasnat and Leshner (2022) reviewed 58 articles published in eight issues (2019–20) of the *Place Branding and Public Diplomacy*. They reviewed 58 articles and found 12 theoretical and conceptual articles, and 46 other types of articles. As expected, they found a wide range of methodologies from discourse analysis to big data. Again, as expected, the most popular methodology was case studies (18 articles or 39 percent), followed by surveys (8 or 17 percent). Content analysis and interviews were also very common, each sharing 7 or 15 percent of the articles. Other methodologies like discourse analysis, network analysis, and experiments were scarcely used.

Since 2003, Gregory (2003–) publishes several times a year a comprehensive list of *Diplomacy's Public Dimension: Books, Articles, Websites*. His lists demonstrate a substantial growth of high-quality publications in PD. The Oxford Bibliographies published two lists of works on PD, one from the perspective of communication (Gilboa, 2019) and the other from the perspective of international relations (Huijgh, Gregory, & Melissen, 2020).

Scholarly independence

Two major periodicals exclusively publish PD research: *Place Branding and Public Diplomacy* and *Journal of Public Diplomacy*. The *Public Diplomacy Magazine* publishes special issues on various aspects of PD. *The Hague Journal of Diplomacy, Public Relations Review, American Behavioral Scientist, International Affairs, International Journal of Communication*, and *International Communication Gazette* also frequently publish articles and sometimes special issues on PD. The Palgrave Macmillan "Global Public Diplomacy" series, the Anthem Press series "Soft Power and Public Diplomacy," Routledge's series on "New Diplomacy Studies," Brill and the Public Diplomacy Council among others offer venues for publication of book-length works in the field.

Textbooks and handbooks also demonstrate the strength of any scientific field. The growing literature in PD includes the second edition of *The Routledge Handbook of Public Diplomacy* (Snow & Cull, 2020), *International Public Relations and Public Diplomacy* (Golan, Yang, & Kinsey, 2014), *The Routledge International Handbook of Diaspora Diplomacy* (Kennedy, 2022), and *City*

Diplomacy (Amiri & Sevin, 2020). The USC Center on Public Diplomacy publishes *Perspectives on Public Diplomacy*, an excellent series of extended papers and monographs in PD. Clingendael, the Netherlands Institute of International Relations, has a similar series. Surprisingly, perhaps, texts in international relations often ignore PD, but any major text or survey of diplomacy, international communication, or international public relations includes a chapter on PD.

The field has been expanded significantly in international scholarly associations, especially in the areas most relevant to PD: international relations and communication. Two divisions at the International Studies Association (ISA), Diplomatic Studies and International Communication, have been regularly sponsoring panels, roundtables, and posters on PD at their annual conferences. The International Communication Association (ICA) has been doing the same at their divisions of Public Relations and Political Communication. In 2015, ICA established for the first time, an Interest Group exclusively dedicated to PD. The Association for Education in Journalism and Mass Communication (AEJMC) and the International Association for Media and Communication Research (IAMCR) have been sponsoring papers and sometimes panels on PD, mostly by its divisions of Public Relations and International Communication.

Several universities in the US and around the world offer various degree programs in PD including the University of Southern California (the first graduate program), Syracuse University, George Washington University, University of Siena in Italy, Reichman University in Israel, The Jagiellonian University in Kraków in Poland, Beijing Foreign Studies University in China, and the Kyoto University of Foreign Studies in Japan. Most schools of international or global studies and foreign service, especially members of the Association of Professional Schools of International Affairs (APSIA), include certificate programs, concentrations, or at least a few courses in PD.

Several states and universities established research centers dedicated exclusively to PD such as the Center on Public Diplomacy (CPD) at the University of Southern California, the Institute for Public Diplomacy and Global Communication at George Washington University, the Biden Center for Diplomacy and Engagement at the University of Pennsylvania, and the Centers for Public Diplomacy at the Ewha Womans University in South Korea and Tsinghua University in China. The University of Shanghai for Science and Technology established the Shanghai Institute of Public Diplomacy (SIPD). Many research centers on international relations, diplomacy, or international communication, such as Clingendael or the Oxford Digital Diplomacy

Research Group at Oxford University, conduct significant research projects in PD. Several Centers, like CPD and the Center for International Communication at Bar-Ilan University, offer basic and advance training programs for practitioners in PD.

Almost simultaneously with the evolution of the academic field of PD, many international actors: governments, international and supranational organizations, and nonstate actors, have recognized the importance and value of PD and established administrative bodies to plan and manage PD programs and activities with different titles such as departments, units, divisions, or bureaus. Embassies, consulates, and diplomatic legations have also added special units for PD and appoint specialists to manage them. These units have required allocation of resources and manpower as well as training and coordination with both other functions at the embassies and the relevant departments back home at the foreign ministry. Much research has been conducted on the use of PD by ministries of foreign affairs and embassies, especially of digital media, but to date, no comprehensive study has been done on how actors organize and manage PD in terms of organizational units, hierarchies, manpower, and budgets. This should be a major topic in the new agenda for PD research.

Ministries of foreign affairs and various organizations published specific manuals for PD or included chapters on PD in general manuals for foreign policy and diplomacy. With a few exceptions, however, these manuals are kept for internal use only and are not available to scholars. The US Department of State and the Philippine Department of Foreign Affairs for example, published manuals for PD available to the public. The NATO Handbook includes a chapter on PD. The Asia–Europe Foundation (2021) published a *Handbook for Public Diplomacy* practitioners in a unique format of combining academic articles with interviews with practitioners. It might be interesting to note the topics this publication assumed PD officials should know including essentials of PD, strategic communications, digital diplomacy, stakeholder engagement, evaluation, cultural diplomacy, and dangers and annoyances, and opportunities: the contemporary communications environment.

Boundaries

Scholars have attempted to map boundaries of PD. Gregory (2016) drew boundaries based on what he thought PD is and *is not*. He suggested four boundaries: (1) a distinction between diplomacy and foreign policy; (2) a framework for diplomacy's public dimension; (3) a separation between diplomacy and civil society; and (4) differences between diplomacy and governance. Boundaries 1, 3, and 4 share several similarities but are also different. Gregory is right to claim that fine tuning of these boundaries is difficult and keeps changing. For example, actors employ civil-society actors to achieve goals and values, but these actors also independently employ PD to advance their own goals and values. Thus, civil-society actors are both actors and instruments. Those who deny the autonomous role of civil-society actors in diplomacy draw the line too narrowly. But those who claim that any civil-society actor or a private multinational firm is a diplomatic actor, draw the line too broadly. The space in between these extreme polars is difficult to pinpoint. Gregory's attempt has been useful but limited in scope and methodology. He did not sufficiently explain how to do the fine tuning between too narrow or too broad boundaries.

Ayhan (2019) sought to clarify boundaries based on the approach to nonstate actors in PD studies. He analyzed 160 articles published between 1985 and 2017 with the term PD in their title to create a taxonomy of perspectives. He identified five main perspectives:

1. State-centric perspectives that restrict PD to state agencies in a coherent way rejecting diplomatic actorness of nonstate actors completely.
2. Neo-statist perspectives that reserve the term PD for states only, while offering alternative terms such as *social diplomacy* or *grassroots diplomacy* for similar nonstate actor activities.
3. Nontraditional perspectives that define diplomacy based not on status, but on capabilities, accepting some nonstate actor activities as PD.
4. Society-centric perspectives that share most traits with nontraditional perspectives, except that they define the public as people in the global public sphere.
5. Accommodative perspectives that accommodate nonstate actor activities within the realm of PD, but only if those activities meet certain criteria.

This analysis is useful and to a certain extent is based on Gregory's formulations, but it represents perspectives mainly within international relations and is limited to actors and to the interplay between states and nonstate actors.

PD scholars have used very different concepts and terms to understand and advance the field such as *layers, components, functions, foundations, pathways, perspectives*, and *logics*. Cowan and Arsenault (2008) suggested 3 *layers* of PD: monologic, one-way communication; dialogic, two-way or multidirectional communication; and collaborative relationship building. Cull (2008) thought that research and practice in PD should focus on 5 *components*: listening, advocacy, cultural diplomacy, international exchanges, and international broadcasting. Ten years later (Cull, 2019b), he incorporated these components into a larger framework which he called foundations for global engagement in the digital age. He added nation branding and partnership to his original five components.

Fitzpatrick (2010) surveyed the PD literature and found six main *functions*: advocacy, communication, relationship management, promotion, political engagement, and warfare. Sevin (2017) identified six *pathways* of connection to public opinion: attraction, benefit of doubt, socialization, direct influence, agenda setting, and framing. Ayhan (2019) explored five *perspectives*. Zaharna (2022) developed and elaborated on three *logics* in PD: individual, relational, and holistic. Each scholar used a different concept to capture the essence of PD, but the multiple terms do not help to consolidate the field. Attempts to analyze boundaries are done mostly horizontally instead of building blocks and moving in stages towards a more comprehensive and multidisciplinary approach. This deficiency must be corrected in the new agenda for PD research, and researchers have to agree on fewer terms that would be the most succinct, relevant, and useful.

One of the most neglected areas in PD research is ethics. Efforts to influence or change public opinion, particularly in the social media in an era of disinformation, fake news, sharp power, and digital authoritarianism, requires more transparency and strict adherence to ethical norms and principles (Bjola & Pamment, 2018). Several scholars extended and applied to PD ethical standards practiced in specific relevant disciplines. Seib (2009a) explained that ethical principles in journalism were very similar to standards that should guide PD practitioners. Fitzpatrick (2017, p. 88) extended ethics in PR to PD and presented the following research questions: "Who decides whose or what interests are served in public interest communications campaigns and programs? How is public interest defined? Who determines what positive behavioral change looks like?" These questions remain very relevant today. Comor and Bean (2012) concluded that only ethical PD, one that "embraces genuine (rather than contrived) dialogue," can be effective. Ethical PD certainly expands the boundaries of PD and should receive more attention in the new research agenda for PD.

Methodologies

The building of any new scholarly field requires development of adequate methodologies. Very few scholars attempted to develop models and theories of PD, let alone paradigms. Most have used case studies and a few conducted comparative analyses. Most researchers used qualitative techniques, only a few collected empirical data and analyzed it via quantitative methods. Popular techniques include content analysis and interviews with policymakers, practitioners, journalists, and scholars. New, more integrated methods would have to be developed and used in the next research phase.

Only states conducted traditional PD towards public opinion in specific states or around the world. In recent decades, PD scholars have emphasized the need to add nonstate actors to research on PD (Lee & Ayhan, 2015). Part I of this volume also includes primarily nonstate actors. A few experts thought that adding nonstate actors combined with digital media has revolutionized PD so much, that it should be called "the new public diplomacy" (Melissen, 2005; Seib, 2009b; Pamment, 2012). Today, most PD scholars have abandoned the term and use only PD, but they still consider the distinction between states and nonstate actors as a major factor in the attempts to chart the boundaries of the field and develop new theories. Yun (2022), however, argued that moving too much and too fast in research on the PD of nonstate actors has distorted the centrality of states in the conduct of PD. The obvious answer is to create a reasonable balance in research of PD between states and nonstate actors.

Scholars have been lamenting the absence of operational models for research on PD. This is still a major deficiency. Most of the existing models have been anchored in specific disciplines. Entman's (2008) highly popular model of mediated PD emerged from communication, constructed around the American political system, and was mostly relevant to liberal democracies. At the same time, Gilboa (2008, pp. 72–3) suggested an integrative framework for analysis of PD based on time frames and matching instruments of PD, that is, immediate (advocacy), intermediate (diaspora diplomacy), or long (international exchanges). Golan (2013) adopted a similar approach. More recent attempts include Zhu's (2021) adaptive model, designed to offer a framework for the selection of PD tools; and Zhang's (2020) PD radar framework consisting of two crossing axes representing ethics (compassion and manipulation) and efficacy (narratives and rational arguments), and five concentric circles that represent goals of PD, power of PD, "worldviews" underlying PD practices, and relevant theories. These two recent models are interesting, but they are very complex, cover too many variables, and would be difficult to apply.

Several studies dealt with methodologies in PD research. But a special issue of *Place Branding and Public Diplomacy* (Vol. 18, Issue 3, 2022) deserves a special citation. The various articles combine disciplinary methods in history, sociology, and communications with techniques including statistical analysis, interviews, and experiments, and applications to case studies of global media, digital media, culture, and evaluation. In the new research agenda, methodologies have to cross much more disciplinary boundaries.

Case studies and qualitative techniques are still the main methodologies in PD research. Case studies provide the foundations for an emerging field, but much more comparative analysis and quantitative techniques are needed to develop, construct, and test theories and models of PD (Gilboa, 2008; Ociepka, 2018). Case studies would be still useful in studying exceptional or neglected actors, strategies, or programs in PD. Ociepka (2017) and Lam (2023) produced two of the best books on the PD of a single country (Poland and Vietnam, respectively). Studies of the PD of terrorist organizations have also been very useful. Melki and Jabado (2016) examined the PD conducted by a terrorist organization, the Islamic State in Iraq and Syria (ISIS). They applied Entman's model of mediated PD and found interesting results including the use of sophisticated branding tactics to recruit fighters and deter foes.

Bos and Melissen (2019) argued that PD researchers should pay more attention to nonstate actors using PD in conflict situations outside the Western world. They examined how two rebel groups in Mali used digital media to enhance their communications with global audiences. They found that social media increased the power and influence of the rebel groups on the international stage. Golan, Arceneaux, and Soule (2019, p. 95) investigated the PD of the Catholic Church via qualitative textual analysis of Pope Francis speeches. His speeches, they found, rely mostly "on narratives of universal identity and values, shared responsibility, and calls to action."

Similarly, in the last decade, there has been more interesting and useful comparative research in PD that has advanced theoretical and empirical dimensions of PD. The comparative research output can be divided into three groups: frameworks for analysis, comparisons between two actors and comparative analysis of several countries. Brown (2012) distinguished among four paradigms of PD that could be used for comparative analysis: extension of diplomacy, national projection, cultural relations, and political warfare. Pamment (2012) applied comparatively a three-category framework: overview, evaluation, and campaigns to the PD of the US, the UK, and Sweden. Sevin (2017) developed his own framework for analysis consisting of six pathways described earlier, and applied them to the PD of the US, Sweden, and Turkey. White and Radic (2014) compared message strategies adopted by ministries of foreign affairs of eight countries in transition – recent members or candidates to join the European Union including Iceland, Croatia, Bulgaria, Romania, Serbia, Montenegro, Macedonia, and Turkey. They conducted content analysis of the PD messages these ministries posted on their websites and correlated them with economic development, level of democracy, and perceptions of the country.

Lee and Lin (2017) did a comparative analysis of information subsidies for PD, the governments of the US, China, and Singapore used through online newsrooms. In PR, information subsidies refer to controlled access to information and materials that come with little effort or cost to the recipient. This is a comparative analysis of the traditional classic one-way communication via means such as press releases. Arif, Golan, and Moritz (2014) produced an interesting case study of mediated PD via a comparison of the relations the US and the Taliban pursued with the Pakistani media. Bali, Karim, and Rached (2018) also conducted an interesting comparison by looking at how the US Consulate General in Erbil and the Kurdistan Regional Government (KRG) representation in Washington used Facebook as a PD tool to influence their intended foreign audiences.

Another interesting example is the study by Lien and Tang (2022) who compared the Chinese Confucius Centers in the US with the US Cultural Centers in China. They found that the development paths of both institutions were closely related to the development and transformation of Sino–US political relations. Comparative analysis appeared also in specific areas of PD such as cultural diplomacy (Kizlari & Fouseki, 2018), digital diplomacy (Bjola & Jiang, 2015), international exchanges (Mawer, 2017; Ayhan & Snow, 2021), sports diplomacy (Kobierecki, 2020), and diaspora diplomacy (Gilboa, 2022).

Evaluation

Evaluation of PD strategies and programs has always been a critical issue because it exposes effective versus ineffective policies. There has not been much good scholarly research on evaluation, but certain progress has been made in the last decade. Scholars identified several obstacles to evaluation: structural, financial, cultural, conceptual, and administrative (Banks, 2011, 2020). Researchers (Buhmann & Sommerfeldt, 2019; Sommerfeldt & Buhmann, 2019) found that officials in the Department of State were under organizational pressure to pursue evaluation, but faced major obstacles such as unclear goals, not knowing how to evaluate, the difficulty of measuring long-term results, lack of training and resources, lack of a standardized set of evaluation practices, the absence of a single authority that directs how evaluation should be done, and tension between diplomacy practitioners in Washington, D.C. and those in the field.

Directors of PD units, however, are not always interested in evaluation either because they think it would be a waste of scarce resources, believe they know in advance what the results would be, or fear revelations of failures that opponents of PD would use to limit or even eliminate the entire PD program. When they do try to evaluate what they do, they often confuse outputs with outcomes. They count activities and investments but not actual results. Without serious evaluation, however, policymakers are operating in the dark not knowing whether their initiatives and programs are achieving the intended results. Banks (2020) explained that three elements determine successful evaluation: strong and effective leadership that values evaluation, an administrative structure that supports evaluation, and sufficient resources.

An excellent evaluation study with significant theoretical and empirical implications for the next phase of research in PD, is a study of the effects of an important instrument of PD, high-level visits by national leaders to other countries, on public opinion in those countries (Goldsmith, Horiuchi, & Matush, 2021). The authors combined a dataset of the international travels of 15 leaders from nine countries over 11 years, with surveys conducted in 38 host countries. They successfully proved a causation between the visits and positive approval levels of the visiting leaders in the eyes of the local publics. Moreover, they also found that PD activities: increasing awareness of the leaders themselves and their country and conveying positive messages, often on the hosts, were a significant factor in facilitating the positive results. This research was significant because it dealt with a crucial measurement issue in PD and employs quantitative statistical data to test a possible causation relationship.

Evaluation is related to planning and decision-making. Cortés and Jamieson (2020) suggested how to design evaluative research in PD. They focused on listening to foreign publics as the main variable, but with little modification, their model could be broadened to the entire planning and decision-making processes in PD. The authors made three recommendations for any research design in PD:

1. Identify an issue requiring PD programs and investigate why it exists in the first place.
2. Design a PD program that could effectively address the issue including the setting of clear and measurable goals.
3. Determine effectiveness via collection of public opinion data at several points of time.

The authors proposed a sequence that starts with a perceived issue and moves through stages of listening to programs and evaluation. The process, however, could begin with listening to identify an issue, following the design and implementation of PD programs, listening could become a feedback instrument.

Global crises

The world has been facing several growing global crises that are threatening humanity: health pandemics like Covid-19, climate change, disinformation, growing gaps between poor and rich states, refugees, populism, warfare, nuclear proliferation, and nuclear war. Coping with all these challenges requires much adaption, cooperation, and coordination among all international actors including public and private, states, international and non-governmental organizations, and multinational corporations. PD can help to promote the understanding and cooperation needed to deal effectively with these global crises, primarily via networking and building relations (Zaharna, Arsenault, & Fisher, 2013; Zaharna, 2022).

Manor and Pamment (2022) devoted a special journal issue to the effects of Covid-19 on PD policies and activities. It took on a unique format of 12 short case studies about the impact of Covid-19 on the present and future of PD. The format was unique but not the fundamental approach to research in PD. The articles were written on states only including Brazil, China, France, Germany, India, Japan, Mexico, Norway, Romania, Russia, Sweden, the UK, and the US. The method was the classic case study, and the topics were human-centered PD, museum diplomacy, diaspora diplomacy, reputational security, digital diplomacy, the 2020/21 Tokyo Olympic Games, and celebrity diplomacy. The issue only laid down ideas for more fundamental research on global pandemics.

Hellmann and Oppermann (2022) provided an example of innovative research on Covid-19 and PD by investigating the Chinese government use of photographs to cope with worldwide criticism of its handling of the pandemic. They combined PD concepts: strategic narratives, non-verbal communication, and public opinion surveys to explore the impact of photographs – distributed by the regime's news agency, Xinhua – on international public opinion. The photographs had a positive effect on China's international image, but this effect was moderated by levels of political knowledge among the target audiences.

Pamment (2021) used the Swedish handling of the Covid-19 pandemic to propose adding a theoretical layer to the classic PD communication process between two actors. He suggested a "theory of disruption" that described the activities of a third party, nonstate actors such as a group of motivated trolls, an organized advocacy group, or agents of a hostile country, that challenge and disrupt governmental messages. This approach may be relevant to the coping with other global crises discussed in this section.

Fewer studies with less insights have been conducted on the potential of PD to deal with other global crises. Climate diplomacy refers mostly to normative studies and manuals telling officials how diplomacy could be used to deal with the global climate crisis (Hsu et al., 2015; Hale, 2018; Tänzler, Ivleva, & Hausotter, 2021). Effective strategy in this case requires a substantial effort to convince elites and audiences around the world how serious the climate change crisis is and how urgent is the need to adopt effective measures to limit it. Sukhorolska (2016) wrote on Western utilization of PD to promote democracy, and Cooper (2019) advocated changes in PD needed to fight populism; Pamment, Dolea, and Ingenhoff (2017) edited an interesting special issue on PD and the refugee crisis in Europe, and Kothari and Tsakarestou (2021) wrote about PD and the refugee crisis in Greece. Yet, most proposals for combatting global crises do not include PD programs in their strategies, and this is another new idea for both research and cooperation between scholars and practitioners.

There are many obstacles PD faces in combatting global crises including fundamental disagreements on the nature of the crises; differing or contradictory national or international interests and rivalries; domestic constraints; disagreement on the right ways to solve the crises; lack of cooperation among international actors; the decline of democracy, the rise of political populism and digital authoritarianism; and the combination of social media and fake news. Thus, the first task is to recognize the obstacles and their myriad sources and develop a joint comprehensive PD strategy and programs that would utilize all the available PD instruments, both to overcome the obstacles and promote the policies needed to cope with the crises. The UN would be the natural place for building such an initiative, but this international body has become a corrupt, highly politicized, and ineffective organization. To create an alternative, the powers will have to adjust an existing international body such as the World Trade Organization or set up an entirely new international mechanism. The alternative body will have to build a strong department of PD, and this should also be a topic on the new PD research agenda.

Any new research agenda for PD must include considerable attention to possible effects of the global crises on PD, ways PD can be employed to resolve or limit them, and obstacles to that employment. Preliminary research on

PD and global crises has already begun. More attention has been given to Covid-19 compared to the other crises, but the whole area should be much more expanded and developed. This would be also an opportunity to use and integrate much better multidisciplinary approaches to PD.

Conclusion

There has been much debate on whether PD is an independent field of study or not. Scholars and practitioners have debated definitions, theories, boundaries, disciplines, models, principles, instruments, and methodologies. This analysis of the field reveals that PD is already meeting some of the major criteria for the establishment of a new field of science. There are many more students and faculty interested and specializing in PD, more academic programs and research centers, and many more practitioners who run and conduct PD activities. Despite the gaps between scholars and practitioners, a PD community has already been established.

This chapter and the other chapters in this volume show that much progress has been made in the field during the last two decades, and it seems now that there is less confusion and debate and more agreement on the value of PD to foreign policy and international relations. But there is still a long road to go. Most PD scholars agree that progress must include the construction of broad bridges, between disciplines, between islands of theory, and between theory and practice. Today, there are more islands of theory, big and small, and the next phase requires expansion and construction of new bridges among them. PD is a very multidisciplinary field. Much of contemporary research is still conducted within disciplinary boundaries. There are gaps between disciplinary approaches to PD, and the next phase of research will have to develop ways to overcome these gaps, create and integrate multidisciplinary research mainly by close cooperation between scholars from different fields.

There could be a way to develop an approach to PD, an "instrumental approach," which has the potential of promoting a theoretical core, overcoming disciplinary barriers, and encouraging closer linkages among scholars and between scholars and practitioners. Diplomacy is an instrument of foreign policy, and PD is an instrument of diplomacy. There are various PD instruments or tools practitioners employ and scholars study. These include advocacy, media relations, international broadcasting, international exchanges, cultural diplomacy, foreign aid, economic diplomacy, sports diplomacy, international public relations, place branding, corporate/business diplomacy, diaspora diplomacy, city diplomacy, citizen diplomacy, NGOs, international law/ lawfare, digital diplomacy, and science diplomacy.

The instrumental approach has several advantages. Several instruments are discipline dependent, but a few such as foreign aid, corporate diplomacy, or diaspora diplomacy cut across several disciplines. The instrumental approach may help to clarify the place of actors in PD processes. Certain actors such as international organizations, corporations, or NGOs are used as PD tools by states, but they also act as independent actors using PD tools to advance their own agenda. The instrumental approach could also help to amalgamate concepts, models, and methodologies. Although Zhu (2021) did not use this approach, his normative study of PD tools decision-makers select, demonstrated its potential contribution to new PD research.

PD is also a developing field of practice. Scholars are studying what government agencies and NGOs plan and do, especially in areas of digital channels. Scholars also develop normative and prescriptive approaches that tell policymakers and officials what they should do to achieve PD goals. Yet there is still a considerable gap between scholars and officials and between theory and practice. Close collaboration between the two groups can help scholars to improve their research on issues that are important for practitioners, and the latter can help scholars to do more relevant and useful research.

Theory construction is needed not only to guide research but also to unify and consolidate the various subfields and areas in PD into one core. We do not have yet a theory or even competing theories of PD. We have attempts to theorize issues or limited areas in PD (Gilboa, 2022). Theory development requires much abstract thinking, imagination, and creativity. Not enough scholars are devoting time and energy to theory development. Much of contemporary research is based on case studies and qualitative methodology. Case studies are important for the initial phases of research but insufficient for the next phase. There is a greater need to move into comparative analysis across the main issues of PD. Sophisticated comparative analysis also provides vital foundations for theory development and testing.

The next phase in PD research requires much more creativity and innovation. Boden (2004) distinguished among three main roads to true scientific creativity: *exploration* – using existing tools to create a new point in existing space; *combination* – making unfamiliar combinations of familiar ideas, and *transformative* or revolutionary creativity – the most elusive and rare that completely shuffles the cards. Despite criticism over the distinction between combinational and transformational creativity, all of Boden's concepts may be helpful to seek creativity in PD research and practice. This idea may be reinforced by her own application of her theory to history of art (Boden, 2010) and artificial intelligence (Boden, 2014). Given the multidisciplinary nature of PD research, the combination road seems to be the most promising. Creativity is certainly needed to cope with global crises and developing ways to deal with them. The next phase in PD research and practice must be much more creative and innovative.

References

Amiri, S., & Sevin, E. (Eds.) (2020). *City diplomacy*. Palgrave Macmillan.

Arif, R., Golan, G., & Moritz, B. (2014). Mediated public diplomacy: US and Taliban relations with Pakistani media. *Media, War & Conflict, 7*(2), 201–17.

Ayhan, K. J. (2019). The boundaries of public diplomacy and nonstate actors: A taxonomy of perspectives. *International Studies Perspectives, 20*(1), 63–83.

Ayhan, K. J., & Snow, N. (2021). Introduction to special issue – global Korea scholarship: Empirical evaluation of a non-Western scholarship program from a public diplomacy perspective. *Politics & Policy, 49*(6), 1282–91.

Bali, A., Karim, N., & Rached, K. (2018). Public diplomacy effort across Facebook: A comparative analysis of the US consulate in Erbil and the Kurdistan representation in Washington. *Sage Open*, 1–9. https://doi.org/10.1177/2158244018758835.

Banks, R. (2011). *A resource guide to public diplomacy evaluation*. Figueroa Press.

Banks, R. (2020). Public diplomacy evaluation. In N. Snow & N. Cull (Eds.), *Routledge handbook of public diplomacy*, 2nd edn (pp. 64–75). Routledge.

Bjola, C., & Jiang, L. (2015). Social media and public diplomacy: A comparative analysis of the digital diplomatic strategies of the EU, US and Japan in China. In C. Bjola & M. Holmes (Eds.), *Digital diplomacy: Theory and practice* (pp. 71–88). Routledge.

Bjola, C., & Pamment, J. (Eds.) (2018). *Countering online propaganda and extremism: The dark side of digital diplomacy*. Routledge.

Boden, N. (2004). *The creative mind: Myths and mechanisms*, 2nd edn. Routledge.

Boden, N. (2010). *Creativity and art: Three roads to surprise*. Oxford University Press.

Boden, N. (2014). Creativity and artificial intelligence: A contradiction in terms? In E. Paul & S. Kaufman (Eds.), *The philosophy of creativity: New essays* (pp. 224–44). Oxford Academic.

Bos, M., & Melissen, J. (2019). Rebel diplomacy and digital communication: Public diplomacy in the Sahel. *International Affairs, 95*(6), 1331–48.

Brown, R. (2012). The four paradigms of public diplomacy: Building a framework for comparative government external communications research. Paper presented at the International Studies Association Convention, San Diego.

Buhmann, A., & Sommerfeldt, E. (2019). Drivers and barriers in public diplomacy evaluation: Understanding attitudes, norms, and control. *The International Communication Gazette, 83*(2), 105–25.

Comor, E., & Bean, H. (2012). America's "engagement" delusion: Critiquing a public diplomacy consensus. *International Communication Gazette, 74*(3), 203–20.

Cooper, A. F. (2019). Adapting public diplomacy to the populist challenge. *The Hague Journal of Diplomacy, 14*(1–2), 36–50.

Cortés, J., & Jamieson, T. (2020). Incorporating research design in public diplomacy: The role of listening to foreign publics. *International Journal of Communication, 14*, 1214–31.

Cowan, G., & Arsenault, A. (2008). Moving from monologue to dialogue to collaboration: The three layers of public diplomacy. *Annals of the American Academy of Political and Social Science, 616*(1), 10–30.

Cull, N. (2008). Public diplomacy: Taxonomies and histories. *Annals of the American Academy of Political and Social Science, 616*(1), 31–54.

Cull, N. (2012). *The decline and fall of the United States Information Agency: American public diplomacy, 1989–2001.* Palgrave Macmillan.

Cull, N. (2019a). The tightrope to tomorrow: reputational security, collective vision and the future of public diplomacy. *The Hague Journal of Diplomacy, 14*(1–2), 21–35.

Cull, N. (2019b). *Public diplomacy: Foundations for global engagement in the digital age.* Polity.

Entman, R. (2008). Theorizing mediated public diplomacy: The U.S. case. *The International Journal of Press/Politics, 13*(2), 87–102.

Fitzpatrick, K. (2010). *The future of U.S. public diplomacy: An uncertain fate.* Brill.

Fitzpatrick, K. (2017). Public diplomacy in the public interest. *Journal of Public Interest Communications, 1*, 78–93.

Fitzpatrick, K., Fullerton, J., & Kendrick, A. (2013). Public relations and public diplomacy: Conceptual and practical connections. *Public Relations Journal, 7*(4), 1–21.

Gilboa, E. (2008). Searching for a theory of public diplomacy. *Annals of the American Academy of Political and Social Science, 616*(1), 55–77.

Gilboa, E. (2016). Public diplomacy. In G. Mazzoleni (Ed.), *The international encyclopedia of political communication* (Vol. 3, pp. 1297–306). Wiley-Blackwell.

Gilboa, E. (2019). Public diplomacy. In P. Moy (Ed.), *Oxford bibliographies in communication* (pp. 1–17). Oxford University Press.

Gilboa, E. (2022). Theorizing diaspora diplomacy. In L. Kennedy (Ed.), *The Routledge international handbook of diaspora diplomacy* (pp. 379–92). Routledge.

Golan, G. (2013). An integrated approach to public diplomacy. *American Behavioral Scientist, 57*(9), 1251–5.

Golan, G., Arceneaux, P., & Soule, M. (2019). The Catholic Church as a public diplomacy actor: An analysis of the pope's strategic narrative and international engagement. *The Journal of International Communication, 25*(1), 95–115.

Golan, G., Yang, S-U., & Kinsey, D. (Eds.) (2014). *International public relations and public diplomacy: Communication and engagement.* Peter Lang.

Goldsmith, B., Horiuchi, Y., & Matush, K. (2021). Does public diplomacy sway foreign public opinion? Identifying the effect of high-level visits. *American Political Science Review, 115*(4), 1342–57.

Gregory, B. (2003–). Public diplomacy resources. Institute for Public Diplomacy and Global Communication, George Washington University.

Gregory, B. (2008). Public diplomacy: Sunrise of an academic field. *The Annals of the American Academy of Political and Social Science, 616*(1), 274–90.

Gregory, B. (2016). Mapping boundaries in diplomacy's public dimension. *The Hague Journal of Diplomacy, 11*(1), 1–25.

Hale, T. (2018). *The role of sub-state and non-state actors in international climate processes.* Chatham House.

Hasnat, I., & Leshner, G. (2022). Experimental methods in public diplomacy. *Place Branding and Public Diplomacy, 18*(3), 254–60.

Hellmann, O., & Oppermann, K. (2022). Photographs as instruments of public diplomacy: China's visual storytelling during the Covid-19 pandemic. *The Hague Journal of Diplomacy, 17*(2), 177–215.

Hsu, A., et al. (2015). Towards a new climate diplomacy. *Nature Climate Change, 5,* 501–3.

Huijgh, H., Gregory, B., & Melissen, J. (2020). Public diplomacy. In D. Armstrong (Ed.), *Oxford bibliographies in international relations.* Oxford University Press.

Kennedy, L. (Ed.) (2022). *The Routledge international handbook of diaspora diplomacy.* Routledge.

Kizlari, D., & Fouseki, K. (2018). The mechanics of cultural diplomacy: A comparative case study analysis from the European context. *The Journal of Arts Management, Law, and Society, 48*(2), 133–47.

Kobierecki, M. (2020). *Sports diplomacy: Sports in the diplomatic activities of states and non-state actors.* Lexington Books.

Kothari, A., & Tsakarestou, B. (2021). Hack the camp: An entrepreneurial public diplomacy and social intervention initiative to address the refugee crisis in Greece. *The International Communication Gazette, 83*(1), 9–25.

Lam, V. (2023). *Public diplomacy in Vietnam: National interests and identities in the public sphere.* Routledge.

Lee, G., & Ayhan, K. (2015). Why do we need non-state actors in public diplomacy? Theoretical discussion of relational, networked and collaborative public diplomacy. *Journal of International and Area Studies, 22*(1), 57–77.

Lee, S. T., & Lin, L. (2017). An integrated approach to public diplomacy and public relations: A five-year analysis of the information subsidies of the United States, China, and Singapore. *International Journal of Strategic Communication, 11*(1), 1–17.

Lien, D., & Tang, P. (2022). Let's play tic-tac-toe: Confucius Institutes versus American Cultural Centres. *Economic and Political Studies, 10*(2), 129–54. https://doi.org/10.1080/20954816.2021.1920194.

Manor, I., & Pamment, J. (2022). At a crossroads: Examining Covid-19's impact on public and digital diplomacy. *Place Branding and Public Diplomacy, 18*(1), 1–3.

Mawer, M. (2017). Approaches to analyzing the outcomes of international scholarship programs for higher education. *Journal of Studies in International Education, 21*(3), 230–45.

Melissen, J. (Ed.) (2005). *The new public diplomacy: Soft power in international relations.* Palgrave Macmillan.

Melki, J., & Jabado, M. (2016). Mediated public diplomacy of the Islamic State in Iraq and Syria: The synergistic use of terrorism, social media and branding. *Media and Communication, 4*(2), 92–103. https://doi.org/10.17645/mac.v4i2.432.

Nye, J. (2008). Public diplomacy and soft power. *Annals of the American Academy of Political and Social Science, 616*(1), 94–109.

Nye, J. (2019). Soft power and public diplomacy revisited. *The Hague Journal of Diplomacy, 14*(1–2), 7–20.

Ociepka, B. (2017). *Poland's new ways of public diplomacy.* Peter Lang.

Ociepka, B. (2018). Public diplomacy as political communication: Lessons from case studies. *European Journal of Communication, 33*(3), 290–303.

Pamment, J. (2012). *New public diplomacy in the 21st century: A comparative study of policy and practice.* Routledge.

Pamment, J. (2021). Does public diplomacy need a theory of disruption? The role of nonstate actors in counter-branding the Swedish Covid-19 response. *Journal of Public Diplomacy, 1*(1), 80–110.

Pamment, J., Dolea, A., & Ingenhoff, D. (2017). The European refugee crisis: Organizational responses and communication strategies. *Journal of Communication Management, 21*(4), 322–426.

Seib, P. (2009a). Public diplomacy and journalism: Parallels, ethical issues, and practical concerns. *American Behavioral Scientist, 52*(5), 772–86.

Seib, P. (Ed.) (2009b). *Toward a new public diplomacy: Redirecting US foreign policy.* Palgrave Macmillan.

Sevin, E. (2017). *Public diplomacy and the implementation of foreign policy in the US, Sweden and Turkey.* Palgrave Macmillan.

Sevin, E., Metzgar, E., & Hayden, C. (2019). The scholarship of public diplomacy: Analysis of a growing field. *International Journal of Communication, 13*, 4814–37.

Sharp, P. (2005). Revolutionary states, outlaw regimes and the techniques of public diplomacy. In J. Melissen (Ed.), *The new public diplomacy: Soft power in international relations* (pp. 106–23). Brill.

Signitzer, B. H., & Coombs, T. (1992). Public relations and public diplomacy: Conceptual convergences. *Public Relations Review, 18*(2), 137–47.

Snow, N., & Cull, N. (Eds.) (2020). *Routledge handbook of public diplomacy*, 2nd edn. Routledge.

Sommerfeldt, E. J., & Buhmann, A. (2019). The status quo of evaluation in public diplomacy: Insights from the U.S. State Department. *Journal of Communication Management, 23*(3), 198–212.

Sukhorolska, I. (2016). Public diplomacy of Western world countries as a tool of democracy promotion. *Journal of Liberty and International Affairs, 1*(3), 45–54.

Tänzler, D., Ivleva, D., & Hausotter, T. (2021). *EU climate change diplomacy in a post-Covid-19 world.* European Parliament. https:// www .europarl .europa .eu/ thinktank/en/document/EXPO_STU(2021)653643.

The Asia–Europe Foundation (2021). *ASEF public diplomacy handbook: Communicating with purpose and value*, 2nd edn. Singapore. https:// asef .org/ publications/ communicating-with-purpose-and-value/.

Vanc, A., & Fitzpatrick, K. (2016). Scope and status of public diplomacy research by public relations scholars, 1990–2014. *Public Relations Review, 42*(3), 432–40.

Walker, C. (2018). What is "sharp power"? *Journal of Democracy, 29*(3), 9–23.

Wei, C. (2020). Public diplomacy: Functions, functional boundaries and measurement methods. In D. Turcanu-Carutiu (Ed.), *Heritage* (pp. 1–12). IntechOpen. https:// www.intechopen.com/chapters/72251.

White, C., & Radic, D. (2014). Comparative public diplomacy: Message strategies of countries in transition. *Public Relations Review, 40*(3), 459–65.

Wiseman, G. (2019). Public diplomacy and hostile nations. *The Hague Journal of Diplomacy, 14*(1–2), 134–53.

Yun, S.-H. (2022). Against the current: Back to public diplomacy as government communication. *International Journal of Communication, 16*, 3047–64.

Zaharna, R. S. (2022). *Boundary spanners of humanity: Three logics of communications and public diplomacy for global collaboration.* Oxford University Press.

Zaharna, R. S., Arsenault, A., & Fisher, A. (Eds.) (2013). *Relational, networked, and collaborative approaches to public diplomacy.* Routledge.

Zhang, J. (2020). Compassion versus manipulation; narratives versus rational arguments: A PD radar to chart the terrain of public diplomacy. *Place Branding and Public Diplomacy, 16*(3), 195–211. https://doi.org/10.1057/s41254-019-00146-2.

Zhu, B. (2021). Tool selection for public diplomacy flagships: Toward an adaptive model. *Place Branding and Public Diplomacy.* https://doi.org/10.1057/s41254-021-00217-3.

PART I

Actors

2 States: public diplomacy contests in Asia

Caitlin Byrne

Introduction

Across Asia, governments of all persuasions recognise the value of engaging with public audiences in the pursuit of power and influence within and beyond their borders. Scholarship from the field suggests that public diplomacy (PD) in Asia has prima facie, reflected contemporary developments including an emphasis on two-way dialogue, relationship building, and mutual benefit for soft power effect (Lee & Melissen, 2011). But PD in Asia has also attracted criticism. While PD practice is seen as consequential in advancing foreign policy goals, its normative underpinnings are open for question.

Observations that PD reflects elements of representational force, political coercion, and rhetorical entrapment (Bially-Mattern, 2005) and find fertile ground in the contemporary Asian context, with the result that the pursuit of soft power is not always viewed as sufficient conceptual explanation for PD investments (Weissman, 2019). Hall and Smith (2013, p. 11) argue that there is an element of faddishness at play whereby, states "pursue public diplomacy because they see other states doing so as well". Increasingly when it comes to the Asian context, PD might more usefully be described as an instrument of strategic narrative that mobilises various forms of national power in the complex interactions between states and other actors for strategic gain.

China's rising ambitions to shape the regional order in Asia is a driving factor behind PDs new prominence as an instrument of strategic narrative. Narratives, as Seib (2019, p. 162) observes, are the essence of PD; the "stories crafted to appeal to the publics that a government wants to influence". Wang (2011) suggests narratives are more than image promotion, and reflect the way that nations "proclaim their visions of world order". Wesley (2021, p. 4) argues that "nations are particularly reliant on narratives, which speak to the core purposes and values of the national community and help to locate them in the world among other nations."

Narratives take different forms and carry varying levels of importance depending on the nature of their significance and focus. Strategic or grand narratives for example, are the significant and compelling stories that political actors use to convey their mission and purpose while seeking to shape the international system (Miskimmon et al., 2013; Ba, 2019). Antoniades et al. (2010, p. 3) defines strategic narratives as "… a means for political actors to construct shared meanings about past, present and future international politics" in order to "project their values and interests, extend their influence, change the discursive environment in which they operate". Scope exists for a more comprehensive research agenda that examines PD through the lens of strategic narrative's three core domains: formulation, projection, and reception (Miskimmon et al., 2013).

This chapter looks at how emerging research trends frame PD through the lens of strategic narrative drawing on China, Japan, and Australia as the key subjects. The first section focuses on the formulation process to understand factors at play, noting that China sets the pace. Section two examines the way that China, Japan, and Australia project their strategic narratives towards Southeast Asia as a primary target.[1] The third and final section highlights the complexities surrounding Southeast Asia's reception of and response to strategic narrative ambitions of others. The demand for further interdisciplinary exploration is illuminated along the way.

Strategic narrative formulation

Formulating strategic narrative calls on political actors to consider their contextual positioning and aspirations in the world. Miskimmon et al. (2013) describe it as a social process that reflects the interplay of internal and external discourses related to geographic context, national experiences and memories, cultural identities, political values and aspirations. PD scholars recognise the significance of the interwoven dynamics of national identity at play, given that "interests, values, memories and geostrategic contexts shape public diplomacy scope and practice" (Gregory, 2008, p. 274). Recent studies further highlight the role that political leaders can play in this formative stage as they embed their political persona and image at the centre of national and strategic nar-

---

[1]   Southeast Asia is taken to comprise the ten member states of the Association of Southeast Asian States (ASEAN), including Brunei Darussalam, Cambodia, Indonesia, Laos, Malaysia, Myanmar, Philippines, Singapore, Thailand, and Vietnam.

ratives (Ingenhoff & Klein, 2008; Balmas, 2018; Snow, 2009). While much attention has been placed on case studies from the US, the opportunity exists to look more closely at the role that Asia's leaders might also play in this process (Byrne, 2019).

Xi Jinping's rise to leadership—a central marker of China's ambitions to set (or reset) the strategic narrative of regional Asian order—has attracted scholarly attention both within and outside China (d'Hoogue, 2021; Repnokova, 2022; Zhao, 2019; Feng, He, & Liu, 2018; Shambaugh, 2013). Xi's determination to share China's wisdom with the world, and "promote the construction of a new model of international relations and a community with a shared future for mankind" (Zhao, 2019, p. 177) reflects China's broader desire to rectify the loss of international standing and dignity during the "century of humiliation" (Kaufman, 2011). Domestic imperatives—to unify and cohere increasingly fragmented domestic audiences behind the party leadership— are also identified as underpinning Xi's vision for the "great rejuvenation of the Chinese nation" (Jones & Hameiri, 2021). Formulated from the top, China's storytelling is framed through a new-found emphasis on cultural self-confidence—inextricably woven into the "China model" of economic success, global governance, and cultural relevance (Zhao, 2019; Feng, He, & Liu, 2018). Underpinning the intricate web of narrative, scholars also note the increasingly political aim to consolidate the Chinese Communist Party's (CCP) hold on national power, while securing China's preeminent position on the global stage (d'Hoogue, 2021; Gill, 2020).

For authoritarian nations like China the formulation process occurs with a scale, force, and direction that democracies are unable to match. The key features of China's formulation process, including its ideological emphasis, inclusion of both state and party influences, absence of civil society inputs and debate, and emphasis on domestic audiences puts it somewhat out of step with the "core principles" of contemporary Western PD (Cull, 2019; Gregory, 2011). Furthermore, for Xi, "'public diplomacy is taken as another battlefield on which China must win" (Huo & Maude, 2021), thus drawing the fault lines of contemporary contest sharply into view.

How China's contemporary strategic narrative challenges other regional powers to formulate counter-narratives are less explored. For policymakers in Japan and Australia, China's strategic narrative push is seen as a clear challenge to the existing principles of the US established liberal international order that have served middle powers interests well for several decades (Abe, 2013; Australian Government, 2017). Both nations hold serious concerns about the implications of China's narrative taking hold, especially in the proximate

Southeast Asian region, a region characterised by "nascent democracies and weak civil societies" (Kurlantzick, 2006, p. 3). Recognising the significance of PD practice in gaining influence in world affairs far beyond their limited material capabilities (Gilboa, 2008), both Japan and Australia have recalibrated their efforts to formulate counter-narratives—separately and together—in the face of China's more assertive practice.

Japan's evolving PD agenda over decades has attracted scholarly attention from across multiple disciplines. Otmazgin (2021), Watanabe (2017), and Lam (2012) explore the considerations and contours underlying Japan's engagement with its wider region in the post-war years. In doing so, they provide insights into the formulation of strategic narratives and their relevance as a platform for engagement. From ambitions for geopolitical dominance in the 1930s to the more subtle post-war desires for acceptance and influence, Japan's external strategic narratives are seen to have been constructed around the nation's changing identity.

Studies by Lam (2012) and Koga (2017), for example, point to the success of the "The Fukuda Doctrine" as providing the basis for Japan's post-war re-engagement in Southeast Asia through "heart to heart understanding", dialogue, and equal partnership. It is a useful example of strategic narrative that goes beyond the "forging of a new identity for post war Japan in Southeast Asia" (Lam, 2012, p. 2) to establish new norms in the international relations of Asia thus filling the void left by the US while countering growing Soviet influence at the time.

The dynamics underpinning more recent recalibrations in the formulation of Japan's strategic narrative, including the central role played by Japan's former prime minister Shinzo Abe offer potential for further exploration. Particularly, as Sakai (2019) suggests, because they challenge previously taboo security discourses in Japan's domestic debate. Like Xi, Abe sought to connect national and strategic narratives, recalibrating the government's PD engagement to "exemplify Japan's strengths and attractions and embody Japanese virtue". To this end, Abe's "Free and Open Indo Pacific" is seen to serve multiple aims, to: (1) cohere domestic support for Japan's changing international image; (2) engage "like-minded states", including Australia, India, and the US in pushing back on China's strategic narrative; and (3) offer reassurance to others, including Southeast Asian nations via an alternative view of the region that could work to their interests.

Turning to Australia, the release in 2017 of the Australian Government's Foreign Policy White Paper—only the third such document ever developed—

revived old debates about complex national narratives of isolation and powerlessness in an alien region (Gyngell, 2021) while bringing new discussions of strategic or grand narratives to the fore (Wesley, 2021; Medcalf, 2020). The Coalition Government's explicit anchoring of the nation's foreign policy to the strategic narrative of a free and open Indo-Pacific, as a reflection of the nation's "optimism born of ambition rather than anxiety" (Turnbull, 2017) signalled the emerging interest of political leaders in crafting the nation's strategic narrative in response to shifting dynamics (Byrne, 2019).

The location of national values in narrative formation holds significance for PD. Australia's former chief diplomat Peter Varghese (2015) makes the point that "giving expression to our values should be seen as a natural part of our foreign relations ..." and that Australia "should be quietly confident about our values because the best way to engage the world is with a clear sense of who we are and what we believe in". Further, as Wesley (2021) notes:

> The lessons of past narratives are that they do not come from a particular place. Australia, like other societies, is a community of story-tellers, searching among our traditional cultural values, emerging intellectual trends, prevailing national and international moods, and cultural innovations for stories that locate us and give us a sense of direction.

The 2017 Foreign Policy White Paper (p. 2) makes explicit reference to Australia's national values, as setting the "foundations of the nation's success in the world". Whether and how they are applied, including in the construction of strategic narrative remains insufficiently unpacked. Traditional foreign and security studies discourse is dismissive. Further interdisciplinary analysis bringing alternative perspectives to light would bring conceptual depth and understanding to the construction of Australian strategic narratives as important dimensions in the middle power's approach to PD.

The interplay between China, Japan, and Australia—three nations that are markedly different from each other, but highly attuned to each other's engagement in a contested region—offers insights into the emerging significance of strategic narrative as a centrepiece for PD. For each, the formulation of an externally oriented strategic narrative is woven into and strengthened by narratives of national identity. The formulation process underscores the relevance of political leadership in the early formulation and framing processes—with leaders bringing "Janus-faced" attention to messages that resonate with domestic and international constituencies.

Projection of strategic narrative

Since the early 2010s, China, Japan, and Australia have turned to project their strategic narratives particularly towards the nations of Southeast Asia; a region of increasing significance in the contest for influence (Shambaugh, 2021; Lee & Lee, 2020), with PD as a key mobilising instrument. Studies of China in this middling stage of the narrative process, initially framed by Kurlantzick (2006) as a "charm offensive", are prolific and varied—reflecting the recent nature of China's PD activity. Scholars like Custer et al. (2019) have responded with novel approaches to activity tracking through multidimensional data-sets which increasingly appeal to multidisciplinary critique. Unsurprisingly though, the subjects of niche research, middle powers Australia and Japan, remain under-examined when it comes to the projection of coherent strategic narrative.

Recent scholarship, including from Southeast Asia, brings notable emphasis to China's PD activities within the region, noting the role expanding Confucius Institute networks, educational and friendship exchanges, and international broadcast as key mechanisms for building influence through narrative projection (Vannarith, 2021; Lau, 2020; Shambaugh, 2021; Repnokova, 2022). These studies observe China's success in leveraging PD to reinforce narratives of long-standing civilisational, diasporic, and trading connections, within a "good neighbourhood" framing. Further, as Shambaugh (2021), Ba (2019), and Kurlantzick (2006) observe, China displays sophistication in leveraging bilateral narratives with Southeast Asian nations in ways that connect to strategic ambitions in the region.

The PD advantage brought by China's vast diaspora linkages in Southeast Asian region is less understood. An (2019) points out that the vast majority of China's 60 million strong diaspora community—including Chinese nationals living in the region as well as Chinese descendants who are citizens of their own country—are dispersed through Southeast Asia. The relationship between the Chinese state and its diaspora communities is complex and evolving. Shared cultural affinities, language, and traditions hold influence in regional conversations, making Chinese diaspora communities increasing central to the (re)production and reception of China's strategic narratives (Barr et al., 2015; Li, 2011). The significance of diaspora communities has not been missed by China's political leadership and is both sustained and activated through China's growing network of traditional and social media (Li, 2011).

In 2018 the CCP Central Committee called on all diaspora to help "realise the great rejuvenation of the Chinese nation and build a community with a shared future for humanity" by "telling Chinese stories, assisting economic development of China, upholding the greater national interests [meaning national reunion], and promoting Chinese culture" (China National People's Congress, 2018). Tan (2021) notes that the Overseas Chinese Affairs Office based within the United Front Department of the CCP has been reorganised to mobilise this effort. How the Chinese government and CCP apparatus continues to manage and cultivate diasporic relationships—as a target and feature of its growing influence in Southeast Asia—warrants further study.

Questions surrounding China's strategic narrative aspirations in Southeast Asia have generated multidisciplinary interests in the value of less conventional PD activity. PD, international relations, and political economy scholars alike draw on analysis of overseas development, debt financed infrastructure programmes—promoted under Xi's Belt and Road Initiative (BRI)—in their considerations of China's global positioning (Dreher et al., 2022; Repnokova, 2022; Shambaugh, 2021; Yu, 2021; Kurlantzick, 2006). International political and development economists note the competing narratives to emerge (Dreher et al., 2022, p. 5).

For example, while critics decry the BRI's reputation for poor governance, labour, and environmental standards, advocates note the fact that China's financing model demands fewer conditions from recipients and as such provides an attractive offering for political elites also seeking popular appeal across the region. Yet, turning to a data-driven analysis of Chinese government-financed projects around the globe, Dreher et al. (2022) brings an important critique of the narrative approach to the fore, and establishes the need for greater emphasis on the empirical tracking and evaluation of PD activities "to assess the volume, direction, and downstream consequences of China" while also dispelling the narrative.

Middle powers Japan and Australia offer fruitful research subjects when it comes to the projection of strategic narrative, but for different reasons, remain relatively under-explored. Despite arguments that PD remains an unfamiliar concept in Japan except within elite diplomatic circles (Ogawa, 2020), the evolution of Japan's conventional public diplomacy holds niche appeal for scholars in Asia (Snow, 2019, 2022; Otmazgin, 2021; Heng, 2014; Watanabe, 2017). Studies of Japanese cultural and educational exchange, including as promoted through the Japan Foundation[2] underline the nation's concerted effort to build constructive people-to-people ties, while gaining influence in Southeast Asia. The evolving role of Japan's international broadcaster NHK as "a dominant global source for news about Japan and the Asian region" (Snow, 2019, p. 17) complements Japan's wider PD efforts to provide an alternative voice in Southeast Asia.

The establishment of the Cool Japan Division within the Japanese Ministry of Economy, Trade and Industry (METI) brought a new global relevance to Japan's cool exposure within the region, especially as Otmazgin (2021, p. 626) notes, in "the realm of anime (animation), manga (comic publications), and, more recently, fashion and culinary culture". A scan of the Japanese government's official Facebook sites across Southeast Asia points to the breadth and depth of cultural engagement that offers significant appeal to Southeast Asian audiences. Though as some commentators note, Japan has been less successful in weaving bilateral and regional narratives more overtly into the strategic concept of a "free and open Indo-Pacific" (Beaty, 2021).

Though well known to international political and development economists, and consequential for Southeast Asia, Japan's economic statecraft towards Southeast Asia is rarely examined for its PD value. The "Partner for Quality Infrastructure" (PQI) initiative launched by Abe in 2015 offers an example of Japan seeking to frame investment initiatives through the lens of strategic narrative, with the deliberate emphasis on "quality" aimed at providing contrast to China's BRI (*The Economist*, 2021). As a major donor nation, Japan's development assistance (amounting to USD 3.6 billion in 2019) is similarly consequential for Southeast Asia (MFA, 2021). And it is increasingly clear that Japan aims to link development assistance investments to broader strategic narratives. For example, in the 2020 White Paper on Development Cooperation, Foreign Minister Motegi explicitly notes the role of development initiatives as contributing to the "realization of a 'Free and Open Indo-Pacific' aiming to establish a free and open order based on the rule of law in the Indo-Pacific region, the core of the world's vitality" (MFA, 2021).

Covid-19 raised the stakes for Japan's development agenda in Southeast Asia and, despite Olympic miscalculations at home (Snow, 2022), the middle power was able to establish itself as a "leader in vaccine donations" particularly in Southeast Asia (Beaty, 2021). Indeed, Japan's government has made "vaccine

---

[2]   The Japan Foundation is represented in eight of the ten Southeast Asian nations with Brunei Darussalam and Singapore being the two exceptions.

diplomacy" a key component of its foreign policy and leadership strategy as the nation seeks "to strengthen its image as a humanitarian aid donor and to capitalise on China's failure to improve its global reputation" (Beaty, 2021). Yet again the strategic narrative opportunities surrounding these initiatives have not been mobilised by Japan in the same way that China has done, leading some to suggest that Japan must lift its storytelling efforts (Stanislaus, 2017; *The Economist*, 2021).

Like Japan, Australia points to long-standing diplomatic relationships across Southeast Asia (Adamson, 2021). Scholar-practitioners observe that long-standing resistance of soft power coupled with declining investments in PD resourcing have undermined the middle power's visibility and reach (Wise, 2021; Wiseman, 2018; Byrne, 2021; Spry, 2020).[3] Niche investments in flagship programmes, including outbound scholarships, global alumni engagement, and cultural and sports diplomacy bring special emphasis to Southeast Asia but attract limited research. Monitoring the effectiveness of these programmes over time could add much needed ballast to Australia's PD profile. In the meantime, and without strong evidence to the contrary, Australia's conventional PD activity in Southeast Asia appears to remain comparatively limited in practice with few opportunities for projecting strategic narrative.

More recently, Australia has leveraged Covid-19 development assistance to project subtle narratives towards Southeast Asia, while highlighting the deficiencies in China's strategic narrative. Australia's A$500 million "Partnership for Recovery" initiative, was framed as delivering access to "safe and effective vaccines" plus "wrap around support" for Southeast Asia and the Pacific nations, in the aftermath of Covid-19. It was a clear bid to build influence as a reliable, dependable, and capable partner in the region (Byrne, 2021) and one that is "standing by our neighbours when it counts" (Australian Government, 2021).

The language used provides a centrepiece for official speeches, statements, and media targeting opinion leaders at home and in the region, although some suggest Australia could be more strategic with its messaging (Huo & Maude, 2021). Australia's position is also bolstered by the strategic heft of its recent multilateral contributions, including those made through the "Quad" alongside the US, Japan, and India (Jennett, 2021). While these developments are

---

[3]   Although a scan conducted by the author of the official Chinese, Japanese, and Australian diplomatic Facebook sites across Southeast Asia indicates that at March 2022 Australia leads in followership overall.

the subject of numerous foreign and security studies projects, there is limited analysis of their nature, conduct, or efficacy from a PD perspective.

China, Japan, and Australia utilise different mechanisms and platforms to project their strategic narratives towards the nations of Southeast Asia, and the scale of their engagement and reach is varied. Yet, emerging patterns point to opportunities for further study. First, that the projection of strategic narratives is initiated and increasingly controlled by central actors, with political and official actors playing a key role in the projection. Second, it appears that increasing emphasis is placed on the PD value derived from strategic activities including via economic and vaccine statecraft that aims to reflect a prevailing normative global leadership system. Third, where systems of leadership are in competition, narratives are projected in ways that seek to maximise strategic gain, while also diminishing the credibility of others.

Strategic narrative reception: Southeast Asia's response

As with broader PD activities, the evaluation of strategic narratives "requires—at a minimum—analysis of [the target audience] attitudes, opinions, and behaviour" (Miskimmon et al., 2013, p. 12). The task itself presents multiple challenges that are not unfamiliar to PD scholars (Sevin, 2017). These challenges are reinforced when reviewing Southeast Asian responses to strategic narratives projected towards the region by China, Japan, and Australia. Emerging scholarship, largely reflecting International Relations perspectives has generated helpful insights (Shambaugh, 2021; Kuik, 2021; Strangio, 2020; Weissman & Li, 2019) but the view remains patchy. As Custer et al. (2019, p. 1) observe, "despite the prominence of these debates, there has been a relative dearth of data-driven studies on the scope, tactics, and influence of Beijing's efforts to tell China's story." Scope exists for wider disciplinary perspectives and the application of empirical research methods to ensure more comprehensive understanding.

Shambaugh (2021) emphasises the diversity of response that exists across Southeast Asia noting that while the nations of the region "seek to maintain their independence and freedom of choice and action" there is a "pervasive ambivalence" towards external powers (p. 237). It is an important observation that underscores the agency of Southeast Asian nations—seeking to maximise their own interests—in an increasingly volatile environment. Weissmann and Li's (2019) exploration of the power of narrative in East Asian International Affairs expands understanding through a collection of single country case studies. Although not solely focused on Southeast Asia, the work casts light on the interplay of strategic, national, and issue-based narratives particularly relevant to Southeast Asia. They highlight the variability of responses shaped by relational and temporal dynamism of narratives.

Data offers important insights. For example, the US State Department-funded AidData Research Lab, which enables the collection, tracking, and analysis of activity-based data relevant to China's global PD efforts is generating useful insights about the nature and extent of the great power's influence (Custer et al., 2019; Dreher et al., 2022). Polling and survey data adds further granularity. For example, the 2021 State of Southeast Asia Survey Report suggests that the views of Southeast Asian elites towards external actors are largely shaped by how they see those actors responding to the key interests and needs of the region (Seah et al., 2022). According to the survey, the impact of Covid-19 on human health currently ranks as the most pressing concern across the region, followed by unemployment and economic recession, and climate change. Unsurprisingly China is viewed as "the undisputed economic power" and "the most significant political and strategic power" in the region (Seah et al., 2022, p. 22).

The extent of China's reach—in all domains—also generates considerable anxiety, with concerns expressed that China "intends to turn Southeast Asia into its sphere of influence". By contrast, and though trailing on measures of economic and political influence in the region, Japan is seen as the clear front-runner for ASEAN's "most favoured and trusted strategic partner" (Seah et al., 2022). Australia follows in second place. Data collected by the Pew Research Center's Global Attitudes Survey (2019) reflects a similar trajectory on Southeast Asian views towards China noting an emerging complexity aligned to shifts in the powerhouse nation's narrative.

Nascent scholarship into Southeast Asia's reception of strategic narratives suggests that informed audiences across the region are increasingly alive to the grand storytelling by external forces. Several moderating factors at play. First, "Southeast Asians have deeply ingrained postcolonial identities across the region and are quick to react to larger powers seeking to establish asymmetrical relationships and acting with arrogance" (Shambaugh, 2021, p. 14). The strategic narratives posed by China, Japan, and Australia might all be viewed and critiqued, to varying degrees through this lens. Second, public audiences across Southeast Asia are increasingly informed and engaged. The unprecedented uptake of education and mobility opportunities by students, academics, and policymakers has enabled a new generation of political and intellectual elites whose contributions to shaping political discourse and preferences are proving important. Southeast Asia, now home to the prestigious annual Shangri-La Dialogue and other important regional forums offers a venue in which policies and narratives are more thoroughly critiqued from within, although there is a yawning gap between public and elite perceptions of external power narratives within the region (Strangio, 2020). Third, disconnects between the strategic narratives projected and policy action executed on the ground undermine credibility and trust. China's expanding military and economic influence remains a source of deep suspicion and trust deficit in Southeast Asia, undermining its strategic narrative of benevolent leadership (Strangio, 2020).

Conclusion

This chapter draws attention to PD's strategic turn in the contest for strategic narrative in Asia. The race to determine "whose story wins?" has revealed a harder edge to PD practice in Asia. Under Xi, China has ratcheted its national investment and effort directed towards achieving Xi's ambitious aspirations for global leadership. And while it is neither unsurprising nor unreasonable that China, as a rising power, would seek to make its mark on the global order, it nonetheless represents a challenge to the status quo. China's emphasis on strategic narrative has thickened the nature of its PD activity—with political, business, academic, and policy elites engaged at multiple levels of activity. The culmination of these factors plays firmly into Xi's narrative of China as a generous provider of global public goods. However, suspicions about China's broad ambitions remain.

Middle powers, Australia and Japan—both beneficiaries of the existing order—are clearly recalibrating their efforts, including through PD to counter China's strategic narrative. The intent is to push back on China's influence in the region, while also seeking to preserve the status quo and shape the regional order as one more conducive to their interests. While their efforts are significant and complementary and play on factors of credibility, quality, and trust, they remain less overt and do not appear to have cultivated the same quality of thickness as those produced by China.

When viewed through the lens of strategic narrative, emerging trends in PD practice are evident. First, practice is increasingly centralised and controlled, with political leaders playing a central role to engage publics at home and abroad in the storytelling process. Second, while conventional people-to-people and international broadcasting activities remain prominent, a wider range of activities—including economic statecraft—are leveraged for their PD impact. Third, in an era of competition where PD seeks to mobilise a strategic narrative, the aim is not only to maximise strategic gain, but also to diminish the credibility of, competitors.

As the proving ground for the competing strategic narratives at play Southeast Asian nations are under pressure to respond. While more research is required to fully evaluate the perceptions of target Southeast Asian nations, it is clear that audiences are increasingly sophisticated. Evidence suggests that their views will be shaped by multiple factors, yet PD efforts that highlight substantive tangible benefits will hold the most sway over the short term. How public audiences receive and respond to projected strategic narratives, both separately and collectively is underdone and offers fertile ground for further interdisciplinary exploration.

References

Abe, S. (2013, February 22). Japan is Back. Speech delivered to the CSIS. https://www.mofa.go.jp/announce/pm/abe/us_20130222en.html.

Adamson, F. (2021, April 21). Leaders on Asia address. Lowy Institute for International Policy.

An, W. X. (2019). China's evolving policy towards the Chinese diaspora in Southeast Asia (1949–2018). *Trends in Southeast Asia*, 14, ISEAS Yusof Ishak Institute. https://bookshop.iseas.edu.sg/publication/2404

Antoniades, A. et al. (2010). Great power politics and strategic narratives. Working Paper No. 7, The Centre for Global Political Economy. https://pure.qub.ac.uk/en/publications/great-power-politics-and-strategic-narratives.

Australian Government (2017). *Opportunity, Security, Strength: 2017 Foreign Policy White Paper*. Commonwealth of Australia.

Australian Government (2021). *Partnerships for Recovery: Australian Official Development Assistance*. Department of Foreign Affairs and Trade.

Ba, A. (2019). China's "Belt and Road" in Southeast Asia: Constructing the strategic narrative in Singapore. *Asian Perspective*, *43*(2), 249–72.

Balmas, M. (2018). Tell me who is your leader, and I will tell you who you are: Foreign leaders' perceived personality and public attitudes toward their countries and citizenry. *American Journal of Political Science*, *62*(2), 499–514.

Barr, M. et al. (2015). Introduction: The soft power of hard states. *Politics*, *35*(3–4), 213–15.

Beaty, C. (2021, August 8). Japan and vaccine diplomacy. *New Perspectives on Asia*, CSIS.

Bially-Mattern, J. (2005). *Ordering international politics*. Routledge.

Byrne, C. (2019). Political leaders and public diplomacy in the contested Indo-Pacific. *The Hague Journal of Diplomacy*, *14*(1–2), 182–97.

Byrne, C. (2021). Vaccine diplomacy: Tensions and contestation in Southeast Asia. *La Trobe Asia Issue Brief* 5, p. 6. https://www.csis.org/blogs/new-perspectives-asia/japan-and-vaccine-diplomacy.

China National People's Congress (2018, April 25). Report of the State Council on the protection of overseas Chinese rights and interests. *The National People's Congress of the People's Republic of China.* https://cset.georgetown.edu/publication/report-to-the-state-council-on-work-to-protect-the-rights-and-interests-of-overseas-chinese/.

Cull, N. (2019). *Public diplomacy: Foundations for global engagement in the digital age.* Polity.

Custer, S., Prakash, M., Solis, J., Knight, R., & Lin, J. (2019). *Influencing the narrative: How the Chinese government mobilizes students and media to burnish its image.* Aid data at William & Mary. https://www.aiddata.org/publications/influencing-the-narrative.

d'Hoogue, I. (2021). China's public diplomacy goes political. *The Hague Journal of Diplomacy, 16*(2–3), 299–322.

Dreher, A., Fuchs, A., Parks, B., Strange, A., & Tierney, M. (2022). *Banking on Beijing: The aims and impacts of China's overseas development program.* Cambridge University Press.

Feng, H., He, K., & Liu, F. (2018). *Chinese scholars debate world politics: A reader.* Oxford University Press.

Gilboa, E. (2008). Searching for a theory of public diplomacy. *The Annals of the American Academy of Political and Social Science, 616*(1), 55–77.

Gill, B. (2020). China's global influence: Post-COVID prospects for soft power. *The Washington Quarterly, 43*(2), 97–115.

Gregory, B. (2008). Public diplomacy: Sunrise of an academic field. *The Annals of the American Academy of Political and Social Science, 616*(1), 274–90.

Gregory, B. (2011). American public diplomacy: Enduring characteristics, elusive transformation. *The Hague Journal of Diplomacy, 6*(3–4), 351–72.

Gyngell, A. (2021). *Fear of abandonment: Australia in the world since 1942.* La Trobe University Press.

Hall, I., & Smith, F. (2013). The struggle for soft power in Asia: Public diplomacy and regional competition. *Asian Security, 9*(1), 1–18.

Heng, Y.-K. (2014). Beyond "Kawaii" pop culture: Japan's normative soft power as global trouble shooter. *The Pacific Review, 27*(2), 169–92.

Huo, F., & Maude, R. (2021, September 21). Chinese digital diplomacy in Southeast Asia during the pandemic. *Asia Society Policy Institute.* https://asiasociety.org/policy-institute/chinese-diplomacy-southeast-asia-during-covid-19-pandemic.

Ingenhoff, D., & Klein, S. (2008). A political leaders' image in public diplomacy and nation brand: The impact of competence, charisma, integrity and gender. *International Journal of Communication, 12,* 4507–32.

Jennett, G. (2021, March 12). Australia joins US, India and Japan in "unprecedented" deal for coronavirus vaccines after historic Quad meeting. *ABC News.* https://www.abc.net.au/news/2021-03-13/quad-australia-us-india-japan-in-massive-covid-vaccine-deal/13245198.

Jones, L., & Hameiri, S. (2021). *Fractured China: How state transformation is shaping China's rise.* Cambridge University Press.

Kaufman, A. (2011, March 10). The "Century of Humiliation" and China's national narratives. Testimony before the U.S.–China Economic and Security Review

Commission Hearing on China's narratives regarding national security policy. https://www.uscc.gov/sites/default/files/3.10.11Kaufman.pdf.

Koga, K. (2017). Transcending the Fukuda Doctrine: Japan, ASEAN and the future of regional order. *Strategic Japan 2017 Series*, Centre for Strategic and International Studies. file:///C:/Users/user/Downloads/170401_Japan_SEAsia.pdf.

Kuik, C. (2021). Asymmetry and authority: Theorizing Southeast Asian responses to China's Belt and Road initiative. *Asian Perspective*, 45(2), 255–76.

Kurlantzick, J. (2006, September 1). China's charm offensive in Southeast Asia. *Carnegie Endowment Policy Brief*. https://carnegieendowment.org/files/Kurlantzick_SoutheastAsia_China.pdf.

Lam, P. E. (2012). *Japan's relations with Southeast Asia: the Fukuda Doctrine and beyond*. Routledge.

Lau, J. (2020, November 6). Coronavirus: Hope for stranded Southeast Asian students after being shut out of China for nearly 2 years. *South China Morning Post*. https://www.scmp.com/news/china/diplomacy/article/3157380/coronavirus-hope-stranded-southeast-asian-students-after-being.

Lee, L., & Lee, J. (2020, April 10). Countering China's grand narratives: The American interest. https://www.the-american-interest.com/2020/04/10/countering-chinas-grand-narratives/.

Lee, S. J., & Melissen, J. (2011). *Public diplomacy and soft power in East Asia*. Palgrave Macmillan.

Li, H. (2011). Chinese diaspora and the image of China. In J. Wang (Ed.), *Soft power in China: Public diplomacy through communication* (pp. 135–56). Palgrave Macmillan.

Medcalf, R. (2020). *Contest for the Indo-Pacific: Why China won't map the future*. La Trobe University Press.

MFA [Ministry of Foreign Affairs] Japan (2021). International cooperation in the COVID-19 era: Our commitment to the future. White Paper on Japan's Development Cooperation. https://www.mofa.go.jp/mofaj/gaiko/oda/files/100343083.pdf.

Miskimmon, A. et al. (2013). *Strategic narratives: Communication power and the new world order*. Routledge.

Ogawa, T. (2020). Japan's public diplomacy at the crossroads. In N. Snow & N. Cull (Eds.), *Routledge handbook of public diplomacy*, 2nd edn (pp. 273–83). Routledge.

Otmazgin, N. (2021). An East Asian public diplomacy? Lessons from Japan, South Korea, and China. *Asian Perspective*, 45(3), 621–44.

Pew Research Center (2019). *Global Attitudes Survey*. https://www.pewresearch.org/global/category/publications/.

Repnokova, M. (2022). *Chinese soft power*. Cambridge University Press.

Sakai, H. (2019). Return to geopolitics: The changes in Japanese strategic narratives. *Asian Perspectives*, 43(2), 297–322.

Seah, S. et al. (2022). *The state of Southeast Asia: 2022 survey report*. ISEAS-Yusof Ishak Institute. https://www.iseas.edu.sg/articles-commentaries/state-of-southeast-asia-survey/the-state-of-southeast-asia-2022-survey-report/.

Seib, P. (2019). US public diplomacy and the terrorism challenge. *The Hague Journal of Diplomacy*, 14(1–2), 154–68.

Sevin, E. (2017). A multilayered approach to public diplomacy evaluation: Pathways of connection. *Politics & Policy*, 45(5), 879–901.

Shambaugh, D. (2013). *China goes global: The partial power*. Oxford University Press.

Shambaugh, D. (2021). *Where great powers meet: America and China in Southeast Asia*. Oxford University Press.

Snow, N. (2009). *Persuader-in-chief: Global opinion and public diplomacy in the age of Obama*. Nimble Books.

Snow, N. (2019). NHK, Abe and the world: Japan's pressing needs in the path to 2020. *Asian Journal of Journalism and Media Studies, 2*, 15–27.

Snow, N. (2022). Japan's strategic miscommunications in the shadow of the pandemic Olympics. *Place Branding and Public Diplomacy, 18*, 30–32. https://doi.org/10.1057/s41254-022-00259-1.

Spry, D. (2020, June 2). Winning hearts and likes: How foreign affairs and defence agencies use Facebook. *Australian Strategic Policy Institute*. https://www.aspi.org.au/report/winning-hearts-and-likes.

Stanislaus, W. (2017, July 22). Japan house: Tokyo's new public diplomacy push. *The Diplomat*. https://thediplomat.com/2017/07/japan-house-tokyos-new-public-diplomacy-push/.

Strangio, S. (2020). *In the dragon's shadow: Southeast Asia in the Chinese century*. Yale University Press.

Tan, Y. (2021, November 10). China's diaspora engagement policy and its powerful effect outside its borders. *Melbourne Asia Review*. https://doi.org/10.37839/MAR2652-550X8.9.

The Economist (2021, August 14). A glimpse into Japan's understated financial heft in the region. *The Economist*. https://www.economist.com/finance-and-economics/2021/08/14/a-glimpse-into-japans-understated-financial-heft-in-south-east-asia.

Turnbull, M. (2017, June 3). Keynote address at the 16th IISS Asia Security Summit, Shangri-La Dialogue. https://www.malcolmturnbull.com.au/media/keynote-address-at-the-16th-iiss-asia-security-summit-shangri-la-dialogue.

Vannarith, C. (2021, March 21). Confucius Institutes accepted in SEA and embraced by Cambodia, unlike in the West. *Think China*. https://www.thinkchina.sg/confucius-institutes-accepted-sea-and-embraced-cambodia-unlike-west.

Varghese, P. (2015, August 20). An Australian world view: A practitioner's perspective. Address to the Lowy Institute for International Affairs. https://www.dfat.gov.au/news/speeches/Pages/an-australian-world-view-a-practitioners-perspective.

Wang, H. (2011). China's image projection and its impact. In J. Wang (Ed.), *Soft power in China: Public diplomacy through communication* (pp. 37–56). Palgrave Macmillan.

Watanabe, Y. (2017). The pivot shift of Japan's public diplomacy. In N. Chitty, L. Ji, G. Rawnsley, & C. Hayden (Eds.), *Routledge handbook of soft power* (pp. 400–413). Routledge.

Weissmann, M. (2019). Capturing power shift in East Asia: Toward an analytical framework for understanding soft power. *Asian Perspective, 44*(3), 353–82.

Weissmann, M., & Li, M. (2019). Introduction to the Special Issue. *Asian Perspective, 43*(2), 215–21.

Wesley, M. (2021). *Finding Australia's new Asian narrative*. Asialink. https://asialink.unimelb.edu.au/stories/finding-australias-new-asia-narrative.

Wise, J. (2021, February 11). The costs of discounted diplomacy. *ASPI Insights*. https://www.aspi.org.au/report/costs-discounted-diplomacy.

Wiseman, G. (2018, August 24). Soft power and reviewing Australia's global appeal. *The Interpreter*. https://uscpublicdiplomacy.org/blog/soft-power-and-reviewing-australia%E2%80%99s-global-appeal.

Yu, K. (2021, April 6). The Belt and Road Initiative in Southeast Asia after COVID-19: China's energy and infrastructure investments in Myanmar. *ISEAS Perspective*. https://www.iseas.edu.sg/articles-commentaries/iseas-perspective/2021-39-the

-belt -and -road -initiative -in -southeast -asia -after -covid -19 -chinas -energy -and
-infrastructure-investments-in-myanmar-by-kaho-yu/.

Zhao, K. (2019). The China model of public diplomacy and its future. *The Hague
Journal of Diplomacy, 14*(1–2), 169–81.

3 International organizations

Phillip Arceneaux

Introduction

Traditionally, public diplomacy (PD) is understood as purposeful communication with foreign audiences in the advancement of a state's foreign policy (Cull, 2019). *New PD* challenges this definition (Melissen, 2005; Fitzpatrick, 2007), considering nonstate actors as PD practitioners, including corporations, nonprofits, NGOs, and diasporas. Indeed, PD scholarship has grown substantively since the beginning of the 21st century, in such areas as international exchanges (Hayden, 2009), nation branding (Buhmann et al., 2019), and digital diplomacy (Manor, 2019).

The premise of new PD stresses two-way, mutually beneficial communication between an expanded range of actors, publics, and stakeholders (Fitzpatrick, 2007; Melissen, 2005). Subsequent research on foreign public engagement by nonstate actors such as cities (Amiri & Sevin, 2020), NGOs (Pamment, 2013), corporations (Kochhar, 2018), think tanks (Li et al., 2019), and diasporas (Kennedy, 2022) has also grown to varying extents. Additionally, Gilboa (2008) asserted the need to better understand the role of international law surrounding PD. While new and traditional PD serve as polar ends of a continuum, this chapter proposes a blended framework, considering states, venues of international law, and international organizations as actors and targets of PD.

International organizations like the United Nations (UN), European Union (EU), Association of Southeast Asian Nations (ASEAN), and North Atlantic Treaty Organization (NATO) are central to 21st-century international relations, yet scholarship lacks the context for studying international organizations as primary (1) venues for PD, (2) targets of PD, or (3) as PD actors themselves. Exploring this gap, this chapter offers an overview of international organizations as a rife research agenda for PD. Taken in stride, this chapter exposes a critical context for understanding what scholars lack on the practice and conceptual understanding of new PD.

International organizations are defined as supranational institutions founded by multilateral treaty, governed by international law, and possessing legal personality. This ranges from the UN and its various organs (WHO, UNICEF, UNESCO, UNHRC), to NATO, the World Bank, International Monetary Fund, and Interpol to name a few. This definition excludes international non-governmental organizations (NGOs), which are recognized as civil entities within the jurisdiction of a given country, who conduct their work across international borders. This ranges from Doctors Without Borders, to Human Rights Watch, Amnesty International, Sister Cities International, Save the Children, and Mercy Corps.

The traditional unit of analysis in PD research is the nation state, with increasing attention paid to public and private NGOs. This chapter, rather, looks to supranational geopolitics to advocate for a research agenda analyzing PD efforts at, toward, and by international organizations. The chapter highlights PD by states *within* international organizations, including campaigning during UN Security Council elections, China's use of the International Court of Arbitration as a tactic of lawfare, and NATO's military personnel exchange programs. It also addresses PD aimed *at* international organizations, in the case of *Palestine 194* and the global justice movement. Lastly, the chapter highlights the use of PD *by* international organizations, ranging from EU supranationalism, the African Union's "African Renaissance" and ASEAN's people-to-people connectivity, to debt-trap diplomacy by the International Monetary Fund and World Bank. Taken in stride, this chapter shines a light on critical gaps in the study of modern PD practice.

Public diplomacy within international organizations

International relations scholarship considers anarchy to be the state of persistent competition within the international political theater, caused by the lack of a central authority or governing body to instill rules, regulations, and processes that govern state behavior. While often voluntary, international organizations, like the UN for example, provide such an executive authority with legislative processes designed to impact state behavior. Understanding states may behave differently within this context; it is natural to assume PD may equally be different, necessitating scholarly attention and analysis. Thus, research treating international organizations as venues for states engaging in PD is necessary.

Though states may target foreign audiences within their PD efforts, such audiences do not have to be civil society. Such is the case within the United Nations General Assembly (UNGA), a body populated by diplomats and international bureaucrats. A context for states engaging in PD within the venue of international organizations is evident in various lobbying and campaign efforts, such as those conducted by states interested in being elected to rotating seats on the Security Council.

Offering an initial lens into this research context, Arceneaux (2021) analyzed the storytelling strategies, or strategic narratives (Miskimmon et al., 2017), in Ireland's two-year PD campaign to be elected to the UN Security Council for 2021–23 in one of Western Europe's two allotted seats. Built on themes of Empathy, Partnership, and Independence, the Irish PD campaign spent two years melding system, identity, and issue narratives of its own foreign policy interests to those of the UN (peacekeeping, climate change, humanitarian aid), and to the foreign policy interests of strategic mid- to small-sized states in the UNGA spanning the Asia-Pacific (technological regulation), sub-Saharan Africa (disarmament), and the Middle East (two-state solution in the West Bank). This study highlights a context for the practice of PD within the venue of an international organization.

Understanding isolated cases of PD behavior within an international organization, as in the case of Ireland's Security Council campaign, only paints part of the picture. International organizations present new venues for state competition; thus, PD scholarship addressing this new venue should consider both case studies of single states, but also PD competition within the international organization (IO) venue. Considering the Security Council election, Ireland competed with both Norway and Canada to fill Western Europe's two available seats. Based in the notion of frame-building in elite competitive environments (Chong & Druckman, 2007), researchers should also consider such a context within their analysis. Ireland, Norway, and Canada are particularly apt for study as their PD campaigns constituted friendly competition, a unique context compared to the kinds of adversarial PD competition present in the Security Council, as evidenced by the US and Russia sparring over Ukraine (Davis & Kelemen, 2022).

Though international organizations like the UN and NATO may provide executive or legislative structure, other international organizations provide a judicial basis for the regulation of state behavior. A driving premise in the international system is the power of image within the international community, and some of the only concrete repercussions that can be levied against states behaving poorly is the image and reputation damage of being expelled from the community. Such is the case of North Korea from the UN, and Russia from the Group of 8. Understanding the image and reputation damage such expulsion could cause to the narrative of its peaceful rise, China has doubled down on its efforts to work within the international community, and its IO structures, to improve its image and advance its interests.

While China has pursued increasing sovereignty in the South China Sea, it was brought to the Permanent Court of Arbitration by the Philippines. Though China initially attempted to circumvent the IO, it eventually shifted tactics, using the court as a form of lawfare (Kittrie, 2016), merging PD influence over public opinion with international law (Gilboa & Shai, 2011). This was a strategic move to illustrate that, despite China's growing global influence and military capacity, both of which could easily overwhelm Filipino regional interests, its actions are in line with its words of seeking a peaceful international presence. The use of the internal legal system, as a tactic of lawfare, is an additional context of the advancement of PD scholarship (Arceneaux, 2020).

Lastly, a third context for studying PD through the venue of international organizations involves exchange programs. A people-to-people pillar of Cull's (2008) taxonomy of PD, militaries often engage in officer exchanges to promote tactical knowledge, but also to facilitate inter-military integration (Davis, 2020; Waller, 2020), that is, build relational bonds and cultural understanding between allies. NATO is a common IO through which member states regularly facilitate officer exchanges across all branches of various militaries. This includes officer exchanges across the army, marines, and air force branches of the US, UK, Canada, France, Italy, and Poland, to reference only a few. While some exchanges are short-term programs, others are permanent exchange appointments. The USS *Winston S. Churchill* is the only ship in the US Navy to have a British Royal Navy officer permanently assigned to its command staff (Fisher, 2020).

Public diplomacy targeting international organizations

PD can also be targeted externally at IOs. Such was the case in the *Palestine 194* campaign. Ahead of the 2011 UNGA, the Palestinian Authority applied to become the 194th member of the UN, an effort supported by the launch of the *Palestine 194* campaign to curry favor and support for the UN's adoption of Palestine (Esposito, 2011). The campaign was devised by the Palestinian Liberation Organization (PLO) as a soft power means to look for a multilateral solution to the bi-lateral impasse between Palestinian and Israeli interests stemming from the Oslo Agreement (Deas, 2021). The Palestinians have also successfully used PD in other UN organizations such as the UN Human Rights Council (Gilboa, 2021).

Another such example involves PD efforts by the global justice movement against financial international organizations like the World Trade Organization. This network of movements promotes equitable distribution of economic wealth and resources across the globe, blaming existing global economic institutions for the present lack of international financial equity. While a decentralized network of movements presenting its share of continuity challenges (Oglesby, 2010), the global justice movement's PD efforts have been more concrete, mobilizing coherent campaigns that utilize various tactics, including celebrity diplomacy (Cooper, 2016). One such example involves the *Make Poverty History* campaign featuring celebrities Bob Geldof, Bono, and Richard Curtis (Brown, 2009). Though generally unsuccessful to date, the movement has consistently advocated for the adoption of more fair-trading practices and regulations by financial international organizations.

Public diplomacy by international organizations

Perhaps the most novel approach to a new agenda of scholarship surrounding international organizations is the application of PD by these supranational organizations. Such is the case, for example, in EU efforts to promote a European identity both abroad but also within its member states (van Ham, 2013). While countries like France and Germany are traditionally pro-European integration, EU favorability ranges widely across member states. Tarasevish et al. (2019) found that nationalistic sentiment in the UK and Poland were determining factors in decreased support for EU policy and the broader status of regional integration. Understanding this, the EU uses PD to communicate with diverse national audiences across Europe to promote pan-European values, and the inherent benefits of the continent cooperating as a unified bargaining block (Davis Cross, 2013).

While both Europe and the EU are mainstays in PD scholarship, new research agendas should turn outward to explore the role of international organizations in supporting regional integration and soft power in other contexts. The African Union (AU), for example, wages extensive PD campaigns promoting pan-Africanism to solve many of the continent's struggles, from conflict, to corruption, famine, disease, and so on (Agupusi, 2021). Though an "African

Renaissance" was coined by Cheikh Anta Diop in the mid-20th century, the AU adopted the concept as the centerpiece of its pan-Africa PD campaign.

The "African Renaissance" campaign has manifested itself in a variety of forms, such as public artwork including the *Monument de la Renaissance Africaine* in Senegal. It has also led to the adoption of ceremonial "Doors of Return" in Nigeria, Ghana, and Zimbabwe. The "Door of Return" initiative looks to advance engagement with the global African diaspora, as well as drive economic cooperation with respective governments, like Jamaica and others across the Caribbean (ATQ News, 2017).

Beyond the physical manifestation of people-to-people PD programming, the AU has explored the digitalization of such efforts, through the adoption of extensive digital diplomacy programming. Outlined in its Digital Transformation Strategy for Africa (2020–30), the adoption of both digital strategies and infrastructure has catalyzed the AU's capacity to promote continental diplomacy (Ayodele, 2021). This constitutes AU efforts to achieve *Pax Africana*, or regional integration through peaceful cohabitation, if not cooperation, across the continent based on mutual interests in self-establishing the continent's own economic development and political stability.

Shifting analysis on the digitalization of PD in regional rather than continental international organizations, from the AU to NATO for example, Bjola and Manor (2020) explored the digital outreach of an international organization during the flashpoint of the Covid-19 pandemic. As they point out, NATO is a military-based international organization, and is not designed to respond to public health crises. Based on this, the Twitter handles for both NATO and its missions altered their digital diplomacy approaches, using their existing campaigns and hashtags to reframe NATO as a secondary international actor looking to assist member states in their own public health responses. Overall, the study found a general lack of issue and message coordination across NATO and its missions' handles, which was executed in a rigid and largely analog manner, with the virtualization of traditional, one-way press conferences and ministerial meetings.

After considering the PD work of international organizations across Europe and Africa, this chapter now turns to consider Asia, specifically the ASEAN. Founded in 1967 and chartered in 2008, the ASEAN has adopted internal PD programming to promote regional cooperation and community more so than integration, as in the case of the EU and AU (Pagovski, 2015). Constituted largely by mid- to low-power states, ASEAN PD has primarily been aimed externally at creating perceptions that the international organization is a strong, significant actor both in Asia and the international theater. This is partly based on the notion that ASEAN interests are not necessarily aligned with those of regional powerbrokers including China, Japan, or South Korea.

Based in non-Western vernacular, the ASEAN tends to not overtly reference PD or its incorporation in organizational programming. Rather, the body prefers "people-to-people connectivity" (Anantasirikiat, 2021). Such efforts at cultural diplomacy have manifested in a variety of programs, such as the online games "Next Top Chef," "The Legend of the Golden Talisman," and "ASEAN Quiz Program" aimed at generating global exposure for the international organization (Pagovski, 2015). Divisions within ASEAN also recently cooperated to produce a cookbook, *Table for 10: ASEAN Shared Food Traditions*, highlighting the cuisine and culinary cultures of ASEAN members (Philippines Department of Foreign Affairs, 2021). ASEAN has also begun establishing academic scholarships through its member states to promote and support educational exchange programs (Pagovski, 2015).

Moving from legislative to judicial international organizations as PD actors, some existing scholarship has successfully addressed the application of PD by international judiciaries. Eichert (2021) applied a qualitative content analysis to investigate the digital diplomacy efforts of the International Criminal Court (ICC). He found that while the ICC used its digital diplomacy to promote narratives of the international court acting in the name of a unified global fight for justice, it strategically tried to generate political support from influential diplomatic powers and fellow international organizations. In the effort to engage with foreign publics, however, the ICC's digital diplomacy was also guilty of over-simplifying complex geopolitical issues. Overall, Eichert (2021) concluded that though the ICC portrays itself as a politically neutral and objective judicial international organization, its digital diplomacy adopts a markedly political tone and stance.

Lastly, while PD is largely situated in the framework of soft power (Nye, 2021), recent work has addressed the purview of *sharp power* as means of manipulative influence through less reputable modes of communication, including censorship and disinformation campaigns (Walker, 2018). PD tends to be studied through normative, and at times utopian, lenses. Understanding this tendency, this chapter purposefully highlights a more predatory context of PD by an international organization, that of debt-trap diplomacy.

The concept of "debt-trap diplomacy" was coined during the Trump administration as a reference point to articulate Chinese economic manipulation in *One Belt One Road* initiatives in Africa (McConnell & Woon, 2021) and Asia

(Gopaldas, 2018). More specifically, the concept illustrates how China offers financial capital to fund infrastructure projects in developing countries which can likely not be repaid, strategically indebting the receiving country to China and its geopolitical interests (Kulsoom, 2020). While the concept was developed to explain such behavior by state actors, it is increasingly being employed by financial international organizations, including the International Monetary Fund (IMF) and World Bank.

Advancing their geopolitical and economic interests, the IMF and World Bank have strategically sought out loan ventures with poorer states to leverage influence over their policies. Such has been the drive behind foreign financial aid provided by the World Bank to the Philippines since the 1960s (Toussaint, 2020). A more recent context for debt-trap diplomacy is evident in relief loans provided by the IMF during the Covid-19 pandemic. The conditions of the financial aid have strategically driven policies of austerity in approximately 80 percent of the weakest economies and poorest governments across the globe (Oxfam, 2020).

Most of the topics overviewed span diverse academic backgrounds: communication, political science, law, economics, diplomatic studies, tourism, and so on. While largely approached from disparate theoretical and methodological backgrounds, the only way to move the understanding of public diplomacy surrounding international organizations forward is to span ideological bridges to pursue interdisciplinary, collaborative research. For example, scholars need more analysis on organizational aspects, such how international organizations conduct PD. This spans which departments within these organizations, what manpower and budgets they have, and what strategies they employ, if any.

Beyond spanning academic disciplines, scholars must work with both practitioners and policymakers to best understand this niche practice. Organizational structures that might serve as starting points include NATO's Strategic Communications Centre of Excellence (StraCom COE). Though appearing to have ended in 2016, StraCom COE's PD forum (nato.int/pdforum) was a primary venue for connecting the practitioners of PD within international organizations with scholars. NATO employs an Assistant Secretary for PD and a head of the Engagement Section within the PD Division. NATO PD programming is under the direction of the North Atlantic Council (NAC) and NATO's Secretary General, while the Committee on Public Diplomacy (CPD) is a part of NAC that advises the council on policy and programming. NATO also staffs a Public Diplomacy Division (PDD) to execute the organization's PD efforts. In carrying out NATO's PD programming, PDD works with the Public Affairs and Strategic Communications Advisor to the Chairman of the

Military Committee. They also collaborate with Allied Command Operations and Allied Command Transformation to communicate on NATO operations (NATO, 2016).

Looking elsewhere, the UN's Department of Global Communications is apt for both organizational study and collaboration. The department is responsible for the organization's strategic communications, news and media engagement, and public outreach. Today, specific collaborators who are friendly to PD research include Charlotte Scaddan and Karin Orantes of the UN Department of Public Information, who oversee the international organization's flagship social media accounts. Additionally, Nancy Groves of the UN's Environmental Program currently serves as digital strategy chief and has actively participated in digital diplomacy programming within the academic PD community.

Conclusion

Scholarship on supranational PD (i.e., global strategic communications within, targeting, and by IOs), is a context of new PD that has yet to be substantively explored. As international organizations exist to provide executive, legislative, or judicial capacities external to any one state, they fundamentally impact the way states behave and engage with each other in the international system. As such, they offer vital contexts for the application of both soft and sharp power toward both internal and external stakeholders.

To understand the forces at work within the international system more accurately, scholars must be more flexible in the unit of analysis within PD research, moving to new actors that are both above (supranational) and below (infranational) the narrow thresholds of states alone. Even when considering states, the venues in which they engage in PD should be considered, such as the role of states campaigning within supranational legislative bodies like the UN, to the role of states seeking arbitration in supranational judicial bodies like the International Court of Justice, or even the transitive capacity of international organizations to facilitate exchange programs.

Looking outward, there are apt contexts of the study of PD campaigns aimed at influencing the opinions and behavior of international organizations. This can begin with *Palestine 194* or the effort to advance sovereign statehood through grassroots efforts to fight universal inequality through the global justice movement. While the cases highlighted in this chapter focus on public interest social movements, such a context for future PD research need not focus solely on global publics, but also on governmental and political actors seeking to advance their interests through impacting international organization behavior.

Lastly, and arguably most important to a chapter centered on international organizations and PD, is the application of PD programming by international organizations. Contexts for such research should consider a wide range of variables, from continental bodies (EU and AU) to sub-regional units (ASEAN or NATO), to infranational efforts (identity formation and regional integration) to supranational efforts (block negotiating and value or norm sharing), and soft (culture and exchanges) versus sharp (debt-trap diplomacy) applications of PD programming. Considering all these research permutations, this chapter shines a light on critical gaps in the study of modern PD practice in the supranational capacity of international organizations.

To conceptualize a path forward for the study of PD surrounding international organizations, this chapter closes with questions aimed at inspiring future research at this niche intersection. Scholars should look to answer: What disciplines, theories, and methodologies are best equipped to illuminate the use of strategic communications by, toward, and within international organizations? What kinds of international organizations or campaigns might serve as successful models or case studies of supranational PD, and what organizational structures lent to the success or failure of PD programming by such actors? How do systemic factors within international relations and communications impact the goals, outcomes, and outputs of international organizations as they engage in PD programming? And lastly, what kinds of metrics are used inter-organizationally to measure the effectiveness of PD programming, whether by, toward, or within international organizations? As international organizations, states, and societal actors all tend to present with limited resources, in terms of both fiscal assets and manpower, performance evaluation is an optimal area for future research.

References

Agupusi, P. (2021). The African Union and the path to an African Renaissance. *Journal of Contemporary African Studies*, *39*(2), 261–84. https://doi.org/10.1080/02589001.2021.1874611.

Amiri, S., & Sevin, E. (2020). Introduction. In: S. Amiri & E. Sevin (Eds.), *City diplomacy: Current trends and future prospects* (pp. 1–10). Palgrave Macmillan.

Anantasirikiat, S. (2021, May 11). Public diplomacy matters for the future of ASEAN. USC Center for Public Diplomacy Blog. Available at: https://uscpublicdiplomacy.org/blog/public-diplomacy-matters-future-asean.

Arceneaux, P. (2020). International law provides new context for public diplomacy scholarship. USC Center for Public Diplomacy. Retrieved February 10, 2022 from https://uscpublicdiplomacy.org/blog/international-law-provides-new-context-public-diplomacy-scholarship.

Arceneaux, P. (2021). Political public relations within foreign affairs: Ireland's public diplomacy campaign for a Security Council seat. *Public Relations Inquiry.* https://doi.org/10.1177/2046147X211055194.

ATQ News (2017, March 31). Four nations sign up on Door of Return with Accompong, Jamaica to drive tourism with diaspora. Available at: https://atqnews.com/4-nations-door-drive-tourism-diaspora/.

Ayodele, O. (2021). The digital transformation of diplomacy: Implications for the African Union and continental diplomacy. *South African Journal of International Affairs, 28*(3), 379–401. https://doi.org/10.1080/10220461.2021.1968944.

Bjola, C., & Manor, I. (2020). NATO's digital public diplomacy during the COVID-19 pandemic. *Turkish Policy, 19*(2), 77–87.

Brown, J. (2009). Publicizing the African cause: Evaluating global media discourses regarding the celebrity-led "Make Poverty History" campaign. Southern Illinois University. Available at: https://opensiuc.lib.siu.edu/dissertations/101/.

Buhmann, A., Ingenhoff, D., White, C., & Kiousis, S. (2019). Charting the landscape in research on country image, reputation, brand and identity: A transdisciplinary overview. In: D. Ingenhoff, C. White, A. Buhmann, & S. Kiousis (Eds.), *Bridging disciplinary perspectives of country image, reputation, brand, and identity* (pp. 1–11). Routledge.

Chong, D., & Druckman, J. N. (2007). Framing public opinion in competitive democracies. *American Political Science Review, 101*(4), 637–55. https://doi.org/10.1017/S0003055407070554.

Cooper, A. F. (2016). *Celebrity diplomacy.* Routledge.

Cull, N. J. (2008). Public diplomacy: Taxonomies and histories. *The Annals of the American Academy of Political and Social Science, 616*(1), 31–54.

Cull, N. J. (2019). *Public diplomacy: Foundations for global engagement in the digital age.* Polity.

Davis, C. (2020, January 27). JB Charleston benefits from Military Personnel Exchange Program. United States Air Force. Retrieved February 10, 2022 from https://www.af.mil/News/Article-Display/Article/2233168/jb-charleston-benefits-from-military-personnel-exchange-program/.

Davis, W., & Kelemen, M. (2022, January 31). U.S. and Russia share tense exchange at U.N. Security Council meeting. National Public Radio. Available at: https://www.npr.org/2022/01/31/1077069002/russia-united-states-ukraine-un-security-council.

Davis Cross, M. K. (2013). Conceptualizing European public diplomacy. In: M. K. Davis Cross (Ed.), *European public diplomacy: Soft power at work* (pp. 1–11). Springer.

Deas, J. (2021). Thinking outside the bilateral box: Can the Palestinian leadership reshape a post-Oslo diplomatic strategy? *Confluences Méditerranée, 117*(2), 133–47.

Eichert, D. (2021). Hashtagging justice: Digital diplomacy and the International Criminal Court on Twitter. *The Hague Journal of Diplomacy.* https://doi.org/10.1163/1871191X-bja10074.

Esposito, M. K. (2011). Update on conflict and diplomacy. *Journal of Palestine Studies, 41*(1), 147–88. https://doi.org/10.1525/jps.2011.XLI.1.147.

Fisher, C. (2020, September 18). USS *Winston S. Churchill* conducts interoperability operations with British Royal Navy. U.S. Naval Forces Europe-Africa/U.S. 6th Fleet. Retrieved February 10, 2022 from https://www.c6f.navy.mil/Press-Room/News/

News-Display/Article/2352428/uss-winston-s-churchill-conducts-interoperability-operations-with-british-royal/.

Fitzpatrick, K. (2007). Advancing the new public diplomacy: A public relations perspective. *The Hague Journal of Diplomacy*, *2*(3), 187–211. https://doi.org/10.1163/187119007X240497.

Gilboa, E. (2008). Searching for a theory of public diplomacy. *The Annals of the American Academy of Political and Social Science*, *616*(1), 55–77. https://doi.org/10.1177/0002716207312142.

Gilboa, E. (2021). The Palestinian campaign against Israel at the United Nations Human Rights Council. *Israel Affairs*, *27*(1), 68–88. https://doi.org/10.1080/13537121.2021.1864849.

Gilboa, E., & Shai, N. (2011). Rebuilding public diplomacy: The case of Israel. In: A. Fisher & S. Lucas (Eds.), *Trials of engagement: The future of US public diplomacy* (pp. 33–54). Brill.

Gopaldas, R. (2018, February 21). Lessons from Sri Lanka on China's "debt-trap diplomacy." Institute for Security Studies. Available at: https://issafrica.org/iss-today/lessons-from-sri-lanka-on-chinas-debt-trap-diplomacy.

Hayden, C. (2009). Applied public diplomacy: A marketing communications exchange program in Saudi Arabia. *American Behavioral Scientist*, *53*(4), 533–48. https://doi.org/10.1177/0002764209347629.

Kennedy, L. (Ed.) (2022). *The Routledge international handbook of diaspora diplomacy*. Routledge.

Kittrie, O. (2016). *Lawfare: Law as a weapon of war*. Oxford University Press.

Kochhar, S. (2018). Corporate diplomacy as an engagement strategy of the nonmarket business environment. In: K. A. Johnson & M. Taylor (Eds.), *The handbook of communication engagement* (pp. 347–56). Wiley.

Kulsoom, S. (2020). Economic determinants in India's public diplomacy towards South Asia. In: P. Surowiec & I. Manor (Eds.), *Public diplomacy and the politics of uncertainty* (pp. 255–76). Springer.

Li, L., Chen, X., & Hanson, E. C. (2019). Private think tanks and public–private partnerships in Chinese public diplomacy. *The Hague Journal of Diplomacy*, *14*(3), 293–318. https://doi.org/10.1163/1871191X-14301024.

Manor, I. (2019). *The digitalization of public diplomacy*. Palgrave Macmillan.

McConnell, F., & Woon, C. Y. (2021). Mapping Chinese diplomacy: Relational contradictions and spatial tensions. *Geopolitics*. https://doi.org/10.1080/14650045.2021.1966417.

Melissen, J. (2005). The new public diplomacy: Between theory and practice. In: J. Melissen (Ed.), *The new public diplomacy: Soft power in international relations* (pp. 3–27). Springer.

Miskimmon, A., O'Loughlin, B., & Roselle, L. (2017). *Forging the world: Strategic narratives and international relations*. University of Michigan Press.

NATO (2016, June 20). Communications and public diplomacy. Available at: https://www.nato.int/cps/en/natohq/topics_69275.htm.

Nye, J. S. (2021). Soft power: The evolution of a concept. *Journal of Political Power*, *14*(1), 196–208. https://doi.org/10.1080/2158379X.2021.1879572.

Oglesby, D. M. (2010). Spectacle in Copenhagen: Public diplomacy on parade. USC Center for Public Diplomacy, Perspectives on Public Diplomacy. Available at: https://uscpublicdiplomacy.org/sites/uscpublicdiplomacy.org/files/useruploads/u35361/2010%20Paper%204.pdf.

Oxfam (2020, October 12). Over 80 percent of IMF COVID-19 loans will push austerity on poor countries. UN Office for the Coordination of Humanitarian Affairs. Available at: https:// reliefweb .int/ report/ world/ over -80 -cent -imf -covid - 19 -loans -will-push-austerity-poor-countries.

Pagovski, Z. Z. (2015). Public diplomacy of multilateral organizations: The cases of NATO, EU, and ASEAN. USC Center for Public Diplomacy, Perspectives on Public Diplomacy. Available at: https:// uscpublicdiplomacy.org/ sites/ uscpublicdiplomacy .org/ files/ useruploads/ u33041/ Public %20Diplomacy %20of %20Multilateral %20 - %20Full%20June%202015.pdf.

Pamment, J. (2013). *New public diplomacy in the 21st century: A comparative study of policy and practice*. Routledge.

Philippines Department of Foreign Affairs (2021, December 31). DFA, ASEAN Ladies Foundation launch "Table for Ten: ASEAN Shared Food Traditions." Available at: https://dfa.gov.ph/ibf-releases/30018-dfa-asean-ladies-foundation-launch-table-for -ten-asean-shared-food-traditions.

Tarasevish, S., Khalitova, L., Arceneaux, P., Myslik, B., & Kiousis, S. (2019). Ethnic nationalism and gatekeeping in the European media: Linking agenda setting, agenda building, and agenda indexing. *The Agenda Setting Journal*, 3(1), 23–42. https://doi .org/10.1075/asj.18014.tar.

Toussaint, T. (2020, April 17). The World Bank and the Philippines. Committee for the Abolition of Illegitimate Debt. Available at: https://www.cadtm.org/The-World -Bank-and-the-Philippines.

van Ham, P. (2013). The European Union's social power in international politics. In: M. Cross & J. Melissen (Eds.), *European public diplomacy: Soft power at work* (pp. 157–81). Palgrave Macmillan.

Walker, C. (2018). What is "sharp power"? *Journal of Democracy*, 29(3), 9–23.

Waller, R. (2020, April 27). Military personnel exchange program officers strengthen partner countries' military response. United States Air Force. Retrieved February 10, 2022 from https://www.af.mil/ News/ Article -Display/ Article/ 2166275/ military -personnel-exchange-program-officers-strengthen-partner-countries-milit/.

4   Corporate diplomacy

Candace L. White and Wilfried Bolewski

Introduction

Public diplomacy (PD) is a process driven by a nation state's[1] actions and communication directed toward foreign publics with the goal of generating beneficial relations that support the country's foreign policy agenda and increase its attraction and soft power. "PD is a communication process that states, nonstate actors, and organizations employ to influence the policies of a foreign government by influencing its citizens. PD is designed to bring about understanding for a nation's ideas and ideals, its institutions and culture, as well as its national goals and policies" (Gilboa, 2016, pp. 1297–8). Twenty-first-century PD is increasingly multi-lateral, with governments as part of a network of actors rather in full control of messages emanating from a nation. Globalized communication networks and political and commercial entities that transcend the borders of nation states have blurred the line between "official messages" from a government and the cacophony of communication from nonstate actors that also greatly affects perceptions and opinions about the nation from which the communications originate (White, 2020).

Globalization has made the boundaries of diplomacy porous (Saner & Yiu, 2003) and has created a power shift in international relations with greater interdependence between global business and international politics that has transformed the relationship between state and nonstate actors in PD (Ban & Dutta, 2012). Furthermore, the publics of diplomatic messages often are global audiences, rather than citizens of a particular country, composed of a variety of interest groups based on values, religion, and other ideologies that can transcend the boundaries of nation states (White, 2015). In light of sociological globalism and growing uncertainties in a transnational risk society (Manor & Surowiec, 2021) the expected purpose and mission of PD is extending – by

---

[1]   In this chapter, the terms country and nation state are used interchangeably, recognizing they do not mean the same to everyone. An explanation of the complexity of the differences is beyond the scope of the chapter.

popular support – from listening, messaging, informing, communicating and influencing publics and governments to a public-involvement emphasis and collaborative problem-solving to address global societal challenges such as pandemics, climate, and others (Cotton & Sebastiao, 2022).

While governments are at the center of PD, the multi-directional nature of new PD has resulted in new roles for nonstate actors such as international corporations and non-governmental organizations (NGOs) that contribute to diplomatic outcomes. Sources outside governments have increasing influence on policy and diplomatic activities. The Center on Public Diplomacy (CPD) at the University of Southern California purports that PD includes not only government-sponsored cultural, educational, and informational programs, but also citizen exchanges, private media broadcasts, and corporate communications used to promote the national interests of a country. It defines PD as a country's efforts, through official and private individuals and institutions, to communicate with publics in other countries and societies (http://www.uscpublicdiplomacy.com). Multinational corporations hold economic power, media have power over public opinion, and citizen interest groups hold power in policy implementation (White, 2015).

Corporate diplomacy (CD), which is the involvement of corporations as nonstate actors in public diplomacy, is carried out by working intentionally with governments through partnerships and strategic coordination, or independently through activities that include cultural exchanges, direct involvement with foreign governments, and an array of other activities that affect country image and produce diplomatic outcomes. Multinational corporations spend more money on communication than do many governments with access to research, extensive networks, and locals on the ground. They have the propensity to listen to local markets with expertise in intercultural communication (Reinhard, 2009). They also seek to influence political decisions and to affect policy and media agendas in foreign countries, in consort with their own government, or independently. Hocking (2004) notes, for example, that Shell Oil has developed a diplomatic structure in Nigeria that rivals that of developed nations. He observes, as do other scholars (Westermann-Behaylo, Rehbein, & Fort, 2015) that global problems require multi-lateral, global solutions that international companies can help provide. Global corporations from all countries have the power and resources to be a force for change and to enrich the soft power and diplomatic efforts of the nation with which they are associated.

The concept of CD has gained traction in recent years, but the motivations, functions, and country and cultural differences are understudied. Thus, this chapter sets forth a research agenda for exploring CD that recognizes the evolving nature of PD perpetuated by global communication networks and increasing reliance on nonstate actors. Key issues are understanding the nuances in defining CD for research purposes and recognizing motivations and intentions for companies' involvement in PD. Studies are needed to separate the concept of CD from the related concept of business diplomacy, to differentiate diplomatic activities that only benefit corporations from benefits to broader social issues. CD implies that companies act beyond pure self-interests.

Embracing and enhancing CD does not mean undermining state diplomacy. Transnational corporations can profit from traditional state diplomacy to create an enabling business environment to anticipate and avoid costly conflicts, and nation states can benefit from the resources of businesses. In some cases, the private sector can even play the role of initiator and facilitator of diplomatic efforts. In tackling grand challenges, corporations are becoming diplomatic co-actors in PD and acquiring access to the diplomatic arena. Thus, multinational corporations are to be acknowledged both as objects and actors in diplomatic processes and international affairs (Sevin & Karaca, 2016).

Motivations, intentions, and enlightened self-interests

A purpose of this volume is to help existing and future PD scholars find a common language. CD is an evolving concept that is often defined differently from different disciplinary perspectives, and a clearer and more uniform operational definition is needed to help scholars examine the phenomenon. Research that examines the motivations and intentions behind corporate engagement in diplomatic activities will help parse out an operational definition for research purposes. Conceptually, motivations for CD can range from purely profit-driven motives based on corporate self-interests to a broader concern for building country image and/or solving global problems. In terms of developing a common language to clarify CD, it may be helpful to separate the notion of diplomacy motivated solely for corporate interests, and diplomacy used with intentions for benefits that go beyond increasing profits for the corporation. The first would be "business diplomacy" and the second "corporate diplomacy." Of course, corporations can use diplomacy for mixed motives that benefit business goals while also serving broader interests, which is described as "enlightened self-interests" (Reinhard, 2009).

Business diplomacy

Business diplomacy describes the efforts of a corporation operating abroad to develop a hospitable operating environment in host countries, the goal of which is to achieve corporate objectives for instrumental, profit-driven motives and benefits. Kesteleyn, Roirdan, and Ruël (2014) note that businesses often carry out their own diplomacy in foreign countries, working independently from their embassies, to negotiate directly with governments and other stakeholders in their own interests, and in doing so, corporations take on many functions that were previously performed by government diplomats. In some cases, corporations may even hire former government diplomats to carry out these activities.

In the business literature, the terms CD and business diplomacy are used interchangeably, and the conceptualizations are the same, both falling on the profit-motive end of the continuum. Studies by Amann et al. (2007) and Asquer (2012) used the term CD, but the motivations and intentions were to achieve business goals (business diplomacy). Amann et al. (2007) defined CD as the attempt to manage the business environment systematically and professionally to ensure that business is done smoothly, and Asquer (2012) defined CD "as strategically managing relationships, through various means and methods, to achieve corporate objectives." In these conceptualizations of CD there has been little or no emphasis on diplomatic activities to advance broader state interests. The primary goal of these types of diplomatic activities is to achieve business goals, which would fall on the business diplomacy end of an operational definition continuum.

Corporate diplomacy

On the CD end of the definitional continuum are diplomatic activities that benefit both the business and the home country, and often the host country in which the corporation operates. As early as 1966, U.S. corporate executive Christian A. Herter (1966), general manager of government relations for Socony Mobil Oil, observed a need for corporate policies abroad to reflect the larger interests of a corporation's home country "or at least try to accommodate itself to them, without sacrificing completely its proper, profit-oriented motivation" (p. 408). Herter purported that CD had dual objectives of establishing relationships abroad that are essential to the corporation, as well as building an enduring feeling of goodwill for the U.S., its people, its economic system, its business organizations, its political institutions, and the validity of its culture (p. 409). He noted that in this sense corporate and political diplomacy are virtually indistinguishable.

Saner and Yiu (2003) consider that CD includes influencing policy to achieve corporate goals while taking into account the needs of other stakeholders, working with rule-making international bodies, forestalling potential conflicts with governments, using international media to safeguard the image and reputation of the corporation's home country, sustaining credibility and legitimacy, and creating social capital through dialog with stakeholders who might be impacted by the process of economic development and globalization. Thus, CD could advance both corporate and state goals.

Bolewski (2017) refers to CD as symbiotic transnational governance that has emerged as a result of the growing power and influence of multinational corporations, as well as public expectations that corporations will be politically involved in advancing human rights, improving global economic stability, and promoting peace. CD includes creating a favorable environment for corporate goals (business diplomacy) while also contributing to the resolution of societal conflicts. He defined CD as "the behavioral craft to peacefully and sustainably manage the needs and interests of all concerned transnational parties, which can serve as a bridge into a mix of complementary political, economic, and social and cultural dynamics" (p. 4).

A conceptualization of CD from a PD perspective would place CD as a component of PD in which private sector corporations build relationships with foreign entities that not only benefit the corporation but enhance the image of the corporation's home country, which could be described as serving enlightened self-interests. CD, in this sense, can be implemented by various means, including corporate social responsibility (CSR), cultural diplomacy, and other strategic initiatives, which may include intentional coordination of effort with governments, or may be conducted independently (White, 2015).

For example, the U.S. corporation ALCOA was instrumental in helping the country of Romania achieve water quality goals that helped Romania qualify for European Union membership, which in turn helped create favorable perceptions about the U.S. (White, Vanc, & Coman, 2011). The corporation had profit-based motives in that it needed water quality for its own operations but recognized the broader benefits. In 2011, three Estonian companies opened a Skype station in Tallinn Airport as a reminder that Skype originated in their nation in a deliberate attempt to improve the image of their country. Corporate influence, both direct and indirect, on the foreign policies of home and host countries warrants further study. More case studies are needed to track the roles corporations have played influencing policy outcomes and bolstering country image in host countries, and through what means.

The globalization of economies has increased the power of international corporations, and with this power and political influence comes a greater obligation for corporate social responsibility. Corporations face increased demands and expectations from stakeholders to use corporate resources to address social and political issues and have a responsibility to reconcile their economic interests with public interests (Bolewski, 2018). This includes such things as corporate governance, workplace standards, environmental sustainability, corporate philanthropy, and corporate citizenship, corporate-sponsored cultural activities, and other non-governmental exchanges. Long-term relational diplomacy as a managerial practice of non-marketing strategy is not only an option for internationalized companies, but also provides new opportunities and thus becomes "imperative" (Burmester, 2021; Doh, Dahan & Casario, 2021). Future research should consider the diplomatic activities on a continuum ranging from instrumental profit-driven motives to social and/or political goals that extend beyond corporate interests and include responsibilities related to global governance and solving global problems.

Symbiotic relationships and complementary roles

Operating in an increasingly complex and volatile global environment, transnational corporations are recognizing the importance of the diplomatic mindset and practices. To navigate the ship of business through these challenges, it is imperative that global corporations integrate CD as a governance compass into their strategic planning to successfully match the liabilities that come with operating in a foreign market (Doherty, 2014). When CD activities are aimed at economically as well as socially sustainable business solutions, they can improve public perception through political influence by filling government gaps (Mogensen, 2020). Bolewski (2017) noted that when governments are unstable or unpopular (citing Trump's climate change policy), CD can play a balancing role that is as important as political diplomacy. Reappraising their moral and civilizing virtues, a socially embodied diplomacy – not tied solely to the state – could become a form of "third culture" (Bolewski, 2008; Leira, 2017).

The symbiotic relationship between corporate and government actors creates a synergy between the private and public spheres. It should take the form of an unconventional deliberative "multilogue" among all concerned on vital societal issues, moving toward a more human-centered economy with a shared sense of what change is needed and how to secure it (Bolewski, 2021). The purpose of international management is not merely business. Changing societal expectations demand that future managers contribute also to social and environmental issues as problem-solvers in order to secure general acceptance, sustainability, and social credit. For such a reorientation of professional mindsets, transnational business management needs to embrace the practices of CD as a competitive edge in future business–society relations (Bolewski, 2022).

Intentionality

Corporate behavior plays a role in building relationships, promoting trust, cultivating positive public opinion, and affecting the image of a corporation's home country, all of which affect PD outcomes, even when that is not the primary intention. CSR efforts by companies operating abroad have a halo effect on national image. In addition to CSR practices, brands and products as well as corporate communication affect how the country with which an international corporation is associated is perceived abroad (White, 2012). For example, Lee, Toth, and Shin (2008) found consumption of products from South Korea caused people to perceive the reputation of the country as "high technology" and "advanced economy." Popular culture, including music and games, news and entertainment that are produced and exported by the private sector contribute to a country's attraction, which plays a role in PD whether intentional or not.

As scholars study the role of the private sector in PD, a key concept to examine is intentionality of CD. Gregory (2008) contends that PD is a function of governance above, below, and around the state. CD could be viewed as around or beside the state, but not necessarily under the state since PD is increasingly a function of networks rather than a hierarchical function with government at the top. The concept of intentionality may play a role in studying the relationship between CD and PD. Furthermore, CD can be intentional even though it is not conducted in direct consort with government.

Strategic partnerships

Intentional involvement of the private sector in government PD includes strategic and direct involvement with government entities for the purpose of affecting policy and perceptions. Examples of intentional CD efforts are partnerships and contracts with government agencies. In the U.S., there is a history of government officials inviting chief executive officers (CEOs) to play a role in diplomatic endeavors. Corporate actors are interested in doing so if it is good for the image of the corporation as well as the country. "They are happy to do it for the country, but they also see that it is quite good for the corporation, or they wouldn't be doing it" (Bruce Gregory, personal interview, 2011, cited in White, 2015, p. 315).

As Chief of Protocol to German Chancellors Schröder and Merkel, Bolewski (2019) observed the partnered practices between government and transnational corporations when global business leaders accompanied them on diplomatic visits. These contacts were mostly marked by symbiotic relationships. Occasional corporate reluctance to the application of CD was grounded either in the lack of knowledge of the diplomatic mindset or an economic prevalence of commercial profit thinking over social, societal, and political concerns of sustainability. On the government side, shortcomings resulted from economic, political, and educational objections to participative leadership in foreign affairs. These difficulties could be overcome by bringing public, private, and civil society actors together to build relationships for collectively addressing transnational problems through diplomacy as society-craft for whole-of-society governance.

An emerging area of the applicability of strategic partnerships is in the collaborative relationships and conviviality of G7, G8, and G20 summit multilateralism among governments, markets, and civil society actors to promote stronger commitments to social dialogue at the global level and a sense of collective belonging (Louis, 2022). The dual purpose of the inclusion of non-state actors in these events are establishing political recognition of the business community on the international stage and influencing government policies as well as business strategies for global solutions and governance. More research on these events is called for to gain further insight into diplomatic working methods and any transformative impact (Li et al., 2022; McDonald, 2022).

Political leaders and many foreign policy experts agree that governments must find ways to benefit more strategically from the talents and resources of the corporate sector (White, 2020), and business could benefit symbiotically from the government sector (Bolewski, 2021). Fitzpatrick, White, and Bier (2019) note that more research is needed to deepen understanding of the network of influences in the new PD environment that could help identify common elements of successful collaborations.

Strategic coordination: differences among nation states

The willingness to engage in intentional CD as part of a government's PD efforts may vary based on the different cultural, economic, and political structures of nation states that may affect strategic coordination and partnerships. In Switzerland and the United Kingdom (U.K.), the corporate sector plays a role in PD through direct interactions with foreign governments. In the U.K., business interests have been formally integrated into diplomatic structures, particularly for the function of commercial diplomacy (Lee, 2004). Swiss multinational corporations have entered in direct negotiation with the European Union and other countries to benefit the economy of Switzerland (Saner & Yiu, 2005).

White and Alkandari (2019) found strong cooperation between the public and private sectors in Kuwait for promoting country image, related to the collectivistic sociocultural context of the country and the entwined economic and political structure. Internationally, Kuwaiti companies consider their work outside Kuwait as more than business and have a sense of obligation to represent their country when operating abroad. Kuwait Energy, for example, intentionally and purposefully coordinates activities with governments abroad to strengthen the relationship between other governments and the government of Kuwait. Particularly for smaller countries and for countries with intertwined political and economic relationships, governments could benefit from corporate involvement in PD.

Fitzpatrick, White, and Bier (2019), in a study based on interviews with corporate executives, found that corporate leaders of U.S.-based companies believed positive diplomatic relationships between the U.S. and the countries in which their companies do business have positive impacts on business. However, they felt no responsibility to engage in PD directly. One participant stated, "Using the U.S. government as an ally is probably the exception rather than the rule." However, in the same study, participants working for non-U.S. corporations were more likely to align the corporation with their home countries. A Swiss executive of a multinational corporation based in Switzerland reported an ongoing dialogue between the corporation and the home country's government and as well as corporate efforts to promote Switzerland's country image and national values; he said, "We can't think of any time we might not want to be associated with the Swiss" (p. 32).

There may be political reasons for reluctance of corporate involvement in PD. For some international corporations based in the U.S., the existence of anti-American sentiments throughout the world has created a propensity for them to distance themselves from the U.S. government (White, 2015). In countries transitioning from communism to democracy, there may be a desire for international businesses operating in global free markets to distance themselves from previously authoritarian governments (Szondi, 2008). In some cases, international corporations try to position themselves as global, international brands or seek to establish a transnational identity by developing different brands for different countries and maintaining an array of corporate websites in different languages and internet domains to make their products and activities seem indigenous to their markets (White, 2020).

It should be noted that there are instances where a government may want to disassociate itself from a corporation. Corporations sometime abuse their power, particularly in third-world countries. Corporations are guilty of harming natural environments (pollution, waste, habitat destruction, deforest-ation), human rights violations and labor abuses (unfair treatment of women, children, and vulnerable and indigenous populations), as well as corruption and the encouragement of hyper-consumerism and wasteful consumption (Prieto-Carrón et al., 2006). The imbalance of power between multinational corporations and the countries in which they operate and the potential for environmental and societal harm that are often casualties of profit-driven goals can have a detrimental effect on PD, and can therefore mitigate inten-tional, strategic involvement with the corporate sector by governments. The potential downsides of corporate involvement in PD should also be on the CD research agenda. Fitzpatrick (2009) suggested a need to consider whether in some instances the PD mission might be compromised by private sector involvement.

Many questions remain about how CD can be strategically coordinated between business and governments, and how strategic government/corporate partnerships are managed by different nations as well as the reasons for the dif-ferences. More research is needed to explore these notions. Future research also is needed to consider motivations for CD as well as the motivations of nation states in different parts of the world to involve corporations in state-centered PD, including motivations for *not* engaging in strategic partnerships.

Developing a research agenda

Much of the extant professional and scholarly literature about CD is based on conceptual essays. More empirical studies using different units of analyses are needed to test and refine the concepts. Interviews with government diplomats and business executives based in different countries, studies of perceptions of foreign audiences that focus on diplomatic outcomes, and case studies from understudied parts of the world can provide insights into the opportunities and challenges of CD.

Studies to date, discussed and cited in this chapter, have uncovered the following general presumptions that can be points of departure for future research, all of which need to be tested empirically in different contextual conditions.

- Motivations for conducting CD range from purely profit-driven motives to broader concerns for country image and the improvement of global society. In many cases, motivations align with the societal culture of the corporation's home country.
- As well as a variety of motivations for being involved in CD, corporations have reasons for *not* being involved in PD. The political environment of a nation state affects the propensity of corporations based in the country to feel responsibility to "carry the flag" abroad and to consciously work to enhance country image. Political reasons for the reluctance of corporate involvement in diplomacy vary among countries.
- Infrastructural variables affect strategic coordination between corporations and governments in the processes of PD implementation. The willingness to engage in intentional, strategic CD as part of a government's PD efforts vary based on the different economic structures of nation states, with greater likelihood in countries in which government and economic entities are entwined.
- CD can be intentional even though it is not conducted in direct consort with government. The concept of intentionality may play a role in studying the relationship between CD and PD.
- Activities associated with corporate social responsibility (CSR) often are associated with the implementation of CD. Such activities can have the impact and effect of PD +, regardless of whether diplomacy was the primary motive.

Conclusions

Research about CD to date has focused primarily on the presumptions listed above and the unit of analyses almost always have been the corporation or the country–corporation interaction. There are gaps in the literature that need to be addressed in future studies. The effects, outcomes, and impacts of CD on foreign audiences need exploration. Few studies were found that present data that examines perceptions of publics in host countries in assessing the impacts of corporate diplomatic activities. Empirical data from different regions of the world are needed to examine perceptions and stakeholder expectations and impacts of corporate diplomatic activities to provide practical implications for governments as well as corporations to benefit from corporate diplomacy.

While a few studies have noted the role corporations have played in influencing policy outcomes in host countries, more studies are needed to document the circumstances in which this occurs and through what means, as well as dilemmas corporations occasionally face in reconciling the interests of their home country, their own interests, and the interests of the country in which they operate. Related to this is exploration of the role of corporations in government-sponsored confederations such as G8 summits and other multilateral efforts. Furthermore, research is needed to consider the role of corporations in sub-state diplomacy such as city diplomacy.

As Gilboa (2008) notes, much of the scholarship about PD is based on the study, experiences, and observation of the U.S. and Western Europe. Research is needed to access how intentionality, strategic coordination, and implementation of CD differ among countries based on political, economic, and sociocultural structures from the points of view of scholars from multiple countries. Future studies examining an array of perspectives will help to inform the constructs of CD and will be useful in identifying common elements and strategies for successful collaborations.

The future of PD depends on the willingness and openness of key players in the broad international political and business context to combine the effort of understanding the other's interests with a modern transformational leadership approach. CD as a new management communication and engagement doxa can link best managerial practices with the diplomatic tools of ethically principled pragmatism to control and balance turbulences and uncertainties in ways that benefit both corporations and the governments with which they are associated. The practice of CD with engagement in social and societal concerns (migration, poverty) and issues for public good (climate, public health, human rights) secures a stable socio-political environment for the conduct of corporate activities. At the same time, as a form of civil society participation by corporations, CD fosters their political and moral legitimacy (social license to operate) and societal usefulness and reputation at home and in foreign countries. CD also can assist governments in the fight against public evils such as corruption, cyber-criminality, and terrorism through the application of sanctions. Corporations that voluntarily pulled out of Russia during the invasion of Ukraine intensified the economic sanctions imposed by governments. This enlargement of purpose provides companies with influence in shaping a one-voice foreign policy (Bolewski, 2019).

A new mindset with new results could navigate present and future business and government leaders through turbulent times. Turbulent times require creative and innovative solutions on a global level; thus, constructive diplomatic relationships need to be maintained. Shared vision and motivation among foreign policymakers and their diplomatic assemblages that included corporations could mobilize the appropriate sustainable solutions for future challenges (Bolewski, 2021).

References

Amann, W., Khan, S., Salzmann, O., Steger, U., & Ionescu-Somers, A. (2007). Managing external pressures through corporate diplomacy. *Journal of General Management, 3,* 33–50. http://dx.doi.org/10.1177/030630700703300103.

Asquer, A. (2012). What is corporate diplomacy? And why does it matter? *Journal of Multidisciplinary Research, 4*(3), 53–63.

Ban, Z., & Dutta, M. J. (2012). Minding their business: discourses of colonialism and neoliberalism in the commercial guide for US companies in China. *Public Relations Inquiry, 1*(2), 197–220. http://dx.doi.org/10.1177/2046147X11435079.

Bolewski, W. (2008). Diplomatic processes and cultural variation: the relevance of culture in diplomacy. *Whitehead Journal of Diplomacy and International Relations* (Winter/Spring), 145–60.

Bolewski, W. (2017). Corporate diplomacy as symbiotic transnational governance. Working paper, Project Diplomacy in the 21st Century, German Institute for International and Security Affairs.

Bolewski, W. (2018). Corporate diplomacy as global management. *International Journal of Diplomacy and Economy, 4*(2), 107–38. http://dx.doi.org/10.1504/IJDIPE.2018.094089.

Bolewski, W. (2019). Diplomatic engagement with transnational corporations: a path to sustainable governance. *International Journal of Diplomacy and Economy, 5*(1), 42–52. http://dx.doi.org/10.1504/IJDIPE.2019.099140.

Bolewski, W. (2021). Compass for public/private management in turbulent times: corporate diplomacy. *International Journal of Diplomacy and Economy*, 7(1), 4–18. http://dx.doi.org/10.1504/IJDIPE.2021.10037505.

Bolewski, W. (2022). Corporate diplomacy: compass for public/private management in turbulent times. In S. P. Sebastiao & S. de Carvalho Spinola (Eds.), *Diplomacy, Organisations and Citizens* (pp. 139–53). Springer. http://dx.doi.org/10.1007/978-3-030-81877-7_8.

Burmester, B. (2021). The diplomatic imperative: MNEs as international actors. In Ö. Bozkurt & M. Geppert (Eds.), *A Research Agenda for International Business and Management* (pp. 109–28). Edward Elgar Publishing. http://dx.doi.org/10.4337/9781789902044.00015.

Cotton, A.-M., & Sebastiao, S. P. (2022). From diplomacy to (new) public diplomacy: a communication perspective. In S. P. Sebastiao & S. de Carvalho Spinola (Eds.), *Diplomacy, Organisations and Citizens* (pp. 39–62). Springer. http://dx.doi.org/10.1007/978-3-030-81877-7_3.

Doh, J. P., Dahan, N. M., & Casario, M. (2021). MNEs and the practice of international business diplomacy. *International Business Review*. https://doi.org/10.1016/j.ibusrev.2021.101926.

Doherty, C. L. (2014). Business diplomacy: the compass rose of foreign markets. Master's thesis, Escola Brasileira de Administraçao Publica e de Empresas, Rio de Janeiro.

Fitzpatrick, K. (2009). Privatized public diplomacy. In P. Seib (Ed.), *Toward a New Public Diplomacy: Redirecting US Foreign Policy* (pp. 155–72). Palgrave Macmillan.

Fitzpatrick, K., White, C., & Bier, L. (2019). C-suite perspectives on corporate diplomacy as a component of public diplomacy. *Place Branding and Public Diplomacy*, 16(1), 25–35.

Gilboa, E. (2008). Searching for a theory of public diplomacy. *Annals of the American Academy of Political and Social Science*, 616(1), 55–77.

Gilboa, E. (2016). Public diplomacy. In G. Mazzoleni (Ed.), *The International Encyclopedia of Political Communication* (pp. 1297–306). Wiley-Blackwell. http://dx.doi.org/10.1002/9781118541555.wbiepc232.

Gregory, B. (2008). Public diplomacy sunrise of an academic field. *The Annals of the American Academy of Political and Social Science*, 616(1), 274–90.

Herter, C. A. (1966). Corporate diplomacy in foreign countries. *Vital Speeches of the Day*, 32, 407–9.

Hocking, B. (2004). Privatizing diplomacy? *International Studies Perspectives*, 5(2), 147–52.

Kesteleyn, J., Riordan, S., & Ruël, H. (2014). Introduction: business diplomacy. *The Hague Journal of Diplomacy*, 9(4), 303–9.

Lee, D. (2004). The growing influence of business in UK diplomacy. *International Studies Perspectives*, 5(1), 50–54.

Lee, S., Toth, E. L., & Shin, H. (2008). Cognitive categorization and routes of national reputation formation: US opinion leaders' view on South Korea. *Place Branding and Public Diplomacy*, 4(4), 272–86.

Leira, H. (2017). The making of a classic: on diplomacy 30 years on. *New Perspectives Relations*, 25(3), 67–73. http://dx.doi.org/10.1177/2336825X1702500305.

Li, J., Shapiro, D., Peng, M., & Ufimtseva, A. (2022). Corporate diplomacy in the age of US–China rivalry. *Academy of Management Perspectives*. https://doi.org/10.5465/amp.2021.0076.

Louis, M. (2022). The G8, G7 and G20 summits as professional events: business as usual or new opportunities for business organizations? In A. Béliard, S. Naulin, & V. Potier (Eds.), *Trade shows in the 21st Century: The Role of Events in Structuring Careers and Professions* (pp. 178–97). Edward Elgar Publishing.

Manor, I., & Surowiec, P. (2021). Conclusions. In P. Surowiec & I. Manor (Eds.), *Public Diplomacy and the Politics of Uncertainty* (pp. 329–42). Palgrave Macmillan.

McDonald, C. (2022, August 5–9). Extending the continuum of corporate diplomacy: insights for effective implementation of the SDGs. Working paper prepared for the AOM Annual Meeting, Seattle. https://doi.org/10.5465/AMBPP.2022.16256abstract.

Mogensen, K. (2020). Legitimacy issues in corporate public diplomacy. In J. D. Rendtorff (Ed.), *Handbook of Business Legitimacy: Responsibility, Ethics and Society* (pp. 1277–93). Springer.

Prieto-Carrón, M., Lund-Thomsen, P., Chan, A., Muro, A., & Bhushan, C. (2006). Critical perspectives on CSR and development: what we know, what we don't know, and what we need to know. *International Affairs, 82*(5), 977–87. http://dx.doi.org/10.1111/j.1468-2346.2006.00581.x.

Reinhard, K. (2009). American business and its role in public diplomacy. In N. Snow & P. M. Taylor (Eds.), *Routledge Handbook of Public Diplomacy* (pp. 195–200). Routledge.

Saner, R., & Yiu, L. (2003). International economic diplomacy: mutations in post-modern times. Discussion Papers in Diplomacy. The Netherlands Institute of International Relations Clingendael. http://www.clingendael.nl.

Saner, R., & Yiu, L. (2005). Swiss executives as business diplomats in the new Europe: evidence from Swiss pharmaceutical and agro-industrial global companies. *Organizational Dynamics, 34*(3), 298–312.

Sevin, E., & Karaca, H. S. (2016). Corporations as diplomatic actors: conceptualizing international communication tools. In N. Zakaria, A. Abdul-Talib, & N. Osman (Eds.), *Handbook of Research on Impacts of International Business and Political Affairs on the Global Economy*. IGI Global. http://dx.doi.org/10.4018/978-1-4666-9806-2.ch019.

Szondi, G. (2008). Public diplomacy and nation branding: conceptual similarities and differences. The Netherlands Institute of International Relations Clingendael. http://www.clingendael.nl.

Westermann-Behaylo, M. K., Rehbein, K., & Fort, T. (2015). Enhancing the concept of corporate diplomacy: encompassing political corporate social responsibility, international relations, and peace through commerce. *Academy of Management Perspectives, 29*(4), 387–404. http://dx.doi.org/10.5465/amp.2013.0133.

White, C. (2012). Brands and national image: an exploration of inverse country-of-origin effect. *Place Branding and Public Diplomacy, 8*(2), 110–18.

White, C. (2015). Exploring the role of private-sector corporations in public diplomacy. *Public Relations Inquiry, 4*(3), 305–21. http://dx.doi.org/10.1177/2046147X15614883.

White, C. (2020). Corporate diplomacy. In N. Snow & N. Cull (Eds.), *Routledge Handbook of Public Diplomacy*, 2nd edn (pp. 413–21). Routledge.

White, C., & Alkandari, K. (2019). The influence of culture and infrastructure on CSR and country image: the case of Kuwait. *Public Relations Review, 45*(3), 101783. http://dx.doi.org/10.1016/j.pubrev.2019.05.004.

White, C., Vanc, A., & Coman, I. (2011). Corporate social responsibility in transitional countries: public relations as a component of public diplomacy in Romania. *International Journal of Strategic Communication, 5*(4), 1–12. http://dx.doi.org/10.1080/1553118X.2010.549815.

5   City diplomacy

Efe Sevin and Sohaela Amiri

Introduction

The practice and study of public diplomacy (PD) has expanded the concept of diplomacy by introducing new actors, activities, and objectives (Golan, 2013). Traditional approaches to international relations looked at diplomacy as "the system and the art of communication between powers" (Wight, 1977, p. 177) in which powers refer exclusively to states (Nicolson, 1964), while communication is limited to negotiations and debates among professional diplomatic corps representing these powers to advance their interests (James, 1980). With PD practice, we observe the inclusion of nonstate actors (e.g. non-governmental organizations, grassroots movements) engaging in various communication activities (e.g. cultural exchanges, broadcasting, sports competitions) to "manage the international environment" (Cull, 2009, p. 12). This expansion led to a phenomenon labeled as "hyphenated diplomacy" in which various qualifiers are used to describe a different focus in diplomatic processes (Hayden, 2011) such as health diplomacy (Bliss, 2011), gastro-diplomacy (Rockower, 2012), and grassroots diplomacy (Payne, 2009a).

City diplomacy (CityDip) can be seen as a part of this new tradition. The concept, technically, predates PD. There have been historical examples, such as cities in ancient Greece sending and receiving ambassadors (Pluijm & Melissen, 2007) or Italian city states in the Middle Ages building networks and alliances (Kurbalija, 2021). PD didn't create CityDip – but rather, helped this already existing practice gain more traction and interest. Acuto (2013, p. 2) called cities "the invisible gorillas of international studies," alluding to a prominent selective attention experiment in which participants are shown a video with people passing a basketball around while a person in a gorilla suit walks across the scene (Simons & Chabris, 1999). Just as participants focusing on ball players miss the gorilla, scholars focusing on state-level analyses have been missing CityDip.

The winds have started to turn for cities recently. They are more often called on to tackle issues faced by our global community, ranging from climate change (Lee, 2015) to terrorism (Marchetti, 2021), and even to the Covid-19 pandemic (Wang & Amiri, 2020). Cities are, once again, starting to receive the attention they deserve in the international arena. A recent report by the Advisory Commission on Public Diplomacy in the U.S. repeatedly underlined the importance of city-to-city relations and city-level diplomacy (Walker et al., 2022). There are debates on establishing an Office of Subnational Diplomacy within the State Department (Office of Chris Murphy, 2020). An increasing number of city networks are facilitating interactions and collaborations among local governments (Acuto & Leffel, 2021). CityDip is likely to continue its rise in popularity.

This chapter includes three sections. The first provides a brief overview of conceptual discussions on CityDip and a concise summary of existing studies. The second outlines a research agenda under three headings: learning from the mishaps of PD, digitalization of activities, and policies and governance. The third section draws some conclusions.

What is city diplomacy?

A frequent statistic on the growth of urban population cited in CityDip studies shows that around 57 percent of the world population lives in cities (Buchholz, 2020). These areas are not only home to people, but generate larger economic outputs (Florida, 2019; Florida et al., 2008). Cities are different from rural areas in the sense that they provide the density and interaction necessary to reach these output levels (Florida, 2011). It is, then, not unexpected that diplomatic relations will come to these new powerhouses.

Amiri and Sevin (2020, p. 1) argued that this city identity is particularly important for PD as "public diplomacy activities are run through or by city governments." CityDip at its core is about fostering good relations with international actors through collaboration, cooperation, cultural ties, civic exchanges, and shows of goodwill while promoting trade, policies, and the city's global image (Amiri, 2022b). Various actors might be engaging in CityDip activities within a city. In larger cities, such as New York and Budapest, there are dedicated offices and units for foreign affairs (Amiri, 2020; Budapest, 2022). In other cases, political leaders (i.e. mayors) take charge and represent their cities in the global arena (Kosovac et al., 2020). Cities gain their attraction power through international exchange programs, cultural diplomacy, branding, involving local communities in international affairs, and networked policy collaborations. An explanation of diplomatic relations that does not incorporate local governments misses a considerable volume of activity as the diplomatic actions of the cities continue to grow. But to enhance the study and practice of CityDip, we need to better understand and design government institutions that manage international affairs at the local level.

Inadvertently, cities might have advocacy or policy agendas that are incompatible with their nation states. To date, cities have shown that they can form networks and partnerships for policy collaboration and advocacy even when they do not have the full support of their national government. In 2017, Pittsburgh found itself in a mediatized conflict over climate change with the White House when former president Donald Trump argued he "was elected to represent the citizens of Pittsburgh, not Paris" whereas former mayor Peduto responded by saying Pittsburgh sided with Paris (Gambino, 2017), referring to the Climate Accords signed a year earlier. Amiri (2022a) presents a visualization and high-level assessment of the synergy between national and CityDip to help identify potential missed opportunities, trends, and potential conflict areas to highlight the growing need for more research on understanding how national foreign policymaking should become more inclusive of perspectives and recommendations from local governments.

Briefly, CityDip is the conducting of international affairs by a city government to benefit the security and prosperity of local constituents (Amiri, 2022a). The term covers a variety of activities through which cities conduct external relations with other actors, including other cities and nation states (Kosovac et al., 2020). Any activity, within this definition, that puts cities on the international stage can be seen as CityDip. It is possible to build another connection between fields of city and PD at this moment. Gregory (2011, 2016) proposes using a public dimension of diplomacy as opposed to PD as the latter marginalizes the importance of the practice by demoting it to a subcategory. Similarly, CityDip can be seen as an *international dimension of city activities* (Sevin, 2021). Such an approach is useful in providing a more inclusive picture of the international presence of cities.

Existing research on city diplomacy

Amiri and Sevin (2020) demonstrated a new direction in CityDip studies. The field expanded both in the number and foci of international city networks (Acuto, 2013). While there have been exceptions (e.g. La Porte, 2013; Sizoo & Musch, 2008), the majority of the work had been around how cities used networking as a cooperation mechanism mostly to combat climate change. With the new wave, we hint at the complexity and the variety of global urban forces at play in the international sphere (Acuto, 2020, p. ix). Our objective was to cast a line on what else was being practiced and studied. We didn't discredit existing work. On the contrary, we probably were closer to Barber's (2014) observation "if mayors ruled the world." We asked what else cities are capable of doing. We organized our volume under three thematic headings and included a fourth section for case studies. These three themes were, eventually, about *governance*.

In the first section, we welcomed works discussing city networking and networks. Though authors moved beyond solely looking at how networks worked, and asked other relevant questions such as do city networks eventually become independent actors in foreign politics (Lecavalier & Gordon, 2020), or how these networks coordinate behavior (Abdullah & Garcia-Chueca, 2020). The second part of the book moved from a discussion on platforms to communication strategies used in CityDip. After all, CityDip is about local actors engaging with global audiences. Ranging from leveraging cultural assets (Grincheva, 2020) to tourism marketing (Crilley & Manor, 2020), there are a variety of strategies at their disposal. The third section highlighted the intricacies of governance systems that CityDip is embedded in, at the local, national, and international levels. In the case studies section, works showed that CityDip was not a monopoly of global cities – those that command considerable resources and are well-known by audiences. These cities are influential and will actively engage in international affairs. Yet, our authors depicted how small cities, city states, and young democracies, are advancing their local interests globally.

Cities have the potential to bring global publics together, enhance mutual understanding, advance mutual goals, and shared challenges. The in-between power of cities (Amiri, 2020) is key for establishing the role of cities as international actors who possess both the administrative structures and authority of the nation state and the sense of community, loyalty, and legitimacy that is usually associated with non-governmental organizations (NGOs). Moreover, cities have a wide range of tools available to establish their presence in the international arena. Moving beyond their networked diplomacy, the implementation of digital communication platforms, natural and infrastructural assets, and even international summits were identified as means to reach a global audience. There are conceptual explanations of how cities can interject themselves into national and global governance systems. The cases discussed showed examples of "less acknowledged" actors in CityDip as the practice is no longer in the exclusive domain of metropolitan areas or Western cities.

Cities are not leaving world politics to nation states. On the contrary, as existing literature shows through conceptual discussions, empirical studies, and examples from practitioners, cities are assuming responsibility to tackle international challenges and advance their political interest. However, a commonly accepted framework, and the governance system that supports it has been missing to shape research and scholarship. Amiri (2022b) outlined the key parameters of such a framework for CityDip to inspire future research in a more systematic and comprehensive way that is well integrated with the practice. Through better integration of research and practice, CityDip, and ultimately global PD, can become more strategic and policy oriented. In the next section, we outline research trajectories on three possible areas.

Research agenda

Learning from the mishaps of public diplomacy

We introduce three areas for future research. Advancing research on CityDip requires an understanding of the link with research of PD as the latter grew from a compilation of normative works to a rigorous field of study. Second, it must consider digitalization of activities. Last, we propose governance as the most important aspect of CityDip studies and highlight their potential to contribute to policymaking. With the practice and study of CityDip growing from its roots in global PD, we need to shape and guide research, policies, and strategies that bring local populations closer to their global aspirations. Yet, such an ambitious agenda is not without challenges, some of which have been faced by scholars already.

First, CityDip is currently undergoing the same conceptual limitations and stretches that PD has been. Who can engage in CityDip activities? Who has the authority to represent the city in the international arena? There is, technically, not a consensus on what constitutes an acceptable actor in PD (see Ayhan, 2019 for a taxonomy). While some scholars (Bátora, 2005; Lee, 2018; Sevin, 2017) argue that it is almost exclusively nation states and actors sanctioned by nation states that can engage, others have proposed nonstate actors (La Porte, 2015), including individuals (Payne, 2009b), NGOs (Cevik, 2015), and even corporations (Macnamara, 2012). While this ambiguity might be useful in empowering different constituents, it brings PD – and by extension CityDip – closer to being a vague catch-all term, rather than a precisely defined field. Together with agent and agency come activities. What are the conceptual criteria for an activity to be counted as CityDip, international dimension of city activities, or any other applicable label?

Second, measurement and evaluation need to be further discussed. The PD field has been going through debates on even what should be measured, let alone how to measure (Pamment, 2014). The crucial but often hard-to-measure value of global engagement remains an area that can benefit from innovative approaches to impact assessment. The CityDip field has offered various single case studies (Amiri & Sevin, 2020). There are a few examples of other empirical works, using social network analysis to look at how cities use networking to advance policy interests (Acuto & Leffel, 2021) and large-scale descriptive surveys to understand the variance in CityDip practices (Kosovac et al., 2020). For example, indicators may be designed to assess and rank cities based on the strength of their international networks. Based on such ranking and metrics, the integration of cities into global governance can become more systematic, transparent, and sustainable. Further, metrics need to be developed to assess aspects of the three categories of contextual factors, to assess the impact of CityDip, and to capture how and why this practice enhances a country's international affairs.

Third, the link between CityDip and foreign policy should be better articulated. This connection has been difficult to operationalize and demonstrate in PD – how does a country move from hosting an exchange student to advancing foreign policy interests (Sevin, 2017)? Yet, without such pieces of evidences, practices face the threat of losing funding (Schuman, 2014). CityDip faces another layer of complexity within this link – agency. When discussing foreign policy, should scholars refer to that of nation states or can cities have their own agendas? If so, what is the relationship between the agendas of cities and nation states?

There are four areas of PD that would be most beneficial for researchers of CityDip. One is the focus on the domestic dimension of diplomacy which would entail engaging the domestic audiences to raise their knowledge and awareness about the values of international engagement; another is re-envisioning and enhancing programs such as Sister Cities International to better fit today's context of international affairs, partnerships, and to be resilient in the face of politicization. A third area is reimagining international broadcasting and communication efforts with local governance and city-to-city interactions. A fourth area is international aid and collaboration such as the work that USAID undertakes which may benefit from closer collaboration with local governments.

In 2022, the Advisory Commission on Public Diplomacy (ACPD) and the USC CPD published a report urging that "at a time when many American cities are reinvigorating sister city and similar international links, there are opportunities for cities to become more significant partners in foreign policy" (Walker et al., 2022, p. 7) The report specifically encourages the design of policies that would on one hand enhance the public's understanding of and appreciation for diplomacy, and on the other create a mechanism, perhaps through CityDip, to inform the country's foreign policies.

U.S. CityDip is centered on building and maintaining relationships. Therefore, it plays a crucial role for American attraction of power and global influence. This is why and how the practice can benefit from an examination that is done through the lens of PD, and vice versa. CityDip contributes to a nation's attraction power, its relationship building and global engagement, and is possible through five functions: (1) trade and economic development, (2) diplomatic representation and protocol, (3) international exchange, cultural ties, and aid, (4) civic engagement and education, and (5) policy collaboration, advocacy, and action (Amiri, 2022a).

The benefits of strong international ties may not always be directly apparent or quantifiable. More research is needed to inform the assessment of such activities. Since the measures depend on the views or perceptions of the receiving audiences, a mechanism for making and maintaining relationships allows an environment for perceptions to be shaped. In a closed loop, such relationship building and maintaining will in turn help an actor to further enhance its legitimacy, authority, and competence or to better promote its attributes.

Digitalization of activities

Digital diplomacy, which can be seen as another hyphenated diplomacy or offshoot of PD, has already established itself as a viable practice covering different uses of communication technologies to conduct diplomacy (Ross, 2011). Ministries, diplomats, and international organizations alike are adopting such technologies including social media platforms, multimedia sharing sites, and intranets as part of their daily activities (Manor, 2015, 2019). One promising research area, in that sense, is the digitization of existing CityDip activities (Dietrichsen & van Niekerk, 2021). In other words, how will e-learning systems, virtual meetings, and webinars change the landscape of CityDip?

Additionally, it is possible to consider the additional functions brought in by these technologies. While the former area described, for instance, considers what will happen to city network structure if digital communication technologies can replace face-to-face meetings, the latter focuses more on the new areas opening up such as how the concept of smart cities can expand existing collaborations (Cheng, 2020). An exciting area of possibilities lies within metaverse, an interactive virtual world experience supported by prominent technology companies (Ravenscraft, 2022). Discussing metaverse requires further qualifiers since the term is not necessarily new.

Around a decade ago, Second Life – a computer game built on a premise of an interactive virtual world – became popular among diplomats and scholars. There have been multiple embassies on Second Life and numerous works on their impacts (Manor, 2016; Pamment, 2011). Both the platform and its diplomatic functions lost their popularity over the years. What probably makes metaverse and CityDip is the platform's relationship with cities. From a domestic perspective, metaverse might facilitate community building (Geragthy et al., 2022) and create actors that might want to have a say in CityDip. From an international perspective, metaverse makes the movement of goods, services, and money across borders easier (Kilzi, 2022). Cities might – or rather should – try to regulate and benefit from these processes.

Policies and governance

More research is needed to inform policies related to the national–local dynamics when it comes to international affairs. For example, the role that CityDip can or should play in shaping foreign policies remains an area that needs further exploration and thought leadership. Similarly, the role that cities can play to engage domestic constituents and connect them to foreign policies that represent them needs to be better envisioned to inform the future direction of the practice and how it can be strategically integrated into a country's statecraft.

Cities can be seen as the "in-between power" in global governance. On the one hand, they have the authority that comes from being a part of the government system, and on the other, they have the legitimacy that comes from being closer to the people they serve, ideologically and physically. To ensure the sustainability of the practice of CityDip, its dynamics with the state and other government entities as well as its dynamics with non-states, such as the citizens, remain valuable areas of study. For the latter, a better understanding of the role of nonstate actors, from diaspora groups to international companies as actors in CityDip would be insightful.

We also encourage analytical attention to cities, especially within the field of international relations, and more specifically to soft power and PD scholars. While CityDip as a topic of study is gaining more attention, the practice is often approached through fields other than the study of diplomacy or international relations. The links between CityDip and PD, as well as traditional diplomacy, are important areas for future research. PD has already expanded our understanding of what diplomacy should entail (Gregory, 2016). The continued rise of cities, similarly, is pushing the boundaries of diplomacy.

One example of this will be using a CityDip framework to discover policy issues, beyond climate change and terrorism. This argument warrants further unpacking. Indeed, climate change and terrorism are pressing issues that require immediate global attention and can benefit from intercity cooperation – yet, so can many others including income inequality (Hachigian, 2019), pandemics (Amiri & Dossani, 2019), disaster response (Ayres, 2018), and cultural heritage preservation (Beall & Adam, 2017). As argued in a joint brief by the Atlantic Council, U.S. Advisory Commission on Public Diplomacy (Cabral et al., 2014) and Amiri and Sevin (2020), diffused power structures in one international area of research remains an inquiry into the platforms that allow for CityDip, such as various city networks and the diplomatic agency of various actors in these networks. The broader area of study that networks as systems belong to is global governance and understanding the intricacies of governance systems that CityDip is embedded in, at the local, national, and international levels. Another area of inquiry can focus on the role of small cities, city states, and young democracies, that are not necessarily "global cities" in global affairs.

As researchers delve deeper into understanding the boundaries and the evolving nature of the practice, we encourage them to apply theories and concepts from various fields including but not limited to public administration, foreign policy analysis, and communications, to better understand CityDip within the broader practice of diplomacy. The authors of this chapter have already embarked on this approach to research. For example, Amiri (2022a) has adopted theories in physics to guide thinking about CityDip and adopted architectural design methods to further enhance data analysis. The results have been an outline of a framework for CityDip as well as a systematic analysis of the dynamics between CityDip and PD. Scholars can build on this groundwork as they view CityDip through the lens of international affairs.

The key parameters of a framework for CityDip analysis include: (1) contextual factors that affect the success or failure of a city's international affairs, and (2) functions of CityDip as a mechanism of statecraft. Contextual factors range from fixed (e.g. geographic location) to dynamic (e.g. leader's popularity). These contextual factors are inputs necessary for any international actor to successfully conduct international affairs, engage globally and enhance the prosperity and security of the citizens it serves. The contextual factors can be divided into three categories: (1) relational, (2) instrumental, and (3) discursive. The first category, relational, includes factors such as culture, values, beliefs, and identity. Policy positions and attitudes towards policies fall under this category as well. The instrumental category refers to the condition of being official, having sovereignty, stability, and the authority to enact policies and enforce law and order. The discursive category refers to the possession of capital, geographic assets, skilled labor and access to information, technology, networks, allies or partnerships. Depending on how a CityDip activity is bound by time and target audience, the categorization of contextual factors and appropriate measurements varies (Amiri, 2022a).

Literature on CityDip can be further enriched by bringing scholars and practitioners from diverse backgrounds together, who can introduce new viewpoints and bridge the gap between policy and scholarship. Research needs to catch up with the new developments in the practice to, in return, make the practice more strategic. At the same time, such research should not be solely normative or theoretical. Hence, examination of cases remains an informative contribution to the field. A combination of practitioner and academic scholarship is meant to celebrate the importance of collaboration between the two.

Conclusions

In this chapter, we have highlighted three domains of inquiry for future research in CityDip. We mainly asked how we can move the conversations about CityDip to further advance both study and practice. We presented our answers with an eye on PD literature as CityDip has benefited – and should continue learning – from the contributions of PD scholars in the last few decades.

Our proposed research agenda started with this claim – CityDip literature can expedite its development by drawing lessons from PD. A clear articulation of what CityDip is, including expected actors and activities, and how it contributes to achieving foreign policy objectives will be useful for scholars and practitioners. Second, we highlighted digitalization of diplomatic activities as a plausible arena. While we were cautious to argue for or against the future of metaverse, we encouraged cities and scholars of CityDip to be aware of the developments. Last – and most importantly – we underlined the need for research that can inform policies.

Fundamental research questions should outline the boundaries of the field, such as: How can CityDip be sustainably integrated within the broader system of statecraft? How can CityDip inform foreign policies that are set at the national level? What is the dynamic between city and national diplomacy, and how can a better synergy between the two be created? How can international governance systems evolve to allow for the systematic integration of local governments? And how can outcomes of CityDip be measured? Given the importance of mediatization, scholars should ask: What are the impacts of digitalization on CityDip? Most importantly, the field should work towards answering how research can inform practice.

Given the diverse nature of the practice, it is important that researchers and scholars work more closely with practitioners in the field of CityDip. This is further enhanced if the attention is given to diversity in terms of geographic location, various government structures, and political systems. This would both enrich the literature by introducing new viewpoints and bridge the gap between policy and scholarship. Cities are famous for being practical and pragmatic. Hence the study of CityDip cannot ignore practical implications. Research needs to catch up with the new developments in the practice to, in return, make the practice more strategic. At the same time, such research should not be solely normative or theoretical. The combination of practitioner and academic scholarship goes beyond a mere celebration of the importance of collaboration between the two and becomes a necessity for practice by local governments.

While it is true that the practice and study of CityDip should remain in constant contact, it is equally important to have a guiding and theoretical framework to stay focused. Scholarly investigations into how public policies can be shaped to improve and enhance global governance practices by better incorporating cities into the broader governance system at various levels: local, federal, and international can help craft more effective CityDip strategies. Practitioners can tap into the body of research to identify policy needs, design and advocate for newer policies that will make CityDip more strategic, efficient, and effective. But having the theoretical underpinning will ensure that the study of CityDip is not derailed by policy needs.

References

Abdullah, H., & Garcia-Chueca, E. (2020). Cacophony or complementarity? The expanding ecosystem of city networks under scrutiny. In S. Amiri & E. Sevin (Eds.), *City diplomacy* (pp. 13–36). Palgrave Macmillan.

Acuto, M. (2013). *Global cities, governance and diplomacy: the urban link*. Routledge.

Acuto, M. (2020). Prologue. In S. Amiri & E. Sevin (Eds.), *City diplomacy* (pp. vii–xi). Palgrave Macmillan.

Acuto, M., & Leffel, B. (2021). Understanding the global ecosystem of city networks. *Urban Studies*, *58*(9), 1758–74. https://doi.org/10.1177/0042098020929261.

Amiri, S. (2020). Making US MOIA sustainable institutions for conducting city diplomacy by protecting their precarious values. In S. Amiri & E. Sevin (Eds.), *City diplomacy* (pp. 235–52). Palgrave Macmillan.

Amiri, S. (2022a). Understanding the dynamics between U.S. city diplomacy and public diplomacy. *Journal of Public Diplomacy*, *2*(1), online first. https://doi.org/10.1163/1871191X-bja10095.

Amiri, S. (2022b). City diplomacy: an introduction to the forum. *The Hague Journal of Diplomacy*, *17*(1), 91–5. https://doi.org/10.1163/1871191X-bja10090.

Amiri, S., & Dossani, R. (2019, November 22). *City diplomacy has been on the rise: policies are finally catching up*. https://www.rand.org/blog/2019/11/city-diplomacy -has-been-on-the-rise-policies-are-finally.html.

Amiri, S., & Sevin, E. (Eds.) (2020). *City diplomacy*. Palgrave Macmillan.

Ayhan, K. J. (2019). The boundaries of public diplomacy and nonstate actors: a taxonomy of perspectives. *International Studies Perspectives*, *20*(1), 63–83. https://doi.org/10.1093/isp/eky010.

Ayres, A. (2018). *The new city multilateralism*. Council on Foreign Relations. https://www.cfr.org/expert-brief/new-city-multilateralism.

Barber, B. R. (2014). *If mayors ruled the world: dysfunctional nations, rising cities*. Yale University Press.

Bátora, J. (2005). Public diplomacy in small and medium-sized states: Norway and Canada. *Discussion Papers in Diplomacy*. http://www.peacepalacelibrary.nl/ebooks/files/Clingendael_20050300_cli_paper_dip_issue97.pdf.

Beall, J., & Adam, D. (2017). *Cities, prosperity, and influence: the role of city diplomacy in shaping soft power in the 21st century*. British Council. https://www.britishcouncil .org/sites/default/files/g229_cities_paper.pdf.

Bliss, K. E. (2011). *Health diplomacy of foreign governments*. CSIS. https://csis-website -prod .s3 .amazonaws .com/ s3fs public/legacy_files/files/publication/111222_Bliss_ HealthDiplomacy_Web.pdf.

Buchholz, K. (2020). *UN: how has the world's urban population changed from 1950 to 2020?* World Economic Forum. https://www.weforum.org/agenda/2020/11/global -continent-urban-population-urbanisation-percent/.

Budapest (2022). Budapest portal: The task of the City Diplomacy unit. https://budapest .hu/sites/english/Lapok/2021/the-task-of-the-city-diplomacy-unit.aspx.

Cabral, R., Engelke, P., Brown, K., & Wedner, A. T. (2014). *Diplomacy for a diffuse world*. Atlantic Council. https://www.atlanticcouncil.org/in-depth-research-reports/issue-brief/diplomacy-for-a-diffuse-world/.

Cevik, S. (2015). *The rise of NGOs: Islamic faith diplomacy*. http://uscpublicdiplomacy .org/blog/rise-ngos-islamic-faith-diplomacy.

Cheng, K. (2020). Neglected agents: elucidating Chinese social actors' role in Thai–Sino smart city diplomacy. *International Journal of China Studies*, *11*(1), 1–20.

Crilley, R., & Manor, I. (2020). Un-nation branding: the cities of Tel Aviv and Jerusalem in Israeli soft power. In S. Amiri & E. Sevin (Eds.), *City diplomacy* (pp. 137–60). Palgrave Macmillan.

Cull, N. J. (2009). *Public diplomacy: lessons from the past*. Figueroa Press.

Dietrichsen, P., & van Niekerk, G. (2021). City diplomacy in a changing world of international relations. In *City Diplomacy Papers: Volume 1*. South African CitiesNetwork. https:// www .sacities .net/ wp -content/ uploads/ 2021/ 01/ City -Diplomacy-Papers_Volume-1_.pdf#page=5.

Florida, R. (2011, September 15). Why cities matter. CityLab. http://www.theatlanticcities .com/arts-and-lifestyle/2011/09/why-cities-matter/123/.

Florida, R. (2019, February 28). The real economic powerhouses are mega-regions, not nations. Bloomberg. https://www.bloomberg.com/news/articles/2019-02-28/ mapping-the-mega-regions-powering-the-world-s-economy.

Florida, R., Gulden, T., & Mellander, C. (2008). The rise of the mega-region. *Cambridge Journal of Regions, Economy and Society, 1*(3), 459–76. https://doi.org/10.1093/cjres/ rsn018.

Gambino, L. (2017, June 1). Pittsburgh fires back at Trump: we stand with Paris, not you. *The Guardian.* https://www.theguardian.com/us-news/2017/jun/01/pittsburgh -fires-back-trump-paris-agreement.

Geragthy, L., Lee, T., Glickman, J., & Rainwater, B. (2022). *Cities and the metaverse* (The Future of Cities). National League of Cities. https://www.nlc.org/wp-content/ uploads/2022/04/CS-Cities-and-the-Metaverse_v4-Final-1.pdf.

Golan, G. (2013). An integrated approach to public diplomacy. *American Behavioral Scientist, 57*(9), 1251–5. https://doi.org/10.1177/0002764213487711.

Gregory, B. (2011). American public diplomacy: enduring characteristics, elusive transformation. *The Hague Journal of Diplomacy, 6*(3), 351–72. https://doi.org/10.1163/ 187119111X583941.

Gregory, B. (2016). Mapping boundaries in diplomacy's public dimension. *The Hague Journal of Diplomacy, 11*(1), 1–25. https://doi.org/10.1163/1871191X-12341317.

Grincheva, N. (2020). Museums as actors of city diplomacy: from "hard" assets to "soft" power. In S. Amiri & E. Sevin (Eds.), *City diplomacy* (pp. 111–36). Springer. https:// doi.org/10.1007/978-3-030-45615-3_6.

Hachigian, N. (2019, April 16). Cities will determine the future of diplomacy. *Foreign Policy.* https://foreignpolicy.com/2019/04/16/cities-will-determine-the-future-of -diplomacy/.

Hayden, C. (2011). The lessons of hyphenated diplomacy. *Public Diplomacy Magazine, 2*(4). https://uscpublicdiplomacy.org/pdin_monitor_article/lessons-hyphenated -diplomacy.

James, A. (1980). Diplomacy and international society. *International Relations, 6*(6), 931–48.

Kilzi, M. (2022). Council post: the new virtual economy of the metaverse. Forbes. https://www.forbes.com/sites/forbesbusinesscouncil/2022/05/20/the-new-virtual -economy-of-the-metaverse/.

Kosovac, A., Hartley, K., Acuto, M., & Gunning, D. (2020). *Conducting city diplomacy: a survey of international engagement in 47 cities.* The Chicago Council on Global Affairs. https://www.thechicagocouncil.org/research/report/conducting-city -diplomacy-survey-international-engagement-47-cities.

Kurbalija, J. (2021, August 29). Renaissance diplomacy: compromise as a solution to conflict. *Diplomacy and Technology: A Historical Journey.* https://www.diplomacy .edu/histories/renaissance-diplomacy-compromise-as-a-solution-to-conflict/.

La Porte, T. (2013). City public diplomacy in the European Union. In M. K. D. Cross & J. Melissen (Eds.), *European public diplomacy: soft power at work* (pp. 85–111). Palgrave Macmillan US. https://doi.org/10.1057/9781137315144_5.

La Porte, T. (2015). Improving efficiency in public diplomacy practices: advising non-state actors' strategies in the EU framework. In A. Manero & M. Luisa (Eds.), *Public diplomacy: European and Latin American perspectives* (pp. 125–48). Peter Lang.

Lecavalier, E., & Gordon, D. (2020). Beyond Networking? The agency of city network secretariats in the realm of city diplomacy. In S. Amiri & E. Sevin (Eds.), *City diplomacy* (pp. 13–36). Palgrave Macmillan.

Lee, K. S. (2018). Entitled to benevolence? South Korea's government-sponsored volunteers as public diplomacy and development actors. In J. Pamment & K. G. Wilkins (Eds.), *Communicating national image through development and diplomacy* (pp. 123–41). Palgrave Macmillan. https://doi.org/10.1007/978-3-319-76759-8_6.

Lee, T. (2015). *Global cities and climate change: the translocal relations of environmental governance*. Routledge.

Macnamara, J. (2012). Corporate and organisational diplomacy: an alternative paradigm to PR. *Journal of Communication Management, 16*(3), 312–25. https://doi.org/10.1108/13632541211245794.

Manor, I. (2015, January 9). Framing, tweeting, and branding: a study in the practice of digital diplomacy. *USC CPD Blog.* http://uscpublicdiplomacy.org/blog/framing-tweeting-and-branding-study-practice-digital-diplomacy.

Manor, I. (2016). *Are we there yet: have MFAs realized the potential of digital diplomacy? Results from a cross-national comparison.* Brill. https://brill.com/view/title/33370.

Manor, I. (2019). *The digitalization of public diplomacy.* Palgrave Macmillan. https://doi.org/10.1007/978-3-030-04405-3.

Marchetti, R. (2021). *City diplomacy: from city-states to global cities.* University of Michigan Press.

Nicolson, H. (1964). *Diplomacy* (3rd edn). Oxford University Press.

Office of Chris Murphy (2020). *Murphy, Perdue introduce legislation to establish subnational diplomacy, counter China.* U.S. Senator Chris Murphy of Connecticut. https://www.murphy.senate.gov/newsroom/press-releases/murphy-perdue-introduce-legislation-to-establish-subnational-diplomacy-counter-china.

Pamment, J. (2011). Innovations in public diplomacy and nation brands: inside the House of Sweden. *Place Branding and Public Diplomacy, 7*(2), 127–35. https://doi.org/10.1057/pb.2011.3.

Pamment, J. (2014). Articulating influence: toward a research agenda for interpreting the evaluation of soft power, public diplomacy and nation brands. *Public Relations Review, 40*(1), 50–59.

Payne, G. (2009a). Trends in global public relations and grassroots diplomacy. *American Behavioral Scientist, 53*(4), 487–92. https://doi.org/10.1177/0002764209347635.

Payne, G. (2009b). Reflections on public diplomacy: people-to-people communication. *American Behavioral Scientist, 53*(4), 579–606. https://doi.org/10.1177/0002764209347632.

Pluijm, R. van der, & Melissen, J. (2007). *City diplomacy: the expanding role of cities in international politics.* Netherlands Institute of International Relations Clingendael.

Ravenscraft, E. (2022). What is the metaverse, exactly? *Wired.* https://www.wired.com/story/what-is-the-metaverse/.

Rockower, P. (2012). Recipes for gastrodiplomacy. *Place Branding and Public Diplomacy, 8*(3), 235–46. https://doi.org/10.1057/pb.2012.17.

Ross, A. (2011). Digital diplomacy and US foreign policy. *The Hague Journal of Diplomacy, 6*(3), 451–5. https://doi.org/10.1163/187119111X590556.

Schuman, R. (2014, March 26). Don't extinguish the Fulbright. *Slate.* http://www.slate.com/articles/life/education/2014/03/proposed_fulbright_budget_cuts_the_grant_program_helps_america_exercise.html.

Sevin, E. (2017). *Public diplomacy and the implementation of foreign policy in the US, Sweden and Turkey.* Palgrave Macmillan.

Sevin, E. (2021). Bright future for city diplomacy and soft power. *Diplomatica*, *3*(1), 200–209. https://doi.org/10.1163/25891774-03010013.

Simons, D. J., & Chabris, C. F. (1999). Gorillas in our midst: sustained inattentional blindness for dynamic events. *Perception*, *28*(9), 1059–74. https://doi.org/10.1068/p281059.

Sizoo, A., & Musch, A. (2008). City diplomacy: the role of local governments in conflict prevention, peace-building and post-conflict reconstruction. In A. Musch & A. Sizoo (Eds.), *City diplomacy: the role of local government in conflict prevention, peace-building, post-conflict reconstruction* (pp. 7–26). VNG International. http://edepot.wur.nl/2595.

Walker, V. S., Fitzpatrick, K. R., & Wang, J. (2022). *Exploring U.S. public diplomacy's domestic dimensions: purviews, publics, and policies.* Advisory Commission on Public Diplomacy. https://www .state .gov/ exploring -u -s -public -diplomacys -domestic -dimensions-purviews-publics-and-policies-2022/.

Wang, J., & Amiri, S. (2020, April 14). *Five takeaways on U.S. city diplomacy during the COVID-19 Crisis.* USC Center on Public Diplomacy. https:// uscpublicdiplomacy .org/blog/5-takeaways-us-city-diplomacy-during-covid-19-crisis.

Wight, M. (1977). *Systems of states.* Leicester University Press.

6   Citizen diplomacy

Paul Lachelier and Sherry Lee Mueller

Introduction

> While accepting the Fulbright Prize in 2019, Angela Merkel said that "Senator Fulbright firmly believed in citizen diplomacy – in the idea that it is not only politicians and diplomats who foster peace, but above all citizens who establish and maintain friendly relations with people in other countries."[1]

The world is changing in both troubling and promising ways. On one hand, terrorism, resurgent authoritarianism, nuclear weapons proliferation, cyber-attacks, disinformation, pervasive inequalities, pandemics, and worsening climate change pose serious, even existential threats to life on Earth. On the other hand, increasing economic interdependence alongside rising education levels and expanding internet access have spurred more connections among citizens in different countries. Still, the Earth is vast, human experience varies widely, and so do ways of being and seeing. In this fragmented and often contentious global context, the inclination and ability of people to communicate and cooperate internationally becomes increasingly important to piece together the fragments of our humanity. In this context, citizen diplomacy (CD) grows more vital.

CD can be understood as the right, even the responsibility, every person has to help shape international relations (Mueller, 2020). How people who are not government officials go about shaping international relations takes an increasing variety of individual and organizational forms. Moreover, for better or worse, those forms are not necessarily government sponsored, as public diplomacy (PD) is. This chapter traces historical highlights of CD, current research

---

[1]   Remarks by Dr. Angela Merkel, Chancellor of Germany at Fulbright Prize Ceremony AXICA Congress and Convention Centre, Berlin, Germany, January 28, 2019. Authors' personal communication with Dr. John Bader, Executive Director, Fulbright Association, November 17, 2022.

and questions, CD dimensions and varieties, and priorities for advancing both research and practice.[2]

The concept of citizen diplomacy

Whether studying the international campaign that resulted in the 1997 Treaty to Ban Landmines (Cameron, 1998; Rutherford, 2010; Williams et al., 2008), or the Hebei–Iowa Sister State relationship as told by Lande (2017), there are many illustrations of the impact of citizens on international affairs. The individual as an actor in intercultural affairs began in ancient times and certainly predates the establishment of the nation state. The Jesuit priest Matteo Ricci, who lived in China from 1583 to 1610, is just one example (Arndt, 2005, p. 6).

The use of the term "citizen diplomacy" to describe the idea that the individual plays a role in shaping international relations precedes the use of "PD," articulated in 1965 by Edmund Gullion. PD was defined as a national government's efforts to communicate with and build relationships with foreign publics – to influence public opinion with the intent to influence the behavior of their leaders. Given U.S. culture's emphasis on the idea that the individual has a responsibility to make a difference, it is perhaps not surprising that the few early publications on CD appeared in the U.S. They were sparked by reactions to the horror of war. In 1922, Secretary of State Elihu Root (1937) wrote "A Requisite for the Success of Popular Diplomacy." In distilling the lessons derived from participation in World War I, he argued persuasively

---

[2]   In order to better assess the research and practice, we assembled a bibliography of more than 600 CD-related articles, books, reports, and videos. We also interviewed 21 diplomacy scholars and practitioners in seven countries to explore CD definitions, varieties and research questions, extant research, and suggestions for ways to further develop the field. Several sections in this chapter are based on these interviews. We thank the interviewees, who are listed here in parentheses by the country where they reside: Canada (Roopa Trilokekar), Israel (Lior Lehrs, Ilan Manor), South Korea (Kadir Jun Ayan), Thailand (Kian Cheng Lee), the Netherlands (John Marks, Willem Post, Giles Scott-Smith), U.K. (Andreas Fulda, Carne Ross), U.S. (Ibrahim Anli, George Brown, Nicholas Cull, Ed Gragert, Jay Harris, Robert Kelley, Siobhan Lyons, Kenneth Quinn, Hannes Richter, Linda Staheli, Andreas Stroehl). We also thank our research assistants, Jibbi Bah (George Mason University) and River Stone (University of Virginia), for their help with the research and editing of this chapter, and the development of the CD bibliography.

that American citizens must learn about international relations and actively participate.

Marshall (1949), a law professional who worked for a wide range of U.S.-based public sector organizations after World War II, apparently first articulated the concept of CD. Marshall argued that diplomacy must open to the public domain to regain democratic legitimacy. He fervently made the case for the inclusion of "laymen" in foreign policymaking and expressed his frustration "the political technician and the bureaucrat [who] simply treat the layman as one who lives on the wrong side of the tracks of wisdom" (p. 85).

In 1956, President Dwight Eisenhower convened a White House Summit on CD. As People to People International and Sister Cities International grew out of these deliberations, the concept of CD gained traction and was used by these and other organizations to describe their work. Embracing the notion, in 1959 the U.S. State Department Advisory Commission on Educational Exchange published the booklet: "The Citizen's Role in Cultural Relations." Stanley (1983, p. 1) made one of the most eloquent arguments in support of CD: "The problems we face are global in proportion, but their solution begins with individuals." Since, international non-governmental organizations (NGOs) and inter-governmental bodies have proliferated worldwide, especially with the spread of the internet starting in the 1990s. Scholarly interest in CD has grown accordingly, and it is to that interest that we now turn.

Existing research on citizen diplomacy

Several interrelated bodies of international research now exist, and often precede and inform both the study and practice of CD. These bodies include globalization and global governance (Dingwerth & Pattberg, 2006; Ludwig & Kok, 2018; Marx & Wouters, 2018), global citizenship and global citizenship education (Bosniak, 2000; Goren & Yemini, 2017; Hazama et al., 2019), transnational social networks and movements (Bhattacharya & Jairath, 2012; Earle, 2011; Herz & Olivier, 2012), conflict resolution and peacebuilding (Alger, 2007; Chetail & Jütersonke, 2015; Hauss, 2010), and PD (Chahine, 2010; Sevin et al., 2019; Snow & Cull, 2020). These literatures may not mention CD, but they often focus on cross-national citizen communication and collaboration.

To explore existing CD research, we developed a bibliography of CD books, articles, reports, and videos that is available online. That growing bibliography, numbering more than 600 items as of this writing, reveals several patterns worth noting. First, there has been a marked increase in publications on CD since the earliest entry in the bibliography (Root, 1922) particularly after 2010, then even more in 2020 onward (Figure 6.1).

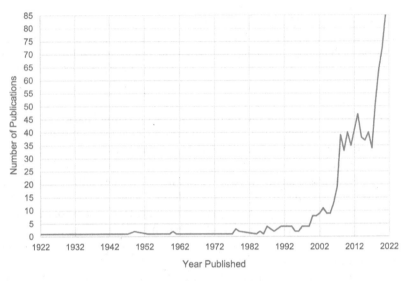

Figure 6.1   Trend in citizen diplomacy publications

Second, an increasing number of academic and professional journals are publishing on CD or closely related topics. The growing number reflects mounting scholarly interest in diplomacy, including PD. The proliferation of explicitly diplomacy-focused journals since 2000 parallels the spread of the internet and social media worldwide, a sharp rise in the number of international organizations mobilizing publics transnationally, and corresponding changes in diplomacy's context and actors (Cooper et al., 2013).

Third, with some exceptions (e.g., Lee, 2019, 2020; Oshewolo, 2020; Yu, 2018), most authors in the CD bibliography are based in the U.S. or Europe although more publications appear elsewhere as the years progress. This geographic imbalance may indicate real paucity of CD research and practice in Latin America, Africa, and Asia, and greater U.S. and European interest in CD, perhaps due to more widespread individualism and liberal democratic values. The imbalance may also be due to our U.S. experience, and our internet search engine algorithms' steering to U.S. and European sources. Regardless of the cause, the relative absence of CD literature originating from Latin America, Africa, and Asia is striking.

Fourth, when scholars examine CD, it is often under the umbrella of PD or a government's efforts to influence foreign publics. Hence, much CD research focuses on government-funded programs and campaigns rather than independent, citizen-initiated CD. For instance, the U.S. government has conducted, or paid scholars and private sector organizations, such as the Institute of International Education, to conduct evaluations of federal programs involving citizen diplomats (Arndt & Rubin, 1993; Bhandari & Belyavina, 2011; Gullahorn & Gullahorn, 1966). The International Visitor Leadership Program (IVLP) is one prominent example in the CD literature (Adams, 1999; Gibson, 1979; Opitz et al., 2022; Popkova, 2022).

Fifth, four CD-related forms of diplomacy come up more often, especially since the 2010s: city, health, digital and, above all, sports diplomacy. It is perhaps no surprise that sports diplomacy is the most common focus in the CD literature, given wildly popular international sports like soccer and cricket, the longstanding prominence of the Olympic Games, and the often-intense emotions these contests inspire. Yet, our research uncovers no "sports diplomacy" publications before 2000, just four from 2000 to 2009, 15 from 2010 to 2019, and 15 just from 2020 to the present. Scholars writing about sports diplomacy aptly question whether it advances international peace or national ambitions, particularly amidst tense relations between prominent countries, like Iran and the U.S. (Chehabi, 2007), or India and Pakistan (Aslam et al., 2017), and the ban on Russian participation in international sports events following its invasion of Ukraine in 2022. Conversely, the literature on health diplomacy often calls for training of both official diplomats and medical professionals in health diplomacy because intensifying globalization has spawned more global health issues, from obesity to Covid, and correspondingly more international cooperation, with consequences for both diplomacy and public health (Hunter, 2013; Katz et al., 2011; Luh, 2021).

Similarly, since the 2010s, scholarly and professional attention to city diplomacy has burgeoned in light of transnational issues directly impacting cities (e.g., terrorism, global trade, climate change, refugees, immigration) and the perceived inability or unwillingness of national governments to effectively address them (See Chapter 5 in this volume and Acuto et al., 2021; Amiri & Sevin, 2020; Leffel, 2018). Some kinds of city diplomacy, like that of the Global Parliament of Mayors and C40 Cities, gather government officials more than citizen diplomats, but others, such as Sister Cities International and the International Urban Development Association, convene varied stakeholders. Thus, city diplomacy may bring international diplomacy closer to people's lives in communities, but it does not necessarily advance CD research or practice.

The earliest significant work we found addressing CD on the internet is *Cyberpolitics* (Hill & Hughes, 1998), which focused on domestic and transnational political communication. Since the 2010s though, scholarly interest in "digital diplomacy" – diplomatic interactions online, especially via social media – has grown remarkably. Such research examines mostly governments' diplomatic activities online (Bjola & Holmes, 2015; Duncombe, 2018; Kurbalija, 2013), but also various international organizations (Bjola & Zaiotti, 2021; Grincheva, 2021; Pamment, 2016), diasporas (Dolea, 2021; Kennedy, 2022), and extremist groups (Bjola & Pamment, 2019). These findings point to a sharp increase in scholarly interest in diplomacy, particularly PD, since the 2010s, but less in CD. Hence, as CD practice proliferates worldwide online and off, the opportunities for CD research expand, and so do the questions researchers can pursue.

Research questions

We asked interviewees (experts on PD) to identify CD research and gaps in that research. Significantly, only a few interviewees identified specific scholars or publications focused on CD. As Cull noted, the terms "public diplomacy" and "cultural diplomacy" are used more often than CD, and this research tends to focus on government-driven diplomatic efforts that may not meaningfully involve citizens. However, the interviewees raised useful research questions. A distillation follows. Some questions may be of more interest to CD scholars, others to CD practitioners.

History & Trends: What are historical examples of CD successes and failures, and what explains their success or failure? What trends in diplomacy and society have implications for CD? How will technological developments, such as the developing online "metaverse," influence CD practice?

Identities & Motivations: What kinds of people (demographics, ideologies) identify as citizen diplomats? Why do some people get involved in CD and others do not? How can people be effectively motivated and trained to become citizen diplomats, and how can stakeholders be motivated to invest in CD? Can crises, like climate change, and trends, like growth in tourism, be harnessed to inspire CD practice and research?

Quantity & Quality: What is the quantity and quality of past and present CD practice? Quantity could be measured by numbers of participants, countries, and resources involved on a continuum from the smallest to the largest scale of CD operation. Quality could be measured on a continuum from the most superficial to the deepest CD instances (e.g., single, momentary interactions online to the most institutionalized, ongoing, in-person collaborations). In either case, continua can be filled with historical or hypothetical CD cases to convey the range of past practices or future possibilities.

Legitimacy: What is legitimate CD? Who should decide, using what standards? How can citizen diplomats determine the legitimacy of particular issues or organizations? What are the ethical obligations of citizen diplomats, and how can these obligations be enforced?

Relationships & Collaborations: How do citizen diplomats interact and, in some cases, collaborate with official diplomats as well as other institutional players, especially during significant world events or periods of conflict? How do official diplomats view CD? Older generations of official diplomats may be more skeptical and accustomed to one-way communication with citizens while younger generations may be more open to multi-directional communication with publics, and attentive to how publics respond to official diplomacy. How is CD viewed in different countries? For instance, how do stakeholders in countries with more state-centered, authoritarian, and/or collectivist cultures perceive and practice CD? Some analysts report more suspicion of, and less active CD in some East Asian countries (Jones, 2015; Kerr & Taylor, 2013). How are businesses using CD, and for what purposes? How can those inter-viewee Jay Harris called "local-global players" in cities and towns worldwide be made more visible to governments, transnational businesses, nonprofits, and each other to facilitate cooperation and leverage their often-impressive connections, knowledge, and skills?

Effectiveness & Training: What are the qualities of effective citizen diplo-mats? What kinds of knowledge, skills, connections, attitudes, and other resources matter most? How can people be trained to develop these quali-ties and resources? How can citizen diplomats "agree on how to disagree," and also avoid being manipulated to do the bidding of domestic or foreign governments?

Agency: Who controls or drives the CD, to what extent, and in what ways, from creation and planning, to implementation, to evaluation and reporting? How is the CD funded, and how does that funding affect "agency," understood as a continuum from the most "bottom up" (driven by the least advantaged citi-zens) to most "top down" (driven by the most advantaged citizens).

Impact, Success & Benefits: How do CD projects and programs impact participants – from students, to farmers, to activists and nuclear scientists – as well as non-participants? How should success be measured? Is there a way to measure the cost of the absence of CD, perhaps by comparing similar conditions with and without CD? Is there a way to measure the "multiplier effect" or impact of CD on non-participants? Who currently benefits from CD? Some of the preceding questions invite network analysis, life histories and, when resources allow, longitudinal and experimental studies that can better distinguish the impact of CD versus other proximate actors and events (Banks, 2011; Bhandari & Belyavina, 2011).

If diplomacy is "no longer a stiff waltz among states alone, but a jazzy dance of colorful coalitions" (Melissen, 2011), and if diplomats will "increasingly function as facilitators and social entrepreneurs between domestic and foreign civil society groups as they operate in global policy networks" (Hocking et al., 2012), then largely focusing on official diplomacy becomes less tenable. The risk is that diplomacy professionals and scholars miss challenges and opportunities that developments in international civil society pose to diplomacy, governments, and publics. Diplomacy research can and should examine how governments, media, transnational corporations, NGOs, and individual actors influence each other.

Governments can still be at the center of analysis, recognizing their official role and power. However, a broader network approach to diplomacy research recognizes that interactions not immediately or necessarily involving governments – from international organizations collaborating across borders to ban landmines (Cameron, 1998; Rutherford, 2010; Williams et al., 2008), to a Christian preacher in Florida burning Islamic Korans on social media (Nye, 2010) – can and do impact official diplomacy. Further, for CD practitioners, such broader research can deepen understanding of the possibilities for fruitful collaboration among diverse diplomacy actors. This invites attention to the varied dimensions of CD.

Nine dimensions of citizen diplomacy

Scholars and practitioners conceptualize CD in various ways. The following nine dimensions, and corresponding questions, capture some of the complexities involved in CD research. These dimensions can also help scholars analyze

CD activities, practitioners to design CD initiatives, and both to deepen their understanding of this nuanced, growing phenomenon.

1. Identity: Who is playing the role of citizen diplomat, and how do they view themselves? Do they see themselves as citizen diplomats? Some argue that all individuals are citizen diplomats even though many do not realize it. Their behavior toward people from other nations either improves the other's view of their country or tarnishes it. Some define everyone as a citizen diplomat, whether or not they are aware of it. Others define citizen diplomats more narrowly as those who call themselves such, or those who deliberately engage in cross-national dialogue or collaboration. Mueller and Rebstock (2012, pp. 16–17) make a useful distinction between spontaneous CD (those opportunities each person has to affect others' perceptions of their country as they go about their daily lives) and intentional CD (when individuals deliberately pursue international dialogue or collaboration) in how citizens choose to participate – as guest or host – in international exchanges and other activities usually designed to build positive relationships. International gamers and social media influencers are often examples of spontaneous citizen diplomats. Sister City delegations are classic examples of intentional CD.

2. Representation: Closely aligned but distinct from identity is representation. Whom do the citizen diplomats represent? Is the citizen diplomat acting as a lone individual or as a member of an organization or another institution? What is their relationship to government(s)? The U.S. State Department's International Visitor Leadership Program is an excellent example of a longstanding PD program that depends on Global Ties U.S., a network of citizen diplomats (many are volunteers) to administer the program on a daily basis.

3. Variety: What kinds of CD are practiced? What is the focus of their interaction: peacebuilding, religion, education, sports, arts, or something else?

4. Activity: What are citizen diplomats doing together, and with others, such as fellow citizens, foreign citizens, or official diplomats? What is the sequence or process of designing these activities? Activities include home visits and homestays, master classes, conferences, panel discussions, unofficial negotiations, business meetings, sports events, and performances as well as the burgeoning field of online exchanges. Home visits/homestays are viewed as especially impactful because they are a way of experiencing a culture from the inside out rather than looking in from the outside.

5. Scope: How many people are involved? How many countries? Self-described global CD networks such as Sister Cities International (SCI), People to People International, and Friendship Force International (FFI) are excellent examples of large CD networks. FFI has 15,000 active members span-

ning 45 countries on six continents. SCI is the umbrella organization for more than 1,800 partnerships in 142 countries. In contrast, Fulda (2019) documents the experience and profound impact of 12 European citizen diplomats in China. Some interviewees argued that in this era of political divisiveness CD is needed within nations, such as delegations moving between NYC and Pueblos in New Mexico.

6. Resources: What resources (e.g., money, celebrity, expertise, paid staff, volunteer hours, networks, meeting space, lodging) do citizen diplomats bring to the table? Who supplies those resources? Do one or more governments provide funding/structure? If so, how much and which governments?

7. Duration: How long is the CD effort? It may be a one-time event such as the Minnesota Symphony visit to Cuba in 2015, or programs spanning many years. One interviewee asserted that "citizen diplomacy is meaningful interaction over time – substantive and enduring." Many CD efforts depend on the dynamic personality and persistence of a particular leader, then fade once that leader is no longer active.

8. Intentions: Who is the intended audience? What are the goals? Who are the intended beneficiaries? Citizen diplomats' intentions are myriad, from broader peacebuilding or economic development between two or more countries, to more specific cultural, educational, commercial, or political goals to benefit particular groups, clients, or organizations. While the CD literature often implies that citizen diplomats mean to do good in the world, it must be acknowledged that CD actors' intentions are not always productive or benign (Long et al., 2021; Sharp, 2001).

9. Impact: What are the results? Who and/or what is affected? How are results measured and reported? Who is monitoring impact? To what extent does impact evaluation inform subsequent CD practice?

Priorities to advance CD research and practice

Straddling the study and practice of CD, we suggest three priorities to further both the research and implementation of CD. These priorities are listed from the smallest to the largest in scale. First, several interviewees expressed the need for a comprehensive hub online to find past and present CD research, stories, models, guides, and other resources for the benefit of scholars and practitioners. There is no lack of diplomacy or foreign service training programs at institutes and universities worldwide, and some of these offer CD information online, but there is no comprehensive resource hub. The University of Southern California's Center on Public Diplomacy serves as a hub for PD news, research, and discussion, which sometimes focuses on CD.

Second, and relatedly, there is a need for an international network that can sustainably connect and facilitate collaboration among the growing numbers of CD scholars, students, and practitioners across the globe. Scholars can enrich practitioners' understanding of the history, theory, and practice of CD. They can also advise or assist in the evaluation research practitioners need to assess their impact, engage in advocacy, and garner resources. In turn, practitioners can offer their frontline insights, access to data, and jobs or internships.

Learning Life's Citizen Diplomacy Initiative (CDI) aspires to be such an international CD network. Launched in 2019 by Paul Lachelier as the Public Diplomacy Council of America's Citizen Diplomacy Research Group, the CDI now holds open meetings every three months to discuss CD research, practice, and news. With every meeting, the CDI issues a *CDI Bulletin* with the latest CD articles, books, videos, reports, and events found online. Participation in the CDI is free. As of April 13, 2024 more than 1,150 diplomacy students, scholars, and practitioners across the world are on its listserv. However, the CDI is run by volunteers, and has no funding, which limits its capacity to expand the network and foster more collaborations. The U.S. Center for Citizen Diplomacy was founded in 2006 to establish a network and to promote CD. The Center has been part of PYXERA Global, an international NGO headquartered in Washington, D.C., since 2012. PYXERA staff members have conducted some training programs, but the Center has been constrained by limited resources.

Whether based at a university or nonprofit, a vibrant CD research and practice network should endure and thrive when start-up enthusiasm fades, or a charismatic founder leaves the organization. A sustainable funding model, whether based on individual donations, grants, sponsorships, member dues, advertising revenue, or else, is key to longevity. Funding could provide for an office which could, among other things, serve as an archive and even a museum for CD materials and literature. Researchers and interested citizens could visit such a museum or archive to better understand the history and potential of CD.

Third, researchers and practitioners interested in advancing CD globally should collaborate to design and build a larger CD ecosystem. That ecosystem can support an online resource hub and international network, but also strengthen the web of international individuals, organizations, and agencies (world affairs councils, international businesses, nonprofits and interest groups, high school and university global studies programs, local and regional government foreign trade offices, language schools, culture clubs, etc.) that can connect residents and foreign visitors in localities throughout the world.

Here, we draw some inspiration from the peacebuilding Alger's (1978, 2007, 2013) vision of a more participatory foreign relations. In the 1970s, Alger (1978) noted the existence of the International Council of Mid-Ohio, which boasted "a language bank for emergency translation service, a handbook of international services and opportunity for service ... a monthly and quarterly composite calendar of international events in the community, a resource bank of local international experts" (p. 21). Today, more cities and regions offer these and other resources. The Hague, for example, has a Hospitality Center for International Media & Visitors, an Embassy Week when embassies open their doors to the public, The World Class where foreign and Dutch students participate in lectures and socials, and a Bridge Program connecting residents and foreigners via markets, lectures, walking and bike tours, and more.

We also draw inspiration from their own and their interviewees' experiences building or participating in diverse private, nonprofit, and for-profit CD initiatives, such as Learning Life's Family Diplomacy Initiative, or Jay Harris' Carpe Global. Some of the interviewees' paths to diplomacy signal other actual and potential points in a larger CD ecosystem, like an international summer farm labor-lodging exchange in Denmark, an international boarding school and exchange program in Japan, lower school Spanish classes, a U.S. military base in England, and missionaries. An online resource hub, a financially sustainable international network, and a global CD ecosystem do not exhaust the possibilities, but they would considerably advance CD research and practice, and in so doing, nourish peace and democracy in our fragmented world.

References

Acuto, M., Hartley, K., & Kosvac, A. (2021). City diplomacy: Another generational shift? *Diplomatica*, *3*(1), 137–46. http://doi.org/10.1163/25891774-03010007.

Adams, C. M. (1999). *Domestic, social, and economic impacts of the International Visitors Program.* National Council for International Visitors.

Alger, C. F. (1978). Extending responsible public participation in international affairs. *Journal of International Education and Cultural Exchange*, *14*(1), 17–21.

Alger, C. F. (2007). There are peacebuilding tasks for everybody. *International Studies Review*, *9*(3), 534–54. http://doi.org/10.1111/j.1468-2486.2007.00720.x.

Alger, C. F. (2013). *The UN system and cities in global governance.* Springer.

Amiri, S., & Sevin, E. (Eds.) (2020). *City diplomacy: Current trends and future prospects.* Palgrave Macmillan.

Arndt, R. T. (2005). *The first resort of kings: American cultural diplomacy in the twentieth century.* Potomac.

Arndt, R. T., & Rubin, D. L. (1993). *The Fulbright difference: 1948–1992.* Transaction.

Aslam, S., Hussain, S., & Ali, A. (2017). Politics through sport and cricket diplomacy between Pakistan and India: A case study of national daily newspaper (Dawn Pakistan). *The Government: Research Journal of Political Science, 5*(5), 61–75.

Banks, R. (2011). *A resource guide to public diplomacy evaluation.* Figueroa Press.

Bhandari, R., & Belyavina, R. (2011). Evaluating and measuring the impact of citizen diplomacy: Current status and future directions. Institute of International Education. https://www.semanticscholar.org/paper/Evaluating-and-Measuring-the-Impact-of -Citizen-and-Bhandari-Belyavina/3aba2a46fec84faca02ebefe2dfe78f585879285.

Bhattacharya, N., & Jairath, V. K. (2012). Social movements, "popular" spaces, and participation: A review. *Sociological Bulletin, 61*(2), 299–319. http://doi.org/10.1177/0038022920120205.

Bjola, C., & Holmes, M. (2015). *Digital diplomacy theory and practice.* Routledge.

Bjola, C., & Pamment, J. (2019). *Countering online propaganda and extremism: The dark side of digital diplomacy.* Routledge.

Bjola, C., & Zaiotti, R. (2021). *Digital diplomacy and international organizations: Autonomy, legitimacy and contestation.* Routledge.

Bosniak, L. (2000). Citizenship denationalized. *Indiana Journal of Global Legal Studies, 7*(2), 447–509. http://doi.org/10.7282/00000118.

Cameron, M. (1998). *To walk without fear.* Oxford University Press.

Chahine, J. (2010). Public diplomacy: A conceptual framework. PhD thesis. McGill University Library. http:// culturaldiplomacy .org/ academy/ pdf/ research/ books/ public _diplomacy/ Public _Diplomacy _ - _A _Conceptual _Framework _ - _Joumane_Chahine.pdf.

Chehabi, H. E. (2007). Sport diplomacy between the United States and Iran. *Diplomacy & Statecraft, 12*(1), 89–106.

Chetail, V., & Jütersonke, O. (2015). Peacebuilding: A review of the academic literature. *Geneva Peacebuilding Platform,* White Paper Series 13. https:// www .gpplatform .ch/ sites/ default/ files/ WPS %2013 %20 - %20Review %20of %20the %20Academic %20Literature%20-%20Chetail%20and%20Jütersonke.pdf.

Cooper, A. F., Heine, J., & Thakur, R. (2013). Introduction: The challenges of 21st-century diplomacy. In A. F. Cooper, J. Heine, & R. Thakur (Eds.), *The Oxford handbook of modern diplomacy* (pp. 1–31). Oxford University Press.

Dingwerth, K., & Pattberg, P. (2006). Global governance as a perspective on world politics. *Global Governance, 12*(2), 185–203. http://doi.org/10.1163/19426720-01202006.

Dolea, A. (2021). Transnational diaspora diplomacy, emotions and COVID-19: The Romanian diaspora in the UK. *Place Branding and Public Diplomacy, 18,* 12–14. http://doi.org/10.1057/s41254-021-00243-1.

Duncombe, C. (2018). Twitter and the challenges of digital diplomacy. *SAIS Review of International Affairs, 38,* 91–100. http://doi.org/10.1353/sais.2018.0019.

Earle, L. (2011). *Literature review on the dynamics of social movements in fragile and conflict-affected states.* Governance and Social Development Resource Centre, University of Birmingham. https://gsdrc.org/wp-content/uploads/2015/07/EIRS13 .pdf.

Eisenhower, D. D. (1956). *People-to-people partnership: The White House conference* [speech transcript]. NC State University Libraries' Digital Collections: Rare and Unique Materials. https:// avpd .lib .ncsu .edu/ transcript/ AV2 _FM _296 -people2people.

Gibson, J. S. (1979). *The United States International Visitor Program: Strengthening the community organization.* National Council for International Visitors.

Goren, H., & Yemini, M. (2017). Global citizenship education redefined – a systematic review of empirical studies on global citizenship education. *International Journal of Educational Research, 82*(15), 170–83. http://doi.org/10.1016/j.ijer.2017.02.004.

Grincheva, N. (2021). *Museum diplomacy in the digital age.* Routledge.

Gullahorn, J. E., & Gullahorn, J. T. (1966). American students abroad: Professional versus personal development. *The Annals of the American Academy of Political and Social Science, 368,* 43–59. http://doi.org/10.1177/000271626636800106.

Hauss, C. (2010). *International conflict resolution.* Bloomsbury.

Hazama, I., Nyamnjoh, F. B., & Umeya, K. (2019). *Citizenship in motion: South African and Japanese scholars in conversation.* Langaa RPCIG. http:// doi .org/ 10 .2307/ j .ctvhn0d00.5.

Herz, A., & Olivier, C. (2012). Transnational social networks – current perspectives. *Transnational Social Review, 2*(2), 115–19. http:// doi .org/ 10 .1080/ 21931674 .2012 .10820729.

Hill, K. A., & Hughes, J. E. (1998). *Cyberpolitics: Citizen activism in the age of the internet.* Rowman & Littlefield.

Hocking, B., Melissen, J., Riordon, S., & Sharp, P. (2012). *Futures for diplomacy: Integrative diplomacy in the 21st century.* Netherlands Institute of International Relations Clingendael. http://doi.org/10.1163/187119112X625538.

Hunter, A. (2013). Global health diplomacy: An integrative review of the literature and implications for nursing. *Nursing Outlook, 61*(2), 85–92.

Jones, P. (2015). *Track two diplomacy in theory and practice.* Stanford University Press.

Katz, R., Kornblet, S., Arnold, G., Lief, E., & Fischer, J. E. (2011). Defining health diplomacy: Changing demands in the era of globalization. *The Milbank Quarterly, 89*(3), 503–23.

Kennedy, L. (Ed.) (2022). *Routledge international handbook of diaspora diplomacy.* Routledge.

Kerr, P., & Taylor, B. (2013). Track-two diplomacy in East Asia. In P. Kerr, & G. Wiseman (Eds.), *Diplomacy in a globalizing world: Theories and practices* (pp. 226–43). Oxford University Press.

Kurbalija, J. (2013). The impact of the internet and ICT on contemporary diplomacy. In P. Kerr, & G. Wiseman (Eds.), *Diplomacy in a globalizing world: Theories and practices* (pp. 141–59). Oxford University Press.

Lande, S. (2017). *"Old friends": The Xi Jinping–Iowa story.* US China Friendship Education Company. http://www.worldcat.org/title/1049570727.

Lee, K. C. (2019). Negotiating diplomacy: Forging Thai–Sino relations through interactive business workshops. *Journal of Chinese Overseas, 15*(1), 89–105.

Lee, K. C. (2020). Re-envisioning citizen diplomacy: A case study of a multifaceted, transnational, People's Republic of China "Ethnopreneur." *Journal of Current Chinese Affairs, 48*(2), 127–47.

Leffel, B. (2018). Animus of the underling: Theorizing city diplomacy in a world society. *The Hague Journal of Diplomacy, 13*(4), 502–22. http:// doi .org/ 10 .1163/ 1871191X -13040025.

Long, K., Etheridge, C., Hugins, K., & O'Connell, C. (2021). Rising global fears of foreign interference in higher education. *International Higher Education, 107,* 8–10.

Ludwig, K., & Kok, M. (2018). *Exploring new dynamics in global environmental governance – A literature review.* PBL Netherlands Environmental Assessment Agency. https:// www.pbl.nl/ sites/ default/ files/ downloads/ 3253_Exploring_new_dynamics _in_global_environmental_governance_.pdf.

Luh, S. (2021). The role of EU health attaches for global health diplomacy in times of COVID-19. *Global Affairs*. http://doi.org/10.1080/23340460.2021.2008265.

Marshall, J. (1949). Citizen diplomacy. *American Political Science Review, 43*(1), 83–90. http://doi.org/10.2307/1950316.

Marx, A., & Wouters, J. (2018). *Global governance, Vol 1: Different manifestations of, and perspectives on global governance*. Edward Elgar Publishing.

Melissen, J. (2011). *Beyond the new public diplomacy*. Netherlands Institute of International Relations Clingendael.

Mueller, S. L. (2020). The nexus of U.S. public diplomacy and citizen diplomacy. In N. Snow, & P. M. Taylor (Eds.), *Routledge handbook of public diplomacy* (pp. 112–19). Routledge.

Mueller, S. L., & Rebstock, M. (2012). The impact and practice of citizen diplomacy. *Public Diplomacy Magazine, 7*, 15–28.

Nye, J. S., Jr. (2010, October 4). The pros and cons of citizen diplomacy. *The New York Times*. https://www.nytimes.com/2010/10/05/opinion/05iht-ednye.html.

Opitz, C., Geis, A., & Pfeifer, H. (2022). Engaging with public opinion at the micro-level: Citizen dialogue and participation in German foreign policy. *Foreign Policy Analysis, 18*(1). http://doi.org/10.1093/fpa/orab033.

Oshewolo, S. (2020). "Citizens" in foreign policy theorizing: President Yar'Adua and Nigeria's citizen diplomacy. *African Identities, 19*(4), 522–35.

Pamment, J. (2016). Digital diplomacy as transmedia engagement: Aligning theories of participatory culture with international advocacy campaigns. *New Media & Society, 18*(9), 2046–62. http://doi.org/10.1177/1461444815577792.

Popkova, A. (2022). Exploring citizen diplomacy's local impact: The case of Global Ties Kalamazoo. *The Hague Journal of Diplomacy*. http://doi.org/10.1163/1871191X-bja10100.

Root, E. (1922, September 14). A requisite for the success of popular diplomacy. *Foreign Affairs*. https://www.foreignaffairs.com/articles/united-states/1922-09-15/requisite-success-popular-diplomacy.

Root, E. (1937). A requisite for the success of popular diplomacy. *Foreign Affairs*. https://www.foreignaffairs.com/united-states/requisite-success-popular-diplomacy.

Rutherford, K. R. (2010). *Disarming states: The international movement to ban land-mines*. ABC-CLIO.

Sevin, E., Metzgar, E. T., & Hayden, C. (2019). The scholarship of public diplomacy: Analysis of a growing field. *International Journal of Communication, 13*, 4814–37.

Sharp, P. (2001). Making sense of citizen diplomats: The people of Duluth, Minnesota, as international actors. *International Studies Perspectives, 2*(2), 131–50.

Snow, N., & Cull, N. J. (2020). *Routledge handbook of public diplomacy*, 2nd edn. Routledge.

Stanley, M. (1983). *Global citizenship* [speech transcript]. Stanley Center for Peace and Security. https://stanleycenter.org/our-story/global-citizenship/.

U.S. Department of State. (1959). The citizen's role in cultural relations. International Educational Exchange Service, Bureau of International Cultural Relations.

Williams, J., Goose, S. D., & Wareham, M. (2008). *Banning landmines: Disarmament, citizen diplomacy, and human security*. Rowman & Littlefield.

Yu, Z. (2018). Citizen diplomacy – New US public diplomacy strategy in the Middle East under the Obama Administration. *Journal of Middle Eastern and Islamic Studies (in Asia), 9*(4), 36–58. http://doi.org/10.1080/19370679.2015.12023272.

PART II

Disciplines

7   History

Nicholas J. Cull

Introduction

History has an important place as an approach for exploring public diplomacy (PD). While the systematic study of PD can be traced to the American pioneers of public opinion research – Laswell, Lippmann, and their colleagues – writing in response to propaganda in World War I, historians like Squires (1935) came hard on their heels. Their initial task was reconstructing the mechanisms at work in the war and addressing such questions as the role of British government media in breaking down American neutrality. In the century since, history has remained a key discipline for the study of PD. Sevin, Metzgar, and Hayden (2019), in their survey of English-language journal publications in the field from 1965 to 2017, found that history was second only to communication studies as an approach to thinking about PD. Their assessment is almost certainly an undercount given that much historical writing relevant to the field uses terms preferred in the time studied such as the dreaded word "propaganda".

Similarly, many historical and other scholarly pieces have identified their subject by a term other than the umbrella term PD such as cultural diplomacy, exchange, international broadcasting, or public opinion/audience research, even when the work studied took place under the auspices of a PD agency. This chapter will take the field broadly and consider themes and approaches which historians might usefully explore in coming years, from the vantage point of an active historian, but before that it is necessary to look at the existing dynamics of historical writing as it relates to PD. As will be seen, because both the terminology and the idea that the practice of PD is part of an interconnected whole that emerged in the United States (U.S.), the American experience has loomed largest in the literature.

The disproportionately American history of history in public diplomacy studies

As with the entire field of PD studies, the absence of agreed parameters raises an immediate problem. While the term "PD" emerged in regular use only in the mid-1960s and chiefly within the U.S., the practice of advancing foreign policy by engaging foreign publics was as old as statecraft and had been studied sporadically from ancient times by historians and other analysts of government. The emergence of the coherent and interconnected discussion of the topic necessary to constitute a field required a surge in the practice and a bureaucracy keen to make the connections. This surge came with the Great War, in which struggles to win allies, demoralize adversaries, and woo neutrals were central to diplomacy.

The historical study of PD began as the practitioners themselves endeavored to record their deeds. Foundational works include Creel (1920a): the official report of America's Committee on Public Information (CPI) published in the wake of the Great War or British equivalents like Stuart (1920). Later institutionally generated texts included important histories such as Espinosa (1976), commissioned by the State Department's historical unit or Donaldson (1984): the history of the British Council, published to mark its 50th birthday. Today's institutional publication includes a retroactive project by the State Department Historical Branch to integrate documents on the history of PD into the *Foreign Relations of the United States* (FRUS) volumes. During the years when PD was the responsibility of the United States Information Agency (USIA) the historical branch neglected PD, leaving it out of its own account of the Cold War and underplaying it in pre-USIA years. PD now has its own distinct volume for each era some including audiovisual materials (U.S. Department of State, 2017). Each new volume should spark further historical research.

Memoirs

Many key works in U.S. PD history originated as memoirs, starting with Creel's (1920b) notoriously self-serving version of the global U.S. campaign in the Great War or Whitehouse's (1920) account of her work for CPI in Switzerland. There was a surge of similar books in mid-Cold War with works like Sorenson (1969) or in the UK Marett (1968). Such works created a hybrid form that blended history and memoir. At the end of the Cold War a number of veteran practitioners devoted part of their retirement to chronicling the history of their agency or approach. Important books include Dizard's (2004) history of USIA, Heil's (2004) meticulous history of Voice of America (VOA) radio, Morgan and Masey's (2008) treatment of U.S. contributions to Expos, and Arndt's (2006) magisterial history of U.S. cultural diplomacy, all of which appeared in the first decade of the twenty-first century in the immediate aftermath of the demise of USIA.

Subsequent scholarship has built on these foundations. This record is recounted to suggest that institutional self-documentation and the hybrid form of memoir/history will be part of the future of the field also. Recent additions in the U.S. literature of PD include the books by Obama administration veterans Under Secretary of State for Public Diplomacy and Public Affairs, Richard Stengel (2019) and Radio Free Europe/Radio Liberty president/CEO, Thomas Kent (2020). Both books argued for a more vigorous U.S. response to Russian activity in information space.

Archive-based history

Histories by non-participants have typically lagged a generation behind memoirs and hybrid memoir/histories. Memoirs of PD at the Office of War Information (OWI) during World War II such as Carroll (1948) were published early as part of an argument over the need to integrate PD into postwar foreign policy, yet the first book-length overview of the OWI (Winkler, 1978) appeared only in step with standard declassification some 30 years after the closure of the agency, with added time for research and writing. In the U.K., participants in British interwar international outreach like the documentary filmmaker and film theorist John Grierson had their say in print decades before historians. Taylor's (1981) influential *The Projection of Britain* came at the end of the first wave of studies of British interwar foreign policy and was some half a century after the events described.

This indexical feature of historical scholarship whereby historians work as archives become available has established a pattern in PD scholarship and modern political and international history in general whereby research is closely linked to the bulk availability of new materials. The field has reproduced the evolution of practice as the focus of study has advanced through time. Studies of prewar publicity gave way to wartime psychological outreach, which led to the exploration of postwar global public engagement seen in the Marshall Plan (Ellwood, 1992) or Enemy Reeducation (Pronay & Wilson, 1985), and then on to PD in the high Cold War (Lucas, 1999). This pattern of historical scholarship as a kind of advancing frontier will also doubtless continue. Scholars of the early years of the Cold War have long since begun to publish on the 1970s (Notaker, Scott-Smith, & Snyder, 2016). We can expect that they will remain in step with the archives and follow the same themes into the post-Cold War era as those records open.

The path of declassification does not always run smoothly. Legal restrictions on access to the archives of the USIA held back work on that key agency until after the end of the Cold War but the field swiftly made up for lost time with the American Cold War PD being perhaps the most investigated historical topic on any PD area worldwide, with scholarship skewing to the Eisenhower period especially. The most comprehensive single administration account is Osgood's (2006) treatment of Eisenhower. Scholars have considered particular themes like race (Dudziak, 2000) or the representation of U.S. society (Belmonte, 2008). Others have looked at specific mechanisms such as exchange (Scott-Smith, 2008), art (Krenn, 2006), music (Von Eschen, 2006), exhibitions (Wulf, 2015), culture (Krenn, 2017), dance (Philips, 2019), or documentary film (Real, 2020).

Some scholars have focused on particular targets of U.S. attention such as the Soviet Union (Hixson, 1997) or postwar Germany (Gienow-Hecht, 1999). They have explored particular campaigns like media around the Space Race (Muir-Harmony, 2020), Cuba broadcasting (Walsh, 2011), or the war in Vietnam (Page, 1996). They have looked at complex dynamics such as the way in which PD called forth the notion of a Third World (Parker, 2016). Some personalities have attracted individual coverage, most notably Edward R. Murrow (Tomlin, 2016; Snow, 2013). Cull (2008, 2012) attempted to tell the entire story of U.S. PD from 1945 to 2001, a project that generated two monographs and multiple historical essays.

And so the field grew, transcending its focus on the U.S. Important areas of focus have included Germany and France where works such as Gienow-Hecht (2009) and Evans (2002, 2004) have developed a richer understanding of the foundations of national cultural diplomacy. Insightful works on postwar campaigns include Glover (2011) on Sweden and Rosendorf (2014) on Franco's Spain. The Soviet Union's engagement through culture was explored by David-Fox (2011) and others. Especially interesting contributions have included the handful of parallel studies which look simultaneously at two-actor approaches to the same issue. Vaughan (2005) addressed both British and U.S. PD in the Middle East in the 1950s. Rawnsley (1996) and Nelson (1997) did the same for international broadcasting. Eames (2023) has a parallel study of Anglo-American PD around nuclear weapons in the Reagan/Thatcher era. Still more ambitious are the parallel studies that consider both antagonists in the Cold War as with Peacock's (2017) work on appeals to childhood in the U.S. and U.S.S.R., or the study of U.S. and Soviet cinema produced by Shaw and

Youngblood (2014). Multi-scholar anthologies have proven an effective mechanism for opening a range of cross-regional and Eastern/Western perspectives most especially on the issue of the cultural Cold War (Mitter & Major, 2004; Mikkonen, Parkkinen, & Scott-Smith, 2018; Scott-Smith & Krabbendam, 2004).

Looking ahead

Looking ahead within the declassification cycle within the field of U.S. PD, historians have some clear research tasks. The years leading up to the terrorist attacks on the 9/11 terrorist attacks on the U.S. promise to be especially interesting given the common opinion at the time of the attacks that deficits in U.S. PD in the Middle East were part of the problem. On the positive side, there are important PD dimensions to the response to the crisis in the former Yugoslavia. The approach to Eastern Europe invites studies focused on the confluence of PD and development policy. Both USIA and USAID were tasked to work in the region. Issues worthy of detailed study include media development policies aimed at developing free and democratic communication structures in the region.

The established PD history sub-themes of race and gender need to be traced in detail into the 1990s. The race story will need to explore representation of the Los Angeles riots of 1992 and the beginning of hip-hop as a genre in U.S. cultural diplomacy in the George W. Bush years. In terms of gender scholars will need to chart USIA's role publicizing the Beijing Women's Conference of 1995 on one hand while simultaneously responding to the challenges of President Bill Clinton's distinctly gendered adventures and managing the Agency's loss in 1994 of a massive gender bias lawsuit known as the Hartman Case, formally Civil Action No. 1977-2019 *Hartman, et al. v. Albright, et al.* (now called *Carolee Brady Hartman, et al., v. Michael R. Pompeo, et al.*, under Federal Rule of Civil Procedure 25(d)). There is also a need for a comprehensive treatment of LGBTQ issues in PD given the increased presence of this theme in Western PD generally from the 1990s on.

The preeminence of climate change as an issue for contemporary PD and in the world at large underscores the need for systematic attention to earlier treatment of this issue most especially in the years from the Rio Earth Summit of 1992 onward. Of particular interest is the way in which the U.S. and other international actors began to integrate climate themes into their representations of morality and immorality on the international stage. Case studies should include the emphasis on environmental damage in negative U.S. messaging about Saddam Hussein and the positive claims about stewardship of the environment seen in U.S. PD platforms such as the pavilions at the Genoa Expo of 1992 and Lisbon Expo of 1998, both of which focused on the health of oceans and coastal areas.

Sometimes the declassification cycle is utterly short-circuited, and a body of documents arrives in the public domain without review. The obvious example of this was the dumping of State Department documents onto the Wikileaks site in 2010. The leak of these papers has provided snapshots of practice in advance of archive release. Historians have begun mining this material with first fruits of this research, including work by Moody (2017) on contemporary U.S. embassy use of cinema.

Beyond the declassification cycle

Historians do not merely advance like cattle grazing new territory according to an annual cycle of declassifications. They turn back into old pasture too. Themes which emerge in the present can redirect attention to previously well-explored epochs. Part of a scholar's mission is to seek out ways in which a reexamination of the past can cast fresh light on the present. Hart (2013) revisited the origins of U.S. PD in the era of the Global War on Terror. Hamilton's (2020) complete history of U.S. government's information in the Great War was shaped, if not wholly inspired, by Trump-era debates around falsehood in political media. Scholarship itself draws forth further scholarship. Contemporary debates around nation branding and soft power have encouraged scholars to revisit issues of national image and reputation in the past in search of the nation brand and soft power before the words (Viktorin et al., 2018). The stage is set for more detailed country-specific studies.

Interesting avenues included historical work on the evolution of images during the great political transitions of the recent past such as the attempts to develop post-communist images for the nations of Eastern Europe. Similarly, although issues around human rights emerged to the fore of PD discourse in the 1970s and, in step with the declassification cycle, moved into the historical discourse 30 years later thanks to the work of scholars like Moyn (2010), we are now seeing a reexamination of the previous presentation of human rights in cultural diplomacy across a much broader period (Geinow-Hecht, Kunkel, & Jobs, 2023).

Taking the long view

The combination of the lively scholarship around propaganda and PD and its emergence as a characteristic practice of foreign policy prompted Taylor (2013) to examine the deep historical roots of media in foreign policy, and doubtless the research agenda for coming years will include a quest for the deeper roots of our contemporary PD phenomena, including city diplomacy, diaspora diplomacy, and attention to networks. It is interesting that while celebrity diplomacy is well recognized in the present it rarely shows up in the historical discourse. The missions of Hollywood actor and raconteur Will Rogers to Latin America seldom surface in accounts of the interwar years in U.S. diplomacy, public or otherwise.

Towards geographic diversity

There is scope for regionally specific and country-specific studies focused on the general approach to engaging the wider world, and bilateral relationship with the U.S. The countries of Europe West and East have been well-served. The Nordic countries have developed an especially lively historical literature. Latin America has an emerging scholarship seen presently in historical anthology projects. The Middle East and Africa remain understudied with the key exception of interest in U.S. responses to apartheid. Such currents are in some way predictable, but a truly ambitious research agenda should look to break with the habits of the past and strike against dominant trends in the present.

National diversity

The history of the Cold War period has focused on the transmitting nations of the era. The extent to which media of the era still flowed along lines established in the colonial era – from north to south – was a major issue at the time in key fora such as the MacBride (1980) report. As systematic historical scholarship moves into the post-Cold War period this regional bias will have to change not merely for reasons of equity but because the balance of activity shifted in the world fundamentally during the course of the 1980s. By the early 1990s Manheim (1994) noted that the balance of PD material at that point flowed into the U.S. rather than out.

Looking at the post-Cold War period we already have good accounts of some European actors. Pamment's (2016) history of British PD's entry into the digital era is a model for others. But there are wider stories to tell of elaborate attempts to develop influence. Big spenders of the era include South Korea and Saudi Arabia. There have been long arcs of emerging strength in PD worldwide most especially from China and India, although Turkey also has an interesting trajectory, mixing government communication with strength in the field of popular culture.

The rapid expansion of PD in the early 2000s threw up some remarkable cases of positive PD stories emerging from unexpected places. Thailand's use of gastro diplomacy caught the world by surprise as did the emergence of Peru and Angola as notable contributors to the international exhibition circuit. Angola's win at the 2013 Venice Biennale of art showed what could be done. There have also been interesting shifts from a PD based on narrow self-promotion to a more altruistic strategy. Ireland's use of diaspora diplomacy, setting itself up as a diaspora relations consultant to others, is a good case.

The domestic dimension of public diplomacy

Sometimes fields expand their scope beyond their original limits and the process broadens the agenda for future research. One of the most significant issues to emerge in contemporary PD in recent years is concern over its domestic dimension. For many years the field followed the division of labor in U.S. PD that anything domestic was public affairs. Today, there are many factors mitigating for the inclusion of the domestic within PD. The elimination of the boundary between foreign and domestic audiences in the age of the internet is one. The political significance of diasporic groups for whom foreign language materials are relevant and who might even make significant intermediaries for messaging to their countries of origin is another. It is also clear that many countries worry about domestic support for foreign policy. In China the prime audience for Beijing's PD is the home audience. In the U.S., Secretary of State Blinken (2021) has explicitly emphasized the need for diplomacy to be understood at home. This development will however also direct attention to historical attempts to balance domestic and international priorities and the operation or not of a firewall to insulate international communication from party political or other short-term domestically driven influence. This has been a major theme in the history of the British Council for example.

New technology and media disruption

Technology has played a central role in PD since the end of the Cold War and is part of the reason that governments are so interested in the activity. However, there is a tendency to see the arrival of each new technology or platform in PD as being so different from anything in the past as to render historical inquiry irrelevant. This is a mistake. PD is hurt by presentism. In the case of the internet there is a whole evolution worthy of exploration which includes moments when the digital was brought into PD, from initial reports of technological breakthroughs being integrated into the soft power of science to the integration of early digital systems into embassy communications. But in an age in which a new media has plainly disrupted international relations, it makes sense to systematically study other moments in which media has evolved in a dramatic fashion. Once one begins to look for it, it is striking that there is a historical correlation between new forms of mass media for which audiences have yet to evolve skepticism or media specific literacy and conflict.

The international crisis in the run up to the outbreak of the Great War was made worse by the baying of mass circulation newspapers, each with their national focus and agenda, playing to their own readers' pet hatreds with a view to maximizing circulation. Our tendency to see history in terms of nations and personalities rather than platforms has played up the role of the Kaiser and Tsar in what happened rather than the newspapers they were working to appease. Similarly in crisis, the run up to World War II also shows signs of media disruption. We have the testimony of Dr. Goebbels himself that radio was a key part of the Nazi domination of Germany (Wijfjes, 2014).

One could also add the role that the newsreel played a part in lending an unprecedented reality to selected images on a screen crafted to rouse or deter. The Cold War has an under-explored relationship to the new medium of television. It was certainly exploited to disruptive effect by opportunist voices like Senator Joseph McCarthy or Bishop Fulton Sheen, whose interventions distorted U.S. foreign policy into a populist anti-communism which reduced the freedom of action available to politicians. Internationally television had its role in overlaying political alignments with technological and media connections as both the U.S. and U.S.S.R. helped allies to develop television networks and furnished politically useful content.

Media literacy and peace building

There is a corollary of the disruption caused by new media which also needs systematic historical inquiry. Just as it is possible to see new media disruption in the outbreak of the world wars and escalation of the Cold War, so it is possible to see a learning process and rebalancing of media consumption playing a role in their de-escalation. In fact, the diplomacy at the end of the world wars included discussion of the disruptive role of media, the most famous being the great statement of the preamble to the UNESCO of 1945: "since wars begin in the minds of men, it is in the minds of men that the defences of peace must be constructed." The Cold War also had its media solutions, including information disarmament talks. We live in an era in which media is weaponized. It stands to reason that a weapon requires a disarmament process specifically focused on reducing its damage. Previous processes of taming new media and stepping back from the brink diplomatically deserve historical attention. I have sought to start this ball rolling by examining the media disarmament between the U.S. and Soviet Union in the 1980s (Cull, 2021). There is still much to be done.

Diversifying actors

One powerful critique of PD and its subset (or some say parallel activity) cultural diplomacy is that it overemphasizes the importance of the nation state as an actor and neglects the role of nonstate and especially community interconnection. This statist approach predetermines the field to a top-down perspective. Community level actors include diasporic groups, indigenous communities, and civic institutions such as museums. But not all nonstate activity is bottom up. The post-Cold War period had produced clear examples of corporations mimicking nation states as they seek to enhance their reputation and wield something akin to soft power. The relationship between the corporate sector and state PD around the world is under-explored (see Chapter 4 in this volume). We at least know that the private sector cannot be counted on as an auxiliary of the nation state. It operates more as an ally, helping when it sees mutual interest. In the history of U.S. PD there have been moments of partnership – private cooperation in USIA work in the Eisenhower and Reagan years for example – and moments of crashing disappointment. The failure to raise sufficient private capital to properly underwrite U.S. attendance at World Expos as Congress hoped is an obvious case. By Expo 2020 interest levels were so low that the Emirati government had to pay for the U.S. to be there, like a poor uncle who can't make his own way to the wedding.

The issue of a private and non-governmental presence in PD raises the question of partnerships and multi-stakeholder coalitions. After attracting attention in the scholarship of the early Cold War (Laville & Wilford, 2006) the concept of the state/private network in PD has lain fallow since. The emergence of this partnership in the 1990s for reasons of reduced budgets and in order to maximize the possibilities of working with actors with special sectorial credibility to audiences, increases this need. By extension there is a need to document the kind of multi-stakeholder coalitions that have developed around the great issues of the recent past. My own long-term project has been to chart the PD of the global movement opposing apartheid in South Africa which united a liberation movement with an international organization, sympathetic states, and civil society actors around the world. In that case corporations tended to be the targets of activism rather than partners. Similar cases begging detailed historical analysis include the anti-nuclear and disarmament campaigns and coalitions around environmental issues.

Issues raised by the Russian war in Ukraine

As already noted, issues in the present have always energized the reexamination of the past. The crisis and war between Russia and Ukraine is no exception. A major feature of the buildup to war, dating back to the crisis of 2014 was the Kremlin's emphasis on disinformation as a tactic. This was a substitute for PD and set the communication agenda for many other countries and institutions – including NATO and the EU – as they sought to set the record straight and blunt the attack. Regions that had hitherto enjoyed enviable reputations suddenly found themselves rebutting slander. The Nordic countries had particular difficulties having been branded in Kremlin media as rife with pedophilia and worse.

The return of disinformation calls for its own history, but that should include reminders that disinformation was not invented by Russia but rather has a long history in the West too. There are also disturbing stories in Britain's National Archives of the use of fake news in World War II (Hemming, 2019) and the British army's use of disinformation to discredit the Provisional Irish Republican Army (IRA) during the "troubles" in Northern Ireland (Cormac, 2018, p. 201). It should be remembered that this last case was a domestic use of the tool, much as the IRA wished to be foreign citizens. The gathering of historical evidence that such techniques were counterproductive will help to build a case for restraint in political communication.

There are deeper implications from the return to an open hostility in world affairs. Our uncertain times beg a revision of soft power. It is time to move beyond the idea that being admired for values and culture is some kind of bonus for the most successful countries – the so-called Soft Power 30 – and understand that for the most vulnerable places their fate can be determined by their reputation. Admired countries have friends and support in a crisis. They enjoy reputational security (Cull, 2022). Places whose identity is not understood and whose narrative is unclear to foreign audiences can find themselves losing provinces. A key case is Ukraine, initially little understood by the outside world in its post-Soviet incarnation. From 1992 to the mid-2010s most of Europe saw Ukraine primarily as a former Soviet Socialist Republic and thought in terms of its similarity to Russia rather that its distinctiveness. Ukraine paid the price for this in 2014 as Russia severed entire provinces with a disproportionately underwhelming reaction from Europe.

In the aftermath, Ukraine focused on building a distinct reputation including much cultural work. The value of this work was clear in 2022 when a renewed Russian onslaught was met with exponentially different levels of support frequently framed with expressions of Ukrainian distinctiveness such as displays of its national colors. This notion of reputation security needs historical investigation to see how it has played beyond the obvious cases, like its absence for Czechoslovakia when threatened by Hitler in 1938. Where have countries experienced extra security or its lack as a result of their reputation? Are there other examples of reputations being transformed to the benefit of security? This seems to have happened for Britain during the course of World War II as widespread Anglophobia in the 1930s morphed into adulation in the U.S. for Churchill's Island during 1940 (Cull, 1995), much like the surge of feeling for Zelensky's Ukraine in 2022.

Conclusion

In sum, history remains a vibrant and essential approach for PD scholarship. It has been a vital source for cases and illustrations to flesh out the major theories of the field such as soft power. It has shown clearly what can be done with examples like those illustrating the efficacy of exchanges in building Franco–Germany reconciliation following World War II. Conversely, it has also shown the limits of PD, with the lavish spending on U.S. PD during the Vietnam War failing to compensate for flawed policy. History can be a reality check for other approaches to PD. For PD scholarship, history can serve in place of the laboratory for the life and exact sciences. Researchers can use historical cases to build as well as test theories, and conduct badly needed comparative research across nations, regions, and cultures.

There is still work to be done to fill in the details of the best-known story – that of the U.S. – and a pioneering scholarship necessary to create the first complete accounts of emerging players in the field. We need history to explore the interconnections of different types of players and to document the backstory to the key themes of our time. Finally, perhaps in history we will be able to find a resource to empower new solutions to the world's challenges. At a time when problems from pandemic, climate change, mass migration, and open warfare require collective solutions, the world as a whole needs a clear understanding of how past coalitions have worked and previous generations have rallied to a shared objective. An understanding of such a process may yet be the salvation of us all.

References

Arndt, R. (2006). *The first resort of kings: American cultural diplomacy in the twentieth century*. Potomac.

Belmonte, L. (2008). *Selling the American way: U.S. propaganda and the Cold War*. University of Pennsylvania Press.

Blinken, A. J. (2021, August 9). Domestic renewal as a foreign policy priority. Speech given to A. James Clark School of Engineering, University of Maryland, College Park, MD. Retrieved from https://www.state.gov/domestic-renewal-as-a-foreign-policy-priority/.

Carroll, W. (1948). *Persuade or perish*. Houghton Mifflin.

Cormac, R. (2018). *Disrupt and deny: Spies, special forces, and the secret pursuit of British foreign policy*. Oxford University Press.

Creel, G. (1920a). *Complete report of the chairman of the Committee on Public Information*. US Government Printing Office. https://www.loc.gov/item/20026826/.

Creel, G. (1920b). *How we advertised America: The first telling of the amazing story of the Committee on Public Information that carried the gospel of Americanism to every corner of the globe*. Harper & Brothers.

Cull, N. J. (1995). *Selling war: British propaganda campaign against American "neutrality" in World War II*. Oxford University Press.

Cull, N. J. (2008). *The Cold War and the United States Information Agency: American propaganda and public diplomacy, 1945–1989*. Cambridge University Press.

Cull, N. J. (2012). *The decline and fall of the United States Information Agency: American public diplomacy, 1989–2001*. Palgrave Macmillan.

Cull, N. J. (2021). The forgotten process: Information disarmament in the Soviet/US rapprochement of the 1980s. *Bulletin of St. Petersburg State University, International Relations, 14*(3), 257–72.

Cull, N. J. (2022). From soft power to reputational security: Rethinking public diplomacy and cultural diplomacy for a dangerous age. In B. McKercher (Ed.), *The Routledge handbook of diplomacy and statecraft.* 2nd edn (pp. 409–19). Routledge.

David-Fox, M. (2011). *Showcasing the great experiment: Cultural diplomacy and Western visitors to the Soviet Union, 1921–1941.* Oxford University Press.

Dizard, W. P. Jr. (2004). *Inventing public diplomacy: The story of the U.S. Information Agency.* Lynne Reinner.

Donaldson, F. (1984). *The British Council: The first fifty years.* Jonathan Cape.

Dudziak, M. (2000). *Cold War civil rights.* Princeton University Press.

Eames, A. (2023). *A voice in their own destiny: The triumph of Anglo-American public diplomacy in the nuclear 1980s.* MIT Press.

Ellwood, D. W. (1992). *Rebuilding Europe: Western Europe, America, and postwar reconstruction.* Longman.

Espinosa, J. M. (1976). *Inter-American beginnings of U.S. cultural diplomacy, 1936–1948.* U.S. Department of State.

Evans, M. (2002). *Propaganda and visions of empire in France.* Palgrave Macmillan.

Evans, M. (2004). *Empire and culture: The French experience, 1830–1940.* Palgrave Macmillan.

Fulda, A. (2019). The emergence of citizen diplomacy in EU–China relations: Principles, pillars, pioneers, paradoxes. *Diplomacy & Statecraft, 30*(1), 188–216.

Gienow-Hecht, J. (1999). *Transmission impossible: American journalism as cultural diplomacy in postwar Germany, 1945–1955.* Louisiana State University Press.

Gienow-Hecht, J. (2009). *Sound diplomacy: Music and emotions in transatlantic relations, 1850–1920.* University of Chicago Press.

Gienow-Hecht, J., Kunkel, S., & Jobs, S. (Eds.) (2023) *Visions of humanity.* Berghahn.

Glover, N. (2011). *National relations: Public diplomacy, national identity and the Swedish institute, 1945–1970.* Nordic Academic Press.

Hamilton, J. M. (2020). *Manipulating the masses: Woodrow Wilson and the birth of American propaganda.* Louisiana State University Press.

Hart, J. (2013). *Empire of ideas: The origins of public diplomacy and the transformation of U.S. foreign policy.* Oxford University Press.

Heil, A.L. Jr. (2004). *Voice of America: A history.* Columbia University Press.

Hemming, H. (2019). *Agents of influence: A British campaign, a Canadian spy, and the secret plot to bring America into World War II.* Public Affairs.

Hixson, W. L. (1997). *Parting the curtain: Propaganda, culture and the Cold War, 1945–61.* St. Martin's Press.

Kent, T. (2020). *Striking back: Overt and covert options to combat Russian disinformation.* Jamestown Foundation.

Krenn, M. L. (2006). *Fall-out shelters for the Human Spirit: American art and the Cold War.* University of North Carolina Press.

Krenn, M. L. (2017). The history of United States cultural diplomacy: 1770 to the present day. Bloomsbury.

Laville, H., & Wilford, H. (Eds.) (2006). *The US government, citizen groups and the Cold War: The state private network.* Frank Cass.

Lucas, W. S. (1999). *Freedom's war: The US crusade against the Soviet Union, 1945–1956.* Manchester University Press.

MacBride, S. et al. (1980). *Many voices, one world: Towards a new, more just, and more efficient world information and communication order.* UNESCO.

Manheim, J. B. (1994). *Strategic public diplomacy and American foreign policy: The evolution of influence.* Oxford University Press.

Marett, R. (1968). *Through the back door: Inside view of Britain's overseas information services.* Pergamon Press.

Mikkonen, J., Parkkinen, J., & Scott-Smith, G. (Eds.) (2018). *Entangled East and West: Cultural diplomacy and artistic interaction during the Cold War.* De Gruyter.

Mitter, R., & Major, P. (Eds.) (2004). *Across the blocs: Cold War cultural and social history.* Frank Cass.

Moody, P. (2017). Embassy cinema: What WikiLeaks reveals about US state support for Hollywood. *Media, Culture & Society, 39*(7), 1063–77.

Morgan, C. L., & Masey, J. (2008). *Cold War confrontations: US exhibitions and their role in the cultural Cold War.* Lars Müller.

Moyn, S. (2010). *The last utopia: Human rights in history.* Harvard University Press.

Muir-Harmony, T. (2020). *Operation Moonglow: A political history of Project Apollo.* Basic Books.

Nelson, M. (1997). *War of the black heavens: The battles of Eastern broadcasting in the Cold War.* Brasseys.

Notaker, H., Scott-Smith, G., & Snyder, D. J. (Eds.) (2016). *Reasserting America in the 1970s: U.S. public diplomacy and the rebuilding of America's image abroad.* Manchester University Press.

Osgood, K. (2006). *Total Cold War: Eisenhower's secret propaganda battle at home and abroad.* University of Kansas Press.

Page, C. (1996). *U.S. official propaganda during the Vietnam war, 1965–1973: The limits of persuasion.* Leicester University Press.

Pamment, J. (2016). *British public diplomacy and soft power diplomatic influence and the digital revolution.* Palgrave Macmillan.

Parker, J. (2016). *Hearts, minds, voices: U.S. cold war public diplomacy and the formation of the Third World.* Oxford University Press.

Peacock, M. (2017). *Innocent weapons: The Soviet and American politics of childhood in the Cold War.* University of North Carolina Press.

Philips, V. (2019). *Martha Graham's Cold War: The dance of American diplomacy.* Columbia University Press.

Pronay, N., & Wilson, K. (Eds.) (1985). *The political re-education of Germany and her allies after World War II.* Croom Helm.

Rawnsley, G. D. (1996). Radio *diplomacy and propaganda: The BBC and VOA in international politics, 1956–64.* Palgrave Macmillan.

Real, B. (2020). Private life, public diplomacy: Tibor Hirsch and documentary filmmaking for the Cold War USIA. *Historical Journal of Film, Radio, and Television, 40*(22), 297–324.

Rosendorf, N. (2014). *Franco sells Spain to America: Hollywood, tourism, and public relations as postwar Spanish soft power.* Palgrave Macmillan.

Scott-Smith, G. (2008). *Networks of empire: The US State Department's foreign leader program in the Netherlands, France and Britain, 1950–1970.* Peter Lang.

Scott-Smith, G., & Krabbendam, H. (Eds.) (2004). *The cultural Cold War in Western Europe, 1945–60.* Routledge.

Sevin, E., Metzgar, E., & Hayden, C. (2019). The scholarship of public diplomacy: Analysis of a growing field. *International Journal of Communication, 13*, 4814–37.

Shaw, T., & Youngblood, D. J. (2014). *Cinematic Cold War: The American and Soviet struggle for hearts and minds.* University of Kansas Press.

Snow, N. (2013). *Truth is the best propaganda: Edward R. Murrow's speeches in the Kennedy years.* Miniver Press.

Sorenson, T. (1969). *The word war: The story of American overseas propaganda.* Harper & Row.

Squires, J. D. (1935). *British* propaganda *at home and in the United States from 1914 to 1917.* Harvard University Press.

Stengel, R. (2019). *Information wars: How we lost the global battle against disinformation and what we can do about it.* Atlantic Monthly Press.

Stuart, C. (1920). *The secrets of Crewe House: The story of a famous campaign.* Hodder and Stoughton.

Taylor, P. M. (1981). *The projection of Britain: British overseas publicity and propaganda 1919–1939.* Cambridge University Press.

Taylor, P. M. (2013). *Munitions of the mind: The history of propaganda from the ancient world to the present day.* 3rd edn. Manchester University Press.

Tomlin, G. M. (2016). *Murrow's Cold War: Public diplomacy for the Kennedy administration.* Potomac.

U.S. Department of State (2017). *Foreign relations of the United States, 1917–1972, Volume VI, Public Diplomacy, 1961–1963.* US Government Printing Office.

Vaughan, J. (2005). *The failure of American and British propaganda in the Arab Middle East, 1945–1957: Unconquerable minds.* Palgrave Macmillan.

Viktorin, J. et al. (Eds.) (2018). *Nation branding in modern history.* Berghahn.

Von Eschen, P. M. (2006). *Satchmo blows up the world: Jazz ambassadors play the Cold War.* Harvard University Press.

Walsh, D. (2011). *An air war with Cuba: The United States radio campaign against Castro.* McFarland.

Whitehouse, V. (1920). *A year as a government agent.* Harper.

Wijfjes, H. (2014). Spellbinding and crooning: Sound amplification, radio, and political rhetoric in international comparative perspective, 1900–1945. *Technology and Culture, 55*(1), 148–85.

Winkler, A. (1978). *The politics of propaganda: The Office of War Information 1942–1945.* Yale University Press.

Wulf, A. (2015). *U.S. International exhibitions during the Cold War: Winning hearts and minds through cultural diplomacy.* Rowman & Littlefield.

8   International relations

Craig Hayden

Introduction

In the wake of an unmanaged global pandemic and a shift into populist politics of division, the United States (US) has faced considerable pressure on its capacity for influence on a global stage. Nye's (1990) original concept of soft power described the capacity of the US to lead in the aftermath of the Cold War through means other than military might or economic coercion. US soft power is challenged by an increasingly fractious, multipolar world of competing interests, interdependencies, and identity-based conflict. This condition of potential soft power decline provides an opportunity to reconsider the theoretical assumptions and methods used to assess the role of soft power in foreign affairs – not just for the US but more broadly for the concept (Li, 2018). It also provides an opening to reconsider the utility of soft power's theoretical assumptions for the practical ways through which states seek to influence, such as public diplomacy (PD) and other forms of strategic communication.

Signs of US soft power decline or even disintegration, however, are not necessarily a problem caused by a failure of PD – the ways in which states engage publics to shape belief, deepen relational ties, and manage perceptions in ways that improve understanding (Cull, 2009). However, as this chapter illustrates, the context of soft power decline, combined with converging critiques of the soft power concept, suggest a revised approach to the study of soft power as a tool to explain PD and related forms of strategic communication. How we study soft power, and, the theoretical wagers we make about soft power, can shape the questions we ask, and the methodological choices employed in the study of PD.

This chapter proposes reconsidering soft power through an outcomes-based approach – which is often missing in writing about soft power despite the fact that Nye (1990, p. 156) has sought to distinguish soft power as an outcome-oriented theory, rather than derived from material capabilities. The tension in claims about what drives soft power, how "resources" are translated into the "behaviors," require more clarity on the mechanisms of influence

(Nye, 2011, p. 21). As this chapter argues, these problems are not unique to soft power, and are present in the study of international reputation and credibility. These critical observations serve as an opportunity to rehabilitate the concept for PD research, by driving different kinds of questions about when and where soft power matters.

The first section of the chapter presents and explains the decline in US soft power. It elaborates on problematic ambiguity within the soft power concept, observed in soft power scholarship and, by extension, PD studies around relational approaches to power. The second section presents three studies of relational soft power, to demonstrate the growing centrality of relational approaches, and identifies instructive parallel findings within the study of international credibility and reputation in questions of security and deterrence. How studies of international reputation have wrestled with the problem of contingency across relations provide potential insight into a reformulated approach to the study of soft power through diplomacy. The third section proposes an outcome-oriented approach to PD research that would generate a more grounded typology of how soft power is leveraged in concrete examples of statecraft.

The central argument of this chapter is that if soft power is largely contingent on the characteristics of the *relation* between the agent and the subject or target of soft power activity, then the conceptual framework should accommodate the diverse routes to influence. While "structural" factors such as strategic narratives or identity discourse can contribute to soft power, for soft power to be a theory of *practice*, Nye's identified behaviors of persuasion, agenda setting, and cultivation of attraction need further elaboration as mechanisms of soft power, and it is likely that there may be other such "behaviors" (Nye, 2011, p. 21).

Critical perspectives on soft power point to its indeterminacy. First, is it simply a reflection of other capacities (material power, economic dependency, cultural hegemony, etc.) that shape the intervention of soft power at the level of "preferences" (Layne, 2010; Lukes, 2007; Mattern, 2005)? Second, studies of soft power and in some cases, PD, work to identify existing state activities and efforts as a kind of soft power. While this inventory of what states do to leverage soft power is important, particularly in the context of disinformation, propaganda, and influence operations, what Bennet (2022) calls "malign soft power," this represents only part of a larger question of when and where soft power operates on outcomes. Nor should any study of soft power confuse outputs with outcomes. Third, the logic of influence embedded in soft power often collapses distinctions between different routes to influence – from the media effects impact of agenda setting and framing, to the cumulative impact of historical relations that shape perceptions of legitimacy and value. Soft power has become a catch-all term, a compound theory that effaces differences among theories of influence, persuasion, and identification.

This particular issue makes the concept difficult to attribute in causal arguments about the resources and effects at stake in PD. Finally, the development of soft power scholarship has trended toward recognition of its relational contingency. Soft power is both manifest as a relational concept (rather than material), and, that it is contingent on both the "sender" and the "receiver." This relational perspective has been well established in more practice-oriented PD scholarship. The perspective advocated below is to reorient research toward those pathways of influence.

What are the lessons of soft power decline?

The rapid decline in global public opinion about the US since 2016 has been coupled with increased concern over the rise of China, the decline of democratic governments worldwide, and the outbreak of great power war in Europe as a powerful set of signals for US soft power decline. If soft power is clearly reflected in the global resilience of values and ideas endemic to US interests, then the empirical trends may be a telling warning sign. The popular opinion measures in themselves were illustrative of shifting perceptions, in the wake of unilateralist moves by President Donald Trump and the de-prioritization of diplomatic institutions. A Gallup poll in 2018 showed that only 30 percent of citizens in foreign countries held a positive view of the US (Gass & Seiter, 2020, p. 156).

The steady drift in US domestic politics away from commitments to traditional liberal values and institutions of democratic governance correlates strongly with shifting views of the US abroad. The normalization of political violence and rejection of electoral outcomes for partisan gain likely sends a message to global audiences, who inevitably weigh these trends alongside their historical experience with the US and its dealings with the world. As Kearn (2022) notes in his dire assessment of US soft power, global opinion of US values among key allies and partners had fallen to dismal levels by the conclusion of the Trump presidency, with scant support for US democratic ideals and growing criticism of US hypocrisy. The US default global brand of growing inequality, corruption, and toxic political culture put at risk the US role as champion of universal political ideals. And, simply attributing this decline to Trump's actions misses the wider message that a significant percentage of the American political class embraced this divergence from previous US norms of political culture and values. The persistent message to the world was that the US would embrace a foreign policy not only centered around US interests alone, but that the nature of global politics demanded transnationalism over shared value-based cooperation (Drezner, 2017).

Though global public opinion rebounded quickly after the election of President Joe Biden, questions remain about the durability of the US defense of ideals and values that are, at least in theory, key determinants of US soft power. David Kearn's (2022) argument that US soft power is severely threatened by the rise of anti-democratic forces both within the US and without echoes similar warnings on the rise of authoritarianism around the world, which yokes the question of US soft power to larger claims about the systemic transformation of the global "rules-based order" (Walker & Ludwig, 2021). The global visibility of the US response to the COVID pandemic and the apparent weaknesses of the global supply chain yielded further evidence of challenges to the otherwise durable liberal international order sustained, in part, by a shared commitment to norms and values represented by the US.

The Kearn argument rests on three key assumptions on the nature of soft power. First, that public opinion represents a salient indicator of soft power, or at least a visible trending measure. Second, that the value commitments of the US have sufficient universal attraction to enable the policy outcomes that have sustained US predominance – something Nye has argued consistently since his initial advance of the concept. Finally, that US soft power is itself a significant guarantor of a global order that benefits US interests. Indeed, this claim was central to Nye's early articulations of the concept – that soft power is reflected in a shared perception of common interest, underscoring the durability of international institutions and attitudes toward collaborative problem solving for international problems.

But does the decline of primacy and rise of multilateral order reflect a diagnosis about soft power? Global public opinion data suggest part of the story, but not all. The rapid consolidation of Western countries in opposition to the Russian war of aggression against Ukraine took many by surprise and reflected a potentially latent aspect to the values associated with US soft power. The emergence of consensus around principles justifying the response point to the difficulty of making systemic arguments about soft power, especially when it is used as a proxy term for US de facto influence and cooptation of interest.

The decline of US hegemony more broadly presents a host of methodological issues for the study of soft power, not the least of which is the *attribution* of decline to a measure of soft power (Cooley & Nexon, 2020). As Layne (2010) has argued, soft power may be an outcropping of more fundamental capabilities of military and economic power – the "power" in soft power is a luxury afforded by other measures of power. Given the shifting geopolitical context for the US, what sort of lessons can be derived from existing criticism within soft power studies, and how might those translate into different ways to evaluate and assess soft power in the context of intentional state action like PD?

The growth of relationalism in soft power studies

Nye argues that soft power is a theory of agency, reflecting both the capability and intentionality of state actors to achieve outcomes. If, as Nye (2011, p. 24) argues, soft power is visible in the "conversion" of *resources* through *behaviors*, then analysis should reflect the concatenation of factors (both intentional and contextual) that lead to the observable realization of soft power for state actors. Put differently, what sorts of actions and contexts are both necessary and sufficient to realize soft power? A research design in this framing would need to account for what Bakalov (2019, p. 132) calls "Nye's underlying understanding of power." Soft power has three characteristics in this regard: it is "(1) actor-centric (not structural); (2) relational (not proprietary); and (3) strategic (not contingent)." The pivotal distinction in Nye's writing moves power away from capacity and locates power in the interaction between actors, thus framing the concept in relational terms.

The move to a relational approach evolves in Nye's writing. In 2011, Nye identifies particular behaviors as exemplary of how soft power works: "framing the agenda," persuading," and "eliciting positive attraction" (Nye, 2011, p. 21). These effects underscore the fundamental move away from coercion and force toward cooptation. However, this works on both individuals *and* publics. As Balakov notes, soft power operates on "individual decision-makers and their actions directly," or "indirectly, whereby affected publics exert pressure onto their leaders to act in line with the preference of the country wielding soft power" (Nye, 2011, p. 94). In both cases, the wielding of power is contingent on the subject. This relational perspective opens up an array of questions on how particular resources, such as foreign policy legitimacy or shared values translate into a soft power behavior under particular circumstances. The theory itself doesn't provide clear direction, as Nye argues that different types of resources do not necessarily yield specific outcomes (Nye, 2011, p. 12). There is no prescriptive formula for the translation of resources to outcomes.

What remains, however, is the notion that any soft power outcome is contingent on some form of recognition by the subject. And, the contingency of resources, behaviors, and the relations themselves point toward case-based analysis. As Feklyunina (2016) argues, soft power resources are not significant in themselves, but only in the context of the reaction they trigger in the intended audience. Whether conceived as brand attributes, measures of policy legitimacy, or other forms of cultural value – soft power resources are only significant in so far as they are recognized as such by an audience to soft power. The following three exemplar studies suggest different approaches to explaining the relational element of soft power, in ways that offer some clues on how a relational perspective can be understood both in theory and in data collection.

Cheskin's (2017) depiction of Russia's "structural power" in Ukraine builds on studies centering the role of language and identity in soft power (Solomon, 2014). He argues for a "subject"-based view of soft power. As with Mattern's critique of soft power language as threatening the "ontological security" of its target subjects, Cheskin uses the soft power concept of attraction as a reflection of the "affective investments" of publics – the ways in which identity is formed through symbols, images, and discourse.

Cheskin's theoretical contribution is more than just an assertion that attraction is conditioned by culture and identity. Rather, it offers a theory-driven rationale for why attraction works – at the intersection of pre-existing identity discourses in a target population and what an agent promotes through PD. The conclusion is that "[a]ttraction is not defined by the external agent – but defined by self-identifies, which allows for position in relations" (Cheskin, 2017, p. 279). The fundamental implications of this perspective are well established in relational prescriptions found in PD studies which have long moved on from situating attraction in monological messaging or the force of argument (Lee & Ayhan, 2015). Cheskin's assessment of Russian soft power is relational, however, in that it is conditional on the subject's interpretation. The structural focus on discourse, however, leaves some questions about the agency audiences have to make judgments outside of historical discourse.

The second approach to relational soft power presented here examines the units of relation as the resource itself, where indicators of relational ties correlate with the capability of attraction key to soft power. Wu's (2018) novel "soft power rubric" approach exemplifies the method, as does correlational analysis of on the relationship between exchange programs and political change in target populations (Atkinson, 2010). Wu's approach presupposes empirical measures of connection as indicators of identification crucial to attraction. Specifically, she points to evidence of identification through consumption of media products, the rate of travel to the agent country, study abroad, and emigration. Wu's approach is more firmly grounded as a reflection of identity alignment, in contrast to other soft power indices that more loosely aggregate measures of interconnection, branding, and public opinion on the attributes of states, such as the Soft Power 30 index.

Wu's framework places what subjects do as crucial to any measure of soft power capabilities. Publics vote with their feet and pocketbook to build the density of connections for a durable form of soft power. As such, it provides a replicable framework for the study of PD impact and evaluation efforts (e.g. exchange program growth rates). There are two caveats to this claim. First, Wu's measures are argued to be indicative of identification, which in turn imputes influence through attraction. It is less obvious that this translates into specific policy outcomes. Second, the purpose of PD is often not the accrual of soft power measures *per se*, but the leveraging of soft power capabilities to achieve more specific policy outcomes at the level of mission or regional strategy – such as setting the conditions for bilateral engagement, highlighting humanitarian involvement, and so on. Wu's model narrows the field of relevant measures of relations, but banks heavily on those measures being significant reservoirs of soft power.

The third example of relationalism is Brannagan and Giulianotti's (2018) study of soft power *disempowerment* in Qatar. Their study illustrates how resources can both amplify and diminish soft power potential, thus impacting the translation of soft power resources into tangible policy outcomes. They develop a model that explicitly identifies what they term the "(inter) subjectivities of soft power audiences" as crucial to the realization of power. They identify various attributes, such as Qatar's economic success, its role as a regional mediator, and charitable donations as accumulating soft power, while increased awareness of its domestic human rights record, corruption surrounding the FIFA World Cup hosting bid, and possible role in extremist financing, as contravening soft power capabilities. They describe soft power as a competitive domain for control of narrative and attention, and the exposure of Qatar's record on migrant labor relations, for example, undermined the credibility of its promoted image and narrative.

In Brannagan and Giulianotti's proposed framework, "soft power is an intersubjective and relational process that requires a shared understanding of the constitution of both 'attraction' and 'credibility'" (p. 1144). The juncture between promoted message and the realization of soft power is what they call the "credible attraction filter," which they describe as the "intersubjective mesh through which state soft power resources must pass in order to convert into outcomes" (p. 1151). Brannigan and Giulianotti build a process model of conversion that does not simply replicate the Nye "resource/behavior" equation. Rather, their model accounts for different kinds of successful outcomes and importantly, the consequences of soft power disempowerment, when soft power is eroded, and outcomes fail to materialize.

On its face, the authors' model offers a helpful corrective. Rather than linking resources with behaviors, their model links credibility attraction filters (a conceptual short-hand that would benefit from further elaboration) with a diversity of policy outcomes – a useful analytical tool to map outcomes back through steps of strategic communication and PD efforts. It provides an orientation for PD measurement and evaluation as well. Importantly, this process-driven approach illustrates how *failure* and "disempowerment" show that the attributes and actions of a sender country can work at cross-purposes.

Their observations have two clear methodological implications pertinent to studies of PD programs and campaigns. First, they do infer influence from an inventory of capabilities but also offer a process for retracing efforts to leverage soft power assets (e.g. Sevin, 2015). Second, the disaggregation of soft power allows for different configurations of resources and outcomes, opening the door to a more robust typology of outcomes other than the *behaviors* identified by Nye. These could account for the interplay of discursive "structures" like identity narratives, history, or even competing messaging campaigns (or disinformation campaigns) on PD programs or campaigns. As Hall (2010) argued, the complexity of a relational approach to soft power presents the need for different forms of soft power – such as institutional power, reputational power, and representational power. The goal in this relational model would not be to advance neologisms, but account for the fact that soft power conflates too many routes to influence.

Lessons from reputation, status, and credibility

While soft power has been criticized for its analytical ambiguity, similar issues surface in other kinds of influence-based communication in international relations. The study of reputation, credibility, and status among states is instructive to the problem facing the imprecision of soft power. Reputation studies focus on signaling and perception among states to avert crisis, manage conflict, or engage in coercion, so the research questions often revolve around decision-making and security (Jervis et al., 2021). *Reputation* reflects "beliefs about an actor's persistent characteristics or tendencies" (Dafoe et al., 2014, p. 374). In deterrence scenarios, from Thomas Schelling onward the study of reputation for resolve plays an important role in conflict behavior (Clare & Danilovic, 2012). Likewise, *credibility* is related to reputation. Credibility among states reflects whether an actor's statements or commitments are to be believed (Dafoe et al., 2014, p. 376). In a review of contemporary studies of reputation and credibility, Jervis et al. (2021) observed a recurring finding that attempts to manage reputation and credibility were contingent on the target of communication, "[c]ontrary to what many decision makers may believe about reputation and credibility, the two are relational qualities that actors do not own for themselves" (p. 176).

Much like soft power, reputation and credibility are not static attributes nor resources to be tapped for predictable outcomes. Research on when reputation or credibility matter in foreign affairs indicate that situational factors matter, such that the history of relations between states can affect perceptions of reputation after repeated interactions. Likewise, beliefs about what states believe – prestige – also matter (Dafoe et al., 2014, p. 374). But also, that the psychological and cognitive characteristics of decision-makers were also significant. Jervis et al. (2021) noted that the existing theoretical framework for reputation was insufficient to explain the diversity of circumstances and factors that influenced action. They acknowledge the role of the audience again as key for managing reputation and credibility through communication: "the challenge in creating these desired impressions means that scholarly theories about how signals should be perceived can run aground on the way the observer interprets them" (Jervis et al., 2021, p. 177). While the US fought in Vietnam to demonstrate to allies its resolve and willingness to provide aid, the beliefs of allies did not change and they did not support the war.

This finding resonates across their review of separate studies. "To truly understand why communication between states succeeds or fails, we need theory and empirics that examine what the signaler is trying to say, how the perceiver interprets it, and over what duration these impressions last" (Jervis et al., 2021, p. 177). The need for such a theory emerges from the similarity of findings across separate reputation studies, which note that reputation and credulity are "relational concepts … [that] depend entirely on the perceptions of others" (Jackson, 2016, p. 20). And more generally, state behavior cannot be understood or interpreted in a predictable way by decision-makers. For

Jervis et al. (2021), questions of research design and method emerge from this observation.

The lack of primary document evidence makes it difficult to access the decision-making of leaders that weigh reputation and credibility. If reputation is contingent on circumstance and leader attributes, then does it make sense to study reputation and credibility over time or in particular episodes? Case selection bias is also a problem. When credibility is underestimated, these are cases where conflict has likely occurred, while the overestimation of credibility does not produce "vivid outcomes" or necessarily observable events (Jervis et al., 2021, p. 183). This problem is relevant for PD measurement and evaluation, as often the signs of policy success are non-events, like countering violent extremism.

But this is also a data availability problem. Jervis et al. acknowledge that beliefs held by leaders, organizations, and governments shape not only decisions, but they serve as filters to inferences they draw about other countries. More broadly, foreign policy decision-makers respond to narratives that reflect their theory of how the world works – information that is usually only accessible much later in historical archives.

Reputation and credibility connote different mechanisms that condition influence and behavior among states, particularly during periods of potential conflict. But, as research indicates, how and when reputation and credibility matter is debated. The common thread between both this literature and soft power studies is the contingency of observable influence, and recognition that all of these concepts are likely some reflections of the relation between the agent and the subject. But as Dafoe et al. (2014) observed, a corrective for this would be more refined theory that can capture the differences across situations of communicative coercion.

Rehabilitating soft power in public diplomacy studies

Soft power has a conceptual problem of boundaries. The notion that states can convert particular resources (culture, values, policy legitimacy) into behaviors (persuasion, agenda framing, and attraction) to bring about outcomes collapses a diversity of causal mechanisms of influence under a single umbrella term. The term likewise provides few prescriptions for the design of PD and strategic communication, other than the wager that resources can work to enable strategic outcomes for a soft power agent. And a significant number of studies have charted the embrace of soft power as a logic of influence to justify PD campaigns (Nye, 2008).

While soft power is not solely defined by PD, the practice of PD can serve as a natural experiment for building a more robust typology of effects and scenarios that sufficiently capture the relational aspect between agent and audience. Applying lessons from the relational focus in soft power scholarship through established cases of PD also opens possibilities of theory development through a form of "middle range" approach to research that would reconstruct the mechanisms of influence to elaborate the assumptions baked into the soft power concept (Merton, 1968).

One such approach to a revitalized soft power research agenda would embrace what Nye (2011, p. 24) articulated to elaborate a soft power conversion strategy through a form of process tracing, in order to identify causal mechanisms. This has been appropriated in PD and digital diplomacy studies (Sevin, 2015; Spry & Lockyer, 2022). The purpose would be, in effect, to identify the conditions under which resources, practice, and outcomes align in a way that embodies the intent of Nye's original formulation – a theory of influence focused on effects rather than capabilities. This more modest, stepwise approach toward the "outcomes" of soft power could be a step toward making the soft power concept less a systemic diagnosis of popularity or hegemonic decline, but instantiations of power that spread across networks of (mis)information, emergent from exchange-based relational ties, or shared narratives of policy legitimacy.

A committed "outcomes" approach could be facilitated by a focus on discrete practices, with the objective of building out a typology of soft power mechanisms that would capture the linkage between practices such as exchange programs, key leader engagements, social media campaigns, and so on, with successful foreign policy initiatives and goals. In the US case, the State Department has already identified a range of PD outcomes that are suitable for measurement and evaluation. These include the raising of awareness, attitude change, behavior change, relationship building, skills building and training, and the formation of institutional partnerships (personal communication, 2018). This could be paired with other data, such as regional or Integrated Country Strategies (ICS), to provide a rubric for measuring policy objectives.

Such an approach incorporates the critiques and suggested revisions emerging in the study of soft power. It also is a corrective to potential theory and terminology eclecticism, reframing soft power as a theory of outcomes visible in a reconstructed chains of PD practice, rather than as an inventory of resources or potential capabilities. As a theory of power, the term remains a diagnostic tool, to reconstruct the mechanisms and levers available in how states, often through PD and other forms of strategic communication, shape perceptions, influence opinions, and build social capital in ways that facilitate policy objectives.

This "grounded," piece-meal approach to building a repertoire of soft power practices also makes possible charting how such influence activities work in conjunction with other capabilities and practices. Much like the country team of an embassy, foreign policy is rarely the sole portfolio of a singular diplomatic function. Rather, the case-based reconstruction of policy objectives as a result of diplomatic practice would help to situate the role of PD and soft power in the longer chain of diplomatic engagement, through functional and regional authorities and under various circumstances and contexts. This does not preclude large-N empirical analysis of social media data, nor structured, focused comparisons of policy action. Rather, the objective would be to reconstruct episodes of diplomatic influence in order to identify what is likely a diverse typology of soft power mechanisms leveraged in the combination of diplomacy and outcomes. The objectives of PD offer a readily available data outcropping to test the levers of soft power – even if the outcomes are not always positive.

The bottom-up approach presented here presumes that any international order does not hang together through soft power operating as a kind of invisible hand of shared assumptions or preferences, but through the steady accumulation of soft power efforts, through diplomacy over time, to build trust, lay down a demonstrative record value commitment, and frame actions as credible to foreign publics.

Conclusion

Much has been written about how soft power functions to sustain a systemic order, often through terms borrowed from other treatments of power (Gallarotti, 2011). The argument presented here calls for more research that addresses soft power as a compound set of influence mechanisms observable in how states seek to influence and achieve outcomes. The analytical ambiguity of soft power is not unique to the concept as this chapter elaborates. The research into reputation and credibility in international security affirms the significance of a relational focus. The relational perspective in turn, invites investigating the particular, granular instances of when soft power is leveraged through engagement or communication.

Therefore PD, rather than being somehow justified *by* soft power, provides a variety of sites of inquiry, a sampling through which to assess and elaborate a more accurate definition of the concept. And as the so-called soft power of the international rules-based order recedes, prompting some to speculate on the disintegration of US soft power, understanding how actors seek to manage the perceptions of their actions in a complex world of weaponized interdependence will become more necessary, rather than less.

The prospect of a soft power research agenda animated by focused attention on state-based influence activities is a foundational move to rebuild the currency of the concept. It also acknowledges that the conceptual imprecision of soft power may be remediated by disaggregating the component theories of influence at stake in what we might call soft power practices. The prospect of states "getting what they want" through means other than military force or coercion clearly involves more than PD and strategic communication, but the role of PD within the configuration of diplomatic efforts to achieve policy ends is an available set of practices to test assumptions, establish boundary conditions for causal mechanisms, and build up a testable inventory of soft power "conversion strategies" that more robustly capture the range of influence attempts, from exchange programs to disinformation.

References

Atkinson, C. (2010). Does soft power matter? A comparative analysis of student exchange programs 1980–2006. *Foreign Policy Analysis, 6*(1), 1–22.

Bakalov, I. (2019). Whither soft power? Divisions, milestones, and prospects of a research programme in the making. *Journal of Political Power, 12*(1), 129–51. http://doi.org/10.1080/2158379X.2019.1573613.

Bennet, R. M. (2022). Soft power's dark side. *Journal of Political Power, 15*(3), 437–55. https://doi.org/10.1080/2158379X.2022.2128278.

Brannagan, P. M., & Giulianotti, R. (2018). The soft power–soft disempowerment nexus: The case of Qatar. *International Affairs, 94*(5), 1139–57. https://doi.org/10.1093/ia/iiy125.

Cheskin, A. (2017). Russian soft power in Ukraine: A structural perspective. *Communist and Post-Communist Studies, 50*(4), 277–87. http://doi.org/10.1016/j.postcomstud.2017.09.001.

Clare, J., & Danilovic, V. (2012). Reputation for resolve, interests, and conflict. *Conflict Management and Peace Science, 29*(1), 3–27. https://doi.org/10.1177/0738894211430190.

Cooley, A., & Nexon, D. (2020). How hegemony ends: The unraveling of American power. *Foreign Affairs.* https://www.foreignaffairs.com/articles/united-states/2020-06-09/how-hegemony-ends.

Cull, N. (2009). *Public diplomacy: Lessons from the past.* Figueroa Press.

Dafoe, A., et al. (2014). Reputation and status as motives for war. *Annual Review of Political Science*, *17*(1), 371–93.

Drezner, D. (2017, June 1). The most extraordinary op-ed of 2017. *Washington Post*. https://www.washingtonpost.com/posteverything/wp/2017/06/01/the-most-extraordinary-op-ed-of-2017/.

Feklyunina, V. (2016). Soft power and identity: Russia, Ukraine and the Russian World(s). *European Journal of International Relations*, *22*(4), 773–96. http://doi.org/10.1177/1354066115601200.

Gallarotti, G. (2011). Soft power: What it is, why it's important, and the conditions for its effective use. *Journal of Political Power*, *4*(1), 25–47. http://doi.org/10.1080/2158379X.2011.557886.

Gass, R., & Seiter, J. (2020). Credibility and public diplomacy. In N. Snow & N. Cull, *The Routledge Handbook of Public Diplomacy* (pp. 155–68). Routledge.

Hall, T. (2010). An unclear attraction: A critical examination of soft power as an analytical category. *The Chinese Journal of International Politics*, *3*(2), 189–211. http://doi.org/10.1093/cjip/poq005.

Jackson, V. (2016). *Rival reputations: Coercion and credibility in US–North Korea relations*. Cambridge University Press.

Jervis, R., et al. (2021). Redefining the debate over reputation and credibility in international security: Promises and limits of new scholarship. *World Politics*, *73*(1), 167–203.

Kearn, D. (2022). The crisis of American soft power. *Journal of Political Power*, *15*(3), 397–414. http://doi.org/10.1080/2158379X.2022.2127277.

Layne, C. (2010). The unbearable lightness of soft power. In I. Parmar & M. Cox (Eds.), *Soft power and US foreign policy: Theoretical, historical and contemporary perspectives* (pp. 51–82). Routledge.

Lee, G., & Ayhan, K. (2015) Why Do We Need Non-state Actors in Public Diplomacy? Theoretical Discussion of Relational, Networked and Collaborative Public Diplomacy. *Journal of International and Area Studies*, *22*(1), 57–77.

Li, E. (2018, August 20). The rise and fall of soft power. *Foreign Policy*. https://foreignpolicy.com/2018/08/20/the-rise-and-fall-of-soft-power/.

Lukes, S. (2007). Power and the battle for hearts and minds: On the bluntness of soft power. In F. Berenskoetter & M. J. Williams (Eds.), *Power in world politics* (pp. 83–97). Routledge.

Mattern, J. B. (2005). Why "Soft Power" isn't so soft: Representational force and the sociolinguistic construction of attraction in world politics. *Millennium*, *33*(3), 583–612.

Merton, R. K. (1968). Social theory and social structure. Free Press.

Nye, J. Jr. (1990). *Bound to lead: The changing nature of American power*. Basic Books.

Nye, J. Jr. (2008). Public diplomacy and soft power. *The Annals of the American Academy of Political and Social Science*, *616*(1), 94–109.

Nye, J. Jr. (2011). *The future of power*. Public Affairs.

Sevin, E. (2015). Pathways of connection: An analytical approach to the impacts of public diplomacy. *Public Relations Review*, *41*(4), 562–8.

Solomon, T. (2014). The affective underpinnings of soft power. *European Journal of International Relations, 20*(3), 720–41. https://doi.org/10.1177/1354066113503479.

Spry, D., & Lockyer, K. (2022). Large data and small stories: A triangulation approach to evaluating digital diplomacy. *Place Branding & Public Diplomacy, 18,* 272–86. https://doi.org/10.1057/s41254-021-00248-w.

Walker, C., & Ludwig, J. (2021). *A full-spectrum response to sharp power: The vulnerabilities and strengths of open societies.* National Endowment for Democracy.

Wu, I. (2018). *Soft Power amid great power competition.* Wilson Center Asia Program. https:// www .wilsoncenter .org/ publication/ soft -power -amidst -great -power -competition.

9   Public relations

Kathy R. Fitzpatrick

Introduction

The multidisciplinary nature of public diplomacy (PD) has been well documented, indicating a need for PD research that "embraces the potential contributions of other social and behavioral disciplines" (Gilboa, 2008, p. 73). Yet, in research and in practice, scholars and practitioners often neglect relevant knowledge outside their disciplinary homes. As an example, Robson (2021) found in reviewing the literature on place branding and public relations that "the two fields are on the whole siloed and have failed to consider insights from the other" (p. 2). Notwithstanding "a significant overlap in the scholarly interests of the two fields, particularly around relationships, engagement, strategic communication, and reputation," place branding researchers "tend to see public relations as a promotional tactic centered around publicity rather than an academic field" (p. 2). As a result, the perceived value of public relations scholarship to place branding is limited, with "one field largely dismiss[ing] the other" (p. 7).

In a comprehensive review of PD literature from 1965 through mid-2017, Sevin et al. (2019) noted the impact of discipline-specific inquiries "in narrowing the scope of questions being asked about public diplomacy" (p. 4832). When disciplinary approaches do not intersect, "there is the loss of explanatory power" (p. 4832). Calling for researchers to look for synergies with scholars working in other disciplines, they suggested that "if the study of public diplomacy is to deserve the description of *cross-disciplinary*, then researchers might work more consciously toward incorporation of literature and insights outside their own" (pp. 4832–3).

This chapter explores public relations (PR) concepts relevant to the study and practice of PD. The discussion begins by reviewing conceptual and practical connections between the two fields. It then discusses aspects of theory building related to relationships, power, publics, and ethics. Next, the chapter considers the developing domain of strategic communication and its possible impact on PD as a multidisciplinary enterprise. The aim is to spark new ways of thinking about and studying PD and to suggest insights from PR that can help move PD forward. The work identifies gaps in PD scholarship that could be addressed in future research.

Conceptual and practical connections

Of all of PD's disciplinary relatives, PR is arguably its closest kin (L'Etang, 2009). The two fields, both of which emerged from propagandistic roots, share a history involving many of the same characters and developed along strikingly similar lines (Cutlip, 1994; Maxwell, 2020). For example, the story of US PD's rise and fall in times of war and peace illustrates the same crisis mentality of organizational leaders that has influenced the advancement of PR. The attainment of professional maturity in both fields has been stifled by a lack of clear identities and perceptions of PR and PD, respectively, as peripheral to or of limited value to organizational success (Sharp, 2009; Thurlow, 2009). Such views might be attributed in part to the lack of commonly accepted definitions of the respective functions. As Gregory (2008) said about PD, its "meaning is evolving and contested", and "there is no consensus on its analytical boundaries" (p. 274).

A close look at what PR and PD specialists do and how and why they do it reveals substantial commonalities. For example, the Public Relations Society of America (2021) describes PR as "a strategic communication process that builds mutually beneficial relationships between organizations and their publics … in order to shape and frame the public perception of an organization." International PR is widely viewed as "the planned and organized effort of a company, institution, or government to establish mutually beneficial relationships with the publics of other nations" (p. 409). These definitions track Sharp's (2005) description of PD as "the process by which direct relations are pursued with a country's people to advance the interests and extend the values of those being represented" (p. 106) and Gregory's (2008) presentation of PD as a communication instrument used in governance by states, associations of states and nonstate actors to "*understand* cultures, attitudes, and behavior; *build and manage* relationships; and *influence* opinions and actions to advance their interests and values" (p. 276).

There are also parallels in the principles, values, and capabilities that define the work of professionals in the two fields. A comparative analysis of knowledge and skills considered important for success in PR and PD, respectively, showed considerable overlap with public diplomats routinely engaging in PR activities

(Fitzpatrick et al., 2016). The researchers concluded that "public relations concepts could contribute to the development of a coherent and integrated framework for public diplomacy research and practice" (Fitzpatrick et al., 2013, p. 17). Of particular note were similarities in the principles and values considered important to the success of PR and PD efforts, including credibility, mutuality, collaboration, honesty, respect, and trust.

Citing PD as a "distinctive new trend" in the global PR literature, Ki et al. (2021) identified the conceptual basis of practical connections between the two fields, observing that PD as a function of government PR "extends the importance of cultivating favorable relationships between a government and foreign publics" (p. 9). "As public diplomacy focuses on relationship building (a primary paradigm of public relations) rather than image cultivation, its primary function is well-suited to the field" (p. 13).

At the same time, the suitability of PR concepts and practices in specific PD contexts should be considered. Incongruences in strategic goals and desired outcomes could limit the extent of disciplinary cross-fertilization. For example, Sevin (2015) argued that because PD is a "unique phenomenon" developed by multiple disciplines and "an inherently foreign policy tool" used to advance national interests and achieve foreign policy goals, linkages between PR and PD "should not be stretched too far" (p. 562). Signitzer (2008) similarly suggested that three distinct approaches to PR – organizational, societal, and marketing – might be applicable in PD practice but for different purposes. Organizational public relations concepts could be useful in managing and maintaining a diplomatic environment and relationships with publics that support the achievement of organizational goals. Societal public relations concepts could help to foster a positive role for PD in society through the advancement of values, principles, and interests that contribute to "a peaceful development of the world system" (p. 215). Marketing public relations and "place branding" could be useful in advancing specific trade and tourism goals (p. 215).

In contemplating the convergence of PR and PD, Van Dyke and Verčič (2009) observed both opportunities and risks, noting that the convergence occurring in practice has progressed more rapidly than in theory, and the integration of strategic communication practices used to support both soft and hard power objectives could serve to diminish the credibility and efficacy of both PR and PD. If communication is not guided by theory and ethics, they argued, "mismanagement of information power could erode the value of public relations and diplomacy, undermine public trust in government and private institutions, increase the likelihood that nations will resort to hard power, and prolong or amplify the adverse consequences of conflict" (p. 838). Such assertions suggest a need for empirical research exploring the analytical and practical boundaries of PR and PD, respectively, and areas in which cross-fertilization is most likely to advance – or perhaps impede – theory and practice development.

Building theory

Ferguson's (2018) proposal in 1984 that relationships should be the central focus of PR research changed the trajectory of PR scholarship. At the time, she suggested a paradigm focus on three areas – social responsibility and ethics, social issues and issue management, and public relationships – noting that if she were "to put her public relations theory development eggs in one basket," it would be public relationships (p. 164). Such focus, she argued, "would speed the development of theory in this field" (p. 164). To get there, however, she said researchers would need to clarify the meanings of core concepts (e.g., public, relationship, organization, communication) to allow researchers to communicate with one another.

Nearly four decades later, PR scholars have built a substantial body of knowledge illustrating the centrality of public relationships in effective and ethical PR practices. In addition to explicating a theory of relationship management (Ledingham, 2003), researchers have examined myriad dimensions of organization–public relationships ranging from relationship antecedents (Valentini, 2021; Grunig & Huang, 2000) to relationship quality (Shen, 2017) to relationship outcomes (Ki & Hon, 2012) to relationship types (Hung, 2005). At the same time, PR scholars recognize the value of multiple theoretical perspectives in building theory and advancing practices in a dynamic communication environment and, for the most part, agree that a general theory of PR may not be possible or desirable. According to Brunner (2019), "[t]here needs to be a diversity of theories and perspectives for public relations to grow" (p. 9).

PD is similarly challenged to define a "paradigm focus" for theory development (Ferguson, 2018, p. 167), while at the same time integrating multiple theoretical perspectives that can contribute to the field's advancement. In a recent examination of the state of PD, Zhang (2020) found the field to be "extremely fragmented" (p. 195), observing that "[t]he complicated theoretical underpinnings of PD are partially caused by the interdisciplinarity of the field" and "ever changing technologies, PD practices, actors, and the global environment" (p. 197). Sevin et al. (2019) similarly observed that "the breadth of what falls under the shifting rubric of public diplomacy" (p. 4814) has resulted in "no single theoretical perspective" that unites PD work (p. 4815). Rather than view this as a shortcoming, however, they viewed it as a strength. What is needed, they said, "is appropriate theory to guide research questions and ensure coherence in analysis of results" (p. 4833).

Notably, their comprehensive review of the literature showed that the most common concept-based research topic in PD is soft power, "confirming its status as a predominant framework for the field" (Sevin et al., 2019, p. 4830). This finding suggests a need for PD researchers to heed Ferguson's (2018) advice and take a close look at core concepts in PD that must be clarified in meaningful ways for future research. The fact that soft power remains a guiding light for researchers suggests that a necessary step in building theory is to consider whether soft power is desirable and/or sustainable as a foundational framework for PD research and practice going forward. According to Pamment (2015), "soft power has failed to provide sufficient support for theories of PD" (p. 204).

In PR scholarship, the concept of power is addressed in research examining power dynamics in organization–public relationships and the social role and impact of PR in practice. For example, in considering the role of PR in deliberative systems, Edwards (2016) pointed out that while research has shown the valuable role PR can play in building democracy, PR also can be used to "reduce the quality of deliberation, depending on who is using it and what they are using it for" (p. 74). In challenging the normative conception of symmetrical communication as a model for excellent and ethical PR, Roper (2005) argued that inequalities in resources and the negotiating power of organizations and their publics may lead to hegemonic outcomes. The symmetrical communication process, she said, "is often one of compromise to deflect criticism and maintain power relations rather than one of open, collaborative negotiation" (p. 69).

In PD, critical research is needed to challenge assumptions regarding PD's aims and impacts, as well as the interests that are – or should be – served. As Shin and Heath (2020) observed, "Critical theorists reason that if the foundations of a discipline are flawed, then so too is its theory" (p. 166). Future research should address the question: If not soft power, then what is the conceptual basis of PD?

One alternative model that PR scholars have explored is social capital. Drawing on sociological and business perspectives, Dodd (2016) proposed a social capital model of PR based on the idea that PR specialists "have expertise, knowledge, training, and education appropriate for maintaining, gaining and exchanging intangible resources as social capital" (p. 295). These intangible resources, including trust, reputation, credibility, and legitimacy, she said, "are managed through strategic and directed communication behaviors" (p. 290). Social capital theory, it is argued, much like relational theory, provides a rationale for both the existence of PR and the value of PR in organizations and society (Brunner, 2019; Dodd, 2016).

Another concept that has received considerable attention in PR research is engagement (Johnston, 2014; Johnston & Taylor, 2018; Koya et al., 2021). In proposing a new model of engagement in PR, Dhanesh (2017) summarized key points in the engagement literature that have relevance for PD: (1) engagement is often equated with communicative interactions between organizations and their publics; (2) engagement involves forms of interaction ranging from collaboration to control, with collaboration the preferred approach; and (3) even collaborative forms of engagement may involve asymmetries of power and inequality among interacting entities.

Noting that the "basic building block" of her proposed model is salience, Dhanesh (2017) noted the need to acknowledge the "situational relevance and importance of all models of engagement, ranging from one-way, transactional forms of engagement as control to two-way or multi-way forms of engagement as collaboration" (p. 930). Decisions regarding which models are best suited for specific situations, she said, should be based on the types of publics targeted for engagement. There is much to unpack here in future PD research, including the notion of engagement as the foundation of both power-based (controlling) and relationship-based (collaborative) approaches to PD, as well as the role and involvement of publics in engagement efforts.

Somewhat ironically, the "public" in PD has received limited attention in PD scholarship, with most works citing the need for more strategic approaches in defining, categorizing, and engaging publics. For example, Zaharna (2010) reviewed emerging best practices in strategic stakeholder engagement, noting the need for research in PD contexts that could help define both "strategic stakeholders" and "strategic engagement" (p. 229). Zaharna and Uysal (2016) later introduced "relationalism" as an analytical tool for constructing a model of PD based on the relational dynamics between a state and its publics (p. 109). Tam and Kim (2018) proposed that "the segmentation of publics is critical for guiding countries to strategically invest resources into building relationships with prioritized publics" (p. 28). They argued that "publics should be understood and segmented based on an intersection between symbolic environment and behavioral experiences" into categories of "ambassadorial publics," "advocational publics," accusational publics," and "adversarial publics" (p. 34).

Future empirical research aimed at testing these ideas in practice might be informed by PR research on inactive publics (Hallahan, 2000); segmentation of publics (Kim et al., 2020; Vardeman-Winter et al., 2013); prioritizing publics (Rawlins, 2006); dialogue with publics (Chen et al., 2020; Kent & Taylor, 2002; Theunissen & Wan Noordin, 2012); and managing relationships with publics (Ledingham, 2003; Ni et al., 2019). The still evolving situational theory of publics – viewed as perhaps "one of the most useful theories for understanding why publics communicate and when they are most likely to do so" (Aldoory & Sha, 2007, p. 339) – also provides valuable insights for theory development in PD.

A topic drawing increased interest among PD scholars and practitioners is domestic publics, which are viewed as both publics and potential partners in PD efforts (Bravo & De Moya, 2021; Pisarska, 2016). Huijgh (2012) observed that the domestic dimension "can be seen as a steppingstone to moving ahead with a more inclusive or 'intermestic' approach to public involvement at home and abroad in diplomacy" (p. 364). In applying business and PR concepts related to stakeholders and publics, Fitzpatrick (2012) proposed a new framework involving domestic and foreign publics that recognizes networks of influence in the contemporary diplomatic environment. Pacher (2018) introduced a conceptual typology of strategic publics based on the strategic importance and power of respective publics, including governmental and nongovernmental, foreign and domestic, and elite and non-elite publics.

In proposing a conceptual model of diaspora diplomacy, Ho and McConnell (2019) challenged distinctions between foreign and domestic publics, observing that "[a]s liminal actors, diasporas can mobilize resources outside of the national territory, perform bridging functions or play peace-building roles in the services of the state" (p. 250). At the same time, they pointed out that diasporas also can mobilize resources in support of alternative political visions, illustrating the strategic influence of diaspora and other domestic publics on PD outcomes. This thinking is in line with PR definitions of strategic publics as individuals or groups that have the ability to enhance or constrain an organization's ability to accomplish its goals (Fitzpatrick, 2012).

Going forward, researchers and practitioners will be challenged to define both what publics matter most to the achievement of PD goals and how to effectively engage those publics in various situations. For example, in writing about PR in global cultural contexts, Bardhan and Weaver (2011) cited the importance of engaging "ethically and critically with matters of cultural differences in a globalizing and multicultural world" (p. 8). PD researchers also should consider whether and how the inclusion of domestic publics could change the roles and responsibilities, as well as institutional structures, of PD and the potential impact of a domestic dimension on how PD is viewed and practiced.

Another avenue for future research related to publics is the connection between public relationships and national reputations. As Melissen (2005) observed, "the strength of firm relationships largely determines the receipt and success of individual messages and overall attitudes" (p. 21). While there has been considerable research on national reputation and its various dimensions, much of which is informed by PR concepts (Ingenhoff et al., 2019), the connections between relationships and reputations should be further explored.

Recent studies illustrate the potential benefits of such research. In a study involving China and South Korea, Kim et al. (2020) found that "variations in reputation formation and relationship building patterns may exist in foreign publics from different countries" (p. 9), suggesting a need to consider "cultural and societal characteristics of foreign publics, as well as the diplomatic history between the two countries" in reputation management efforts (p. 9). In a case study on Danish–Middle Eastern relations, Pultz (2012) also found links between country image and relationship-building strategies. This work showed that "[s]upporting dialogue activities and engaging in dialogue can be effective PD, particularly when a country has a negative image among the recipients of the public diplomacy campaign" (p. 163). Whether such efforts would be effective with "the general public," she said, was unclear, leaving the door open for future research.

Ferguson's (2018) recognition that the social aspects of PR would be important to the growth and development of the field is also relevant to PD. Looking back, her emphasis on social responsibility and ethics seems a prescient prediction for how the role and value of PR would expand in a dynamic and increasingly globalized communication environment (Capizzo, 2020; Ki et al., 2021). PD is similarly evolving into a more socially conscious function with increased demands for attention to global and social concerns that extend beyond national borders (Fitzpatrick, 2017; Kelley, 2014).

This new "societized" form of diplomacy (Melissen, 2011, p. 13) indicates a need for scholarly attention to social responsibility and ethics. While ethical principles and values are recognized as important in the practice of PD, they have not been robustly explored in scholarship. As Zaharna (2010) observed, "[p]ublic diplomacy may be politically motivated, but as a communicative activity will invariably contain an ethical boundary whenever it operates in a social context" (p. 183). Future studies might be informed by PR research that has helped to mark the ethical margins of PR (Baker & Martinson, 2001;

Bortree & DiStaso, 2014; Bowen, 2005; Edgett, 2002). Research on public diplomats as social actors also would deepen understanding of the role and relevance of PD beyond its organizational function.

As PD scholars and practitioners contemplate an expanded role for PD in global society, fundamental questions related to both how and why PD is conducted must be addressed. For example, what is the central purpose of PD? What is PD's role in global society? Whose interests are or should be served by PD and how should competing interests be balanced? How does *PD* serve the *public* interest? What principles and values should guide the work of public diplomats? What does *ethical* PD require?

Strategic communication

In exploring Ferguson's (2018) views on theory building in PR, it is interesting to note that although she recognized the central role of public communication in the study and practice of PR, she argued that the field "is concerned with more than communication" (p. 173) and that "understanding relationships requires more than understanding communication processes and effects" (p. 173). This is true, although recent developments related to strategic communication warrant attention as PD scholars continue "searching for a theory of public diplomacy" (Gilboa, 2008).

In research and in practice, strategic communication and PD are sometimes linked as associated or analogous functions, often without explanation or clear meaning. Other times, they are viewed as either distinct functions or umbrella terms with one subsumed within the other (Creswell, 2019; Loffelholz et al., 2014). The same is true in PR. As Aldoory and Toth (2021) observed, "Strategic communication is a deliberative, holistic, and convergent communication domain, and it is considered a part of, as well as separate from, the scholarly boundaries of public relations" (p. 25).

Since the early 2010s, strategic communication has gained traction in the academy and in industry as a new area of scholarship and practice that integrates PR and other communication functions in efforts to build a body of knowledge focused on the use of communication to achieve organizational goals. The definition of strategic communication has evolved over time, with the most recent offering based on a decade of research aimed at clarifying the meaning of the discipline:

> Strategic communication encompasses all communication that is substantial for the survival and sustained success of an entity. Specifically, strategic communication is the purposeful use of communication by an organization or other entity to engage in conversations of strategic significance to its goals. (Zerfass et al., 2018, p. 493)

In PR, strategic communication is a "contested concept," with debates focused primarily on whether there is room in such definitions for "the interests and perspectives of publics and stakeholders" (Shin & Heath, 2020, pp. 343–4). Additionally, there is concern that the increasing use of "strategic communication" in academic studies and professional practice diminishes the traditional role and integrity of PR as an academic discipline with a discrete body of knowledge and a profession with defined standards of practice.

In contemplating these terminological shifts, Falkheimer and Heide (2014) argued for "the use of strategic communication as a conceptual and holistic framework that better captures that complex phenomenon of an organization's communication than do traditional, boundary-maintaining concepts," such as PR (p. 133). The concept of strategic communication, they said, "is in better accordance with the contemporary social, cultural and economic structural transformation taking place in late-modern society" (p. 133). Future research should consider the strength of such arguments in PD.

The need for such inquiry was shown in a recent analysis of the literature on PD and strategic communication across world regions, in which Loffelholz et al. (2014) found that research on PD and its relationship to strategic communication "is deficient and highly fragmented in its attributions" with most publications relating PD and strategic communication without clear definitions (p. 441). These authors concluded that "public diplomacy can be regarded as strategic communication but is not strategic per se" (p. 453). Thus, "a theoretical grounding of public diplomacy, strategy and strategic communication needs to be accomplished" (p. 439).

The emergence of strategic communication as a new interdisciplinary domain has forced new ways of thinking about the roles and responsibilities, as well as the value, of communication-related functions in organizations and in society. Notably, leading strategic communication scholars point to the interdisciplinary nature of strategic communication as "its defining attribute" (Werder et al., 2018, p. 333). According to Werder et al. (2018), "Interdisciplinary integration brings interdependent parts or knowledge into harmonious relationships to build new knowledge and theoretical solutions" (p. 336). In order to take advantage of the innovation that may result from such encounters, they called for strategic communication scholars "to adopt an interdisciplinary worldview toward research and theory building" based on strategic communication as "an integrated, interdisciplinary approach" (pp. 344–5, 347).

This thinking echoes Sevin et al.'s (2019) argument for greater consideration of multidisciplinary perspectives in PD research. Whether it suggests a movement toward the adoption of strategic communication as a replacement for PD is another matter. Although links between PR and strategic communication are widely acknowledged, strategic communication is not viewed as a *substitute* for PR but rather as a descriptor for how PR is carried out in practice. The same may be true in PD. For example, Zaharna (2010) defined strategic communication as "the systematic design and implementation of a communication initiative to achieve a pre-defined goal" (p. 6). PD, she said, "is viewed as the strategic communication of a political entity – state or nonstate actor – in the international political arena" (p. 6).

Strategic communication scholars have observed increasing interest in strategic communication as "an integral element in warfare," as well as in PD, which is described as "a more 'civilized' way of exercising soft power through global and intercultural communication that influences international relations" (Zerfass et al., 2018, p. 490). Such discussions would benefit from the participation of PD experts familiar with diplomatic and military views on and uses of strategic communication in research and in practice (Michelsen & Colley, 2019).

Conclusion

As the convergence of PR and PD continues, increased scholarly focus on the relational and communicative dimensions of PD could well lead to a shift away from power-based views of PD and contribute to the development of a new analytical framework for PD research and practice. This chapter demonstrates the potential for interdisciplinary concepts to advance thinking and practices in PD through the application of PR concepts and approaches. It also shows that ignoring relevant knowledge from related fields may stifle or slow understanding of how and why PD works the way it works and how it might work better, leading to the "loss of explanatory power" (Sevin et al., 2019, p. 4832). Dismissive attitudes toward PR (as well as other related disciplines) may stifle innovation and hinder the theoretical and practical development of PD going forward. Future studies are needed to help gauge both the strength of the connections between PR and PD and the benefits of bringing multiple communication perspectives to bear in PD research. As Vanc and Fitzpatrick (2016) suggested, to fully understand the potential for cross-fertilization between the two fields, the applicability, as well as the geographic and practical boundaries, of PR concepts and strategies must be tested in diplomatic domains and contexts.

References

Aldoory, L., & Sha, B. L. (2007). The situational theory of publics: Practical applications, methodological challenges, and theoretical horizons. In E. L. Toth (Ed.), *The future of excellence in public relations and communication management: Challenges for the next generation* (pp. 339–55). Routledge.

Aldoory, L., & Toth, E. L. (2021). *The future of feminism in public relations and strategic communication: A socio-ecological model of influences.* Rowman & Littlefield.

Baker, S., & Martinson, D. L. (2001). The TARES test: Five principles for ethical persuasion. *Journal of Mass Media Ethics, 16*(2–3), 148–75. https:// doi .org/ 10 .1080/ 08900523.2001.9679610.

Bardhan, N., & Weaver, C. K. (2011). Introduction: Public relations in global cultural contexts. In N. Bardhan & C. K. Weaver (Eds.), *Public relations in global cultural contexts* (pp. 1–28). Routledge.

Bortree, D., & DiStaso, M. W. (2014). *Ethical practice of social media in public relations.* Routledge.

Bowen, S. A. (2005). A practical model for ethical decision making in issues management and public relations. *Journal of Public Relations Research, 17*(3), 191–216.

Bravo, V., & De Moya, M. (2021). *Latin American diasporas in public diplomacy.* Palgrave Macmillan.

Brunner, B. R. (Ed.) (2019). *Public relations theory: Application and understanding.* John Wiley & Sons.

Capizzo, L. (2020). The right side of history, Inc.: Social issues management, social license to operate, and the Obergefell v. Hodges decision. *Public Relations Review, 46*(5). https://doi.org/10.1016/j.pubrev.2020.101957.

Chen, Y.-R. R., Hung-Baesecke, C.-J. F., & Chen, X. (2020). Moving forward the dialogic theory of public relations: Concepts, methods and applications of organization–public dialogue. *Public Relations Review, 46*(1), 101878. https:// doi .org/ 10 .1016/ j .pubrev.2019.101878.

Creswell, M. H. (2019). Wasted words? The limitations of US strategic communication and public diplomacy. *Studies in Conflict & Terrorism, 42*(5), 464–92. https:// doi .org/10.1080/1057610X.2017.1392097.

Cutlip, S. M. (1994). *The unseen power: Public relations: A history.* Routledge.

Dhanesh, G. S. (2017). Putting engagement in its proper place: State of the field, definition and model of engagement in public relations. *Public Relations Review, 43*(5), 925–33. https://doi.org/10.1016/j.pubrev.2017.04.001.

Dodd, M. D. (2016). Intangible resource management: Social capital theory development for public relations. *Journal of Communication Management, 20*(4), 289–311. https://doi.org/10.1108/JCOM-12-2015-0095.

Edgett, R. (2002). Toward an ethical framework for advocacy in public relations. *Journal of Public Relations Research, 14*(1), 1–26. https:// doi .org/ 10 .1207/ S1532754XJPRR1401_1.

Edwards, L. (2016). The role of public relations in deliberative systems. *Journal of Communication, 66*(1), 60–81. https://doi.org/10.1111/jcom.12199.

Falkheimer, J., & Heide, M. (2014). From public relations to strategic communication in Sweden: The emergence of a transboundary field of knowledge. *Nordicom Review, 35*(2), 123–38. https://doi.org/10.2478/nor-2014-0019.

Ferguson, M. A. (2018). Building theory in public relations: Interorganizational relationships as a public relations paradigm. *Journal of Public Relations Research, 30*(4), 164–78. https://doi.org/10.1080/1062726X.2018.1514810.

Fitzpatrick, K. R. (2012). Defining strategic publics in a networked world: Public diplomacy's challenge at home and abroad, *The Hague Journal of Diplomacy, 7*(4), 421–40. https://doi.org/10.1163/1871191X-12341236.

Fitzpatrick, K. R. (2017). Public diplomacy in the public interest. *The Journal of Public Interest Communications, 1*(1), 78–92. https://doi.org/10.32473/jpic.v1.i1.p78.

Fitzpatrick, K. R., Fullerton, J., & Kendrick, K. (2013). Public relations and public diplomacy: Conceptual and practical connections. *Public Relations Journal, 7*(4), 1–21.

Gilboa, E. (2008). Searching for a theory of public diplomacy. *The Annals of the American Academy of Political and Social Science, 616*(1), 55–77.

Gregory, B. (2008). Public diplomacy: Sunrise of an academic field. *The Annals of the American Academy of Political and Social Science, 616*(1), 274–90.

Grunig, J. E., & Huang, Y. H. (2000). From organizational effectiveness to relationship indicators: Antecedents of relationships, public relations strategies, and relationship outcomes. In J. A. Ledingham & S. D. Bruning (Eds.), *Public relations as relationship management* (pp. 23–53). Lawrence Erlbaum.

Hallahan, K. (2000). Inactive publics: The forgotten publics in public relations. *Public Relations Review, 26*(4), 499–515. https://doi.org/10.1016/S0363-8111(00)00061-8.

Ho, E. L. E., & McConnell, F. (2019). Conceptualizing "diaspora diplomacy": Territory and populations betwixt the domestic and foreign. *Progress in Human Geography, 43*(2), 235–55. https://doi.org/10.1177/0309132517740217.

Huijgh, E. (2012). Public diplomacy in flux: Introducing the domestic dimension. *The Hague Journal of Diplomacy, 7*(4), 359–67. https:// doi .org/ 10 .1163/ 1871191X -12341240.

Hung, C. J. F. (2005). Exploring types of organization–public relationships and their implications for relationship management in public relations. *Journal of Public Relations Research, 17*(4), 393–426. https://doi.org/10.1207/s1532754xjprr1704_4.

Ingenhoff, D., White, C., Buhmann, A., & Kiousis, S. (Eds.) (2019). *Bridging disciplinary perspectives of country image reputation, brand, and identity: Reputation, brand, and identity.* Routledge.

Johnston, K. A. (2014). Public relations and engagement: Theoretical imperatives of a multidimensional concept. *Journal of Public Relations Research, 26*(5), 381–3. https://doi.org/10.1080/1062726X.2014.959863.

Johnston, K. A., & Taylor, M. (Eds.) (2018). *The handbook of communication engagement.* John Wiley & Sons.

Kelley, J. R. (2014). *Agency change: Diplomatic action beyond the state.* Rowman & Littlefield.

Kent, M., & Taylor, M. (2002). Toward a dialogic theory of public relations. *Public Relations Review, 28*(1), 21–37. https://doi.org/10.1016/S0363-8111(02)00108-X.

Ki, E.-J., & Hon, L. C. (2012). Causal linkages among relationship quality perception, attitude, and behavior intention in a membership organization. *Corporate Communications, 17*(2), 187–208. http://dx.doi.org/10.1108/13563281211220274.

Ki, E.-J., Pasadeos, Y., & Ertem-Eray, T. (2021). The structure and evolution of global public relations: A citation and co-citation analysis 1983–2019. *Public Relations Review, 47*(1), 102012. https://doi.org/10.1016/j.pubrev.2021.102012.

Kim, S. Y., Choi, S., Kim, J.-N., & Cai, L. A. (2020). Dual modes of "Good will hunting": Untangling the reputation and relationship correlations en route to foreign amity. *Public Relations Review, 46*(3), 101922. https:// doi .org/ 10 .1016/ j .pubrev.2020.101922.

Koya, N., Hurst, B., & Roper, J. (2021). In whose interests? When relational engagement to obtain a social license leads to paradoxical outcomes. *Public Relations Review, 47*(1), 101987. https://doi.org/10.1016/j.pubrev.2020.101987.

Ledingham, J. A. (2003). Explicating relationship management as a general theory of public relations. *Journal of Public Relations Research, 15*(2), 181–98. https://doi.org/ 10.1207/S1532754XJPRR1502_4.

L'Etang, J. (2009). Public relations and diplomacy in a globalized world: An issue of public communication. *American Behavioral Scientist, 53*(4), 607–26. https:// doi .org/10.1177/0002764209347633.

Loffelholz, M., Auer, C., & Srugis, A. (2014). Strategic dimensions of public diplomacy. In D. Holtzhausen & A. Zerfass (Eds.), *The Routledge handbook of strategic communication* (pp. 439–58). Routledge. https://doi.org/10.4324/9780203094440-39.

Maxwell, J. M. (2020). *Manipulating the masses: Woodrow Wilson and the birth of American propaganda.* Louisiana State University Press.

Melissen, J. (2005). The new public diplomacy: Between theory and practice. In J. Melissen (Ed.), *The new public diplomacy* (pp. 3–27). Palgrave Macmillan.

Melissen, J. (2011). *Beyond the new public diplomacy.* Clingendael. https:// www .clingendael.org/sites/default/files/pdfs/20111014_cdsp_paper_jmelissen.pdf.

Michelsen, N., & Colley, T. (2019). The field of strategic communications professionals: A new research agenda for international security. *European Journal of International Security, 4*(1), 61–78. https://doi.org/10.1017/eis.2018.9.

Ni, L., Xiao, Z., Liu, W., & Wang, Q. (2019). Relationship management as antecedents to public communication behaviors: Examining empowerment and public health among Asian Americans. *Public Relations Review, 45*(5), 101835. https://doi.org/10 .1016/j.pubrev.2019.101835.

Pacher, A. (2018). Strategic publics in public diplomacy: A typology and a heuristic device for multiple publics. *The Hague Journal of Diplomacy, 13*(3), 272–96. https:// doi.org/10.1163/1871191X-13020004.

Pamment, J. (2015). Media influence, ontological transformation, and social change: Conceptual overlaps between development communication and public diplomacy. *Communication Theory, 25*(2), 188–207. https://doi.org/10.1111/comt.12064.

Pisarska, K. (2016). *Domestic dimension of public diplomacy.* Palgrave Macmillan.

Public Relations Society of America (2021). About public relations. https://www.prsa .org/about/all-about-pr.

Pultz, K. (2012). Dialogue and power: Understanding Danish public diplomacy efforts in the Middle East. *The Hague Journal of Diplomacy, 7*(2), 161–80. https://doi.org/10 .1163/187119112X625529.

Rawlins, B. L. (2006). Prioritizing stakeholders for public relations. *Institute for Public Relations,* 1–14. https:// www .instituteforpr .org/ wp -content/ uploads/ 2006 _Stakeholders_1.pdf.

Robson, P. (2021). Public relations and place branding: Friend, foe or just ignored? A systematic review. *Public Relations Review*, *47*(5), 102096. https://doi.org/10.1016/j.pubrev.2021.102096.

Roper, J. (2005). Symmetrical communication: Excellent public relations or a strategy for hegemony? *Journal of Public Relations Research*, *17*(1), 69–86. https://doi.org/10.1207/s1532754xjprr1701_6.

Sevin, E. (2015). Pathways of connection: An analytical approach to the impacts of public diplomacy. *Public Relations Review*, *41*(4), 562–8. https://doi.org/10.1016/j.pubrev.2015.07.003.

Sevin, E., Metzgar, E. T., & Hayden, C. (2019). The scholarship of public diplomacy: Analysis of a growing field. *International Journal of Communication*, *13*, 4814–37.

Sharp, P. (2005). Revolutionary states, outlaw regimes and the techniques of public diplomacy. In J. Melissen (Ed.), *The new public diplomacy* (pp. 106–23). Palgrave Macmillan.

Sharp, P. (2009). *Diplomatic theory of international relations*. Cambridge University Press.

Shen, H. (2017). Refining organization–public relationship quality measurement in student and employee samples. *Journalism & Mass Communication Quarterly*, *94*(4), 994–1010. https://doi.org/10.1177/1077699016674186.

Shin, J. H., & Heath, R. L. (2020). *Public relations theory: Capabilities and competencies*. John Wiley & Sons.

Signitzer, B. (2008). Public relations and public diplomacy: Some conceptual explorations. In A. Zerfass, B. van Ruler, & K. Sriramesh (Eds.), *Public relations research* (pp. 205–18). VS Verlag für Sozialwissenschaften. https://doi.org/10.1007/978-3-531-90918-9_13.

Tam, L., & Kim, J.-N. (2018). Who are publics in public diplomacy? Proposing a taxonomy of foreign publics as an intersection between symbolic environment and behavioral experiences. *Place Branding and Public Diplomacy*, *15*(1), 28–37. https://doi.org/10.1057/s41254-018-0104-z.

Theunissen, P., & Wan Noordin, W. N. (2012). Revisiting the concept "dialogue" in public relations. *Public Relations Review*, *38*(1), 5–13. https://doi.org/10.1016/j.pubrev.2011.09.006.

Thurlow, A. (2009). "I just say I'm in advertising": Public relations identity crisis? *Canadian Journal of Communication*, *34*(2), 245–63. https://doi.org/10.22230/cjc.2009v34n2a2018.

Valentini, C. (2021). Trust research in public relations: An assessment of its conceptual, theoretical and methodological foundations. *Corporate Communications*, *26*(1), 84–106. http://dx.doi.org/10.1108/CCIJ-01-2020-0030.

Van Dyke, M., & Verčič, D. (2009). Public relations, public diplomacy, and strategic communication: An international model of conceptual convergence. In M. Van Dyke & D. Verčič (Eds.), *Global public relations handbook: Theory, research, and practice* (pp. 822–43). Routledge.

Vanc, A., & Fitzpatrick, K. R. (2016). Scope and status of public diplomacy research by public relations scholars, 1990–2014. *Public Relations Review*, *42*(3), 432–40. https://doi.org/10.1016/j.pubrev.2015.07.012.

Vardeman-Winter, J., Tindall, N., & Jiang, H. (2013). Intersectionality and publics: How exploring publics' multiple identities questions basic public relations concepts. *Public Relations Inquiry*, *2*(3), 279–304. https://doi.org/10.1177/2046147X13491564.

Werder, K. P., Nothhaft, H., Verčič, D., & Zerfass, A. (2018). Strategic communication as an emerging interdisciplinary paradigm. *International Journal of Strategic Communication, 12*(4), 333–51. https://doi.org/10.1080/1553118X.2018.1494181.

Zaharna, R. S. (2010). *Battles to bridges: US strategic communication and public diplomacy after 9/11.* Springer.

Zaharna, R. S., & Uysal, N. (2016). Going for the jugular in public diplomacy: How adversarial publics using social media are challenging state legitimacy. *Public Relations Review, 42*(1), 109–19. https://doi.org/10.1016/j.pubrev.2015.07.006.

Zerfass, A., Verčič, D., Nothhaft, H., & Werder, K. P. (2018). Strategic communication: Defining the field and its contribution to research and practice. *International Journal of Strategic Communication, 12*(4), 487–505. https://doi.org/10.1080/1553118X.2018.1493485.

Zhang, J. (2020). Compassion versus manipulation; narratives versus rational arguments: A PD radar to chart the terrain of public diplomacy. *Place Branding and Public Diplomacy, 16,* 195–211. https://doi.org/10.1057/s41254-019-00146-2.

10 Relational and collaborative approaches

R.S. Zaharna and Amelia Arsenault[1]

Introduction

Today, given the shared global problems that demand joint action, relational and collaborative approaches to public diplomacy (PD) may seem natural. However, looking back over the past couple of decades of scholarship, we see a gradual evolution in thinking about relational approaches. As we see below, initially "relational approaches" in PD focused on individual initiatives aimed at creating, building, and managing relationships with publics. Relational approaches typically meant expanding dialogues, forming partnerships, or building networks. In this chapter we take our discussion deeper by shifting our focus from the various types of relational initiatives that we can see, to the buried, unspoken relational assumptions of separateness and connectivity that shape the goals and functions of PD itself.

A relational lens refers to the mindset that a PD practitioner or scholar brings to an initiative while a relational approach includes the array of program and campaign models that PD practitioners implement. We introduce two relational lenses based on two distinctive assumptions. The first lens assumes no relations between the PD actor and other actors or publics. We call this the lens the "lens of separateness." When viewed through this lens, relational approaches focus on the PD initiatives of individual actors as they seek to create, manage, or strengthen relations with target publics. This lens has been the dominant, and for some, the only considered "relational approach" in PD. There is, however, a second, perhaps overlooked perspective; a lens that assumes that all entities are connected to each other either directly or indirectly.[2] We call this lens the "lens of connectivity." This lens, which was

---

[2]   In many ways, the lens of connectivity shares commonality with Latour and other proponents of Actor Network Theory (ANT) who consider it essential to focus

common in ancient and pre-colonial indigenous diplomacies, is resurfacing with enhanced connectivity facilitated by digital technologies. As we discuss below, the presumption of connectivity takes "relational approaches" beyond creating, building, or managing relations. It represents a new vantage point for viewing PD goals and functions.

We begin this chapter with a brief historical overview of the impetus that gave rise to the relational approach. We then move to the two relational lenses. We look first at relational approaches through the lens of separateness, then through the lens of connectivity. We conclude with a discussion of how these two lenses help shape future research on relational and collaborative approaches to PD.

The contemporary impetus for relational and collaborative approaches

Relational and collaborative PD approaches in many ways reflect an evolution in the thinking and practice of the field. We can see this evolution perhaps most clearly in U.S. PD. When PD made a dramatic resurgence in the aftermath of the 9/11 terrorist attacks on the U.S., the idea of "building relations" was relegated to the narrow purview of education and cultural affairs. Popular wisdom at the time was that the attacks were based on a lack of understanding of U.S. policies and values. As the then U.S. president George Bush stated, "I am surprised there is so much misunderstanding. We have to do a better job of making our case." There was an intensive information and media-driven quest to get the message out. Early initiatives included a factbook and daily briefings in multiple languages along with the first ever U.S. branding campaign. The U.S. also launched a new Arabic-language youth-oriented radio station (Radio Sawa) and a satellite television network (Al-Hurra).

Despite these aggressive efforts to "get the message out," the results were underwhelming. Pew (2003) polling results showed a rise in anti-American sentiment in the very same populations of the targeted campaign. Scholars and pundits criticized the approach as one-way, media-driven initiatives that

---

on associations rather than individuals, organizations, or society. ANT starts with the premise that nothing natural or man-made has any meaning outside those associations. Everyone and everything is relational, embedded within networks. This lens of connectivity starts with the premise that PD in practice is best understood through examining the associations between and among actors.

failed to connect with audiences (Snow, 2007; Wang, 2006). Calls abounded for "more listening" (Council on Foreign Relations, 2002; Cull, 2008).

Scholars began to argue for more relational approaches. Riordan (2004) called dialogue the new diplomacy. Melissen (2005) highlighted relations in his definition of PD: "Public diplomacy ... is first of all about promoting and maintaining smooth international relationships" (p. 21). Fitzpatrick (2007) argued that relationship management represented the core of PD. The relational approach that included mutuality was seen as more ethical (Fitzpatrick, 2007; L'Etang, 2009). In one of the seminal PD pieces of the time, Cowan and Arsenault (2008) suggested a three-layered vision of PD that progressed from monologue to dialogue, to collaboration. The monologue represented the one-way, information delivery, dialogue represented efforts aimed at mutual understanding, and collaboration entailed joint activities.

The lens of separateness

While the relational approach may have appeared new at the time, relational initiatives have always been a feature of PD. Cultural and educational exchanges, which are foundational to building relations, occurred in the ancient world. As Arndt (2007) noted, cultural diplomacy was the "first resort" of kings in building or mending relations.

Early PD scholarship often contrasted such relational approaches with strategic approaches focused on advocating for specific foreign policy objectives. Signitzer and Coombs (1992), for example, labeled the cultural, relational approach as "tender-minded" and distinct from the "tough-minded" purpose of information dissemination and advocacy. Post 9/11, U.S. high-profile efforts focused on information delivery – that meant, getting the message out and controlling the narrative. In terms of PD practice, the U.S. has long conducted cultural exchanges and relationship-building exercises such as the Fulbright Program. However, attention to advocacy and relational approaches tends to shift depending on geopolitical realities. As the information advocacy approach proved to yield few if any shifts in "moving the needle forward" in international public opinion about the U.S., attention returned to relational approaches.

While the contrast between advocacy-based and relationship-focused approaches is helpful, it is rather a blunt analytical tool for appreciating the nuanced nature of relations and relations-based initiatives in PD. To understand relational initiatives, we must delve a little deeper to underlying assumptions about relations with others. Different relational premises can shape PD functions and goals.

One distinctive relational premise is the assumption of separateness, which resonates strongly with Western concepts of individualism, and the idea of the bounded, separate entity (Geertz, 1983). This relational assumption of separateness is echoed in international studies and diplomacy, which view distinct, sovereign states as the foundation of the international system. The implicit assumption of separateness is found in Paul Sharp's (2009) oft-cited conception of traditional diplomacy as a response to "a common problem of living separately and wanting to do so, while having to conduct relations with others" (p. 2). PD similarly assumes that state or nonstate actors are separate from target audiences and other states.

Early definitions of PD as a tool for promoting the interests, needs, and goals of each individual actor echo this buried assumption of separateness. It is also reflected in many relational approaches focusing on building connections between actors and publics to achieve the goals of the individual actor. For example, PD serves to "help a nation establish and maintain mutually beneficial relationships with strategic foreign publics that can affect national interests" (Fitzpatrick, 2010, p. 105). Approaching entities as separate creates a hierarchy of PD functions that prioritizes creating relationships, then building and maintaining them, and finally, expanding relations or relational structures, such as networks. We look at research veins on these different functions below.

Viewing entities as separate reinforces the perspective that PD's first function is creating relationships. PD literature highlights several approaches for establishing or creating relationships. Sporting and cultural events are particularly appealing because they contain visual, physical, and emotional elements that transcend language and cultural differences (Rofe, 2018). Deos (2014), for example, explored New Zealand's use of rugby in relational PD. Ping pong was instrumental in building relationships across the political divide of the U.S. and China in the early 1970s. Other examples include basketball youth programs for Palestinian and Israeli youth (Cowan & Arsenault, 2008) as well as the Olympic Games for building bridges (Price & Dayan, 2008). Many exchange programs are also based on the idea that PD goals are served by generating connections between participants that were not there before. One of the primary goals of the U.S. Youth Ambassadors global exchange program is to "foster relationships among youth from different ethnic, religious, and national groups."

Under this lens, PD's second function is managing and sustaining positive relationships between individuals and/or among network members. Examples include cultural diplomacy outreach efforts that range from newsletters, to workshops, to websites and Twitter feeds that feature the work of prominent exchange program alumni. Scholars point toward managing relationships with diaspora publics as particularly important given the bridging role they can play with foreign publics (Bravo & Moya, 2021; Brinkerhoff, 2019; Gilboa, 2022; Rana, 2013). Twinning arrangements between towns, cities, or provinces of two countries are also examples of efforts to promote cooperation and exchanges in a variety of areas such as security, economic, and trade as well as education, technology, and tourism (van der Pluijm & Melissen, 2007). The major significance in pairing, beyond fostering cross-cultural contact and understanding, is that it serves to institutionalize the relationship-building process. During the Covid-19 pandemic when relations were strained at the state level, the personal and enduring relations of sister-cities stepped in to supply emergency medical equipment.

The lens of separateness, includes, but does not often prioritize, a third PD function – that of growing and expanding networks and person-to-person relationships. Castells, whose influential work on the evolution of a "network society" (1996), extended his vision to PD and the public sphere (2008). In a world increasingly defined by connections, Slaughter (2009, 2017), explored how actors could adopt a network approach power in the global arena. Zaharna (2005) described networks as "the new model of global persuasion," illustrating how a network communication approach creates a "soft to power differential" for PD actors (Zaharna, 2007).

Expanding relations also involved collaborating with other actors as a means of what Fisher (2013) called "increasing the odds" of achieving PD goals. However, in practice the primary verbiage and focus tends to be on building new networks initiated by state actors rather than identifying and strengthening existing networks and relationships that support PD goals. This is a critical area to explore further because academic study of "the network effect"[3] and the cavalcade of failed social network start-ups (e.g. Google Wave, Elo, Vine) have demonstrated that network formation is almost always more difficult than strengthening existing ones.

---

[3]   Defined as the phenomenon whereby the value of the network goes up with increases in the number of members who use it in terms of raw numbers or regularity of use.

Viewed through the lens of separateness, relational approaches in PD focus on creating, managing, and strengthening relationships to advance the individual goals of each individual actor. It has been the dominant PD lens, and for some, the only assumed vantage point for viewing "relational approaches." It is worth noting, however, if we look closer at these "relational initiatives," even though PD initiatives may take a "relational approach" – the result of separate individual actors, each working independently to achieve their own goals, is more competitive than relational. The highly competitive nature of relational initiatives is found in the soft power race among states as well as among non-state actors (Storie, 2017).

Despite the clarity that the lens of separateness provides for individual actors and their actions, it is glaring in the relational dimensions it overlooks. Missing are relational dynamics that may constrain actors or usurp agency. Scholars have noted the irony of how states claim to use relationship-building as a strategic PD approach, when in reality their options are often limited by existing diplomatic relations (Brown, 2013; Qin, 2018). Wiseman (2015) highlights the impact of isolation and engagement in U.S. PD aimed at countries such as Cuba or North Korea. Even network analysis studies often assume an individualistic perspective. In international relations scholarship, for example, ego-centric network analyses abound while whole-of-network studies are comparatively rare (Hafner-Burton et al., 2009). In turning to emerging research and setting a research agenda for PD, we can introduce an alternative or second relational premise, that of connectivity.

The lens of connectivity

A lens of connectivity assumes that all entities are connected to each other either directly or indirectly. This lens has become more visible with the emergence of digital technologies and the globalization of flows of finance, products, and peoples. The assumption of connectivity is an emerging relational assumption in PD scholarship found in studies of networks (Castells, 2008) and digitalization (Bjola & Holmes, 2015; Manor, 2019). Digital society assumes connectivity (Manor, 2019; Lupton, 2014).

While digital technologies and network structures may make connectivity appear as a new relational dimension, many of humanity's ancient traditions envisioned an interconnected relational universe. This assumption of connectivity is reflected in various pre-colonial diplomacies of indigenous societies. De Costa (2007) noted the contrast between "conventional (European) diplomacy that re-inscribe modernity's desire for boundaries and categorization" that "privilege[s] separation and distinctiveness rather than connection and relation" and indigenous diplomacies in places such as Australia that embrace "an expanded idea of diplomacy that acknowledges the interrelatedness and connections of all things" (p. 14).

Indeed, if we adopt a lens of connectivity, most immediately, the vision of PD expands beyond the dyadic focus on the PD actor and target public. Yang et al. (2012), for example, revealed how the focus on dyadic relations misses the relational strategies of "soft balancing" that can occur in relational constellations of polities in their study of PD among Western powers and China during the Libyan crisis. The lens of connectivity shifts the basic unit of analysis from the relational sphere of an individual actor to the holistic relational context or relational universe. Arceneaux's study of the United Nations (Chapter 3 in this volume) is illustrative of the emerging research on how larger relational contexts such as historical norms, legal regulations, trade imbalances, and international institutions shape PD.

When we adopt a lens of connectivity, we see a more expansive view of PD goals as well. The idea of individual actors trying to create relations – in an interconnected relational universe – is not a PD goal. Instead of trying to create relations, PD's relational imperatives center on identifying and defining connections, tracing indirect connections, and developing relational strategies for navigating relational complexities and strains with others and within a larger relational universe. The third function listed under the lens of separateness above, thus becomes, not a nice to have but an imperative.

When we look at "relational approaches" through the lens of connectivity, three areas in particular are becoming increasingly salient for PD: identity, emotion, and collective problem solving. We explore those emerging areas of research and PD functions below.

1.   Mediating identities

Mediating identities, as noted above, has always been a core function of individual actors in traditional diplomacy. However, unlike the lens of separateness that implicitly assumes that identity and image are an attribute of an individual actor, the lens of connectivity assumes that all identities and images are relationally co-constructed. Mediating identities under the lens of connectivity exposes the complexity of identities as a relational construct and approach in PD.

For PD, mediating identity differences can be particularly important in pro-tracted conflicts between neighboring or integrated communities. The parties may be socially or physically connected, but the nature of those relations may be strained, sometimes painfully so. Noll (2008) called identity the front line of conflicts and spotlighted the role of storytelling in co-constructing identities that can perpetuate conflicts. In conflicts, people tell stories that cast each other as perpetrators, victims, or collaborators. Over time, Noll (2008) argued these identity narratives tend to become fixed, polarized, and mutually exclusive (p. 48); if one is the "victim," they cannot be the "perpetrator."

Ogawa (2013) of the Japan Foundation provides an example of how a PD ini-tiative specifically focused on reframing identity narratives in the post-conflict Balkan region. A Japanese conductor, Toshio Yanagisawa, who survived the fighting in Kosovo, worked to bring Macedonian, Albanian, and Serbian musicians together to establish the Balkan Chamber Orchestra. For both the musicians and the audience, the sight of the ensemble playing together helped break through the rigid identity front formed during the bloody conflict.

Identity mediation can also occur informally in what has been called "every-day diplomacies" (Marsden et al., 2016), which build relations even if the participants are not aware of the diplomatic repercussions or even despite strained national relations. An illustrative example comes from Kumar and Semetko (2018), who studied media flows across the Indo–Pakistan border. Prior to the 1947 Partition of the subcontinent, people had a shared past and a shared culture of thousands of years. Whereas the flows of people and print media were easily surveilled and restricted, digital technologies created a space for a citizen-initiated dialogue and exchange (p. 615). This new space is an example of a novel site for identity mediation in PD. In mediating identities, accentuating differences can fuel the perception of mutually exclusive rela-tional identities while finding commonalities such as a shared cultural heritage raise the specter of co-existing relational identities.

2.   Managing and responding to emotions

Managing and responding to public emotions is a second critical PD function highlighted by the lens of connectivity. In contrast to states, which are theo-rized as emotionally neutered "rational actors," emotion is the glue of human relations and is a critical determinant of the PD context. In PD practice and scholarship, emotion has been largely overlooked or treated as a tool of persua-sion, rather than a powerful undercurrent shaping international relations, and by extension, diplomacy (Graham, 2014; Reus-Smit, 2014).

The ability to tap into the power of emotions to facilitate bonding is one of the reasons why PD initiatives involving the arts resonate. Tours of national symphonies, dance troops, or artworks are about sharing heritages as well as emotions (Schneider, 2009). Music, art, and dance express emotion, and are designed to elicit emotion. This is a critical area where more empirical studies that tease out the relationship between emotion, arts, and PD outcomes are needed.

We can see the role of emotion in a pioneering study by Shahin and Huang (2019). As they note, most studies assume an instrumentalist approach to see if the social media tools were "effective in self-promotion and influencing international publics" (p. 5101). The scholars take a different approach, focusing on how different bilateral relationships between countries are produced and reproduced through social – or what they call "techno-social" – practices on Twitter. Through their analysis of tweets, they were able to identify and characterize relations and approaches between other countries as "friend," "ally," or "rival" based on the emotional tenor of the tweets. They called their analysis a "techno-social performance."

The lens of connectivity highlights emotion as an underlying relational dynamic of responsive PD listening. Cull (2008, 2019) included listening as one of the five core PD elements. In traditional diplomacy, listening was key to effective information gathering. Yet, the very act of listening can build relationships. Di Martino (2020) called listening a "communication enabler" that can help create a favorable environment and enhance trust (p. 138). He outlined a spectrum of PD listening activities on social media. A failure to listen, on the other hand, may empower publics to challenge official PD narratives, as Jiménez-Martínez (2022) highlighted in his research on public protests.

Empathy takes the importance of listening in PD to the next level. We witnessed a powerful example of empathetic PD during the Covid-19 pandemic. Queen Elizabeth's televised speech to the Commonwealth resonated with audiences around the world. Recognizing that people were fearful and uncertain of what lay ahead and had already lost loved ones, she opened her brief speech with empathy, acknowledging the "challenging time for all," and the grief and pain of separation in quarantine, which was new to the public. She ended with reassurance of physically reuniting: "we will be with our friends again; we will be with our families again; we will meet again."

Emotions help to distinguish loose-tie networks from communities. However, whereas networks are a buzz word in PD, the idea of communities, as La Porte (2012) argued, has been overlooked. Manor brought attention to the significance of community to the digital diplomacy, citing the work of Bauman and Lyon (2012) and their assertion that "a network is not a community" and emotional connections are a primary reason why. Unlike loose-tie networks that often tend to be goal-oriented and temporary, Bauman and Lyon characterize communities as more permanent with members developing emotional connections: "Over time, people develop a 'sense of community' in that the community becomes an important part of their daily lives and their identity" (Bauman & Lyon, 2012, p. 39, cited in Manor, 2019, p. 45).

3.   Problem solving

The lens of connectivity exposes a third PD functional imperative, that of collective problem solving. The growing frequency and severity of wicked problems have highlighted the need for PD to expand its focus beyond the goals of individual states to those that address the needs, interests, and goals of the global public. Constantinou (2006) suggests a focus on "human diplomacy." Castells (2008) recast PD as "the diplomacy of the public" that should promote the value of public interests over private ones. Zhang and Swartz (2009) suggested the idea of "public diplomacy for Global Public Goods (GPG)," while Fitzpatrick (2017) proposed an ethical focus on "public diplomacy in the public interest." Anholt (2020) underscored the moral imperative that countries have in what he called "the Good Country" equation. Zaharna (2019, 2022) spoke of "humanity-centered public diplomacy," that focuses on the collaborative PD processes.

We see within this research vein, studies that explore how different actors, particularly nonstate actors, first create and then respond to a global vision of problem solving. Iriye (2002), for example, observed that below the drama of the state actors on the world stage, there has be a steady growth of international organizations working to collectively problem solve (p. 2). We have seen this recently in the Global Democracy Forum in December 2021, the 26th UN Climate Change Conference of the Parties (COP26) in Glasgow in October and November 2021, and the planned Summit for the Americas in June 2022. Golan, Arceneaux, and Soule (2019) in their study of Pope Francis showed how individual actors have expanded their traditional state focus to a more "universal" vision. Beyond using phrases such as "we," "us," or "working together," a textual analysis of the Pope's speeches revealed three interwoven themes: "universal identity, shared responsibility, and a global call for action that would benefit all humankind" (p. 108).

The relational dynamics of problem solving appear qualitatively different when viewed through the lens of connectivity. The evolving research on "city diplomacy" is illustrative. As we saw above, traditional city diplomacy focused on individual cities creating exchange-based relationships with specific partners to meet their mutual needs. A new generation of city diplomacy research and practice is qualitatively different, according to Amiri and Sevin (2020). Attention has shifted from individual cities and officials to city networks and "issue-specific networks," such as Energy Cities, "that facilitate interaction, distill, reformulate, or reinvent policy action" (pp. 16–17). These city networks create a relational bridge between the local and the global.

Another unlikely research vein for global problem solving is play and interactive gaming. As game designers will tell you, games are about getting people to constructively engage with challenges, feedback, uncertainty, and problem solving to play the game (De Koven, 2013). During the pandemic, online interactive gaming increased exponentially. In late March 2020, leaders from the interactive gaming industry launched #PlayApartTogether campaign with special events and rewards to help spread the World Health Organization guidelines on social distancing, hygiene, respiratory etiquette, and other preventative actions. As one gaming scholar remarked, "COVID-19 may be the turning point when the world realizes playing video games is potentially a form of empowerment that brings people together to solve real world problems" (Phelps, 2020).

Conclusion

This chapter introduced two distinctive lenses for looking at "relational approaches" in PD. The "lens of separateness" assumes actors are separate from other actors and publics. Actors view relations as a choice and adopt a "relational approach" to create, maintain, or expand PD relations. A second "lens of connectivity" assumes that all PD elements – actors, issues, goals, and publics – are inherently interconnected. "Relational approaches" focus on identifying the nature of those interconnections and developing strategies for navigating relational dynamics.

Because relations are a given rather than a choice, critical questions of emotion and identity that shape relational bonds and community become salient. How can PD move beyond repairing national images to mediating contested or fragmented identities that disrupt relations? How can PD respond to powerful tides of public emotions that can challenge relations? Given the need for global problem solving, how can PD mediate relational strains in unwelcomed partnerships or facilitate collaboration in necessary alliances? More empirical field-based studies are needed to explore the pivotal role of emotion, identity, and collective problem solving to develop a constellation of innovative PD program models. If the lens of separation has been a familiar lens for PD researchers in the past, the lens of connectivity represents the future of PD research.

References

Amiri, S., & Sevin, E. (Eds.) (2020). *City diplomacy: Current trends and future prospects.* Palgrave Macmillan.

Anholt, S. (2020). *The good country equation: How we can repair the world in one generation.* Berrett-Koehler.

Arndt, R. T. (2007). *The first resort of kings: American cultural diplomacy in the twentieth century* (new edn). Potomac Books.

Bauman, Z., & Lyon, D. (2012). *Liquid surveillance: A conversation.* Polity.

Bjola, C., & Holmes, M. (2015). *Digital diplomacy: Theory and practice.* Routledge.

Bravo, V., & Moya, M. D. (2021). *Latin American diasporas in public diplomacy.* Springer Nature.

Brinkerhoff, J. M. (2019). Diasporas and public diplomacy: Distinctions and future prospects. *The Hague Journal of Diplomacy, 14*(1–2), 51–64. https://doi.org/10.1163/1871191X-14101015.

Brown, R. (2013). The politics of relational public diplomacy. In R. S. Zaharna, A. Arsenault, & A. Fisher (Eds.), *Relational, network and collaborative approaches to public diplomacy* (pp. 44–55). Routledge.

Castells, M. (1996). *The rise of the network society.* Blackwell.

Castells, M. (2008). The new public sphere: Global civil society, communication networks, and global governance. *The Annals of the American Academy of Political and Social Science, 616*(1), 78–93.

Constantinou, C. M. (2006). *Human diplomacy and spirituality.* Netherlands Institute of International Relations Clingendael, 21.

Council on Foreign Relations (2002, July 30). *Public diplomacy: A strategy for reform.* http://www.cfr.org/diplomacy-and-statecraft/public-diplomacy-strategy-reform/p4697.

Cowan, G., & Arsenault, A. (2008). Moving from monologue to dialogue to collaboration: The three layers of public diplomacy. *The Annals of the American Academy of Political and Social Science, 616*(1), 10–30.

Cull, N. J. (2008). Public diplomacy: Taxonomies and histories. *The Annals of the American Academy of Political and Social Science, 616*(1), 31–54.

Cull, N. J. (2019). *Public diplomacy: Foundations for global engagement in the digital age.* Polity.

de Costa, R. (2007). Indigenous diplomacies before the nation-state. *Canadian Foreign Policy Journal, 13*(3), 13–28.

De Koven, B. (2013). *The well-played game: A player's philosophy* (illustrated edn). MIT Press.

Deos, A. (2014). Sport and relational public diplomacy: The case of New Zealand and Rugby World Cup 2011. *Sport in Society, 17*(9), 1170–86.

Di Martino, L. (2020). Conceptualizing public diplomacy listening on social media. *Place Branding and Public Diplomacy, 16*(2), 131–42. https://doi.org/10.1057/s41254-019-00135-5.

Fisher, A. (2013). *Collaborative public diplomacy: How transnational networks influenced American studies in Europe.* Palgrave Macmillan.

Fitzpatrick, K. R. (2007). Advancing the new public diplomacy: A public relations perspective. *The Hague Journal of Diplomacy, 2*(3), 187–211. https://doi.org/10.1163/187119007X240497.

Fitzpatrick, K. R. (2010). *The future of US public diplomacy: An uncertain fate.* Brill/Nijhoff.

Fitzpatrick, K. R. (2017). Public diplomacy in the public interest. *Journal of Public Interest Communication, 1*(1), 78–93. https://doi.org/10.32473/jpic.v1.i1.p78.

Geertz, C. (1983). *Local knowledge: Further essays in interpretive anthropology.* Basic Books.

Gilboa, E. (2022). Theorizing diaspora diplomacy. In L. Kennedy (Ed.), *The Routledge international handbook of diaspora diplomacy* (pp. 379–92). Routledge.

Golan, G. J., Arceneaux, P. C., & Soule, M. (2019). The Catholic Church as a public diplomacy actor: An analysis of the Pope's strategic narrative and international engagement. *The Journal of International Communication, 25*(1), 95–115. https://doi.org/10.1080/13216597.2018.1517657.

Graham, S. E. (2014). Emotion and public diplomacy: Dispositions in international communications, dialogue, and persuasion. *International Studies Review, 16*(4), 522–39.

Hafner-Burton, E. M., Kahler, M., & Montgomery, A. H. (2009). Network analysis for international relations. *International Organization, 63*(3), 559–92.

Iriye, A. (2002). *Global community: The role of international organizations in the making of the contemporary world.* University of California Press.

Jiménez-Martínez, C. (2022). The public as a problem: Protest, public diplomacy and the pandemic. *Place Branding and Public Diplomacy, 18*, 33–6. https://doi.org/10.1057/s41254-021-00235-1.

Kumar, A., & Semetko, H. A. (2018). Peace communication in cross-border media flows. *Journal of Communication, 68*(3), 612–35. https://doi.org/10.1093/joc/jqy018.

La Porte, T. (2012). The impact of "intermestic" non-state actors on the conceptual framework of public diplomacy. *The Hague Journal of Diplomacy, 7*(4), 441–58.

L'Etang, J. (2009). Public relations and diplomacy in a globalized world: An issue of public communication. *American Behavioral Scientist, 53*(4), 607–26. https://doi.org/10.1177/0002764209347633.

Lupton, D. (2014). A critical sociology of big data. In D. Lupton (Ed.), *Digital sociology* (pp. 93–116). Routledge.

Manor, I. (2019). *The digitalization of public diplomacy.* Palgrave Macmillan.

Marsden, M., Ibañez-Tirado, D., & Henig, D. (2016). Everyday diplomacy. *The Cambridge Journal of Anthropology, 34*(2), 2–22. https://doi.org/10.3167/ca.2016.340202.

Melissen, J. (2005). The new public diplomacy: Between theory and practice. In J. Melissen (Ed.), *The new public diplomacy: Soft power in international relations* (pp. 3–27). Palgrave Macmillan.

Noll, C. (2008). Narratives: The front line of identity conflicts. *InterCulture, 5*(1), 43–52.

Ogawa, T. (2013). New frontiers in relational public diplomacy: Collaborative cultural initiatives in peace building. In R. S. Zaharna, A. Arsenault, & A. Fisher (Eds.),

Relational, network, and collaborative approaches in public diplomacy (pp. 117–31). Routledge.

Pew (2003, December 10). Anti-Americanism: Causes and characteristics. https://www.pewresearch.org/global/2003/12/10/anti-americanism-causes-and-characteristics/.

Phelps, A. M. (2020, April 13). Gaming fosters social connection at a time of physical distance. *The Conversation.* http://theconversation.com/gaming-fosters-social-connection-at-a-time-of-physical-distance-135809.

Price, M., & Dayan, D. (2008). *Owning the Olympics: Narratives of the new China.* University of Michigan Press.

Qin, Y. (2018). *A relational theory of world politics.* Cambridge University Press.

Rana, K. (2013). Diaspora diplomacy and public diplomacy. In R. S. Zaharna, A. Arsenault, & A. Fisher (Eds.), *Relational, networked and collaborative approaches to public diplomacy* (pp. 70–85). Routledge.

Reus-Smit, C. (2014). Emotions and the social. *International Theory, 6*(3), 568–74.

Riordan, S. (2004). *Dialogue-based public diplomacy: A new foreign policy paradigm?* Netherlands Institute of International Relations Clingendael. https://www.clingendael.org/sites/default/files/2016-02/20041100_cli_paper_dip_issue95.pdf.

Rofe, S. (2018). *Sports and diplomacy: Games within games.* Manchester University Press.

Schneider, C. P. (2009). The unrealized potential of cultural diplomacy: "Best practices" and what could be, if only … *The Journal of Arts Management, Law, and Society, 39*(4), 260–79.

Shahin, S., & Huang, Q. E. (2019). Friend, ally, or rival? Twitter diplomacy as "technosocial" performance of national identity. *International Journal of Communication, 13,* 5100–5118.

Sharp, P. (2009). *Diplomatic theory of international relations.* Cambridge University Press.

Signitzer, B. H., & Coombs, T. (1992). Public relations and public diplomacy: Conceptual convergences. *Public Relations Review, 18*(2), 137–47. https://doi.org/10.1016/0363-8111(92)90005-J.

Slaughter, A. M. (2009). America's edge. *Foreign Affairs, 88*(1), 94–113.

Slaughter, A. M. (2017). *The Chessboard and the Web: Strategies of connection in a networked world.* Yale University Press.

Snow, N. (2007). *The arrogance of American power: What US leaders are doing wrong and why it's our duty to dissent.* Rowman & Littlefield.

Storie, L. K. (2017). Relationship cultivation in public diplomacy: A qualitative study of relational antecedents and cultivation strategies. *Journal of Public Relations Research, 29*(6), 295–310. https://doi.org/10.1080/1062726X.2018.1437443.

van der Pluijm, R., & Melissen, J. (2007). *City diplomacy: The expanding role of cities in international politics.* Netherlands Institute of International Relations Clingendael.

Wang, J. (2006). Managing national reputation and international relations in the global era: Public diplomacy revisited. *Public Relations Review, 32*(2), 91–6. https://doi.org/10.1016/j.pubrev.2005.12.001.

Wiseman, G. (Ed.) (2015). *Isolate or engage: Adversarial states, US foreign policy, and public diplomacy.* Stanford University Press.

Yang, A., Klyueva, A., & Taylor, M. (2012). Beyond a dyadic approach to public diplomacy: Understanding relationships in multipolar world. *Public Relations Review, 38*(5), 652–64.

Zaharna, R. S. (2005). The network paradigm of strategic public diplomacy. *Foreign Policy in Focus, 10*(1), 1–2.

Zaharna, R. S. (2007). The soft power differential: Network communication and mass communication in public diplomacy. *The Hague Journal of Diplomacy, 2*(3), 213–28.

Zaharna, R. S. (2019). Culture, cultural diversity and humanity-centred diplomacies. *The Hague Journal of Diplomacy, 14*(1–2), 117–33. https:// doi .org/ 10 .1163/ 1871191X-14101018.

Zaharna, R. S. (2022). *Boundary spanners of humanity: Three logic of communications and public diplomacy for global collaboration.* Oxford University Press.

Zhang, J., & Swartz, B. C. (2009). Public diplomacy to promote Global Public Goods (GPG): Conceptual expansion, ethical grounds, and rhetoric. *Public Relations Review, 35*(4), 382–7. https://doi:10.1016/j.pubrev.2009.08.001.

11 Disinformation

Alicia Fjällhed and James Pamment

Introduction

Disinformation is of central interest to public diplomacy (PD). As a PD practitioner, how do you get your messages across if they are manipulated as soon as they get picked up by social media discussions? What if the information environment of your host country is so contested that factual communication is dismissed? How do you build trust and credibility with audiences who get their news from unreliable sources? How should PD practitioners engage with countries where the government itself is a major purveyor of disinformation?

At different points in time, discussions on these challenging topics have been captured under various labels—traditionally propaganda, then more recently replaced by disinformation and buzzwords such as fake news and alternative facts (Bennett & Livingston, 2018). The re-awakening discussion on false and misleading information in public communication has led to a spike in scholarly interest. A literature review of all English-language journal articles on disinformation recorded in the Web of Science (WoS, previously known as Web of Knowledge) reveals an exponential transdisciplinary interest in the topic. Only about 10 items per year were published between 1980 and 2015, and they jumped to over 500 in 2021. A total of 1,159 journal articles were published up to the end of 2021 with "disinformation" either in the title, abstract, or among the keywords. Most were published in the last two years.

As may be expected, these modern-day discussions about disinformation have entered PD debates. Both PD scholars (i.e. Cull, 2016; Pamment, 2016) and practitioners of PD (i.e. The U.S. Advisory Commission on Public Diplomacy, 2017) spotted the importance of these emerging trends in the field. Since then, the topic has expanded into a wider discussion within the academic and professional community on how disinformation has affected PD, how strategic counteractivities can cope with it, and to what extent PD practices seeking to build trust, inform, and engage publics in political dialogue could be part of the answer to how society at large could address the challenge. While the importance of disinformation to PD is now well established, we argue that the

PD field still needs to adapt in order to more fully integrate some of the principles emerging from this modern take on propaganda. Building on historical conceptions of propaganda in PD, we argue that the new hybrid media system alongside the rising politicized landscape and deteriorating global security situation present a new context which necessitates a revised understanding of disinformation in its current form.

This chapter argues that disinformation comes with a set of needs as well as opportunities for future PD research. On the one hand, there is a continuous need for empirical studies which follow the development of PD actors' and specialized PD institutions' encounters with disinformation, presenting insights on how to build their resilience and strategic countermeasures. This can be seen for example in terms of embassies' continuous development of personal competences and technical tools to identify and counter disinformation about one's nation abroad (Fjällhed, 2021; Manor, 2019). In addition, the disinformation angle opens new perspectives for pre-existing discussions among the academic community of PD, such as the methodological and theoretical development of the field. For example, disinformation is commonly labeled as unethical practices associated with foreign interference and described as non-compliant with the normative ideals of PD. Thus, it provides a possible gateway for theoretical discussions about what constitutes PD by discussing what it is not.

The challenge for PD research, this chapter argues, is related to disinformation's development in tandem with the equally rapid and continuous development of our political, security, and communication landscape. This necessitates a future research agenda for PD that is designed to evolve in parallel with such volatile empirical phenomena and is able to deliver cutting-edge insights to practitioners of PD before they become outdated. We suggest that research in PD addresses this challenge through continuous dialogue with the transdisciplinary frontier of current academia.

This means learning and integrating knowledge from computer science's technological understanding of disinformation's expression in the algorithmically governed communication landscape, from psychological studies on how people process information and from sociological studies for an understanding of cultural differences. The idea is also to deep dive into philosophical concepts that help make sense of the terminological apparatus formed around different forms of disinformation practices. In doing so, this chapter will argue that PD as a field needs a strategic research agenda which leverages the vast transdisciplinary interest and resources. At the same time, PD-specific studies have unique perspectives that could and must contribute to other researchers investigating the phenomenon.

In sketching a research agenda for disinformation in PD, the chapter starts by situating disinformation in the context of PD in relation to concepts used to frame it theoretically and empirically, especially in communications. Then, we review studies on disinformation within PD and identify a few emerging parallel tracks. The chapter demonstrates how a transdisciplinary perspective could further the research agenda in the future and highlights the need for continuous dialogue with practitioners. This action is needed to ensure an empirically grounded understanding of the phenomenon in relation to PD, and identify new relevant tracks for future research on disinformation within the field. The chapter ends by prescribing how these tracks should be coordinated to chart out a research agenda for disinformation studies in PD with a transdisciplinary edge and how these studies may fit into the wider perspective of building a research agenda for PD.

Disinformation in public diplomacy research

Traditionally, in the PD literature, unethical communication has been tied to concepts of propaganda. The reoccurring historical description starts with the Catholic Church and its *Congregatio de Propaganda Fide* where propaganda was introduced as an ethically neutral, if not positive, concept of communicating truth to the masses. Since then, some scholars have continued to argue that propaganda should be considered a neutral concept designating practices of "the *deliberate* attempt to persuade people to think and behave *in a desired way*" (Taylor, 2003, p. 6). However, as propaganda became associated with practices of modern warfare, in the public eye it has been associated with unethical forms of persuasion.

Insofar as it is unambiguously pejorative, disinformation is a useful demarcation of a relatively narrow technique within propaganda. There is near conceptual consensus on disinformation as (a) false or misleading communication (b) intentionally communicated to deceive audiences. Studies in PD typically define disinformation as "purposefully disseminating inaccurate or untruthful information with an intent to deceive" (Potter, 2019, p. 409). This is contrasted conceptually with "misinformation" which is also false but believed to be true by the communicator and hence is not intentionally communicated to mislead (Fetzer, 2004; Floridi, 2011). Conceptual consensus on both these two terms is not only seen among scholars of PD but also as an established part of the professional terminology used internationally, also by policymakers. Disinformation is therefore intimately connected to a notion of unethical or illegitimate communication. Thus, while this chapter analyzes disinformation, it applies somewhat flexible terminological boundaries when outlining the scope of this aspect of propaganda as it relates to PD.

Discussions of disinformation in PD are not only tied to certain concepts, but also to the context in which it appears. While propaganda is often associated with PD in the context of conflict,[1] this chapter focuses on disinformation in a broader sense—tying it to a landscape where "Western liberal democracies are struggling to support a robust public sphere in the face of political polarisation, media 'echo chambers,' allegations of 'fake news' and contentions that we live in a 'post-truth' world" (Potter, 2019, p. 412). This echoes Cull's (2019, p. 21) argument that "a global crisis exists today, driven by a toxic mix of populist politics and disruptive social media." A review of recent PD literature reveals much emphasis on Russia's use of disinformation in the aftermath of the annexation of Crimea in 2014.

It also appeared in subsequent discussions of hybrid warfare, which includes subversive activities outside of traditional military force and is likely to continue in relation to the 2022 Russian invasion of Ukraine (Elswah & Howard, 2020; Erlich & Garner, 2021; Hedling, 2021; Potter, 2019; Stoycheff & Nisbet, 2017). Studies also cover PD actors' attempts to counter disinformation depicting how this challenge has re-structured PD practices, including at the level of EU institutions (Hedling, 2021).

In this context, scholars have theorized that the Western system for ideal public conversation (in relation to which PD has traditionally conceptualized its practices), disinformation actors target vulnerabilities within the process of information dissemination (Nothhaft et al., 2018). It is possible to identify a wide range of tactics used by disinformation producers spanning from false statements to kinetic movements and deceptive signaling, the use of manipulated text, video, or pictures, and the utilization of technical tools enabling covert actions and manipulation of the public conversation, alongside subtle ways of engaging deceptive cognitive and social influence. Nothhaft et al. (2018, p. 32) present tactics such as various forms of hacking (technical as well as cognitive), the use of amplification tools like bots and fake accounts, messaging strategies

---

[1] This constitutes a focus in PD research which deserves analysis beyond this chapter. In this chapter, disinformation and counter-disinformation as topics for PD in international conflicts will not be included. For a few relevant points, see Van Ham (2003), Zaharna (2010), and Arif et al. (2014).

including the use of memes and malign rhetoric, and information distortion through Potemkin villages or tainted leaks. Such techniques can be combined into strategic information influence operations and information influence campaigns aimed at producing desired outcomes or effects.

Against this background, PD research has either treated disinformation as a form of illegitimate or outlaw PD practiced by, for example, terrorist organizations (Melki & Jabado, 2016) and separatist groups (Endong, 2021) or as part of state-sponsored disinformation campaigns (Nisbet & Kamenchuk, 2019), while others focus on how PD can be used to counter disinformation (Fjällhed, 2021; Vériter et al., 2020).

The discussion of disinformation in the PD literature has also produced new concepts such as sharp power. While soft power was described in relation to hard and smart power (Nye, 2009), the idea of sharp power has been used to describe modern-day unethical PD activities (Nye, 2018, 2019; Walker, 2018). While not yet a mature scholarly concept, it is nonetheless used and often tied to the abuse of soft power—often taking Russia and China as examples—where authors describe how such actors spread false information in liberal democracies, mostly via digital media (Potter, 2019).

PD scholars have also used the disinformation debate to venture ethical reflections about the nature of PD. To take a few examples, la Cour (2020) points to Nye's argument that "propaganda and public diplomacy share a common objective" (p. 717) while adding that "good public diplomacy has to go beyond propaganda" (Nye, 2008, p. 101). Similarly, Chernobrov and Briant (2022) recognize propaganda as a politicized term which covers "mutual accusations of digital interference, disinformation, fake news, and propaganda" (p. 1)—thus showing that such labels are based on political convictions, not on technical evaluation of tactics. Taking U.S. and Russia as empirical examples, the authors illustrate how the two states "represent each other's and their own propaganda." In similar ways, propaganda would be the label powers attribute to other sides which "contribute to popular suspicion on both sides, limiting opportunities for restoring dialogue" (p. 12).

Windows of opportunity

This growing body of research on disinformation within PD presents a window of opportunity for empirical and theoretical investigations which will advance the research agenda for disinformation, but also open new horizons in the theoretical, methodological, and empirical advances in PD. An important key for such advancement lies in leveraging disinformation as a subject of interest beyond PD. A search on the WoS shows 1,159 journal articles published before 2022 that mention "disinformation" in the title, abstract, or among keywords. The top five most common academic disciplines for these publications were communication (31 percent), government law (14 percent), computer science (10 percent), information and library science (9 percent), and international relations (6 percent).

It is possible to chart parallel tracks for future advancement by adding trans-disciplinary aspects to existing PD insights on disinformation. A first track is to develop a research agenda on disinformation that will open new theoretical approaches to PD. Several scholars have long emphasized two-way communication and the strive for dialogue with the public in PD, specifically in relation to the practice of listening (Zaharna, 2008; Zaharna et al., 2014). This has been further stressed in the discussion of disinformation. For example, Cull (2019) argued that PD needs to return to its roots as "for public diplomacy to respond, it must remain true to its core principles" and "begin by listening" (p. 21).

At the same time, the critical debate around cases such as Cambridge Analytica and Bell Pottinger's strategic use of listening to develop psychological profiles of target groups led to critical analysis on what listening could mean in a broader sense—as spanning from tools enabling two-way communication to unethical surveillance and spying (Di Martino, 2020). la Cour (2020) adds to that perspective by acknowledging that while Nye and others emphasize two-way communication for PD activities, "it does not seem too far-fetched to argue that clever disinformation campaigns include an attempt to 'listen' to foreign publics to understand which weaknesses to exploit" (p. 718).

Similarly, discussions go beyond what tools should be used to explore how one should communicate. Duncombe (2019) attributed the effectiveness of digital disinformation to its strategic use of emotions and that "the power of social media in public diplomacy is the role of emotion in digital diplomacy strategies" (p. 115). Just as disinformation practices have widened discussions about listening, we see similarly how a dual perspective on disinformation and PD can give rise to questions on the ethical role of emotions in advocacy.

The examples of listening and emotions demonstrate how a closer review of disinformation practices starts to challenge careless statements about propaganda or foreign interference as unethical without placing clearer borders on what differentiates these cases from PD. In deconstructing such values, the field has much to gain by drawing upon the concepts developed in other fields to separate ethical from unethical practices. Other relevant fields include philosophy of information, which draws the conceptual lines between information, misinformation, and disinformation; and moral philosophy which can help to draw clearer lines around the ethics of PD, possibly tying it to PD-specific communicative practices.

A second track is to develop empirical knowledge of disinformation in PD. Beyond keeping up with how disinformation manifests itself in the communication landscape, this track would also be centered around the effects and possible ways to counter disinformation. Scholars have sought to understand what factors affect the public's ability to distinguish information from disinformation, showing how the topic and audiences may affect the certainty and accuracy of peoples' evaluations (Erlich & Garner, 2021). Such studies also contribute to our knowledge of the nature of publics in the contemporary landscape and how these publics process information in general. This, of course, could not only be beneficial for building effective counterstrategies but also for other types of PD campaigns.

To further this research agenda, the broader transdisciplinary pool of knowledge contains a vast number of studies on people's ability to spot false statements (Allcott et al., 2019; Pennycook & Rand, 2020), or on the effect of factors such as media literacy (Jones-Jang et al., 2021). Such studies also include explorations of social media platform algorithms and online content, including how practitioners may use computational competences to set up systems using a linguistic or network analysis (Schmidt & Wiegand, 2020) to detect false statements (Oshikawa et al., 2020), or fake accounts and bot networks (Kudugunta & Ferrara, 2018). This could also be used as a platform to develop PD-specific technical tools to identify disinformation, hate speech, and other forms of unethical communication on social media. From this empirical interest, we can move from understanding how disinformation manifests in the communication landscape to how it affects publics on a cognitive level. Studies on disinformation within PD and beyond have thus also been built on social psychology and its treatments of cognitive biases. Caputo (2013), Wattanacharoensil and La-ornual (2019), and Hirshberg (1993) published several studies on various cases of cognitive biases.

Simiarily, Nisbet and Kamenchuk (2019) argue that the prior emphasis on how technology enables disinformation has led to a disregard for the "underlying human factors driving the success of state-sponsored disinformation campaigns" and a need to understand the "human factors at play" (p. 65). By reviewing state-sponsored disinformation campaigns in relation to cognitive biases, the authors explore "the implications for designing public diplomacy efforts to counter their influence" (p. 66) and "how to design corrective messaging, technology and other public diplomacy efforts" (p. 67). They conclude that a future research agenda should include "investment in more theory-driven formative and summative evaluation research that draws upon the available social-psychological and communication scholarship on misinformation and false beliefs and applies it to public diplomacy contexts" (p. 81). Such explorations could result in hands-on tools for PD practitioners to understand why false narratives spread and how to best provide an effective counter-response (Cook & Lewandowsky, 2020).

Translating transdisciplinary knowledge into public diplomacy contexts

In parallel to the above research strategy of drawing upon the transdisciplinary pool of knowledge on disinformation, there is a need to translate this knowledge into PD-specific contexts. This requires continuous engagement with PD practitioners to understand their experiences of disinformation—spanning from which concepts they use, how they are related to pre-existing PD-concepts, what forms of disinformation they observe and how they assess such cases, how they build structures and competences designed to manage the issue, what counterstrategies they choose to engage in and on what grounds they make all those decisions.

In addition to previously presented empirical studies by academics, we have also seen how practitioners themselves engage in the analysis of disinformation—resulting in valuable resources for scholars to build our understanding of its empirical expression, and as a basis to form future studies on disinformation. As a phenomenon that urgently needs to be understood and managed by PD practitioners, some have initiated projects valuable to PD researchers, in which scholars are often invited as contributors. Through such collaboration, theoretical and professional insights develop in tandem. This chapter argues that such strategically formed research agendas hold value for both parties—with scholars gaining an understanding of the phenomenon's contemporary empirical manifestations and impact on PD, and practitioners being allowed direct access to the aggregated theoretical understanding and best practices identified by scholars through these projects.

First, there is a set of publications by PD actors on disinformation that can be used by researchers to either form an overall understanding of the practical challenges or to be used as empirical material for an analysis of practitioners' ideas of the past, present, and likely future relation between disinformation and PD. This manifests as individual reflections by PD professionals through longer blog posts (such as those published on the Center on Public Diplomacy's website) or shorter entries on social media (right now primarily on Twitter). PD organizations have also engaged in projects to develop their own organizations' knowledge and structures to address the issue, making their findings publicly available online.

Early examples include the U.S. Advisory Commission on Public Diplomacy gathering experts to a workshop as part of their mandate "to help State Department prepare for cutting edge and transformative changes, which have the potential to upend how we think about engaging with foreign publics" (2017). Another example is the report "Information Manipulation: A Challenge for Our Democracies" published by the Policy Planning Staff within the French Ministry for Europe and Foreign Affairs together with the Institute for Strategic Research of the Ministry of the Armed Forces. This report was in direct response to "the repeated interference that has occurred since 2014" and "the attempted interference in the 2017 French presidential election" (Vilmer et al., 2018, p. 7).

The report by Vilmer et al. (2018) described how a joint working group was initially created to explore the possibility of creating an inter-agency task force to combat information manipulation. Through a series of visits to 20 countries and interviews with about 100 national authorities and representatives from civil society in addition to interviews with their own national authorities in France, the result was published as a 200-page report publicly available online—another example of valuable resources available for scholars in PD to gain insights of practitioners about strategic reasoning in relation to disinformation.

Among other valuable insights, the report by Vilmer et al. (2018) shares this chapter's view of "the inherently interdisciplinary nature of information manipulation" described as situated "at the crossroads between international relations, war studies, intelligence studies, media studies, sociology and social psychology" (p. 8) which means that the subject concerns several different administrations. Reports like these point to another important empirical reality in PD professionals' management of disinformation—the need to overcome stovepipes, whether institutional or intellectual.

In addition to these publications issued by PD practitioners and organizations, the sudden need to raise organizational awareness, competence, and capabilities to address disinformation has also led to a series of collaborations among

PD researchers. For example, PD scholars based at Lund University in Sweden helped develop national counter-disinformation guidelines in collaboration with the Swedish, U.K., and Finnish governments, as well as with EU institutions. Knowledge sharing and exchanges typically take place in commissioned projects where the scholars' expertise is directly combined with practitioners in an area where building capabilities is urgent. Training, tabletop exercises, interviews, and participatory observation allow for collaborative development of both policy and operations, drawing on a variety of skill sets. For example, since foreign interference involves diplomats working on security policy, a background in PD can be surprisingly relevant to questions ranging from how communications staff counter disinformation on social media to harder questions of deterrence, attribution, and sanctions.

A related example of collaboration is where PD scholars knowledgeable in disinformation have been invited to organize policy discussions and similar events. In this setting, academic insights into the structure of the current scientific knowledge enable academics to suggest lists of relevant invitees, prepare material on the "state of the art" as grounds for the discussions, moderate the conversation, and draft reports and recommendations emerging from the discussions. In other cases, the competence of PD scholars lies rather in their experience as teachers. Besides offering lectures and training, scholars have been commissioned for developing exercises in which PD actors practice cases of managing disinformation in real time. Here, the experience of preparing teaching material, planning activities, and evaluating performance enables practitioners to directly benefit from skills based at the university.

And while commissioned to contribute to practitioners' understanding and capabilities in managing disinformation, these collaborations give valuable empirical insights for the engaged PD scholars on these actors' first-hand experiences of disinformation, as well as their reflections. This suggests that PD's closeness to the practice can be an advantage in fast-moving policy challenges such as disinformation, but also for researchers to stay tuned with the current challenges facing practitioners in one's own time and within their own virtual and geographical area.

Conclusion

This chapter has argued for a future research agenda on disinformation in PD that focuses on three parallel tracks. First, there is a need to expand knowledge in tandem with the phenomenon's empirical manifestations and continuous transformation. This entails both the development of a practical terminology which could help understand the kinship between related phenomena, as well as producing insights that act as supportive tools for PD actors in their efforts to understand, identify, and counter such phenomena successfully. Second, disinformation opens a new horizon for scholarly reflection on and possibly finding new solutions to wicked problems within the research field. Research on disinformation could help better determine the scope of the PD field, as well as its normative and ethical boundaries.

Third, research would benefit from looking beyond disciplinary stovepipes—leveraging mature concepts from philosophy, for example, or applying insights from computer science for spotting malicious activity online and using findings from social psychology to understand the public appeal of disinformation and how to approach publics effectively. Developed in tandem, these tracks would form a strategic research agenda addressing the inherent challenges embedded in the empirical phenomenon while leveraging the opportunities to translating the transdisciplinary frontier in relation to PD practitioners' experiences.

In conclusion, the chapter argues that future studies on disinformation in PD hold a continuous challenge in following its empirical manifestation in the communication landscape. However, they also create new options and vehicles for advancing PD's tactics designed to monitor the media landscape, understand one's publics, and engage in strategic communication. The research agenda on disinformation within PD should be seen as part of a broader enterprise, in which studies on disinformation can make a broader contribution to PD as one of many parallel advancements in its collective future scholarship.[2]

References

Allcott, H., Gentzkow, M., & Yu, C. (2019). Trends in the diffusion of misinformation on social media. *Research & Politics*, 6(2), 1–8. https:// doi .org/ 10 .1177/ 2053168019848554.

Arif, R., Golan, G. J., & Moritz, B. (2014). Mediated public diplomacy: US and Taliban relations with Pakistani media. *Media, War & Conflict*, 7(2), 201–17.

Bennett, W. L., & Livingston, S. (2018). The disinformation order: Disruptive communication and the decline of democratic institutions. *European Journal of Communication*, 33(2), 122–39.

---

[2]   The authors thank the Marianne and Marcus Wallenberg Foundation for funding the research used for this chapter.

Caputo, A. (2013). A literature review of cognitive biases in negotiation processes. *International Journal of Conflict Management, 24*(4), 374–98.

Chernobrov, D., & Briant, E. (2020). Competing propagandas: How the US and Russia represent mutual propaganda activities. *Politics, 42*(3), 1–17.

Cook, J., & Lewandowsky, S. (2020). *The debunking handbook*. Retrieved from https://www.climatechangecommunication.org/debunking-handbook-2020/.

Cull, N. (2016). Engaging foreign publics in the age of Trump and Putin: Three implications of 2016 for public diplomacy. *Place Branding and Public Diplomacy, 12*(4), 243–6.

Cull, N. J. (2019). The tightrope to tomorrow: Reputational security, collective vision and the future of public diplomacy. *The Hague Journal of Diplomacy, 14*(1–2), 21–35.

Di Martino, L. (2020). Conceptualising public diplomacy listening on social media. *Place Branding and Public Diplomacy, 16*(2), 131–42. https://doi.org/10.1057/s41254-019-00135-5.

Duncombe, C. (2019). Digital diplomacy: Emotion and identity in the public realm. *The Hague Journal of Diplomacy, 14*(1–2), 102–16. https://doi.org/10.1163/1871191X-14101016.

Elswah, M., & Howard, P. N. (2020). Anything that causes chaos: The organizational behavior of Russia Today (RT). *Journal of Communication, 70*(5), 623–45.

Endong, F. P. C. (2021). The "dark side" of African digital diplomacy: The response of Cameroon and Nigeria to separatists' online propaganda. *South African Journal of International Affairs, 28*(3), 449–69. https://doi.org/10.1080/10220461.2021.1966498.

Erlich, A., & Garner, C. (2023). Is pro-Kremlin disinformation effective? Evidence from Ukraine. *International Journal of Press-Politics* (pp. 5–28). https://doi.org/10.1177/19401612211045221.

Fetzer, J. (2004). Disinformation: The use of false information. *Minds and Machines, 14*(2), 231–40.

Fjällhed, A. (2021). Managing disinformation through public diplomacy. In P. Surowiec & I. Manor (Eds.), *Public diplomacy and the politics of uncertainty* (pp. 227–53). Palgrave Macmillan.

Floridi, L. (2011). *The philosophy of information*. Oxford University Press.

Hedling, E. (2021). Transforming practices of diplomacy: The European External Action Service and digital disinformation. *International Affairs, 97*(3), 841–59. https://doi.org/10.1093/ia/iiab035.

Hirshberg, M. S. (1993). The self-perpetuating national self-image: Cognitive biases in perceptions of international interventions. *Political Psychology, 14*(1), 77–98.

Jones-Jang, S. M., Mortensen, T., & Liu, J. J. (2021). Does media literacy help identification of fake news? Information literacy helps, but other literacies don't. *American Behavioral Scientist, 65*(2), 371–88. https://doi.org/10.1177/0002764219869406.

Kudugunta, S., & Ferrara, E. (2018). Deep neural networks for bot detection. *Information Sciences, 467*, 312–22.

la Cour, C. (2020). Theorising digital disinformation in international relations. *International Politics, 57*(4), 704–23. https://doi.org/10.1057/s41311-020-00215-x.

Manor, I. (2019). *The digitalization of public diplomacy*. Palgrave Macmillan.

Melki, J., & Jabado, M. (2016). Mediated public diplomacy of the Islamic State in Iraq and Syria: The synergistic use of terrorism, social media and branding. *Media and Communication, 4*(2), 92–103.

Nisbet, E. C., & Kamenchuk, O. (2019). The psychology of state-sponsored disinformation campaigns and implications for public diplomacy. *The Hague Journal of Diplomacy, 14*(1–2), 65–82. https://doi.org/10.1163/1871191x-11411019.

Nothhaft, H., Pamment, J., Agardh-Twetman, H., & Fjällhed, A. (2018). Information influence in western democracies: A model of systemic vulnerabilities. In C. Bjola & J. Pamment (Eds.), *Countering online propaganda and extremism: The dark side of digital diplomacy* (pp. 28–43). Routledge.

Nye, J. (2008). Public diplomacy and soft power. *The Annals of the American Academy of Political and Social Science, 616*(1), 94–109.

Nye, J. (2009). Get smart: Combining hard and soft power. *Foreign Affairs, 88*(4), 160–63.

Nye, J. (2018). How sharp power threatens soft power: The right and wrong ways to respond to authoritarian influence. *Foreign Affairs.* Retrieved from https:// www .foreignaffairs .com/ articles/ china/ 2018 -01 -24/ how -sharp -power -threatens -soft -power.

Nye, J. S. (2019). Soft power and public diplomacy revisited. *The Hague Journal of Diplomacy, 14*(1–2), 7–20. https://doi.org/10.1163/1871191x-14101013.

Oshikawa, R., Qian, J., & Wang, W. Y. (2020). A survey on natural language processing for fake news detection. Proceedings of the 12th Conference on Language Resources and Evaluation (LREC 2020), Marseille, 11–16 May 2020. European Language Resources Association (ELRA), 6086–93. CC-BY-NC*arXiv preprint arXiv:1811.00770.*

Pamment, J. (2016, November 1). Interview with James Pamment on strategic communication and public diplomacy. Retrieved from https://placebrandobserver.com/ interview-james-pamment/.

Pennycook, G., & Rand, D. G. (2020). Who falls for fake news? The roles of bullshit receptivity, overclaiming, familiarity, and analytic thinking. *Journal of Personality, 88*(2), 185–200. https://doi.org/10.1111/jopy.12476.

Potter, E. H. (2019). Russia's strategy for perception management through public diplomacy and influence operations: The Canadian case. *The Hague Journal of Diplomacy, 14*(4), 402–25.

Schmidt, A., & Wiegand, M. (2019). *A survey on hate speech detection using natural language processing.* Paper presented at the Proceedings of the Fifth International Workshop on Natural Language Processing for Social Media, 3 April, 2017, Valencia, Spain.

Stoycheff, E., & Nisbet, E. C. (2017). Priming the costs of conflict? Russian public opinion about the 2014 Crimean conflict. *International Journal of Public Opinion Research, 29*(4), 657–75. https://doi.org/10.1093/ijpor/edw020.

Taylor, P. M. (2003). *Munitions of the mind: A history of propaganda* (3rd edn). Manchester University Press.

The U.S. Advisory Commission on Public Diplomacy (2017). *Can public diplomacy survive the internet? Bots, echo chambers and disinformation.* Retrieved from https:// www.hsdl.org/?view&did=800873.

Van Ham, P. (2003). War, lies, and videotape: Public diplomacy and the USA's war on terrorism. *Security Dialogue, 34*(4), 427–44.

Vériter, S. L., Bjola, C., & Koops, J. A. (2020). Tackling COVID-19 disinformation: Internal and external challenges for the European Union. *The Hague Journal of Diplomacy, 15*(4), 569–82.

Vilmer, J.-B., Escorcia, A., Guillaume, M., & Herrera, J. (2018). *Information manipulation: A challenge for our democracies.* Retrieved from https://www.diplomatie.gouv.fr/IMG/pdf/information_manipulation_rvb_cle838736.pdf.

Walker, C. (2018). What is "Sharp power"? *Journal of Democracy, 29*(3), 9–23. https://www.journalofdemocracy.org/articles/what-is-sharp-power/.

Wattanacharoensil, W., & La-ornual, D. (2019). A systematic review of cognitive biases in tourist decisions. *Tourism Management, 75*, 353–69.

Zaharna, R. S. (2008). Information and relational communication frameworks of strategic public diplomacy. In N. Snow & P. M. Taylor (Eds.), *The Routledge handbook of public diplomacy* (pp. 86–100). Routledge.

Zaharna, R. S. (2010). *Battles to bridges: US strategic communication and public diplomacy after 9/11.* Springer.

Zaharna, R. S., Arsenault, A., & Fisher, A. (Eds.) (2014). *Relational, networked and collaborative approaches to public diplomacy: The connective mindshift.* Routledge.

12 Management

Steven L. Pike

Introduction

Public diplomacy (PD) is more than a theoretical approach to cross-cultural mass communication in service of a state's foreign policy agenda. It is also an activity that must be carried out on a daily basis, by people and institutions, according to strategic plans, in pursuit of policy goals and tangible results. The institutional management of PD has received relatively little attention by the field, which represents a tremendous opportunity for future scholars. The field lacks a theoretical framework connected to theories of management; without this, it cannot describe the practical, feasible operationalization of theory into policies that institutions can implement, the management practices that can guide people in that implementation, and the strategic management process that would guide the entire enterprise.

This chapter reviews selected areas of PD where initial exploration of management topics does exist, notably the impact of technology on the conduct of public relations (PR), indirect comparisons with the field of PR, and the evaluation of PD programs. This review leads to the inevitable conclusion that much remains to be done. This chapter suggests ways to fill two conceptual gaps in the scholarship of management in PD. First, it offers a theoretical framework of management, derived from its own literature and practice, that may help scholars identify concepts essential to initiating their exploration. Second, it recommends that the most logical and appropriate next step in this line of inquiry would be elaborating a sociology of the profession of PD.

Management

PD scholarship has, since the mid-2010s, produced an impressive quantity of scholarship on many aspects of the discipline. We have a fundamental definition of the field, i.e., a general consensus that PD resides in the realm of soft power (Cull, 2008; Gilboa, 2008; Hart, 2013; Nye, 2008; Snow, 2010) and represents activities and mechanisms by which soft power may be created, deployed, or operationalized to advance the foreign policy aims of an actor in the international system (see Chapter 8 in this volume). We have explored the bounds of actors, tools, contexts, and affordances from other fields, particularly international relations and mass communications. What we have not done, as a discipline, is pierced the strategic veil and analyzed how organizations perform basic managerial and strategic functions with regard to PD. Before we may do that, however, we must develop a theoretical framework for the analysis of management issues within PD, based on a functional theory of management. This requires an understanding of management theory.

Management is exceedingly well defined in its own literature. Griffin (2016) defines management as "a set of activities (including planning and decision-making, organizing, leading, and controlling) directed an organization's resources (human, financial, physical, and information), with the aim of achieving organizational goals in an efficient and effective manner" (p. 4). Smudde (2014) adds that management "involves systematic and ethical ways of directing people, allocating resources, and getting things done according to defined strategic objectives" (p. 14). There are resonances here with common practical definitions of PD as the use of soft power and various programs or tools (resources) by a state (or other organization) according to a strategy in order to achieve set goals (Cull, 2019; Gilboa, 2008).

Griffin (2016) provides further definition of the four activities, or "management functions" (p. 7). Planning means setting an organization's goals and deciding how best to achieve them. Decision-making involves selecting a course of action from a set of alternatives. Organizing determines how activities and resources are to be grouped. Leading describes processes and actions used to get individuals to work together systematically. Controlling involves monitoring the progress of the organization toward its goals.

Management studies also focuses on defining a wide array of skills that practitioners should possess, including technical, knowledge, interpersonal, conceptual, diagnostic, communicative, decision-making, and time-management. Much of the literature related to these skills is focused on their acquisition, development, retention, and deployment. Luthans (2011) adds a human element, dividing management into conceptual, technical, *and human* dimensions. The first two deal with skill and experience; Luthans notes that the third is often regrettably neglected or subject to oversimplification. The distillation of much management literature ultimately distinguishes between the "science" and the "art" of management, connects "science" with the management of tangible and inanimate resources, and connects "art" with the management of people, where interpersonal, psychological, and emotional factors add relatively more complexity.

Management pedagogy generally focuses on methodological approaches to the four functions: planning, strategy-formulation, and decision-making; organization and allocation of tangible resources; direction and leadership of human resources; and control and evaluation (Griffin, 2016; Smudde, 2014). Direction and leadership of human resources encompasses hiring, training, evaluation, discipline, and termination of employees, and a vast body of literature on approaches to managing people (e.g., emotional, transformational, situational), leadership "styles" (e.g., democratic, authoritarian, exclusive, inclusive, team-based, hierarchical), and debates on whether management is principally a traits-based or skills-and-behaviors-based enterprise. Control and evaluation focus on practices to analyze the efficient and effective use of resources by managers to achieve goals, and to generate performance data that can inform subsequent rounds of planning, strategy-formulation, and decision-making.

The field also relies on a conceptualization of management as an ongoing process of developing goals and strategies; environmental scanning; and recalibration of goals and strategy as conditions change. This dynamic process – referred to, with characteristic managerial simplicity, as a *Strategic Management Process* – unites the four functions (planning and decision-making, organizing, leading, and controlling) as a cycle that organizations use to carry out their missions (Griffin, 2016; Smudde, 2014).

Mass communications scholars will recognize this cycle as the core of PR practice: examine your environment; establish goals and objectives; develop strategy for applying resources to the achievement of goals; allocate resources accordingly; and then examine results and impacts with an eye to adjusting strategy for the next round.

Managing public diplomacy

PD scholarship has often revealed management challenges. PD scholars cogently and frequently problematize the PD challenges that leaders and practitioners encounter, identify the sources of those problems, and provide recommendations to policymakers. Those recommendations tend, however, to be tactical, conceptual, or paradigmatic: existing decision-makers should make a different decision; take some previously unconsidered factor into account; or conceptualize the problem differently. PD scholarship has not dived into systemic management considerations or analyzed the systems that made the decisions in the first place. It has not analyzed the criteria and systems by which PD practitioners are hired, trained, and managed; whether those criteria and systems are optimal and productive; whether different criteria and systems might produce better outcomes; and what better criteria and systems we might recommend.

It has not analyzed whether the institutions and organizations producing PD work are properly structured, staffed, and resourced. It has not examined and compared processes for strategic management, nor processes that support such an effort: environmental scanning; gathering and assessment of information; adjusting goals and strategies; realigning strategy; and feeding new information back into the planning process. Within the area of analyzing strategic management processes resides inquiry into the decision-making structure of the institution that manages PD efforts and the various influences upon it: layers of approval; mechanisms for oversight; and scrutiny by the media or the public, just to name a few.

Three areas in which PD scholars have begun to ask the right questions offer a foundation for inquiry and lead on to next steps: technology, evaluation, and PD as PR.

1.   Technology

PD scholars have observed and charted, in impressive detail, the impact of changing technology on PD communications and engagement. The increasing destructiveness of traditional war coupled with the availability and spread of communicative technology shifted the focus of international conflict to battles over image and reputation instead of the more traditional contests for land and resources (Gilboa, 2000, 2002). Changes in technology created "interconnected realities of global relationships" and forced a transformation of PD from "one-way information flow" to dialogue that required not just dissemination of information, but genuine engagement between the communicator and the public (Melissen, 2005). The increasing networking of human communication, the reliance on dialogues centered around human engagement and community, and the contest of narrative, image, and identity in digital communication spaces, has changed the paradigm of communication (Zaharna, 2010). Policymakers must consider different types of communicative networks (e.g., purpose, mode, and time frame – all important management considerations) and elements of network structure, synergy, and strategy (Zaharna, 2013).

Some states make a strategic choice to use electronic networks to exert relational power, while others seek to control or restrict the exertion of such power via policies of blocking, filtering, and censorship (Arsenault, 2013). Communicating and building relationships in the environment of decentralized and participatory networks of communication creates new management challenges, not all of them under the control of the policymakers and the communicators (Causey & Howard, 2013; Seo, 2013). These analyses and cogent case studies show various manifestations of the problems and provide critical and essential insight into the terrain confronting policymakers. The next logical step, from a management point of view, would be to seek instances when policymakers have incorporated such sound counsel into their decision-making and strategic processes, including resource allocation, and to compare management outcomes among those who have, and those who have not.

Golan and Yang (2015) introduced a model of communication, mediated PR, explicitly recognizing that a new paradigm of communication created by digital technologies had replaced the framing battles of traditional media (Entman, 2008). Golan, Manor, and Arceneaux (2019) revisited the mediated PD paradigm in the light of the technology-driven diversification of media into paid, earned, shared, and owned subcategories. A management perspective would inquire how practitioners and institutions manage traditional relationships with the media, where institutions place those relationships in the strategic planning process, and whether there have been changes over time in the allocation of resources – human and non-human – to the function.

The largest question to be explored may be "who speaks?" How are different PD organizations structured to deliver the message? Do they share that responsibility with other entities? What systems and procedures are in place to facilitate message development, decision-making about message strategy, coordination of different operations involved in the process, and the hiring, training, and management of the professionals who carry out the function? Comparing how different PD actors – institutions or even whole countries – manage their PD strategy, resources, and personnel might yield insights into best (or worst) practices for this critical piece of the PD puzzle.

PD has also investigated the dark side of digital technologies that allow malicious actors and states to manipulate public dialogue and interfere with discourse in democratic societies. Malicious actors are updating old theories of reflexive control to suit the digital era (Bjola, 2019) or attacking the epistemic structure on which citizens of democracies depend to govern societal decision-making, rendering those divided and uncertain of what is and is not true (Nothhaft et al., 2019). Pamment and Bjola (2019) offer governments their best suggestions for combatting the onslaught of digital mischief.

Viewing these events through a management lens would urge further inquiry into the implementation of these recommendations and the efforts of states to institutionalize their responses to malicious actors in the digital space. Have governments implemented the recommendations, altered their management structures, hired differently and changed the training of those they employ? Have they instituted procedures to acquire different technology? What systems do they use to monitor the impact of these changes and incorporate insights and learning into subsequent rounds of policy formulation? Which states perform this task successfully, which do not, and is there a difference in out-comes depending on the managerial and strategic approach taken by those different actors?

Several scholars have investigated the impact of digital technology on practice and technique. Gilboa (2016) has looked at the changing use of digital tools by diplomats in the field and suggested that digital tools have required diplomats to do increasingly more broadcasting and messaging versus listening and reporting. Gilboa clearly acknowledges the urgent need to train diplomats for this brave new world, but the content of such training demands further investigation and definition. Manor (2019) has researched, extensively and meticulously, the impact of new communications technology on the practices and structures of foreign ministries. More Ambassadors are engaging in diplomacy in the digital space; there is heavier reliance on visual modes of communication to carry messages; branding of countries, embassies, and even individuals, has become a pervasive occupation. The focus of analysis remains, however, on manifested outcomes, not managerial or strategic process.

A management perspective would ask about the strategy and process behind the activity. Is digital activity increasingly a part of the strategic plan of each embassy, or the performance plan for each diplomat? What levels of training do different foreign ministries provide to their personnel, what technology do they acquire, how do they choose their technology, and how do they evaluate the effectiveness of both the technology and the people? Are there parallel studies of these factors across different countries, which might substantiate which management approaches are more effective or more efficient? How does "digital diplomacy" in its various forms figure in the strategic mission, the overall strategy, or the tactics of different institutions? Do these institutions have processes for setting the goals of their digital diplomacy, allocating resources, and measuring results achieved? Does that information cycle into a revision of the institutional strategy?

In sum, PD scholars have observed the impact of technological change on human communicative interaction. They have noted the propensity for networked, distributed, and egalitarian modes of organization to supplant hierarchical, controlled, and segregated modes, and the presence of such change at every level of social organization: communal, national, societal, or international. They have sought, with considerable success, to describe the policy challenges that such change creates for those who would conduct PD. The field has not yet taken the opportunity to explore whether policymakers are following those recommendations, how they are being implemented, and whether they are successful in producing desired outcomes.

2.   Evaluation

One of the key functions of management is evaluation – determining the effectiveness and efficiency of one's efforts at achieving goals – and evaluating the impact of PD programs has received relatively more attention than management of programs and practitioners per se. This is understandable: virtually every PD practitioner ultimately answers to a legislature or executive that must pay the bills and wants to know how the money has been spent.

Scholars and practitioners have, however, struggled with the challenges of evaluating the impact of PD programs, information operations, exchanges, and even propaganda long before the name "PD" was coined to describe the practice (see the relevant section in Chapter 1). The endeavor suffers from the same methodological problem as the study of media effects: we can show that people are impacted by the media to which they are exposed, but an infinite number of exogenous and uncontrollable variables, including time, makes it virtually impossible to predict the impact that a given media exposure will produce in a particular individual. We know that PD programs impact the thinking of populations, but there is no methodologically sound way to argue that giving person A, PD experience B, will produce outcome C, in time frame D, particularly given the long time frame of a program participant's life and professional career.

Evaluation of programs also suffers from a lack of clarity on the objectives themselves. Different actors (program creators, political leaders, funders, legislators) want different things from the same programs and there is often a lack of agreement on what the outcomes should be. The programs proceed on the assumption that everyone is getting a little piece of the pie, but a methodical examination of actual results would not necessarily make all the actors happy. Political considerations push practitioners essentially to fudge the outcomes desired and the variables measured (Pahlavi, 2007; Pamment,

2014). Additional scholarship has sought to resolve the problem by accepting the political nature of certain objectives and categorizing them as part of the package (Pamment, 2014), suggesting that the time frames be shortened and evaluation rest upon more concrete and measurable outcomes (Sevin, 2017), or developing and applying different methodological approaches that incorporate participants' subjectivity and political outcomes (Pike, 2021) or that propose different models for listening and evaluation of PD interventions and engagements (Ingenhoff & Chariatte, 2020).

These defects may also lead to the politicization of evaluation, a serious impediment to management analysis. The legitimate management question of improving performance degenerates into the political question of assigning blame. The contentious parties conclude that the system would work better if someone else (often themselves) were in charge. "Analysis" degenerates into internal turf wars over who should control the messaging function and promises (or threats) to "get control" of messaging. Gilboa and Shai (2011) describe successive unsuccessful efforts by the government of Israel to reform the organization of PD responsibilities among different government agencies, civilian and military, elected and appointed.

In addition, PD can become a political "football." Politicians who do not get the results they desire are reluctant to hear that their expectations are unreasonable, fixate on practitioner incompetence (or disloyalty), and assert the need for greater political control over messaging (or for bringing practitioners to heel and making them finally obey their political masters). Constant review of American PD effectiveness by the U.S. Advisory Commission on Public Diplomacy rarely goes further than interesting shelf reading, while practitioners and politicians continue to choose emotional sides – for some 20 years, now – in the never-ending debate over whether it was "right" or "wrong" to eliminate the U.S. Information Agency. In-depth analyses of actual managerial practices are rarely done and even less frequently implemented.

Evaluation has come closer to grappling with management-related issues in studying how practitioners managing exchange programs react to the unclear and conflictual standards imposed upon them (Sommerfeldt & Buhmann, 2019). The core of management is getting people to do a job under the assumption that there is some sort of a mission, some goals, a plan, and variety of institutional mechanisms for supporting those people in their work. Examining how professionals attempt to get the job done when different "bosses" are arguing over all those factors, resources may not be adequate, and practitioner input is sometimes desired and sometimes not, frames a brilliant management problem worth further study.

All PD organizations face the challenge of evaluation. Sommerfeldt and Buhmann (2019) showed one, with a particular arrangement of managerial factors. Understanding more about the managerial arrangement of factors in other PD institutions would give ground for comparison. Are there organizations that do it differently, or better? Whatever flaws the system they studied may have, is it rather like Churchill described democracy: the worst, except for every other? There is a foundation here to examine how practitioners perform at creating and managing PD activities given their conditions of work and the management environment in which they function. Such scholarship could produce insights into management structures or principles that would be more effective or efficient, produce better programs, or better insulate practitioners from political pressures.

3. Public diplomacy as public relations

Significant PD scholarship has focused on the similarities between PD and the profession of PR (Fitzpatrick et al., 2013). PR has its own rich literature on management, including both the theoretical and ethical organization of the profession (Grunig, 1992), and the application of management functions and theories described above. Scholars have sought to draw comparisons between PD , corporate diplomacy, and political corporate social responsibility (Ingenhoff & Marschlich, 2019), which may be fruitful ground in the search for comparative management models.

Useful concepts in management of PD may arise from revisiting that which has already been established and probing more deeply into the specific management practices of PR. It will be important to elaborate contextual and professional differences between the two professions during such analysis. For example (and at the risk of gross overgeneralization), PR most often seeks communication and relationship building among organizations and citizens within the context of a civil society or a commercial relationship; PD is conducted in the context of international relations between actors and the citizens of a different state. There are different rules. Nonetheless, much has been invested in studying management in the corporate world, the public sector, government, and organizations. More can be done to identify how these management practices apply and operate within the parameters of PD.

A sociology of the profession of public diplomacy

A signal gap, however, is that the field lacks a well-elaborated professional sociology; this is essential to a robust study of management principles and practices inherent in PD. Pike and Kinsey (2021) argued that the practice of PD met the established conditions of a profession. These include a body of practitioners who possess self-perception as professionals in a practice, an evolving hierarchy, key skills and attributes, group-enforced codes of conduct, a self-perpetuating identity, a sense of special mission and status, and both the will and ability to act to perpetuate and protect the profession per se (Brante, 1988; Millerson, 1964; Parsons, 1964).

The connection to the management perspective is easily elaborated: management defines itself as the practice of applying resources to achieve goals according to a well-elaborated strategy. Furthermore, it asserts that those goals must be consistent with the mission, vision, and values of the organization in question. The sociological elements of the profession and the practitioners – the professional identity, self-definition, and sense of mission of any corps of PD practitioners – also correspond to the mission, vision, and values of a PD organization. Establish the parameters of the sociology of the PD profession and you establish a reliable and robust guide to important management parameters for PD professionals.

A structural referent

This chapter, finally, seeks to create a helpful map of the elements and mechanisms that fit each of the functions of management – planning and decision-making, organizing, leading, controlling – and the overall strategic management process. These elements and mechanisms are the units of analysis and comparison for a robust study of the management aspects of the PD profession. They are explained below and summarized in Table 12.1.

- *Planning and decision-making*: Analysis would begin with mechanisms that precede action, and enable PD organizations to identify challenges, establish their mission, define problems, understand the environment, and establish the parameters of the PD engagements that it wishes to pursue. These mechanisms would include the means for decision-makers to research their environment, understand expectations of stakeholders, define resources needed, and undertake a process of internal discussion and consultation that would lead to the development of a concrete plan of

PD goals, strategies, and desired outcomes. This phase would also include determining the kind of personnel the organization needs and hiring, as well as analysis and evaluation of technological resources that would need to be acquired to properly implement a PD strategy.

- *Organizing*: Now that the plan is established, we need to get the entire organization to the start line. Now that the decision has been made to proceed with a plan, all the implementing aspects need to be put in place. Embassies and consulates need to be staffed and resourced to operate. Programs have to be established and told who their personnel are and what their budgets are. Any processes that involve getting the right resources and the right people to the right place at the right time would be encompassed by the organizing function. How do organizations allocate and assign personnel and resources (logistical or financial)? What are the processes they use to decide to place offices in certain locations and not others?

- *Leading*: Implementation is underway, and the organization is occupied with motivating its people and ensuring that they can do their jobs. What systems are in place for the leadership and management of human resources? How are employees trained, treated, paid, rewarded, assessed, and promoted?

- *Controlling*: The core of the controlling function, at least in management terms, has to do with accountability, effectiveness, and efficiency. These will include any processes for evaluating the outcome and impact of PD activities and programs, but also personnel effectiveness and the proper use of resources. These may be wholly internal processes for self-assessment and monitoring. Given that PD is often a governmental function, attention should be paid to external processes. These may be driven by various forms of oversight from other government bodies and agencies, and even by the media or the public itself.

- *Strategic Management*: Finally, and most importantly, scholars will want to look for those systems and mechanisms that unite before functions in a dynamic cycle. Planning, organizing, leading, and controlling are not static functions that happen in a linear manner. In actual management practice, they occur continuously and concurrently. Scholars will want to look for those processes that enable an organization constantly to monitor internal and external factors, disseminate this information within the decision-making structure, and act as needed to alter any part of the strategic plan, definition of the environment, definition of the problem, goals, strategies, or resource determinations and allocations. International relations scholars will be familiar with the famous phrase of the German general Helmuth von Moltke, that no war plan survives first contact with the enemy. Like war, in business, or in PD, if you are not constantly adapting to changing circumstances, you are failing.

Table 12.1   Units of analysis for the study of PD management

Domain	Elements/Mechanisms
Planning and decision-making	Information collection and assessment; environmental scanning; policy formulation, including mechanisms for staff input; resource analyses; budgeting; human resources planning, including staffing and organizational plans; position descriptions; analysis of personnel needs and hiring of personnel; processes for recommending and evaluating new technology; actors involved (e.g., legislatures, political entities, independent boards or commissions, the media, the public)
Organizing	Processes for allocating human and tangible resources; structural hierarchies, including bureaucratic location of the PD function; allocation of posts (e.g., embassies, consulates, bureaus); acquisition and implementation of technology
Leading	Management of personnel; leadership structure; salaries and compensation regimes; personnel training regimes; performance review systems; systems for promotion, reward, and recognition
Controlling	Evaluation of programs and evaluation of personnel; accountability measures; oversight by other entities (e.g., legislatures, inspectors, outside critics, professional guilds, and associations); oversight and criticism from the media and/or the public
Strategic Management	Integration of the controlling and planning function; frequency of formal and informal strategic review; level of the strategic review function within the organizational hierarchy

Source: Author.

Scholars may also wish to explore a deeper level of management theory, i.e., analysis of the leadership and management styles that pertain to the PD profession. Of the many leadership styles (e.g., democratic, authoritarian, collaborative) and theoretical foundations (trait-based, behavior-based, personality-based, situational, transformational, emotional) that exist, attributes of the PR profession – creativity, education, emotional engagement – seem to favor certain styles and foundations and disfavor others. It would be interesting to categorize the predominant styles of both the international relations and PR professions, and then consider which one the PD profession more closely resembles.

Conclusion

The pressing issue of technological change revolutionizing how humans communicate has, reasonably and logically, occupied significant time and ink. Like most other social, sociological, political, and communications fields, we have answered the call of technological change, and both explored and defined how that change impacts our profession. For all that time spent on what PD is, and how and why PD works, we have much to do to understand how PD practitioners do their work. Fortunately, we have no dearth of theory.

Theories and methodologies for analyzing management practices are robust, well-known, and well-substantiated in academic literature. Scholars have applied them to the analysis of management practices in the private sector and in the government sector, not just in the U.S. or Europe, but in virtually every country on Earth. What remains is to adopt those same tools to the analysis of PD management practices. Additional help will come from first elaborating the precepts of the profession, both in individual countries and collectively, identifying the practices by which professionals affirm, protect, and propagate those precepts, and elaborating a robust sociology of PD.

References

Arsenault, A. (2013). Networks of freedom, networks of control: Internet policy as a platform for and an impediment to relational public diplomacy. In R.S. Zaharna, A. Arsenault, & A. Fisher (Eds.), *Relational, networked, and collaborative approaches to public diplomacy: The connective mindshift* (pp. 192–208). Routledge.

Bjola, C. (2019). Propaganda as reflexive control: The digital dimension. In C. Bjola, & J. Pamment (Eds.), *Countering online propaganda and extremism: The dark side of digital diplomacy* (pp. 13–27). Routledge.

Brante, T. (1988). Sociological approaches to the professions. *Acta Sociologica*, 31(2), 119–42.

Causey, C., & Howard, P. (2013). Delivering digital diplomacy: Information technologies and the changing business of diplomacy. In R.S. Zaharna, A. Arsenault, & A. Fisher (Eds.), *Relational, networked, and collaborative approaches to public diplomacy: The connective mindshift* (pp. 144–56). Routledge.

Cull, N. (2008). Public diplomacy: Taxonomies and histories. *Annals of the American Academy of Political and Social Science*, 616(1), 31–54.

Cull, N. (2019). *Public diplomacy: Foundations for global engagement in the digital age.* Polity.

Entman, R. (2008). Theorizing mediated public diplomacy: The US case. *The International Journal of Press/Politics*, 13(2), 87–102.

Fitzpatrick, K., Fullerton, J., & Kendrick, A. (2013). Public relations and public diplomacy: Conceptual and practical connections. *Public Relations Journal*, 7(4), 1–21.

Gilboa, E. (2000). Mass communication and diplomacy: A theoretical framework. *Communication Theory*, 10(3), 275–309.

Gilboa, E. (2002). Global communication and foreign policy. *Journal of Communication*, 52(4), 731–48.

Gilboa, E. (2008). Searching for a theory of public diplomacy. *Annals of the American Academy of Political and Social Science*, 616(1), 55–77.

Gilboa, E. (2016). Digital diplomacy. In C. Constantinou, P. Kerr, & P. Sharp (Eds.), *The Sage handbook of diplomacy* (pp. 540–51). Sage.

Gilboa, E., & Shai, N. (2011). Rebuilding public diplomacy: The case of Israel. In A. Fisher, & S. Lucas (Eds.), *Trials of engagement: The future of US public diplomacy* (pp. 33–54). Brill.

Golan, G., & Yang, S. (2015). Introduction: The integrated public diplomacy perspective. In G. Golan, S. Yang, & D. Kinsey (Eds.), *International public relations and public diplomacy* (pp. 1–14). Peter Lang.

Golan, G., Manor, I., & Arceneaux, P. (2019). Mediated public diplomacy redefined: Foreign stakeholder engagement via paid, earned, shared, and owned media. *American Behavioral Scientist*, 63(12), 1665–83.

Griffin, R.W. (2016). *Fundamentals of management.* 8th edn. Cengage.

Grunig, J. (1992). *Excellence in public relations and communication management.* Lawrence Erlbaum.

Hart, J. (2013). *Empire of ideas: The origins of public diplomacy and the transformation of U.S. foreign policy.* Oxford University Press.

Ingenhoff, D., & Chariatte, J. (2020). Solving the public diplomacy puzzle – developing a 360-degree integrated public diplomacy listening and evaluation approach to analyzing what constitutes a country image from different perspectives. USC Center on Public Diplomacy. https://uscpublicdiplomacy.org/sites/default/files/useruploads/u47441/Solving%20the%20Public%20Diplomacy%20Puzzle_1.9.21.pdf.

Ingenhoff, D., & Marschlich, S. (2019). Corporate diplomacy and political CSR: Similarities, differences and theoretical implications. *Public Relations Review*, 45, 348–71.

Luthans, F. (2011). *Organizational behavior: An evidence-based approach.* McGraw-Hill/Irwin.

Manor, I. (2019). *The digitalization of public diplomacy.* Palgrave Macmillan.

Melissen, J. (Ed.) (2005). *The new public diplomacy: Soft power in international relations.* Palgrave Macmillan.

Millerson, G. (1964). *The qualifying association.* Routledge & Kegan Paul.

Nothhaft, H., Pamment, J., Agardh-Twetman, H., & Fjällhed, A. (2019). Information influence in western democracies: A model of systemic vulnerabilities. In C. Bjola, & J. Pamment (Eds.), *Countering online propaganda and extremism: The dark side of digital diplomacy* (pp. 28–43). Routledge.

Nye, J. (2008). Public diplomacy and soft power. *Annals of the American Academy of Political and Social Science*, 616(1), 94–109.

Pahlavi, P. (2007). Evaluating public diplomacy programs. *The Hague Journal of Diplomacy*, 2(3), 255–81.

Pamment, J. (2014). Articulating influence: Toward a research agenda for interpreting the evaluation of soft power, public diplomacy and nation brands. *Public Relations Review*, 40(1), 50–59.

Pamment, J., & Bjola, C. (2019). Conclusion: Rethinking strategic communication in the digital age. In C. Bjola, & J. Pamment (Eds.), *Countering online propaganda and extremism: The dark side of digital diplomacy* (pp. 172–80). Routledge.

Parsons, T. (1964). *Essays in sociological theory.* The Free Press.

Pike, S. (2021). Using Q methodology to augment evaluation of public diplomacy programs. *Place Branding and Public Diplomacy.* https:// doi .org/ 10 .1057/ s41254 -021-00229-z.

Pike, S., & Kinsey, D. (2021). Diplomatic identity and communication: Using Q methodology to assess subjective perceptions of diplomatic practitioners. *Place Branding and Public Diplomacy.* https://doi.org/10.1057/s41254-021-00226-2.

Seo, H. (2013). The "Virtual Last Three Feet": Understanding relationship perspectives in network-based public diplomacy. In R.S. Zaharna, A. Arsenault, & A. Fisher (Eds.), *Relational, networked, and collaborative approaches to public diplomacy: The connective mindshift* (pp. 157–71). Routledge.

Sevin, E. (2017). A multilayered approach to public diplomacy evaluation: Pathways of connection. *Politics & Policy*, 45(5), 879–901.

Smudde, P.M. (2014). *Managing public relations.* Oxford University Press.

Snow, N. (2010). *Propaganda, Inc.: Selling America's culture to the world.* Seven Stories Press.

Sommerfeldt, E., & Buhmann, A. (2019). The status quo of evaluation in public diplomacy: Insights from the US State Department. *Journal of Communication Management*, 23(3), 198–212.

Zaharna, R.S. (2010). *Battles to bridges: U.S. strategic communication and public diplomacy after 9/11.* Palgrave Macmillan.

Zaharna, R.S. (2013). Network purpose, network design. In R.S. Zaharna, A. Arsenault, & A. Fisher (Eds.), *Relational, networked, and collaborative approaches to public diplomacy: The connective mindshift* (pp. 173–91). Routledge.

PART III

Instruments

13 Cultural diplomacy

Natalia Grincheva

Introduction

Cultural diplomacy (CUD) as a practice and as a sub-field of a national foreign policy emerged during the Cold War between the U.S. and Soviet Russia. Initially, it was defined by the U.S. Department of State (1969) in 1959 as "the direct and enduring contact between people of different nations [...] to help create a better climate of international trust and understanding in which official relations can operate" (p. iv). CUD is based on international exchanges of different types from artistic to educational that are usually administered through State Departments of Foreign Affairs or Ministers of Culture.

If not mitigating geopolitical conflicts, the ultimate goals of CUD include creating a positive view of the nation in the eyes of the foreign publics, facilitating a stronger cooperation or creating political alliances to manage international positions and security (Melissen, 2005). Predominantly a government activity, CUD has always operated on the instrumentalization of genuine efforts, commitments, and an incredible enthusiasm for a cross-cultural encounter, sharing and dialogue of artists, cultural practitioners, educators, students, and community leaders working on behalf of civil society of their respective countries (Schneider, 2010).

Many countries have been engaged in exchanges and CUD for several decades, and the importance of supporting international arts programs on a national level has been universally recognized (Wyszomirski, 2003). This chapter highlights some of the research on CUD in the past to mainly suggest trajectories for the further development of the scholarship. Exploring major focus and key topics of CUD current literature, the chapter outlines the future research agenda of this growing academic discipline. It argues that while in the past decades CUD has been researched quite extensively, there are still research gaps to be addressed in the future. First, the chapter explores alternative geographies and agencies of diplomacies that have not been extensively covered by the CUD scholarship. The following section proposes new areas for focused research on macro and micro geographical levels which pertain to diplomacies going beyond state-driven bilateral relationships, promoting an exchange of national cultures and traditions.

Understanding CUD as a dynamic practice that brings together artists, educators, policymakers, governments, and civil society, the chapter conceptualizes transformations caused by the emergence of new technologies, new artistic expressions, new cultural trends, and arts practices in the complex processes of globalization, digitalization, and platformization. The last section demonstrates that while CUD is dynamically changing to cope with the pace of all these new developments, there is a growing need to explore more closely new hybrid models and digitally mediated environments of international cultural communications which increasingly engage non-human actors.

Towards post-national cultural diplomacy

The paradigm of national promotion has been especially important, and strongly shaped international cultural exchanges and communication since the times of the structuration of the modern state or Westphalian state. This period was marked by such processes as setting and strengthening strict political, economic, and cultural boundaries among territories belonging to different nations (Batora & Hocking, 2008, p. 4). Reinforced in the 19th century, national promotion remained a dominant diplomatic paradigm which defined how nation states constructed their identities in the international arena and communicated with other countries (Habermas, 2001). Not surprisingly, CUD as a practice was born with major objectives to communicate a positive country image to the outside world, sharing the best of its traditions, national beliefs, arts, and cultural developments. These tendencies have been extensively covered in the CUD scholarship that predominantly focused on the national dimension of foreign policies, operating mostly through a bilateral paradigm.

The legacies of the Cold War between the U.S. and Soviet Russia which gave rise to CUD as a practice and as a field of academic enquiry are reflected in a large body of historical research. From the U.S. perspective, this research reveals how CUD was employed as a political tool operating "very much within the model largely representing the transmission of American skills and values to others" (Scott-Smith, 2009, p. 52). A "triumphant success" and the strong power of CUD as a means of establishing a productive dialogue with foreigners to change their perceptions is largely documented in many historical works and memories (Prevots, 1999; Lucke, 2002; Richmond, 2003; Arndt, 2005). In most cases, they explore CUD activities as powerful platforms which "exposed foreign audiences to American democratic manners" (Schneider, 2003, p. 8) and even "played a great role in undermining the Soviet Union and sowing the seeds for its eventual dissolution" (Schneider, 2006, p. 148).

However, in the conditions of rapidly unfolding processes of globalization that widened, deepened, and accelerated global interconnections between countries (Steger, 2009), new CUD paradigms steadily emerge, going far beyond state-initiated bilateral exchanges. Globalization gave rise to a new ideological dimension in international politics adding new layers of social and cultural "norms, claims, beliefs, and narratives," defining the communicative behavior of nation states confronted with new economic and political realities in the global arena (Steger, 2009, p. 11).

This new power dynamic welcomes theoretical hypotheses and philosophical debates on the growing transnational dimension of politics in the post-modern international system. For example, Habermas questions the implications of globalization in order to comprehend its dramatic influence on contemporary international politics, as well as on the complex processes of forming new transnational identities. Beck (2001, 2006) also contributes to critical analysis of the contemporary international political environment through his "cosmopolitan perspective," which identifies and stresses the power of such important mechanisms of globalization as trans-nationalization (the intensification of trans-border human, informational, media, or financial flows), deterritorialization (the growing disconnection between place and culture), and cosmopolitanizing (the changing relationship between the local and the global), leading to dissolution of the absolute powers of nation states in the global environment.

Under the pressure of global environmental, humanitarian, social, and cultural challenges, diplomacy has acquired a new level, where cross-cultural negotiation and problem solving go beyond exclusively national interests. Some scholars identified a "new dimension" of diplomacy that is placed within a cosmopolitan framework of interests and values, shifting diplomatic outreach to a transnational agenda (Villanueva, 2010). As reflected in emerging CUD scholarship, there are new topics that start to rise on the research agenda. They evolve on the intersections between cultural practices and important issues of global resonance and significance. For example, the climate change crisis as a catalyst for CUD initiatives is explored in several works. Some of them focus on climate diplomacy as a tool for consensus-building and establishing regional (Nagabhatla et al., 2021) or transnational alliances (Strachová, 2021); others look at cases where climate diplomacy takes the form of humanitarian aid and educational cultural activities of powerful country leaders, like the

U.S., in the developing regions (Copeland, 2009). Other issues attracting diplomacy scholars include disability activism (Galmarini, 2021), lesbian, gay, bisexual, trans (LGBT) global rights advocacy (Stephenson, 2020), or transnational feminism movements as a part of CUD activities (Wang et al., 2019).

These studies signal that despite a recent rise of populistic and nationalistic politics across countries, reinforcing human divisions and eroding global collaboration (Stengel et al., 2019), there is still room for "humanity-centered public diplomacy" (Zaharna, 2021). This type of diplomatic communication acquired a new meaning and special significance during the global Covid-19 outbreak (Idowu & Ogunnubi, 2022; Hesse & Rafferty, 2020). Future research should focus more on these cosmopolitan (Villanueva, 2010) or transnational (Chalcraft, 2021) CUD manifestations and their implications to reveal the power dynamics and complex relationships between the global and the local in communicating in the international space, peace building, and establishing channels for mutually beneficial collaborations on common goals. Moving from a macro to micro level of CUD research focus, it is important to note that a few recent articles expose another level of geographical complexities, that have not yet received the required attention from international scholars.

Exploring CUD as a tool of expressing cultural identities of marginalized communities, indigenous people, subregions, and contested territories invites further investigations. Kichuk and Shevchuk (2020) explore the cultural people-to-people diplomacy of Budzhak, the Ukrainian region, bordering on Romania and Moldova, and uniting diaspora of the Albanian, Bulgarian, Gagauze, German, Greek, Jew, Polish, Romanian, and Russian minorities. In this case, CUD activities in the preservation and promotion of local languages and cultural traditions, including rituals, arts, and folk crafts, aim to strengthen the ethnic consciousness of the region. More importantly, though, it helps gain mutual understanding in interethnic relations to "promote intercultural dialogue and tolerance as necessary prerequisites for living in multicultural society" (p. 221).

From a contrasting perspective, Huang (2021) explores how minority ethnic or indigenous culture and heritage can become a powerful tool in the hands of the state leveraging its regional power and identity. This research exposes how Taiwan mobilized its prehistory Austronesian linguistic heritage and indigenous culture "to reposition itself in the Asia-Pacific" by establishing cross-border exchange and partnerships among indigenous communities in Taiwan and the Austronesian peoples (p. 72). The article reveals the extraterritorial role of indigenous heritage that can be strategically mobilized as a tool of CUD to strengthen a small and contested state's position in a wider region.

Both articles open a conversation on more nuanced CUD that exists beyond a traditional bilateral setting in the international relations context. It exposes a high cultural diversity of countries from within, challenging their national status quo.

In a highly globalized world with more diverse multicultural populations residing in different countries, "internal" CUD directed towards domestic populations should become a research priority. As a tool to mitigate cross-cultural conflicts and misunderstanding, CUD as a research focus area can offer a required academic perspective to explore further cultural geographies on the subregional levels and investigate the power dynamics of relationships established with diaspora communities (Kennedy, 2022; Gonzalez, 2011), indigenous people (Giguère, 2018), marginalized cultural groups, and minorities who play an important role in countries' representations and positions on the international arena. As the section demonstrates, a newly emerging but scarce scholarship indicates a growing need to shift the focus of CUD research from national to post-national dimensions. These dimensions should include more nuanced explorations of both global perspectives or "humanity-centered" diplomacies as well as research on sub-national, local, and territorial levels identifying new diplomatic practices exercised by communities with contested cultural identities who still struggle for their status quo.

Towards post-human cultural diplomacy

Human-to-human communication and cross-cultural exchanges have always been a strong component of CUD activities, extensively covered in dedicated scholarship (see Chapter 16 in this volume). Historical research documented that from the era of the Crusades "ordinary people, travelers, pilgrims, missionaries, and interlopers across the globe, concocted ways of [...] establishing relationships with people who did not speak their language, wore different garb, and worshipped other gods" (Trivellato et al., 2014, p. 2). Looking at cultural exchanges in pre-modern and modern times, Bentley (2011) explored cross-cultural interactions and exchanges as a platform to influence others whether by bringing new cultural products to active use or changing the ways people approached various tasks in their daily routines, not to mention historical transformations of cultural beliefs and traditions, or adoptions of new languages.

Exploring CUD from human communication perspectives, the relevant literature has always stressed the importance of a two-way interactive dialogue between people from different cultures. People-to-people dialogue is argued to be a key tool to contest existing misconceptions and stereotypes that is capable to empower participants to negotiate new cultural knowledge, perceptions, and identities (Parkinson, 1977; Snow, 2008). The core principle behind this dialogical power is the claim that bringing people from different countries together through meaningful cultural practices helps to achieve mutual understanding.

Program participants can learn about each other's differences and commonalities through personal connections and artistic co-creation to renegotiate common values (Parkinson, 1977). In CUD activities, art has always played a foundational role in establishing these human bridges across borders to establish a meaningful dialogue and to nurture mutual trust and understanding (Schneider, 2010). The scholarship on arts diplomacy is, indeed, very diverse, encompassing a wide variety of publications which focus on different kinds of artistic practices as the core in international cultural exchanges.

They include dedicated works on museum diplomacy and traveling exhibitions of visual arts (Kong, 2021; Grincheva, 2020, 2019; Harker, 2020), heritage diplomacy (Lähdesmäki, 2021; Winter, 2015), ballet and performance arts (Prevots, 1999; Searcy, 2020), arts festivals (Dines, 2020; Ocón, 2021), as well as research on music tours, from legendary jazz diplomacy during the times of the Cold War (Saito, 2021) to more recent rap and hip hop diplomacy (Dunkel & Nitzsche, 2019). However, one of the most important criticisms of traditional CUD was its focus on high arts as opposed to popular culture, significantly limiting the scope and diversity of audiences that can be targeted by these activities (Ivey, 2007). Addressing this criticism, in the past several decades of CUD scholarship shifted its attention to more subtle channels of diplomatic influence and embraced the role of pop and subcultures in delivering ideological messages to foreign publics and engaging people across borders.

This literature encompasses numerous case studies which gave rise to a whole range of different diplomacies, named according to their cultural form or media channel of delivery, such as cinema diplomacy from the U.S. Hollywood (Chung, 2020) to Indian Bollywood (Thussu, 2020), Japanese manga and anime diplomacy (Lam, 2007), TV show diplomacy (Wang & Hallquist, 2011), circus diplomacy (Sölter, 2015), yoga diplomacy (Gautam & Droogan, 2017), or gastro diplomacy of different countries (Demir & Im, 2019), to name but a few. More recently, though, emerging technologies opened new avenues for exploring completely different art practices which do not necessarily take place in traditional physical environments and even invite interventions of non-human actors on various levels from cultural production and sharing to cultural consumption practices.

Most recently a development of world-like, large-group online environments designed for real-time interactivity among participants visually represented by personalized avatars have significantly advanced with the emergence of new metaverse technologies. First coined by Stephenson (1992) in his highly influential science-fiction novel *Snow Crash*, metaverse as a shared online space that incorporates 3D graphics either on a screen or in virtual reality (VR) has recently got traction. The applications of metaverse technologies in CUD are promising with some countries immediately recognizing new opportunities to engage audiences on a global scale. Since the late 1990s, the South Korean government's investments and efforts in going global by wielding its cultural soft power have produced phenomenal growth and global popularity of Korean culture, known as a Hallyu or Korean Wave (Kim, 2021). Most recently, the Korean Wave agenda and programming have opened new channels through metaverse technologies.

In the challenging times of restricted traveling in the pandemic conditions of the Covid-19 global outbreak, K-pop groups established in 2021 new practices of interacting with their global fans in virtual spaces through different metaverse platforms which offered an exciting opportunity for audiences not only to virtually meet their idols, but also engage with the cultural content through co-creation and participatory activities (Grincheva, 2022). While new technologies appear and transform human practices of cultural sharing dynamically, CUD scholarship is not progressing with the same speed to cover new cases of technological developments.

The establishment of cultural embassies and implementing cultural events and projects in a virtual world, like Second Life, started more than a decade ago with the Republic of Maldives opening the first "virtual embassy" on Second Life's Diplomacy Island back in May 2007. However, since that time there were only a few publications that explore the value, meaning, and mechanics of Second Life CUD activities and their applications in building cultural relationships across borders (Stevens, 2015). New scholarship should modernize the CUD research agenda, critically interrogating the technological implications and reflecting the need to move along with a rapid development of human cultures and artistic practices of contemporary societies. Future research should embrace new emerging forms of digital and new media arts, cyborg art and art robotics, online multiplayer games, metaverse worlds, and artificial intelligence (AI) arts to explore new artistic mediums of the future which transform, automate but complicate, diversify, and challenge CUD (Grincheva, 2022).

Moreover, it is important to explore if digitalization of diplomacy actually supports or at least permits to maintain the same level of cross-cultural relationships, based on human-to-human communications. The digital environment does not necessarily offer the climate of trust and privacy in conversations and online encounters across borders have strict limitations. While diplomatic exchanges have traditionally been based on long-lasting personal connections promoting "international goodwill and understanding" (Mulcahy, 1999, p. 22), a lack of physical contact between participants in digital settings prevents the development of deeper personal relationships. Only a few most recent research works addressed these questions to reveal that, in fact, digital contacts can be very productive in exposing online participants to new cultural knowledge. They can unearth cross-cultural stereotypes, stimulate interest in other people's cultures and traditions, and even generate cross-cultural curiosity leading to personal engagements across countries (Grincheva, 2020).

Nevertheless, future research should continue this line of work to contribute to the current academic scholarship that pays scarce attention to these issues. Furthermore, the increasing digitalization (Peters, 2016) and platformization processes (Jin, 2017) significantly redefine the conduct of global communications impacting the environments where CUD is operating. Digital platforms, including social networks and instant communication providers are powerful governing systems that control public communications, mediate economic, political, and cultural transactions among multiple actors and become important surveillance machines which track and record users' data with an immense economic and political value (Lane, 2020). Platforms' algorithms govern the news and content consumption as well as intervene in users' interactions, actively shaping the social world of people. They are powerful enough to accelerate the cultural and political fragmentation of society, in many cases exacerbating the differences between cultural communities and negatively impacting digital diplomatic initiatives (Riordan, 2019).

Despite the growing number of focused research works on digital diplomacy (Bjola & Pamment, 2018), digital CUD remains largely underexplored (Clarke, 2014; Grincheva, 2020). There are a few works which investigate cultural and political implications of digital archiving technologies (Thylstrup, 2019) and analyze cultural heritage digital platforms, like Google Arts and Culture, from the politico-economic perspective (Valtysson, 2020) or as a new force of cultural colonialism (Kizhner et al., 2021). Nevertheless, more research is required to situate these activities in the framework of CUD that consistently moves into the world of digital and virtual communications, with these trends being significantly amplified by the global pandemic crisis (Grincheva, 2021).

New modes of global communications are rapidly evolving and increasingly bring in the impact of the non-human factor.

The power of algorithms and AI technologies has been actively employed to address tasks in born-digital art creation and even in automation of cross-cultural communications. In online communications among cultural organizations and their global audiences, a human effort to deliver information is increasingly replaced with chatbots. Chatbots are algorithms designed to react to online conversations imitating a dialogue among people (Dahiya, 2017). Cultural and heritage institutions increasingly use chatbots to sustain live conversations online, answer frequently asked questions, guide visitors to the door, or help them to find useful information from ticketing to collections search. In 2020, Europeana, the largest digital heritage aggregator in Europe connecting 3,000 institutions and featuring online over 50 million cultural and scientific artifacts, implemented the Culture Chatbot Generic Services project. It developed a chatbot platform and several different versions of chatbots, analyzing the use-cases of museums to explore the value of AI and algorithms for sharing cultural heritage across borders (Katz, 2020).

Algorithmic help with users' navigation, curation of cultural material, instant translation of content into different languages and responding to users' queries, indeed, replace a direct contact with a human being, making a cross-cultural encounter in virtual realities a completely different endeavor. However, the impact of such a cross-cultural communication has not yet been researched and it is important to interrogate further the capacity of AI to sustain an engaging cross-cultural dialogue and to shape a meaningful perception of another culture. The research agenda of CUD should engage closer with these raising social and technological issues which affect the focus, forms of delivery, and nature of contemporary diplomacy. Future studies should particularly focus on the fundamental components of CUD such as building long-term international cultural relations to conceptualize digital relationships and examine cross-cultural trust, credibility, and reputation management in the post-truth environments in the post-human conditions.

While there has been excitement around deep fakes used in museums to bring to life historical figures (Mihailova, 2021), robots giving addresses for the United Nations Assembly (United Nations, 2017), or works of art created by AI (Manovich, 2018; Zylinska, 2020), the focused examination of the pitfalls of post-humanism, in fact, reveals growing challenges that emerge around issues of technological ethics and post-human rights, digital democracy, and conceptualization of reality under the overshadowing fantasies of cyber-utopianism (Levin, 2020). Understanding better premises and perils of post-human conditions and their impact on human culture and CUD would require further critical engagement with all these questions as well as a more focused interrogation of anthropocentrism and human exceptionalism in the narratives created through newly emerged technological manifestations and their after-effects (Baelo-Allué & Calvo-Pascual, 2021).

This section reveals a high diversity of CUD diplomacy practices from early human-to-human cultural exchanges to the most recent virtual encounters in online environments. It urges to focus the scholarly attention to explore new conditions in which CUD operates in the 21st century, including virtual and algorithmic environments, new artistic practices and cultural norms and expectations, as well as the emergence of non-human actors who increasingly intervene in cross-cultural communications.

Conclusion

The chapter suggests further trajectories for the development of CUD research so it could more proactively shape an academic enquiry focusing on different diplomatic channels, modes of operation, structures, actors, meanings, and applications. First, it advocates for more nuanced geographies of explorations, going beyond the traditional nation state or country focus. On the micro level, the chapter invites future research to scrutinize the communication modes, power dynamics, and implications of various sub-diplomacies of contested territories, marginalized or indigenous communities, who acquired stronger powers of political representation in the age of digital globalization. On the macro levels, it identifies important themes of contemporary CUD that engage closer with global concerns and issues from LGBT activism to climate change crisis to reveal the importance of cosmopolitan dimensions in diplomacy or "humanities centered" narratives that provide a different rationale for diplomatic practices, diminishing the role of national cultural promotion.

Second, the chapter stresses significant impacts of such processes as the digitalization and platformization of contemporary international communications. These processes invite further research on new CUD channels urging to investigate their direct opportunities for involved stakeholders as well as limitations in targeting and meaningfully engaging digital audiences across borders. Considering that the essence of CUD is a creation of a "shared zone" or a meta-space for human contacts and exchanges of cultures, ideas, and beliefs, there is still a limited understanding how the digital environment can accommodate the development of mutual trust and long-term relationships.

CUD scholarship needs to prioritize the exploration of these questions on its future research agenda, also focusing on seizing opportunities and risks emerging in the post-human conditions.

References

Arndt, R. (2005). *First resort of kings: American cultural diplomacy in the 20th century.* Potomac.

Baelo-Allué, S., & Calvo-Pascual, M. (2021). *Transhumanism and posthumanism in twenty-first-century narrative.* Routledge.

Batora, J., & Hocking, B. (2008). Bilateral diplomacy in the European Union: Towards "post-modern" patterns? *Discussion Papers in Diplomacy.* Netherlands Institute of International Relations Clingendael.

Beck, U. (2001). Redefining power in the global age: Eight theses. *Dissent, 3,* 83–9.

Beck, U. (2006). *The cosmopolitan vision.* Polity.

Bentley, J. (2011). Cultural exchanges in world history. In J. Bentley (Ed.), *The Oxford handbook of world history* (pp. 343–60). Oxford University Press.

Bjola, C., & Pamment, J. (Eds.) (2018). *Countering online propaganda and extremism: The dark side of digital diplomacy.* Routledge.

Chalcraft, J. (2021). Into the contact zones of heritage diplomacy: Local realities, transnational themes and international expectations. *International Journal of Politics, Culture, and Society, 34*(4), 487–501.

Chung, H. S. (2020). *Hollywood diplomacy.* Amsterdam University Press.

Clarke, D. (2014). Theorising the role of cultural products in cultural diplomacy from a Cultural Studies perspective. *International Journal of Cultural Policy, 22*(2), 147–63.

Copeland, D. (2009). Transformational public diplomacy: Rethinking advocacy for the globalisation age. *Place Branding and Public Diplomacy, 5*(2), 97–102.

Dahiya, M. (2017). A tool of conversation: Chatbot. *International Journal of Computer Sciences and Engineering, 5*(5), 158–61.

Demir, F., & Im, H. (2019). Effects of cultural institutes on bilateral trade and FDI flows: Cultural diplomacy or economic altruism? *The World Economy, 43*(9), 2463–89.

Dines, N. (2020). Moroccan city festivals, cultural diplomacy and urban political agency. *International Journal of Politics, Culture, and Society, 34*(4), 471–85.

Dunkel, M., & Nitzsche, S. A. (2019). *Popular music and public diplomacy: Transnational and transdisciplinary perspectives.* Columbia University Press.

Galmarini, M. C. (2021). A common space of international work: Disability activism, socialist internationalism, and the Russian union of the blind. *The Russian Review, 80*(4), 624–40.

Gautam, A., & Droogan, J. (2017). Yoga soft power: How flexible is the posture? *The Journal of International Communication, 24*(1), 18–36.

Giguère, M. (2018). Bridging worlds: The ambiguities of *La Mission Ambulante* with the Métis, Plains Cree and Blackfoot during the Great Transformation (1860–1880). *Religious Studies and Theology, 37*(2), 178–205.

Gonzalez, J. J. (2011). *Diaspora diplomacy: Philippine migration and its soft power influences.* Mill City Press.

Grincheva, N. (2019). *Global trends in museum diplomacy*. Routledge.

Grincheva, N. (2020). *Museum diplomacy in the digital age*. Routledge.

Grincheva, N. (2021). Cultural diplomacy under the "digital lockdown": Pandemic challenges and opportunities in museum diplomacy. *Place Branding and Public Diplomacy*, *18*(1), 8–11.

Grincheva, N. (2022). The future of cultural diplomacy: From digital to algorithmic. In Y. Jung, N. Vakharia, & M. Vecco (Eds.), *The Oxford handbook of arts and cultural management*. Oxford University Press.

Habermas, J. (2001). *The postnational constellation*. MIT Press.

Harker, R. J. W. (2020). *Museum diplomacy: Transnational public history and the U.S. Department of State*. University of Massachusetts Press.

Hesse, M., & Rafferty, M. (2020). Relational cities disrupted: Reflections on the particular geographies of Covid-19 for small but global urbanisation in Dublin, Ireland, and Luxembourg City, Luxembourg. *Tijdschrift Voor Economische En Sociale Geografie*, *111*(3), 451–64.

Huang, S. M. (2021). Indigenous heritage in diplomacy: Repositioning Taiwan in the Austronesian network and its cultural implications. *Journal of Cultural Heritage Management and Sustainable Development*, *12*(1), 72–86.

Idowu, D. L., & Ogunnubi, O. (2022). Soft power in therapeutic comedy: Outlining Nigeria's creative industry through digital comic skits. *Creative Industries Journal*, 1–22. https://doi.org/10.1080/17510694.2022.2025703.

Ivey, B. (2007). *Cultural diplomacy and the national interest*. Arts Industry Policy Forum. http://www.interarts.net/descargas/interarts673.pdf.

Jin, D. Y. (2017). *Digital platforms, imperialism and political culture*. Routledge.

Katz, P. (2020). Interacting with the culture chatbot. Europeana pro. https://bit.ly/31VlDM7.

Kennedy, L. (Ed.) (2022). *Routledge international handbook of diaspora diplomacy*. Routledge.

Kichuk, Y., & Shevchuk, T. (2020). Public movement of the national minorities in Budzhak Poliethnic Society as a factor of intercultural interaction. *History Museum of Galati*, *38*(1), 221–37. https://www.ceeol.com/search/article-detail?id=921317.

Kim, Y. (2021). *The soft power of the Korean Wave*. Routledge.

Kizhner, I., Terras, M., Rumyantsev, M., Khokhlova, V., Demeshkova, E., Rudov, I., & Afanasieva, J. (2021). Digital cultural colonialism: Measuring bias in aggregated digitized content held in Google Arts and Culture. *Digital Scholarship in the Humanities*, *36*(3), 607–40.

Kong, D. (2021). *Museums, international exhibitions and China's cultural diplomacy*. Routledge.

Lähdesmäki, T. (2021). Heritage diplomacy discourses in the EU: Notions on cultural diplomacy, cultural heritage, and intercultural dialogue among EU officials and heritage practitioners. *Ethnologia Europaea*, *51*(2), 48–71.

Lam, P. E. (2007). Japan's quest for "Soft Power": Attraction and limitation. *East Asia*, *24*(4), 349–63.

Lane, J. (2020). *Democratizing our data: A manifesto*. MIT Press.

Levin, S. B. (2020). *Posthuman bliss?* Oxford University Press.

Lucke, M. (2002). Vilified, venerated, forbidden: Jazz in the Stalinist era. *Music and Politics*, *1*(2), 1–9.

Manovich, L. (2018). *AI aesthetics*. Strelka Press.

Melissen, J. (Ed.) (2005). *The new public diplomacy: Soft power in international relations*. Palgrave Macmillan.

Mihailova, M. (2021). To dally with Dal'ı: deepfake (inter)faces in the art museum. *Convergence, 27*(4), 882–98.

Mulcahy, K. (1999). Cultural diplomacy and the exchange programs: 1938–1978. *Journal of Arts Management, Law & Society, 29*(1), 7–28.

Nagabhatla, N., Cassidy-Neumiller, M., Francine, N. N., & Maatta, N. (2021). Water, conflicts and migration and the role of regional diplomacy: Lake Chad, Congo Basin, and the Mbororo pastoralist. *Environmental Science & Policy, 122,* 35–48.

Ocón, D. (2021). Cultural diplomacy and co-operation in ASEAN: The role of arts and culture festivals. *The Hague Journal of Diplomacy,* 1–29. https://ink.library.smu.edu .sg/soss_research/3475.

Parkinson, F. (1977). *The Philosophy of international relations: A study in the history of thought.* Sage.

Peters, B. (2016). *Digital keywords: A vocabulary of information society and culture.* Princeton University Press.

Prevots, N. (1999). *Dance for export: Cultural diplomacy and the Cold War.* Wesleyan University Press.

Richmond, Y. (2003). *Cultural exchange and the cold war: Raising the iron curtain.* Penn State University Press.

Riordan, S. (2019). *Cyber diplomacy: Managing security and governance online.* Polity.

Saito, Y. (2021). *The global politics of jazz in the twentieth century.* Routledge.

Schneider, C. (2003). *Diplomacy that works: Best practices in cultural diplomacy.* Center for Arts and Culture. http://www.interarts.net/descargas/interarts645.pdf.

Schneider, C. (2006). Culture communicates: US diplomacy that works. In J. Melissen, D. Lee, & P. Sharp (Eds.), *The new public diplomacy* (pp. 147–68). Palgrave Macmillan.

Schneider, C. (2010). Cultural diplomacy: The humanizing factor. In J. Singh (Ed.), *International cultural policies and power* (pp. 101–12). Palgrave Macmillan.

Scott-Smith, G. (2009). Exchange programs and public diplomacy. In N. Snow & P. Taylor (Eds.), *Routledge handbook of public diplomacy* (pp. 50–56). Routledge.

Searcy, A. (2020). *Ballet in the Cold War: A Soviet–American exchange.* Oxford University Press.

Snow, N. (2008). International exchanges and the U.S. image. *Annals of the American Academy of Political and Social Science, 616*(1), 198–222.

Sölter, A. A. (2015). Festival circus, golden gnomes and cultural diplomacy: The Audi Festival of German films in the context of multicultural festivals in Australia. *Studies in Australasian Cinema, 9*(2), 190–204.

Steger, M. (2009). *Globalization: A very short introduction.* Oxford University Press.

Stengel, F. A., MacDonald, D. B., & Nabers, D. (2019). *Populism and world politics.* Springer.

Stephenson, E. (2020). Invisible while visible: An Australian perspective on queer women leaders in international affairs. *European Journal of Politics and Gender, 3*(3), 427–43.

Stephenson, N. (1992). *Snow crash.* Random House.

Stevens, T. (2015). Security and surveillance in virtual worlds: Who is watching the warlocks and why? *International Political Sociology, 1*(9), 230–47.

Strachová, N. (2021). Cities towards global climate governance: How the practices of city diplomacy foster hybrid multilateralism. *Przegląd Strategiczny, 14,* 365–77.

Thussu, D. K. (2020). Populism and public diplomacy. In N. Snow & N. Cull (Eds.), *Routledge handbook of public diplomacy* (pp. 314–22). Routledge.

Thylstrup, N. B. (2019). *The politics of mass digitization.* MIT Press.

Trivellato, F., Halevi, L. & Antunes, C. (2014). *Religion and trade: Cross-cultural exchanges in world history, 1000–1900*. Oxford University Press.

United Nations (2017, October 11). At UN, robot Sophia joins meeting on artificial intelligence and sustainable development. *UN News*. https://bit.ly/3jBxxQb.

U.S. Department of State (1969). *Cultural diplomacy*. International Education Exchange Service, US Department of State Bureau of International Cultural Relations.

Valtysson, B. (2020). *Digital cultural politics: From policy to practice*. Palgrave Macmillan.

Villanueva, R. (2010). Cosmopolitan constructivism: Mapping a road to the future of cultural diplomacy. *Public Diplomacy Magazine, 4*, 45–56.

Wang, D. R., Hajjar, D. P., & Cole, C. L. (2019). International partnerships for the development of STEM and medical education of Middle Eastern women. *International Journal of Higher Education, 9*(2), 1–15.

Wang, J., & Hallquist, M. (2011). The comic imagination of China: The Beijing Olympics in American TV comedy and implications for public diplomacy. *Place Branding and Public Diplomacy, 7*(4), 232–43.

Winter, T. (2015). Heritage diplomacy. *International Journal of Heritage Studies, 21*(10), 997–1015.

Wyszomirski, M. J. (2003). *International cultural relations: A multi-country comparison*. Americans for the Arts.

Zaharna, R. S. (2021). *Boundary spanners of humanity: Three logics of communications and public diplomacy for global collaboration*. Oxford University Press.

Zylinska, J. (2020). *AI art*. Open Humanities Press.

14   Nation as brand

Simon Anholt

Introduction

It was in the late 1990s when I first became interested in the idea of national image and began to write about a concept I called *nation brand*. My preliminary observation seems like a fairly banal one today, but it created something of a stir at the time: that the images of countries, cities and regions behave very much like the brand images of companies and their products and services; and they are an equally critical driver of the progress and prosperity of places.

But as the expression *nation/country brand* caught on it soon became distorted, with the assistance of ambitious consulting firms that scented a large new marketplace coming into existence, into *nation/country branding*: an epithet which seems to contain a promise that the images of countries can be directly manipulated by means of marketing communications. So simple and appealing was the idea of "nation brand*ing*", I even started to use it myself, long before it dawned on me what a difference that three-letter suffix actually made.

Despite searching and calling for it over the last 20 years, I have never yet seen any good evidence to suggest that "brand*ing*" (in the sense of marketing communications and messaging) has ever produced any change in international perceptions of any country: no case studies, no research, and not even any very persuasive arguments. My conclusion, until I'm persuaded otherwise, remains that countries are judged by what they do, not by what they say, as they always have been. But perhaps not surprisingly, the prospect of a country (or indeed a city or region) being able to advertise its way into a better reputation has proved enduringly attractive, both to communications professionals – who stand to make a fortune if what they offer really does work, and perhaps even if it doesn't – and to the governments they serve.

Despite having pondered this topic for many years, I have to admit that I'm not at all sure I even know what "branding" is. In the commercial context, the term "brand" is used to imply at least three very different things: first, it can refer to the *designed identity* of a product (the look of the product itself, its packaging, its logo, its livery, its communications, and so forth); second, it is sometimes used more ambitiously to refer to the tone, the values, the culture of the organisation behind the product; and third, it can refer to the product's or corporation's *reputation* in the minds of its target audience: this is the sense in which I used the term in an early essay on the subject, although the term "brand image" is a more precise one in this context (Anholt, 1998).

In consequence, one might suppose, the practice of brand*ing* must relate to one or another of these meanings: it is either the business of designing the visual elements of the packaging or communications of products, and/or the products themselves (this is indeed the main activity of branding agencies); or else it is connected with enhancing a sense of corporate culture or "mission" inside the organisation (in fact the word is not often used in this context); or, finally, it is the means by which the product acquires its image and reputation. This is where the trouble starts.

Used in its first sense, branding does have some relevance to countries and the ways they present themselves to the rest of the world, but it is an essentially humble craft, the exercise of which hardly justifies the excitement about "nation branding", or the extravagant sums spent on it. Countries, through their many state agencies, have dealings with many professional audiences around the world, and one can certainly argue that it gives a better impression of the country if those agencies all use consistent, well-designed materials when they carry out their transactions. A single logo, a professional "look and feel" on their stationery, business cards, corporate videos, information leaflets, communiqués, press releases, websites and so forth, undoubtedly reinforce the impression of a well-organised, modern, self-respecting state with effective and efficient structures, processes and mechanisms.

If this is "nation branding" then I withdraw my objections: it's a logical and achievable standard to aspire to; it makes sense for countries to try to do it well; and it's certainly just as important as, for example, making sure that diplomats offer the right kinds of canapés when entertaining foreign officials; but it's hard to understand why anybody in their right mind would want to spend time theorising about it, still less spend millions of dollars of taxpayers' money on it. "Branding" in this sense of the word is a fundamentally *passive* phenomenon. Even very good graphic design can't reach out and attract new talent, investment or tourists, and it simply doesn't have the power to change anybody's mind about the country or affect its prospects in any significant way. It is good practice, a useful exercise of reassurance, a piece of housekeeping: nothing more.

So why all the excitement? Certainly, the impact of graphic design is a different matter in its native context of consumer goods, and this is where the confusion originates. For fast-moving consumer products in a busy retail environment, the branding of a product can become nearly as important as the product itself, because design is often one of the few things that distinguish a product from its competitors; the attractiveness of the product and its wrapper may in some circumstances even be a more significant driver of consumer choice than advertising, although the two usually work closely together. This is why, branding agencies, accustomed to the emphasis placed on brand identity in their native field of commerce, talk so convincingly about such matters, and why public officials are so often swayed by their talk. But countries aren't for sale, aren't easily mistaken one for another (and when they are, it's a bigger problem than graphic design), they aren't fast-moving consumer goods, and certainly don't come in wrappers or live on supermarket shelves, so most of the principles just don't apply.

The confusion becomes acute when people start implying, as per my third definition, that "branding" is a technique for directly building or enhancing brand *image* (or wishing that it was): "Nike's excellent brand image is the result of excellent branding." It is not. Nike's excellent brand image is the result of excellent products, effectively sold in very large numbers at the right price. Brand *building* is the result of excellence and innovation in product development and marketing, the consequence of a long and happy relationship between product and purchaser, and, once again, logo and packaging design are important tools in the marketing mix that supports these activities.

If there is a lesson to be learned by countries from companies, it is simply this: a country that's committed to enhancing its international image should concentrate on "product development" (i.e. improving the quality and relevance of its exports, investment opportunities, cultural, educational and tourism offerings) and "marketing" (i.e. effective promotion of these offerings to their overseas target audiences) rather than chase after the chimera of "branding" (i.e. attempting directly to manipulate international perceptions of the country).

There are no short cuts. Only a consistent, coordinated and unbroken stream of useful, noticeable, world-class and above all *relevant* policies, ideas, people and products can, gradually, enhance the reputation of the country that produces them.

Why does country image matter?

In an effort to resolve or at least avoid some of the confusion caused by careless use of the word "brand" by myself and others, I coined the deliberately unglamorous term *Competitive Identity* as the title of a book on this topic (Anholt, 2007). I doubt it helped sales of the book very much, but it did help make my point that the images of countries have more to do with national identity and the politics and economics of competitiveness than with branding as the term is usually understood. But most governments, as well as the companies and consultants that work for them, still seem a long way from understanding the basic principles of place image. Many if not most countries, as well as many cities and regions, clearly want to enhance, reverse, adapt or otherwise manage their international reputations: yet we are very far from a general understanding of what this means in practice, and just how far commercial approaches can be effectively and responsibly applied to the public sphere (and when or whether it is justifiable to spend taxpayers' money on such approaches).

Many governments, most consultants and even some scholars persist in a superficial (but commercially useful) interpretation of "place branding" that is nothing more than standard product promotion, public relations and corporate identity: the product just happens to be a country, a city or a region rather than a running shoe or a can of beer. It would be invidious to single out examples in this context, but in any list of "country branding" campaigns created during the last 20 years, it is very rare to find cases where the slogans and promises are consistently backed up by policies and behaviours, and very common to find the opposite.

The problem is perpetuated by an almost universal habit of conflating or confusing the promotion of a country's sectors, products and services (such as tourism, export and investment promotion), which can and should be promoted; and the management of its overall image, which is not about selling or promoting anything.

Yet this is a topic that governments must understand. In today's hyper-connected and interdependent world, countries can't operate in a vacuum – whatever they need to attract (investors, aid, tourists, business visitors, students, major events, researchers, commentators and talented entrepreneurs), and whatever they need to promote (products, services, policies, people, policies, culture and ideas) – all of it is discounted if the country's image is weak or negative, and all of it attracts a premium if the image is strong and positive. A poor reputation is truly a structural deficit.

I have even argued that a bad "brand image" easily becomes a security issue. Politicians tend to have a keen instinct for how their own populations regard or respect other countries, and they understand that if they want to stay in favour, they should rush to defend the countries their populations admire and spend blood and treasure on doing so if necessary. By the same token, they understand equally well that they can safely ignore the pleas of countries their populations are unaware of or indifferent to, no matter how urgent their needs or how deep their suffering. Governments in rich countries can implement brutal aid cuts to the world's poorest countries without significantly diminishing their chances of re-election, secure in the knowledge that a healthy majority of their voters are thoroughly ignorant about those countries and only associate them with poverty and starvation: a perception that, tragically, becomes their destiny.

In a similar way, the extreme reluctance of most countries to provide any meaningful assistance to Ukraine following the illegal annexation of Crimea by Vladimir Putin in 2014, and indeed their initial reluctance to come to Ukraine's aid immediately following his full-scale invasion of the country in 2022 is a mark of how little international profile, understanding or affection Ukraine had been able to achieve since it re-emerged into the community of nations at the end of the Soviet era. Those countries' leaders probably felt that they were unlikely to be penalised at the ballot box for contributing fine words and nothing much more to the cause of Ukrainian security. On the other hand, they might well have been penalised for putting boots on the ground, spending public money or offering to take in large numbers of refugees. Of course, sanctions imposed on Russia in retaliation for the invasion will also have a negative impact on the image of Russia – effectively creating a "double punishment" for the aggressor – but this effect pales in comparison to the direct damage done to the image of Russia by the invasion itself. It seems beyond question that however this disgraceful episode ends, the damage done to Russia's already weak image will be catastrophic and will last for decades, effectively barring Russia from normal or profitable transactions with the international community for generations to come.

These dynamics only exist because of our ignorance about other countries. In this crowded modern global marketplace, people have neither the time nor the patience to learn much about the places where they don't actually live. It is a human habit to navigate through the complexity of the modern world armed with a few simple clichés, and those clichés form our opinions, even if we don't like to admit it to ourselves: Paris is chic, Japan is technology, Switzerland is wealth and precision, Rio de Janeiro is carnival and football, Tuscany is the good life, and most African nations stand only for poverty, corruption, war, famine and disease. Very few of us will take the trouble to acquire balanced and informed views about eight billion other people, two hundred other countries and thousands of cities: we make do with summaries for the vast majority of people and places – the ones we will probably never know or visit – and will only expand or refine these impressions when for some reason we acquire a particular interest in them. When we haven't time to read a book, we judge it by its cover.

These clichés and stereotypes – whether positive or negative, fair or unfair – profoundly affect our behaviour towards places, people and products. When attention spans are so short, and the deluge of information so unrelenting, it's a huge challenge for any country to persuade people around the world to think beyond these simple images and begin to appreciate the rich complexity that lies behind them. Yet when it comes into office, a government unquestionably inherits a responsibility for its electorate's most valuable asset: the good name of its country: and one of its key tasks is to hand that good name down to its successors in at least as good condition as it received it.

It is an act of responsible governance to measure and monitor international perceptions of the nation and its principal cities and even regions, and if possible, to develop a strategy for preserving or even enhancing those perceptions. It is a key part of the modern policymaker's job to earn a national reputation that is true, powerful, attractive, materially useful to the economic, political and social aims of the country; one which honestly reflects the spirit, the genius and the will of its population. This daunting task has become one of the primary skills of administrations in the twenty-first century. No wonder, perhaps, that so many Western politicians now come from the fields of public relations and journalism rather than the legal background that until recently was the standard route to public office: but whether this helps them do their jobs more effectively is another question entirely.

Why is rich good?

Surely, therefore, the very last thing countries should want is a "brand". If a brand image is the catchy reduction of something rich and complex into a naive, one-dimensional formula, then many of the countries which already have one would do well to get rid of it, if only they could. Seen in this light, "nation branding" is the problem, not the solution: branding is what the media and public opinion do to countries, not what governments should try to do to their own states and populations. Countries need people around the world to have a richer, deeper, more nuanced view of their land, their population and their civilisation – not a fabricated stereotype to replace the inherited stereotype.

It's worth asking why Egyptian respondents' scores for Denmark dropped by an unprecedented 36 places in the Nation Brands Index (NBI) following the publication in 2006 of cartoons lampooning the Prophet Mohammed, while their scores for the US never fell further than six, despite the invasion and military occupation of two Muslim countries. Perhaps because Denmark had a simple brand image, while America moved beyond a brand centuries ago. Most Egyptians only knew one thing about Denmark – that it was a Scandinavian country – so they admired it; then they learned one new thing – that it had insulted their Prophet – so a large part of its image became negative, and that was enough to sink the ship. By contrast, Egyptians knew (or thought they knew) a great many things about America, so one new negative fact only formed a small proportion of the whole, and the damage was contained.

Countries should surely aspire to something more like education than branding: to find ways of helping people in other countries to get to know them; to explore and celebrate rather than reduce their own complexity. This is why I have often remarked that cultural relations is the only demonstrably effective form of "nation branding" (see Chapter 13 in this volume). The experience of countries that have successfully practised cultural relations over many years shows that consistent, imaginative cultural exchange does eventually create an environment where respect and tolerance flourish, and this undoubtedly also favours increased trade in skills, knowledge, products, capital and people. People who understand each other get on better, and people who get on better tend to trade with each other more frequently, more freely and with greater mutual profit.

Governmental social responsibility?

I believe that if a country wants to be admired, it must be relevant, and in order to become relevant, it must participate usefully, productively and imaginatively in the global conversation on the topics that matter to people elsewhere and everywhere. The list of those topics is a long one: climate change, poverty, famine, narcotics, migration, economic stability, human rights, women's rights, indigenous people's rights, children's rights, religious and cultural tolerance, nuclear proliferation, water, education, corruption, terrorism, crime, war and arms control are just a few of the most obvious ones.

Surely any country could select at least one item on this list that has a special relevance to its own needs, experiences or resources, and find a way to contribute meaningfully towards tackling it – in partnership with others, of course, because there is no rule to say that earning a better national reputation is necessarily a solitary or even competitive activity. There is a strong precedent for this kind of behaviour in the commercial world, which presents us with a far more useful metaphor than branding. For at least 30 years, it has become more and more evident that corporations which fail to demonstrate and maintain high ethical standards, transparency and social responsibility will soon lose the trust and respect of their consumers. I say "30 years" but as I have argued elsewhere corporate social responsibility has existed for as long as commerce and was particularly highly developed by certain Florentine banks in the Middle Ages (Anholt, 2005).

The critics of corporate social responsibility, or what is more frequently referred to today as environmental, social and governance (ESG) criteria, claim that the notion has become devalued because, in many cases, it is no more than window dressing. But even if one is cynical and believes that 75 per cent of organisations that claim to follow ESG principles are merely virtue-signalling, still, it sends out an important message to others that these are the qualities to aspire to; and even if only a fraction of those companies have reviewed the way they do business and its real consequences, and have cleaned up their act as a result, this is revolutionary. It would certainly be revolutionary if countries, cities and regions – today nearly as obsessed with their reputations as companies are – started adhering to the same principles.

The NBI suggests that people around the world are less and less inclined to admire or respect countries and governments that pollute the oceans, cut down forests, permit or sustain corruption, ignore human rights or flout the rule of law. It's the same audience beginning to apply the same standards to places as they apply to products and the companies that make them. In a few decades, the power of consumer choice has influenced the rules of business and transformed the behaviour of corporations. Perhaps there is some hope that consumer power can achieve a similar transformation in the way that countries, cities and regions are governed in the future.

The MARSS model: an account of national influence

Nye's (2005) model of soft, hard and smart power has provided a useful distinction in this context. Of course, there are many different types of power, influence, appeal and authority that a country can wield over the public imagination and over reality (see Chapter 8 in this volume). Most are "soft" (in the sense that they draw people towards them) and a handful are truly "hard" (in the sense that they can be used on people against their will): but it is instructive to explore in more detail the different ways in which national appeal can manifest itself.

The MARSS model is a hypothetical model of the key drivers of country appeal, based on analysis of the 17 large-scale surveys of international perceptions of 64 countries and 71 cities which I carried out between 2005 when the Anholt Nation Brands Index was first fielded, and 2011 when I conducted the analysis. The Anholt Ipsos Nation Brands Index today polls around 60,000 people in 20 countries each year to measure their perceptions of 60 countries (and 50 cities every two years): its cumulative database contains over a billion data points.

Observation of the NBI over the previous six years suggested that the key drivers of overall national standing could be characterised as *Morality*, *Aesthetics*, *Relevance*, *Sophistication* and *Strength*. These five drivers – which together form the MARSS model – appear to co-exist and overlap in a wide variety of combinations (Anholt, 2020).

People may know very little about what certain countries do, make, or look like, but still tend to have fairly clear ideas about whether each is "good" or "bad", beautiful or ugly, strong or weak, sophisticated or primitive, and whether it is relevant to their lives or not.

Morality is concerned with whether people *approve* of the country (or some combination of its leaders, its population and its commercial and public institutions), and believe that it contributes positively to the world outside its own borders: that it is, in other words, a benign or helpful presence in the international community.

Morality may of course differ (in reality as in perception) depending on whether one is considering the government, the population, or the public or private institutions of a nation, but in most cases, international public opinion *en masse* does not appear to trouble with such fine distinctions. In the case of better-known countries, people may distinguish between all of these moral "players"; in the case of less well-known countries, they are more likely to perceive the entire country as a single moral entity (which is bad news for the populations of "rogue" states). The perception of a country's "morality" is, of course, subjective: the parameters are significantly determined by the culture, politics, value-set, religious beliefs and personal experiences of the individual in question.

Aesthetics is a measure of whether the country (i.e. some combination of its people, its built and natural environment, products, cultural output, etc.) is regarded as pleasing to the eye. Sighted people, at any rate, appear to find it difficult to dislike or disapprove very strongly or for very long of beautiful places, people and products – and humanity has a pronounced tendency to associate beauty with virtue. Intriguingly, the NBI showed that many people around the world started to regard the American *landscape* as less beautiful during the second term in office of George W. Bush; many Muslim respondents had a similar response to the Danish countryside following the publication of the infamous cartoons mentioned earlier. These "halo effects" are not an uncommon finding in the NBI: we are emotional as well as rational beings, with a strong tendency to personalise states.

Relevance is a critical factor when considering national image. One of the most unequivocal early findings of the NBI was that, on average, most people seldom think spontaneously or regularly about more than a tiny handful of countries: their own; the US or perhaps another major power that they see as having a profound influence over their lives; and a small number of other countries with which they have some personal association, experience or ambition.

Relevance is a significant challenge for most countries trying to put themselves on people's mental maps: the more relevant the country is to the target, the better the conditions for rapid and profound change in their perceptions of that country. There's a catch: people who already feel that a country is relevant to their lives are more inclined to notice the things that country does or says or makes, but less likely to change their minds as a result, whereas people who don't feel that a country is relevant are less likely to pay attention, but more likely to change their minds.

Sophistication is a measure of how "modern" a country is perceived to be; whether it is regarded as primitive, unsophisticated and backward, or whether it is modern and highly developed. This question is often associated with technological development as much as human and economic capital, and indeed technology is a useful proxy for measuring this axis of the MARSS model.

Strength is concerned with our perception that a country can wield influence over us or others, independently of the other three attributes. Hard power, as described by Nye, is typically military and economic, but to this one might add media power: the country's ability to impose its views via its influence over, or more likely its ownership of, a substantial portion of the media messages reaching people.

Relative strengths of the MARSS components

To estimate the relative influence of these five hypothetical factors, a group of questions from the standard NBI questionnaire is selected as being most indicative of each. Each country's Morality score is produced by a combination of its average global rankings on the NBI questions related to its perceived contribution to poverty reduction; fair treatment of its own citizens and respect for human rights; competent and honest governance; responsible behaviour in international affairs, its contribution to global peace and security; its care for the environment; and the level of equality in its society.

The Aesthetic score is produced by a combination of questions relating to perceptions of attractive cultural heritage and popular culture, beautiful landscapes, and an attractive built environment. The Relevance score is a combination of personal familiarity with the country and beliefs about its international influence. The Sophistication score is based on perceptions of technological prowess, and the perception that the country has vibrant, modern cities. The Strength score is produced by combining rankings for technological and sporting prowess, investment value and perceptions of global impact.

Simply correlating each country's scores on these groups of questions with its overall position in the NBI ranking suggests that the perception of Morality is by a wide margin the strongest driver of overall national image, and this effect is even more pronounced when the analysis is repeated for survey respondents under 45 years of age.

One possible reason why the perception of Morality is so significant is because younger people tend to be influenced substantially by their moral sense and are perhaps less inclined to cynicism and the corrosive influence of *realpolitik*; and the older people who form the elites and the individually powerful are in turn influenced by younger public opinion. Thus, one of the most effective drivers of positive acceptance (in other words, effective soft power) for any country is a *clearly marked moral position*, accompanied of course by sustained and dramatic evidence that it continues to deserve this position.

This finding strongly corroborates a remark I published back in 2006: "If the world's governments placed even half the value which most wise corporations have learned to place on their good names, the world would be a safer and quieter place than it is today" (Anholt, 2006, p. 14). To this observation, I would today add that if governments do so, they also stand a chance of improving their own national prospects more rapidly, more effectively and more comprehensively than good governance and successful trade can do on their own.

The MARSS construct is a hypothetical working model, not a proven theory: to substantiate it will require more primary research as well as further analysis of other relevant datasets, and this work continues.

In June 2014, I released a new ranking, the Good Country Index (Anholt, 2014). This is the first and only study that attempts to estimate what each country on earth contributes to the rest of humanity and to the planet *outside* its own borders, and what it takes away. By combining 35 large datasets, mainly collected by UN agencies, the World Bank, the Basel Convention and other international bodies, the Good Country Index provides an approximate balance-sheet for each of 125 countries (the remaining 75 or so countries don't return enough data for me to be able to rank them fairly). The more than 70 per cent correlation between the results of the Nation Brands Index and the Good Country Index suggests that here, finally, we may be on the right track when it comes to understanding where this most precious national asset – the country's good name – actually comes from, and, perhaps, how it can be influenced over time.

Conclusion

Bragging about one's assets or achievements could never be regarded as sophisticated marketing, and yet it is what dozens of countries, regions and cities repeatedly do in their attempt to raise their profiles and improve their images. But success does not automatically equal respect.

Governments tend to be interested in success and power, since those are the currencies of politics, and so that's what they instinctively want to brag about (and communications agencies, on the whole, are not in the habit of challenging their clients' instincts). But this viewpoint makes them poor marketers, since it's not what their target audience is interested in. Increasingly, when it comes to other countries, the target audience is more interested in values and purpose.

What *does* interest them, in other words, is simply whether they feel glad that another country exists: whether it appears to be working to tackle the transnational, existential challenges of our age and is playing its part in ensuring the survival of humanity and the well-being of the natural world; whether it is simply a free-rider on the international community; or whether its behaviour poses a threat to the future peace and prosperity of all of us, our children and our grandchildren. In the end, the message to governments is quite simple, and quite obvious: if you want to be admired, you need to become admirable.

References

Anholt, S. (1998). Nation-brands of the twenty-first century. *Journal of Brand Management*, 5(6), 395–406.

Anholt, S. (2005). *Brand new justice: How branding places and products can help the developing world.* Revised edn. Butterworth-Heinemann.

Anholt, S. (2006). Anholt Nation Brands Index, *Special Report Q4 2006*: How has our world view changed since 2005?

Anholt, S. (2007). *Competitive identity: The new brand management for nations, cities and regions* (2nd edn. 2016). Palgrave Macmillan.

Anholt, S. (2014). *The Good Country Index.* https://index.goodcountry.org/.

Anholt, S. (2020). *The good country equation: How we can repair the world in one generation.* Berrett-Koehler.

Nye, J. (2005). *Soft power: The means to success in world politics.* PublicAffairs.

15   International broadcasting

Shawn Powers

Introduction

International broadcasting – state-supported media programming, targeting foreign publics, and guided by a mission in support of state interests – has been a central tool of information statecraft for nearly a century. The emergence of capable, long-distance radio transmission networks in the 1920s, alongside a heightened awareness of the acute role of information in shaping international and ideological conflict, fueled the rise of international broadcasting as a geopolitical tool. Historically, governments invest in international broadcasting institutions as a means of reaching and engaging with foreign audiences at times of acute geopolitical anxiety, especially surrounding violent and ideological conflict.

While references to international broadcasting today often conjure images of Cold War-era radio receivers, or the massive broadcast masts they were tuned to, governments have adapted to deploy these tools in creative, and occasionally, extremely productive ways. Today, international broadcasting plays an important role in an increasingly divisive geopolitical question: the primacy of the free flow of information versus the rise of information sovereignty.

Doctrines supporting the free flow of information, regardless of borders – an underlying premise upon which much of the liberal political order is based – is front and center in discussions of information warfare (Price, 2002). While open media systems are crucial to democratic institutions and governance, they are also susceptible to abuse by powerful, external actors. The presence of undesirable information flows, especially those originating from abroad, has pressured governments around the world to embrace greater information controls – or information sovereignty – to manage their domestic information spaces (Powers & Jablonski, 2015).

From the perspective of non-democratic and authoritarian governments, and perhaps some democratic governments, the Arab Spring was a warning as to what can happen when domestic discontent is fused with powerful, uncontrolled foreign information flows. Moreover, as authoritarian states such as Russia, China or Iran embrace new media platforms to coordinate and publicize attacks, established democratic governments too struggle with the proper balance between information freedom and state security. As a result, today, global press freedom continues to decline. The 2021 World Press Freedom Index compiled by Reporters Without Borders (RSF) found that journalists are completely or partly blocked in 73 percent of the 180 countries reviewed (Reporters Without Borders, 2021).

This dyadic phenomenon, whereby the information freedom often supported by Western governments results in media systems vulnerable to foreign propaganda and domestic controls, needs far greater attention. One outcome is the rise of information proxy wars, whereby great and aspiring powers compete, typically in partnership with local actors, to shape and spoil powerful narratives. Conceptualizing international broadcasting through the lens of information proxy wars calls for greater agility and understanding of audiences and their informational needs and expectations, as well as strengthened local partnerships. It may also require adjusting the short-term and long-term goals of broadcasters.

Providing independent journalism is crucial, of course, but so is combatting disinformation campaigns that aim to create confusion and sow distrust toward democratic political institutions. Moreover, while Western international broadcasters typically aim to "go out of business" by fostering an open and democratic media system, the risks of foreign subversion of these systems, including through the purchase of and control over media distribution systems, may require Western broadcasters to remain engaged in even seemingly healthy, democratic societies for far longer than they, or their parliamentarians, expect.[1]

This chapter provides a brief description of the state of global international broadcasting capabilities and charters, outlines how game theory can be adapted to provide a theoretical framework for understanding the likely success of a particular information intervention, and concludes with a discussion of key topics and research questions in need of scholarly attention and scrutiny.

---

[1]   For example, in 2019, Radio Free Europe/Radio Liberty (RFE/RL) re-established its Hungarian language service in response to growing concerns over freedom of the press and access to fact-based, public interest news media in the country. RFE/RL had closed its previous Hungarian service in 1993 after the end of the Cold War and the emergence of independent media and civil society in Hungary.

International broadcasting today

Despite predictions to the contrary, the 21st century has witnessed a dramatic rise in investments in the international broadcasting operations, as well as some innovations. While this started in the aftermath of 9/11, with American policymakers recognizing the centrality of public diplomacy (PD) to U.S. national security, it has taken on a new form since the early 2010s with China announcing its plans to invest billions in PD, as well as Russia's savvy investments to support niche media in markets where legacy journalism institutions are under severe financial strain. Below, I review the missions and operations of the three largest investors in international broadcasting today: China, Russia, and the United States (U.S.).

China

In 2001, the Chinese Communist Party (CCP) embarked on remaking China Central Television's international broadcaster, CCTV-9. According to Li Changchun, China's head of propaganda and media relations, the goal was to modernize the network, moving its focus away from domestic matters to covering the world's news "objectively and impartially from a Chinese angle, giving foreign readers and viewers a novel perspective" (*Taipei Times*, 2009). The network's director of research and development, Li-Sheng Zhang, described CCTV's international efforts as a complement to China's rise as an economic power: "Our country can't just compete in the international economic market, it must also enter the international ideological and cultural market" (Sina News, 2011). Inspired by Qatar's Al Jazeera, China's "going out" strategy is modeled after the tiny Gulf state's success in inserting a new, non-Western perspective into regional and global news flows (Zhu, 2014). Rather than positioning itself as a competitor to the BBC World Service or Voice of America, CCTV International (CCTV-I) was envisioned as "China's CNN, only cleverer" (Jirik, 2016).

Noting that soft power was "an increasingly important factor in national strength," CCTV president Hu Zhanfan called for a multifaceted, global effort, aiming to compete with other established media actors, both private and public (*Taipei Times*, 2009). For example, Xinhua announced a plan to expand its overseas presence, including the establishment of an overseas bureau in virtually every country, in hopes of challenging the dominance of the U.S.-based Associated Press. It also rebuilt its 24-hour, Beijing-based, English-language station. In addition to revamping its French, Spanish and Chinese foreign broadcast networks, in 2009, CCTV launched two new channels, broadcasting in Arabic and Russian.

The initiatives were firmly tethered to state interests. Hu made little effort to conceal the pro-state mission of its journalism: "The first social responsibility and professional ethic of media staff should be understanding their role clearly and being a good mouthpiece. Journalists who think of themselves as professionals, instead of as propaganda workers, are making a fundamental mistake about identity" (Jacobs, 2012). Speaking at China Radio International's (CRI) 70th anniversary celebration, propaganda chief Changchun emphasized the purpose of these efforts was to create "favorable international opinions about China and constantly boost its soft power" (*The Economic Times*, 2013). David Bandurski, editor of the China Media Project, a research consortium at the University of Hong Kong, sees the expansion as purely geopolitical, noting that Chinese leaders think their country is "constrained, even contained, by the global dominance of Western media groups and Western culture" (Farhi, 2012).

The sheer scale of China's information operations is noteworthy. CCTV's international facelift received additional support in 2009 when President Hu Jintao pledged an additional 45 million yuan (approximately $6.7 billion) for the overseas expansion of Chinese state media. By 2015, China was spending more than $10 billion a year on PD alone, not including foreign aid or its investments in the Belt and Road and Maritime Silk Road initiatives, the Asian Infrastructure Investment Bank, and the New Development Bank (Shambaugh, 2015). China's outlays in soft power, communications technologies and infrastructure, and messaging capabilities have only grown since. For example, several multi-million-dollar influence campaigns have recently been uncovered, including a $500 million advertising campaign to attract cable viewers in Australia, and spending over $20 million to influence U.S. public opinion via the *China Daily* newspaper supplement (Cook, 2020). In 2016, CCTV was rebranded as China Global Television Network (CGTN).

State-supported news organizations submit all material to the General Administration of Press and Publication (GAPP) of the People's Republic of China for clearance prior to publication, and topics sensitive to China's internal politics or issues that paint China in a negative light are avoided and/or censored. According to Zhu (2014), State Administration of Radio, Film and Television (SARFT) provides the central government's daily administrative oversight, including censorship of sensitive content, while the propaganda department issues guidelines and "thought directives."

China's national interests are most clearly reflected by the stories or controversies that are not covered or are downplayed on its media networks. Researchers at Columbia University conducting a systematic review of CGTN's English-language programming found "The government's hand can be seen most clearly in what isn't shown – in the omission of any content that might contradict or criticize the image the Communist Party promotes. There is plenty of criticism of the US (and virtually none of China's leaders)" (Farhi, 2012).

Censorship is clear to anyone watching CGTN for an extended period of time. According to Jacobs (2012), "When it comes to politically delicate subjects like Tibet, jailed dissidents or the maneuvering for power among the party's top leaders, Xinhua and [CGTN] have glaring blind spots." For example, CGTN America offered very limited coverage of the Bo Xilai scandal or the drama surrounding Chen Guangcheng, the blind activist who took refuge in the American Embassy in Beijing and later made his way to the U.S. It also, notoriously, tried to suppress news of the SARS epidemic in 2003 and, more recently, spread disinformation about the origins of the Covid-19 pandemic.

Farah sums up the fundamental difference in approaches to international broadcasting: "Western-style media views itself as a watchdog and a protector of public interests, while the Chinese model seeks to defend the state from jeopardy or questions about its authority" (cited in Fish, 2013). The Chinese model has resonance in parts of the developing world, where the challenge of establishing robust institutions of governance alongside economic growth can make investigative news appear to be a roadblock to developing states' transition into a global economy. This hesitance toward models of Western journalism reflects the re-emergence and salience of "development journalism," whereby the proper role of media is to assist in building a cohesive, productive and stable society (Ogan, 1982).

As China tightens censorship at home, Beijing is expanding its presence on Twitter and other American social media platforms banned in China. The number of Chinese government officials and their surrogates on Twitter has increased dramatically in recent years (Conrad, 2021). Those accounts are openly pushing conspiracy theories, such as how the U.S. brought the coronavirus to Wuhan. Not only are there thousands of accounts that are being centrally controlled, but the Chinese government appears to be hacking and spoofing legitimate accounts – including U.S. government-supported Radio Free Asia – to give their new botnet the appearance of credibility (Kao, 2020). This pattern looks remarkably similar to Russia's aggressive disinformation tactics (sharp power) and could well represent the first major shift in China's propaganda efforts in a generation. At present, the CCP appears to be building its own equivalent to Russia's Internet Research Agency, a notorious source of conspiracy theories and disinformation, using the coronavirus as a test case. These efforts, which are being pushed in multiple languages, relentlessly emphasize the heroism of China's response to the virus and the relative incompetence of America's response (Molter & Diresta, 2020).

These investments are starting to pay off (Wong, Rosenberg & Barnes, 2020). China is increasingly capable of presenting itself both domestically and internationally as an effective and benevolent global leader, one that is ascending as Western powers are faltering and failing to meet the needs of their citizens (Lim, 2020). Relying on disinformation, China has pushed a powerful narrative presenting itself as the successful and experienced expert on the novel coronavirus, willing to share openly a model of effectively defeating Covid-19 while selflessly offering medical supplies, technical assistance and resources to counter this deadly global threat. The CCP is undermining democratic institutions by taking advantage of press freedoms to disseminate a global pro-China message while harshly censoring information within its own borders. Once described as tinfoil-hat diplomacy, China's current efforts are nothing short of a wholescale attack on the credibility and image of Western values and institutions (Xiao et al., 2020).

Russia

In December 2013, President Vladimir Putin issued an executive order creating a new international news agency, Rossiya Segodnya, tasked to "provide information on Russian state policy and Russian life and society for audiences abroad" (President of Russia, 2013). This major reorganization of Russia's international information operations included moving RIA Novosti, Russia's legacy international news agency, The Voice of Russia, and Sputnik News into Rossiya Segodnya (Figure 15.1). The move was widely regarded as an effort to consolidate and strengthen Kremlin control over Russia's propaganda apparatus (Ennis, 2013). Consolidating RIA Novosti resulted in the dismissal of approximately 40 percent of its news staff, including "the news agency's relatively liberal leadership" (Roth, 2014). Putin's new propaganda agency is led by Dmitry Kiselev, a well-known, controversial, pro-Kremlin media personality, who described his mission as restoring a "just attitude to Russia as an important country in the world which has good intentions" (Ennis, 2013).

Russia launched Russia Today (RT), an international, multilingual, government-funded television network, in 2005. The RT network consists of three global news channels broadcasting in English, Spanish (RT Actualidad,

2009) and Arabic (Rusiya Al-Yaum, 2007) and is supplemented by RT America (2010), RT Documentary (2011), RT UK (2014), and RT Deutsch (2014) (Plunkett, 2014). In 2017, the Kremlin launched a French-language version of RT, aiming to reach audiences in France, Belgium, Switzerland and Canada. RT is also the parent company of RUPTLY, a video-wire agency, which owns the Redfish and Maffick digital media companies.

Although Rossiya Segodnya and RT remain separate legal entities, with separate budget allocations, they share missions and are managed concurrently by one editor-in-chief, Margarita Simonyan (U.S. Department of State, 2022).

In 2015, Russia focused on the aggressive expansion of Sputnik news, which is disseminated primarily via the Web and radio in 30 different languages. Sputnik's credibility strategy mirrors that of many traditional surrogate broadcasters: identify and hire local talent so that news content is "prepared locally, by local journalists, taking into account local discussions and the demands of the local audience" (Donnelly, 2015). He added that hubs in Edinburgh, Beijing, Berlin, Paris and Washington, D.C. aim to point "the way to a multi-polar world that respects every country's national interest, culture, history and traditions."

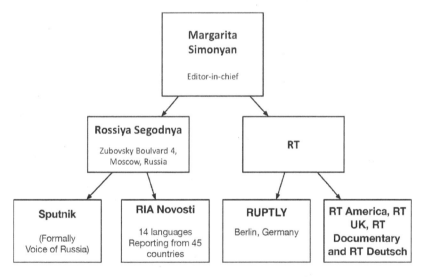

Figure 15.1   Organization of Russia's international information operations

The annual budget in 2022 for Russia's international broadcasting operations, including Rossiya Segodnya and RT, is 38.06 billion rubles, or just under half a million U.S. dollars (Statista, 2022).

Assessing Russia's foreign information operations requires a shift away from the standard PD paradigm, and an understanding of the "active measures" approach to propaganda. Active measures are a Soviet-era term referring to a form of political warfare aiming to influence world events through disinformation, propaganda, counterfeiting official documents, assassinations and political repression.

RT's primary goal is not only to disseminate pro-Kremlin messaging, but rather to leave audiences conflicted, questioning the official or mainstream narratives of current events. Russia does not aim to create anti-Western stories, but rather to challenge faith in existing institutions and governments, leaving audiences questioning what, if anything, can be considered the "truth." For example, Russia's disinformation campaign during its 2014 violent attacks on Ukraine, exemplified the classic KGB doctrine of active measures. The goal was not to establish a fact-based understanding of events, but rather to manipulate stories based on partial truths, combined with speculation, to create uncertainty among elites, divide NATO member states, and undermine the U.S. and its allies in the eyes of the developing world. This tactic allows RT to follow stories in multiple, even contradictory directions, as inconsistency only fosters greater confusion.

Western reactions to RT and other Russian information campaigns feed into the hype of an "anti-Russian narrative" that strengthens Putin domestically, ensuring continued funding for Russian propaganda. According to Russian media expert Snegovaya (2015), "the whole campaign is just to stay relevant and keep Western media pumping out the anti-Russia stuff. Then they can cherry-pick from all the rage and sell it back to the domestic news audience, where they have a media monopoly."

RUPTLY and Sputnik are good examples of how Russia aims to infuse alternative perspectives into global news discourse through micro-interventions into stagnant markets. RUPTLY aims to provide high-quality content and shape the rapidly growing sector of peer-to-peer news aggregation and dissemination. Sputnik adopted a highly localized model, working closely with journalists in strategic markets to ensure Russia's voice is heard via trusted local mediums like FM radio. While much attention is focused on RT, Russia was most aggressive in expanding Sputnik News' operations in former Soviet states, including launching language-specific web and radio services in Poland,

Azerbaijan, Georgia, Armenia and Estonia. Russia's funding of news portals, like Baltnews, targeting audiences in the Baltics, is also of interest, and remains under the radar of most experts and regulators. Moving forward, additional attention needs to be paid to Russia's continued focus on local partnerships, and its co-opting of local news organizations to disseminate its content that remains at arm's length from its more infamous international broadcaster, RT.

In 2022, in the aftermath of Russia's invasion of Ukraine, RT and Sputnik were dealt substantial blows by the international community. The European Union (EU) enacted sanctions on both organizations, prohibiting the broadcast or facilitation of the dissemination of any RT and Sputnik content. Social media platforms, Direct TV, Roku and others all enacted severe restrictions on RT and Sputnik's content, and in many cases the operations were simply banned (Chee, 2022). Two days after the EU announced its sanctions on Russia's media, RT announced the closing of its U.S.-based operations, including terminating all the U.S.-based staff (Darcy, 2022). Following the invasion, several high-profile journalists at RT, including its top editor, have publicly resigned in protest, further straining the credibility of Russia's international media operations (Kirby, 2022).

United States

The U.S. international broadcasting capabilities operate under the purview of the U.S. Agency for Global Media (USAGM), a federally funded entity with a mission to "inform, engage, and connect people around the world in support of freedom and democracy." USAGM's media network comprises two federal organizations – the Voice of America (VOA) and the Office of Cuba Broadcasting (Radio and TV Martí) – and four non-profit organizations – Radio Free Europe/Radio Liberty (RFE/RL), Radio Free Asia (RFA), the Middle East Broadcasting Networks (MBN) and the Open Technology Fund (OTF), an organization that advances global internet freedom. In total, USAGM networks broadcast in 62 languages and reach over 100 countries (U.S. Agency for Global Media, 2022).

Central to USAGM's operations, and likely the most notable difference compared to the Chinese and Russian programs, is the independence of its journalistic enterprises. This independence is protected by a firewall, enshrined in the United States International Broadcasting Act of 1994 (as amended), which prohibits U.S. government entities and authorities from interfering in the editorial process and, thus, ensures the networks have full editorial autonomy. The Act also requires that the agency's journalists reflect the highest professional standards of broadcast journalism, including requiring each of the 62 language services undergo independent programming review to ensure compliance.

The independence of USAGM's journalists has, of course, been tested. Most recently, in 2020, the agency's CEO Michael Pack attempted to remove protections engendered by the firewall and was accused of unlawfully launching investigations into journalists he suspected were not supportive of the Trump administration. A group of career agency executives appealed to the federal courts to intervene to protect the independence of VOA journalists, and in November 2020 the Chief Judge of the United States District Court for D.C. issued an injunction against Pack from taking or influencing any editorial decisions or personnel (Folkenflik, 2020). Chief Judge Beryl Howell (2020) found that Pack and his aides had likely "violated and continue to violate [journalists'] First Amendment rights," adding, "These current and unanticipated harms are sufficient to demonstrate irreparable harm." Pack was forced to stand down his efforts and was removed from his position as USAGM CEO on January 21, 2021. While the agency's newsrooms will inevitably be faced with political pressure again, Howell's ruling, and the resulting legal precedent protecting the networks' first amendment rights, could prove challenging for any political official to overcome.

Using nationally representative surveys conducted by independent research firms, USAGM collects and analyzes data on its audiences and impact in most of the markets in which it operates.[2] In 2021, USAGM's networks reached 394 million adults on a weekly basis, up from 354 million adults the previous year. The agency's networks reached large audiences in countries of strategic importance to U.S. national security, including Russia (7.9 million), China (65.4 million) and Iran (12.2 million). Audiences grew in several key markets – including Turkey (up 287 percent since the agency's previous survey in 2019), Burma (up 132 percent since the previous survey in 2018), and Vietnam (up 241 percent since the previous survey in 2016) – as well as from previously unsurveyed markets, including India (29.4 million) and the Philippines (5.0 million) (U.S. Agency for Global Media, 2022). In the three weeks after Russia's 2022 invasion of Ukraine, the agency verified over 1 billion video views of its Russian-language programs on social platforms alone, a tripling of its Russian-speaking audience from before the war (Osnos, 2022).

---

[2] In certain markets, like North Korea and parts of China, survey research by reputable third-party vendors is not possible, or creates too much risk for the researchers to justify the project.

In 2022, USAGM announced its 2022–26 strategic plan, setting out a vision to ensure access to trusted, compelling and impactful content in order to create a robust response to censorship and disinformation and support democratic ideals and values (U.S. Agency for Global Media, 2022). This new trajectory was driven in part by a recognition that, in the modern media environment, competing with the abundance of content available online, even in closed and quasi-closed societies, requires prioritizing high-impact programming that will command the attention of audiences and the local media. It is also a recognition that, increasingly, USAGM's journalists are operating in markets whereby government censorship and harassment are increasing, and focusing on circumventing these efforts with highly professional, fact-based programming is essential to combat the mainstreaming of disinformation campaigns.

International broadcasting as a multi-layer game

While the Chinese, Russia and American international broadcasting operations are, overall, quite varied and complex, they share a similar strategic dilemma. Today, international broadcasters are required to negotiate with – or tailor their content toward – diverse parties and publics simultaneously in the information age. To be effective, a state's broadcasting efforts need to be modeled as a negotiation, the goal of which is a receptive audience consuming and sharing programing that is supportive of the sponsoring government's broad foreign policy goals. International broadcasting in the information age more closely parallels the mutuality of negotiation than it did in previous eras. This motivates an updated, descriptive model for understanding international broadcasting as a tool of statecraft.

Game theory is an umbrella term for the study of mathematical models of strategic interactions among actors. In the context of international broadcasting, the game being played is among primarily four key actors: (1) the government sponsoring an information intervention (i.e., sponsoring government); (2) the underlying institutions and publics that are concerned with the intervention (i.e., issue publics); (3) the target audience for the intervention (i.e., receiving audience); and finally (4) the government responsible for the territory for which the target audience resides (i.e., receiving government).

From the perspective of the sponsoring government, the game is determining what kind of information intervention meets four primary criteria: (a) is the initiative sufficiently supportive of its values and broad foreign policy goals, (b) will it have at least the tacit support, or is not vocally opposed to, by meaningful issue publics tracking the policies or issues in question, (c) will it provide sufficient value to the target audience ensuring their interest in receiving the program, and ideally returning for more, and (d) doesn't anger the receiving government to such an extent that it puts the target audience in danger or otherwise negatively implicates other bilateral or multilateral initiatives.

This game is similar to Putnam's (1988) two-level game model of international negotiations, which attempts to model how states attempt to reach mutual compacts or treaties. The first level is between diplomats or states' representatives at the international level, and the second level is between these bargainers and their respective domestic publics and/or political institutions. In the case of international broadcasting, the first-level game is between the sponsoring government and the target, foreign audience. Whereas the goal in international negotiations is to strike a bilateral agreement, in this case it is determining the kinds of content sufficiently supportive of the sponsoring government's interests while also being of significant value to the target audience (Figure 15.2).

The second-level game is between each of the respective governments and their citizens and relevant institutions. In the case of the sponsoring government, the preferences and abilities of the institutions and interested issue publics shape the range of options available to the sponsoring government as it considers the types of information intervention it can implement. In the case of the receiving government, concerns over the impact of foreign information flows on domestic politics, as well as the need to be seen as supporting its citizens' fundamental rights to access and share information, shape how it will react to the intervention, among other things.

In the case of international broadcasting, the size of the respective stakeholder win-sets – that is, the range of acceptable outcomes – directly impacts the likely range of options, if any, that will fall within the overlapping win-sets of all four stakeholders. From the perspective of the sending government and its domestic public, larger win-sets provide for more flexibility in determining the ideal content for the intervention. In the case of the receiving public, satisfaction with the existing informational provisions likely directly contributes to its interest and willingness to engage with programing that is sponsored by a foreign government.

When governments establish media aimed at foreign publics, what is negotiated? An international broadcaster is negotiating with a receiving public for its *reception* and eventual *acceptance*, to borrow the first two terms of Zaller's (1992) cognitive processing model. These terms are useful for showing how broadcasting can resemble the rapidly iterative process of bargaining.

Reception refers to a person's attention, and *acceptance* is a function of a message's integration with someone's existing beliefs, systems, identities, and underlying ideologies. In the model outlined here, a broadcaster must adjust its content and programming based on appealing to audience preferences and preexisting attitudes – this is essential to establishing an audience.

Receiving publics will only offer their attention to content that adds value to the existing news ecosystem. In the information age, the audience has more options, and a broadcaster must be adaptable if it hopes to engage audiences. Of course, simply pandering to target public opinion is rarely an option, as the sponsoring government also needs to find value in the content that is created. Thus the "game" is to find content that is valuable to both the sponsoring government and receiving public, while also ensuring the content isn't seen as overly objectionable by either domestic constituencies or the receiving government to motivate either to intervene in the program's implementation.

Game	Putman's Two-Level Game	Negotiating Broadcasting Game
Negotiated Outcome	International Agreement or Treaty	Reception of Broadcasting by Target Public
Success	Ratification & Policy Impact	Acceptance & Policy Impact

Figure 15.2   Comparing Putnam's two-level game to the negotiating communication game

Foreign publics may be open-minded toward foreign, state-subsidized information sources for many reasons. Despite the dramatic growth in news media around the world, market failures – whereby local news providers do not meet citizen information needs – persist. Sometimes international broadcasters have comparative advantages covering certain news stories. For example, in the case of Al Jazeera and the Arab Spring, the Qatar-based broadcaster provided Arab audiences current accounts of protests and the reactions by Tunisian, Egyptian, Libyan and Syrian governments – accounts that were often censored or reported without sufficiently detailed reporting by other local, regional and global news media. Countries where domestic news sources face funding woes may find international news better supplied by international broadcasters.

Even in cases where audiences view particular foreign governments skeptically, international broadcasting can effectively build a loyal community of viewers through creative formats that are not yet available in national systems. For example, the Voice of America's *Parazit* (Persian for "static," a reference to what happens when the Iranian government blocks the satellite airwaves illegally broadcast into Iran) is a program written and produced by a team of young Iranian exiles living in Washington, DC. Modeled after Jon Stewart's *The Daily Show*, *Parazit* is a satire on current events in and about Iran, highlighting hypocrisy among Iranian political, social and religious leaders. The show is critically acclaimed and drives over 22 percent of Iranian households to tune into VOA TV each week (Broadcasting Board of Governors & Gallup, 2012). *Parazit*'s Facebook page receives more than 30 million page views per month, and its YouTube channel generates an additional 45,000 views each week, making it among the most popular shows viewed in Iran (Brown, 2011).

Conclusion

Despite the significant and growing resources devoted to international broadcasting, it remains perhaps the most under-studied aspect of PD. The area is ripe for academic attention. This chapter's review of key players in international broadcasting – China, Russia and the U.S. – barely scratches the surface of this robust field of activities. Australia, Canada, France, Germany, Great Britain, Iran, Israel, Japan, Qatar, Taiwan, Venezuela and other governments are all investing in this space in meaningful ways. Mapping these efforts, how they have evolved to compete in the modern media era, who are they targeting, and which efforts have been especially effective, are all questions the global community of PD scholars is uniquely situated to document and analyze.

Moreover, existing theoretical models for PD simply haven't taken into account the real constraints that shape modern broadcasting efforts. Recognizing that no government is willing to consistently invest in an information intervention strategy unless it can be proven to be effective, and in support of an important national interest, is an essential place to start. This recognition lays the foundation for a game theory approach to international broadcasting, as the negotiative model proposed here recognizes the need to account for not only a sponsoring government's interests, but also the interests of each of the stakeholders with the ability to shape the effectiveness of an information intervention. While global media scholars have long recognized the need to tailor content to the needs of target audiences, scholars have focused less attention on the powerful and essential role that foreign governments play in permitting, sabotaging or competing with foreign information interventions.

Today, the range of tools receiving governments have to obfuscate or obstruct an international broadcasting program are varied and robust, to include the harassment and jailing of journalists, implementation of regulations declaring the journalists foreign agents (i.e., members of the intelligence community), launching competing programs, initiating disinformation campaigns targeting the implementing actors, internet censorship and shutdowns, threatening citizens who are found to have accessed the foreign content, and so on. Understanding the range of tools and approaches being deployed by receiving governments, the effectiveness of these tools, and under which conditions these tools are likely to be deployed is incredibly important for PD practitioners to be able to better plan and implement effective programs in restricted markets.

International broadcasters typically invest in both qualitative and quantitative research to assess their performance, and PD scholars have a unique opportunity to shape the questions this research community aims to address. This is to say, not only is this an area of PD in need of more scholarly attention, but it is also an area where the availability of robust and current data is very real, and collaboration would likely be beneficial to practitioners and scholars of PD alike.

References

Broadcasting Board of Governors & Gallup. (2012, June 12). BBG research series briefing: Iran media use. http://www.bbg.gov/event/new-bbggallup-research-iran-media-use-2012-2.

Brown, J. (2011, February 28). For Iranian TV viewers, "Parazit" offers reprieve from static. *Public Broadcasting Service*. http://www.pbs.org/newshour/bb/world/janjune11/parazit_02-28.html.

Chee, F. Y. (2022, March 2). EU bans RT, Sputnik over Ukraine disinformation. *Reuters*. https://www.reuters.com/world/europe/eu-bans-rt-sputnik-banned-over-ukraine-disinformation-2022-03-02/.

Conrad, J. (2021, July 10). China's nationalistic "Wolf Warriors" blast foes on Twitter. *Wired*. https://www.wired.com/story/chinas-nationalistic-wolf-warriors-blast-foes-twitter/.

Cook, S. (2020). *Beijing's global megaphone*. Freedom House Special Report. https://freedomhouse.org/report/special-report/2020/beijings-global-megaphone.

Darcy, O. (2022, March 4). RT America ceases productions and lays off most of its staff. *CNN*. https://www.cnn.com/2022/03/03/media/rt-america-layoffs/index.html.

Donnelly, B. (2015, September 25). Kremlin mouthpiece sets up UK base in Edinburgh. *The Herald*. https://www.heraldscotland.com/news/13785698.kremlin-mouthpiece-sets-uk-base-edinburgh/.

Ennis, S. (2013, December 9). Putin's RIA Novosti revamp prompts propaganda fears. *BBC Monitoring*. https://www.bbc.com/news/world-europe-25309139.

Farhi, P. (2012, January 17). In Washington, China bids to shape its story. *The Washington Post*.

Fish, I. S. (2013, August 6). Will China ever purchase a U.S. media company? *Foreign Policy*. https://foreignpolicy.com/2013/08/06/will-china-ever-purchase-a-u-s-media -company/.

Folkenflik, D. (2020, November 21). Trump appointee unconstitutionally interfered with VOA, judge rules. *NPR*. https://www.npr.org/2020/11/21/937467457/ceo-over -voa-acted-unconstitutionally-in-pursuing-bias-claims-u-s-judge-rules.

Howell, B. (2020). *Turner et al. v. U.S. Agency for Global Media et al.* Memorandum opinion No. 1:2020cv02885, Document 45. https:// law .justia .com/ cases/ federal/ district-courts/district-of-columbia/dcdce/1:2020cv02885/222894/45/.

Jacobs, A. (2012, August 17). Pursuing soft power, China puts stamp on Africa's news. *The New York Times*. https:// www .nytimes .com/ 2012/ 08/ 17/ world/ africa/ chinas -news-media-make-inroads-in-africa.html.

Jirik, J. (2016). CCTV news and soft power. *International Journal of Communication, 10*, 3536–53.

Kao, J. (2020, March 26). How China built a Twitter propaganda machine then let it loose on coronavirus. *ProPublica*. https:// www .propublica .org/ article/ how -china -built-a-twitter-propaganda-machine-then-let-it-loose-on-coronavirus.

Kirby, P. (2022, March 16). Russia's state TV hit by stream of resignations. *BBC*. https:// www.bbc.com/news/world-europe-60763494.

Lim, L. (2020, March 23). China is trying to rewrite the present. *Foreign Policy*. https:// foreignpolicy.com/2020/03/23/china-is-trying-to-rewrite-the-present/.

Molter, V., & Diresta, R. (2020, June 8). Pandemics & propaganda: How Chinese state media creates and propagates CCP coronavirus narratives. *Misinformation Review*. https://doi.org/10.7910/DVN/5BXL7A.

Ogan, C. (1982). Development journalism/communication: The status of a concept. *International Communication Gazette, 79*(1–2), 3–13.

Osnos, E. (2022, March 24). How to flood Putin's "Information Desert." *The New Yorker*. https:// www .newyorker .com/ news/ daily -comment/ how -to -flood -putins -information-desert.

Plunkett, J. (2014, October 28). Kremlin-backed RT to launch UK TV news channel. *The Guardian*. https:// www .theguardian .com/ media/ 2014/ oct/ 28/ kremlin -rt -uk -news-channel-russia-today.

Powers, S., & Jablonski, M. (2015). *The real cyber war: The political economy of internet freedom*. University of Illinois Press.

President of Russia (2013, December 9). Executive order on measures to raise efficiency in the work of state mass media outlets. *President of Russia*. http:// en .kremlin .ru/ events/president/news/19805.

Price, M. (2002). *Media and sovereignty*. MIT Press.

Putnam, R. (1988). Diplomacy and domestic politics: The logic of two-level games. *International Organization, 42*(3), 427–60.

Reporters Without Borders (2021). 2021 World Press Freedom Index: Journalism, the vaccine against disinformation, blocked in more than 130 countries. https://rsf.org/ en/ 2021 -world -press -freedom -index -journalism -vaccine -against -disinformation -blocked-more-130-countries.

Roth, A. (2014, November 10). Russian News Agency expands global reach. *The New York Times*. https://www.nytimes.com/2014/11/11/world/europe/russian-news -agency-expands-global-reach.html.

Shambaugh, D. (2015). China's soft power push. *Foreign Affairs*. https:// www .foreignaffairs.com/articles/china/2015-06-16/chinas-soft-power-push.

Sina News (2011, January 13). CCTV television transmission. http://news.sina.com.cn/m/2011-01-08/145421782330.shtml.

Snegovaya, M. (2015, September 17). Kremlin is losing the information war. *The Moscow Times.* http://www.themoscowtimes.com/opinion/article/kremlin-is-losing-the-information-war-op-ed/531587.html.

Statista (2022). Federal budget subsidies received by RT (Russia Today) and Rossiya Segodnya in Russia from 2014 to 2020 and planned financing until 2024. https://www.statista.com/statistics/1288564/rt-rossiya-segodnya-budget/.

Taipei Times (2009, October 9). China seeking friendly global image. https://www.taipeitimes.com/News/world/archives/2009/10/09/2003455475.

The Economic Times (2013, May 10). China radio's Tamil service seeks FM carriage in India. https://economictimes.indiatimes.com/industry/media/entertainment/china-radios-tamil-station-to-launch-fm-channel-in-india/articleshow/19986700.cms.

U.S. Agency for Global Media (2022). 2023 Congressional Budget Justification. https://www.usagm.gov/wp-content/uploads/2022/03/USAGMBudget_FY23_CBJ_03-25-22-FINAL.pdf.

U.S. Department of State (2022). *Kremlin-funded media: RT and Sputnik's role in Russia's disinformation and propaganda ecosystem.* https://www.state.gov/wp-content/uploads/2022/01/Kremlin-Funded-Media_January_update-19.pdf.

Wong, E., Rosenberg, M., & Barnes, J. (2020, April 22). Chinese agents helped spread messages that sowed virus panic in U.S. officials say. *The New York Times.* https://www.nytimes.com/2020/04/22/us/politics/coronavirus-china-disinformation.html.

Xiao, M., Jordan, D., Felling, M., & Koettl, C. (2020, March 18). How China is shaping the coronavirus narrative. *The New York Times.* www.nytimes.com/video/world/asia/100000007024807/china-coronavirus-propaganda.html.

Zaller, J. (1992). *The nature and origins of mass opinion.* Cambridge University Press.

Zhu, Y. (2014). *Two billion eyes: The story of China Central Television.* The New Press.

16   International exchanges

Giles Scott-Smith

Introduction

International exchanges – the organised cross-border movement of individuals or groups for the purposes of educational or professional training, teaching, research, or inter-cultural communication – have been a feature of international relations for well over a century, and some would argue much longer. They have always been regarded as a unique activity in public diplomacy (PD), the ultimate form of "slow media" with their own rationale and purpose. Cull (2008a, p. xviii) argued that this uniqueness set them apart as a research field, leading him to leave them out of his otherwise comprehensive study of the United States Information Agency. Even in the field of PD there has been a tendency to bypass exchanges, due partially to the lack of an effective methodology for their evaluation.

Exchanges cover a broad range of activities, from school exchanges to study/research/teaching at university level, to training and development programmes, to more general professional networking. Here it is important to differentiate between official exchanges, the movement of international students as a whole, and the general flux of global interactions *in toto*. Networks of imperial power and influence through history have caused widespread short- and long-term "knowledge migration" from the peripheries to the metropolitan centres (Goebel, 2015; Marrou, 1956). Religion was also a paramount influence for encouraging movement through human history, with advocates travelling to places of worship and instruction according to their faith.

The concept of mobility can be usefully applied to emphasise (among other things) the importance of place, space, and identity formation in movement, and is useful for but not exclusive to the study of exchanges (Cresswell, 2010; Scott-Smith, 2023). Therefore, to narrow down this enquiry, the following definition for exchanges can be applied: "official initiatives by individuals and/or institutions for organizing and structuring regular transnational circulations over a period of time, with some form of learning as the principal goal" (Tournès & Scott-Smith, 2017, p. 2). Research on international education may engage with the specific value and utility of exchanges; it represents a vast field of research largely separate from the concerns of this chapter (Trilokekar & Rasmi, 2011).

This clarifies the study of exchanges to be predominantly about the period during which nation states, empires, and international organisations have sought to utilise exchanges in the pursuit of nationalist, imperial, or internationalist gain – effectively, the modern era since the late 19th century. Yet the scale of this field of activity remains vast. One estimate has it that whereas in 1860 there may have been around 2,000 students studying outside of their home countries, by 2010 there were probably over four million (Perraton, 2020). For the 2018–19 academic year, prior to the onset of Covid-19, almost 1.1 million international students were registered at US universities alone, representing 5.5 per cent of the total student population and contributing $44.7 billion to the US economy (Institute for International Education, 2019). Even if not all of them were travelling via organised exchange, this clarifies the challenges involved in giving these forms of movement intellectual meaning.

The "geography of exchanges" has also been changing, in line with the shifting patterns of world order, the decline of imperial influence and the rise of new powers. The dominant positions of the US and Europe as the central metropoles of global exchange traffic are now challenged by new circuits of transfer, with Japan, India, China, and Singapore playing prominent roles, and south–south transit networks increasingly cutting across the colonial-era north–south lines of passage (Holloway & Jöns, 2012).

Whatever the forms of exchange being referred to, they have always been understood to deliver some form of unique experience for the participant that would not otherwise have occurred. In contrast to other forms of PD, where participants often "consume" information via specific channels or events, "exchanges directly involve the 'human factor', where an engagement with the personality, psychology, and both short- and long-term personal development of participants is central" (Scott-Smith, 2020, p. 38). Despite often being presented in the most neutral possible terms, as if they are solely operative for the purposes of personality enrichment or "mutual understanding", broader assumptions concerning their usefulness for achieving certain goals have always been present in the background, be that national prestige, the transfer of skills, or the promotion of an ideology. At the centre of this lies the assumption that exchanges can cause some level of change in outlook and/or behaviour of the participant, due to the novel, altered social, cultural, and material environment which the participant encounters for a given period of time.

This gives exchanges a political dimension that is not immediately apparent, because changes of outlook and behaviour can have political consequences.

At its most basic level, since the rise of the nation state the movement of people across borders has been an issue of paramount importance, involving complex mechanisms of control and surveillance, from visas and registrations of identity to citizenship and pathways for assimilation and naturalisation (Vaughn-Williams, 2009). The movement of people that exchanges facilitate has also drawn the attention of security agencies over the past century, whether they were in the service of imperial, democratic, or authoritarian regimes (Perraton, 2020). Such a perspective clashes with the liberal ethos that claims a greater circulation of people and ideas will eventually overcome cultural differences and misunderstandings, deliver a reduction in antagonisms, and ultimately lead to more peaceful international relations (Mathews-Aydinli, 2017). Whichever perspective is taken, the political relevance of exchanges is clear enough.

Existing research

There is an extensive literature on the practice and outcomes of specific exchange programmes in the modern era. Historians have begun to piece together the relevance of exchanges for building networks and making ideas travel, with a particular focus on their place within the expansion of US power and influence. This has focused on imperial and bilateral relations, and the influence of internationalist movements in the early 20th century (Ellis & Müller, 2016; Laqua, 2011; Pietsch, 2013). The Boxer Indemnity and China–US educational exchange has received extensive attention (Bevis, 2014; Hunt, 1972), as have US–German exchanges in the higher education sector (Werner, 2013) and the People-to-People programme established by President Eisenhower (Fett, 2021). Exclusive educational exchanges based on stringent selection procedures, such as the Fulbright programme, the Rhodes scholarships, and the Humboldt fellowships have also been scrutinised, both from the perspective of institutional histories, trends over time, and participant experiences (Bettie, 2015; Fu & Zhao, 2017; Johnson & Colligan, 1965; Jöns, 2009; Lebovic, 2013; Pietsch & Chou, 2018; Schaeper & Schaeper, 2010).

Whereas both Rhodes and Humbolt are relatively small in scale, allowing for all-encompassing studies, a full analysis of the Fulbright programme and what it has achieved remains out of reach due to its global scope and, now into its 75th year, its hundreds of thousands of participants. Nevertheless, a reasonable number of country studies examining its impact in academia at national and local levels do now exist, enabling some insight into the contribution of Fulbright towards the shaping of disciplines, institution-building, and its influence on the academic environment as a whole (Garner & Kirby, 2018; Medalis, 2012; Scott-Smith, 2015; Xu, 1999). The US State Department's International Visitor Program (originally the Foreign Leader and Specialist Programs), originating in the late 1930s, has also gathered attention as a prime means of relationship-building for US embassies (Scott-Smith, 2006, 2008a). These studies and others have collectively argued that organised exchanges deserve attention as an activity that has influenced social interaction, inter-cultural communication, and the diffusion of norms over more than a century.

Major gaps still remain, generally due to the sheer scale of exchange activity and the tendency of researchers to focus on elite programmes because of the expectation that they will deliver a stronger set of results regarding their impact. The US- and Europe-focus in much exchange research has in recent years given way to increasing interest in the role of China, but there remains a need to de-centre exchange research away from the global North countries as initiators and receivers. There have also been obstacles related to limitations in measuring effectiveness, and an ongoing scholarly reluctance, connected to this lack of evidence, to grant exchanges a too prominent role in social relations.

On the other hand, specific instances are referred to regularly as evidence of the nefarious potential of exchanges for fuelling negative cultural backlash, the most notorious being the example of Sayyid Qtub's visit to the US in 1948–50 for the purpose of educational management training (Abdel-Malek, 2000; Synnestvedt, 2017; Smith, 2017). This has led to a divergence of discourse between practitioners who believe in the efficacy of the exchanges they facilitate, and researchers who shy away from the at times front-loaded positive claims being put forward. Attempts to position exchanges effectively as a subject of legitimate interest within International Relations theory have also been made, offering a broad basis from which to carry out more focused studies (Scott-Smith, 2008b). Nevertheless, uncertainties exist as to what exchanges have actually achieved over time, and how one can argue for their continuing importance in an era of collapsed distance through digitalisation.

Evaluation

The number one issue at the centre of research into exchanges therefore con-tinues to be evaluation – in short, how to measure "effectiveness", or the (pos-itive) changes that they are supposed to trigger (see also the relevant sections in Chapters 1 and 12 in this volume). To what extent does change in opinion and/or behaviour actually occur through the exchange experience, and in what ways can the results be given a credible explanatory value? Evaluation has been an area of intense interest in PD, a logical focus for a field that is interested in the effectiveness of mechanisms to build cross-border relations and favourably change opinion. However, this is often connected to the narrow interests of the policymaking arena, where funding may be allocated only according to proof of results delivered.

Against this demand, a host of caveats have been levelled, from problems with lack of continuity in staffing to the budget-driven need for success stories and the intangibility of concepts needing to be "measured" (Banks, 2011, pp. 11–14). According to the US State Department, evaluation is conducted "as a basis for making judgments, improving effectiveness and informing decisions" on current programmers, but this may still be carried out with budgetary demands determining how those programmes might be adapted, weakening the feedback "learning loop" (US Department of State, 2017).

Exchanges, being more about the establishment of (longer-term) social rela-tions than the projection of a national image, do not easily fit within the more short-term orientated evaluations conducted for other fields of PD. Approaches to evaluation developed by US social scientists in the 1940s and 1950s were conceived through the narrow visor of wanting to know how the participant had been favourably influenced towards the United States. Recent approaches to public diplomacy evaluation have continued to emphasise the connection to foreign policy, such that "the *true* measure of effectiveness for PD projects is their contribution to advancing national interests" (Sevin, 2017, p. 880, emphasis in original).

Yet exchanges require a broader, longer-term understanding of "effective-ness". It was for a long time widely assumed in the literature – if exchanges were addressed at all – that the engagements and encounters created by exchanges led to "positive" experiences/behaviours, where "success" could be claimed from the perspective of the participant (i.e. exchanges deliver greater personal awareness and opportunity), the organising entity (i.e. exchanges deliver desired changes in outlook and behaviour), and international relations in general (i.e. exchanges deliver improved inter-cultural communications that contribute to a less antagonistic world).

Further, it remains a matter of debate to what extent an empirically viable connection can be made between these three perspectives, and recent research has exactly aimed to tone down such claims by applying more stringent methodologies for measuring "success". Short-term effects are made measurable through opinion surveys, some even conducted both before and after the exchange activity to enable an assessment of changes in attitude due to the given experience. But what of the long term? How do the experiences, opinions, and outlooks generate through the exchange activity factor in decisions and attitudes? Can exchanges be treated as an independent variable for what happens afterwards? These are, of course, questions highly relevant for all public diplomacy activities, but are especially apposite for exchanges (Matwiczak, 2010).

In the 1950s, US social scientists developed tools for assessing the effectiveness of exchanges in changing attitudes and opinions (Brewster Smith, 1955; Padover, 1951; Riegel, 1953; Wilson & Bonilla, 1955). Drawing on assumptions and models applied by communications research and wartime psychological warfare, these studies made use of opinion surveys to test whether exchange participants could be favourably influenced. The approach was based on the "opinion leader" concept, which claimed that the opinions of individuals were influenced by selected trusted sources of information. These statistical-based studies were unable to deliver solid results, leading to a reluctant acceptance of the continuing value of qualitative data based on anecdotal evidence. As one researcher wryly put it, "although the effect doesn't appear to be brilliant, it may in fact be a maximum expectable effect, and therefore a reasonably successful realization of a limited potential" (Riegel, 1953, p. 327).

Since then, the expansion of academic mobility and the investment of universities in the international circulation of researchers and research have led to a large literature on the merits of educational exchange, but evaluation has continued to be a bone of contention. Klineberg (1976), in coordinating a seven-nation study supported by the International Committee for the Study of Educational Exchange, highlighted the need to consider the different goals for exchange depending on whether they are assessed from the perspective of the participants, the universities, the national interest, or the international community.

Messer and Wolter (2007) investigated the increase in student mobility in the late 20th century to question to what extent it contributes to building "human capital" for the participants themselves. Fisher (2010), making use of organisational science methodologies, broadened the use of evaluation to focus on the value of educational programmes for an institution as much as for a participant. This led to a framework that made use of five key parameters: relevance, fiscal efficiency, attaining objectives, impact on participants, and sustainability. Military exchanges from 1980 to 2006 have also been examined in relation to the furtherance of human rights standards and commitment to democracy, with the (perhaps surprising) conclusion that they have functioned as vectors for "the diffusion of liberal values and practices across the borders of authoritarian states" (Atkinson, 2010, p. 1).

An additional path for evaluation, developed recently, concerns a genuine focus on the extent of two-way exchange by addressing the impact and involvement of the local hosting communities. In a pioneering study, Wang and Nisbet (2018) developed an approach that assessed in what ways forms of capital (knowledge, cultural, social, civic, economic) could be created within a community through hosting and engagement with international exchange participants. The focus here is more on capturing the added value of exchange, where value is not reducible to simple metrics. As they emphasise, "Contemporary exchanges are experience-based rather than information-driven."

Testing objectives

Researchers have over the past couple of decades directed their attention to testing the stated objectives of educational exchanges in order to come closer to assessing their actual results. The Erasmus programme was established in 1987 for the purpose of facilitating labour market mobility and generating a common European identity and sense of belonging (Ferreira-Pereira & Pinto, 2021). Between 1987 and 2013, over three million students and 350,000 teachers and administrators spent time in another EU country, and it has become by far the largest educational exchange programme to date (Tournès & Scott-Smith, 2017, pp. 305–21). For this reason, it has attracted probably the most attention of all exchange programmes from scholars aiming to test its purposes and assumptions of success. Despite the claims of the European Commission that it has contributed towards European integration, empirically based studies have been more sceptical. Wilson (2011), Kuhn (2012), and Oborune (2013) argued that participants are predominantly already positively disposed towards the EU and living and working in a "common European space", and hence the Erasmus experience is mainly a confirmation of existing attitudes and behaviours rather than a decisive influence for change.

Similar research has tested the broader assumptions of exchange programmes by applying an analytically rigorous scepticism. The notion that cross-border contacts lead to a reduction in cultural barriers, an increase in interdependence, and so ultimately a higher chance for peaceful relations, is a standard "act of faith" of liberal thinking (Ninkovich, 2008, p. 58). Based on the claim that "educational exchange [is] one of the main types of cross-border contact favored by theorists of international community", Jones (2014) carried out a detailed study of 571 American college students who spent time abroad in order to categorise the effects. Jones found that it was difficult to point to a categorical shift in allegiances among students, according to some sense of international community. And while participation in an exchange did lead to a reduction in the perception of threats from other cultures, it also led to an increased recognition of national identity, difference, and a degree of national pride. Jones concludes that, in terms of changing attitudes and behaviour, a kind of "enlightened nationalism" could be the most achievable outcome, so that "cross-border contact" may indeed encourage peace-promoting norms and a sense of community, just not through the generation of a shared identity (p. 693). As he stated:

> Perhaps a different conception of international community is needed, one that relies less on the realization of fundamental similarities, shared outlooks, and the warmth of human kinship ... and more on the conviction that cultural differences may be profound but need not be threatening ... . The idea of community, then, would be more akin to earlier classic liberal perspectives emphasizing civility and tolerance than to more recent understandings of international community that draw from social psychology and emphasize the growth of a shared identity or common culture. (p. 690)

Jones' work is echoed by other studies that have looked at the special case of Franco–German rapprochement following the Second World War, often pointed to as a major success story regarding the altering of negative opinions and the overcoming of cultural stereotypes through the intensive application of cultural exchange (Cull, 2008b, pp. 40–42; Vion, 2002). Looking to examine the background to these claims, Krotz (2002) introduced the concept of "parapublics" to identify layers of social interaction, "neither strictly public nor properly private", often disregarded when assessing cultural interchange (p. 2). Including youth exchanges in the analysis, Krotz concluded that the results were overall rather limited. The evidence pointed to the creation of only a thin shared Franco–German public sphere, and instead the cross-border channels, including exchanges, were useful for normalising inter-state relations and not for generating new forms of collective identity or altering political processes.

Exchanges, in this case, can therefore contribute as social channels for over-coming obstacles at the micro level that may undermine inter-state coopera-tion – a valuable result in itself – but one needs to be cautious in claiming that they go beyond that towards the stimulation of some form of novel shared public sphere. However, with the Fulbright and Rhodes examples in mind, it is important to recognise the very different effects that exclusivity can deliver when it comes to the formation of alumni networks and their influence over the longer term.

Along the same lines, Wilson (2015) has applied analytical scepticism to the assumptions surrounding the "opinion leader" model, whereby it was intended that foreign nationals selected for (often) elite scholarships would return home afterwards acting voluntarily as positive mouthpieces for improved relations. Examining the motives behind the creation of three prominent British schol-arships, Wilson concluded that although these activities could certainly bring advantages for both the sponsoring nation and the participants themselves, "taking the opinion-leader model of what scholarship programs are for at face value is tempting but may be misleading." After all, "we need to remember that policymaking can be chaotic and unpredictable, that [it] is not safe to assume … that declared objectives correspond with what a program is actually set up to do" (p. 147).

Knowledge circulation

Alongside historians, political scientists, and education specialists, geogra-phers have contributed a great deal to the study of exchanges through their understanding of the circulation of knowledge over given spaces (Heffernan & Jöns, 2013). Mapping this on to broader matrixes of power at the global level, exchanges are seen as "an instrumental strategy to shape cosmopolitan identities, through transnational connections and the patronage of particular disciplines and scholars" (Brooks, 2015, p. 37). Taking this as the starting point, Brooks presented a study of the Ford Foundation in India during the early Cold War, where the foundation's control of the circulation of Western scientific expertise, backed by considerable patronage as part of a strategy over several years, shaped the modernisation of Indian society.

The Ford Foundation was able to project a "modernist imaginary" abroad based on calculations taking place at its headquarters in New York, with the conviction that "educational philanthropy was an investment in a better func-tioning political order." Thus "educational exchange represented a transaction of economic and social capital to control the capillaries of international economic and political power through the individual" (Brooks, 2015, p. 45). From this critical perspective, exchanges acted as an additional form of "capillary power" (Hargreaves, 1987) through which discourses of modernisation and development, and with them the underlying hierarchies of power, could be transmitted.

By drawing on the work of Foucault, Latour, and migration studies in particular, over the past decade geographers have put forward a framework for analysing exchanges in the context of global power relations. For instance, "brain circulation" was a term first introduced by migration studies to encapsulate the longer-term results of professional mobility (Ackers, 2005) but taken further by geographer Jöns (2009) to investigate "the long-term effects of the transnational circulation of academics and its meaning for the constitution of transnational knowledge networks" (p. 316). Analysing the Humboldt fellowships over several decades, Jöns concluded that the cumulative effects pointed to the near-decisive influence of high-end knowledge transfer and network building for the (re-)integration of (West) German centres of expertise into an international context. Without using the same term, similar work has looked at the importance of exchanges such as the Fulbright for establishing American Studies programmes in universities in Europe and around the world (Scott-Smith, 2007). As Welch has argued, exchanges are "important mechanisms to sustain internationalization" (Welch, 1997, p. 340).

Another term useful for linking exchanges as vectors of knowledge transfer with wider power relations and the creation of inequalities is "centres of calculation", taken from Latour (1987). Such centres are sites where knowledge production can take place because of the assembling of resources, materials, and expertise, which over time can lead to the framing of norms and directions for scientific fields of enquiry. Largely applied to unravel and expose the linkage between knowledge production, imperial expansion, and moments of "discovery", the necessity of mobility for the establishment and maintenance of these centres enables a critical assessment of the relationship between exchanges, expertise, and unequal power relations (Jöns, 2011; Jöns, Heffernan, & Meusberger, 2017).

Future directions

The introduction of analytical precision and theoretical perspectives has undoubtedly moved the study of exchanges out of the margins of PD research.

In terms of assessing the contribution of international exchanges for the altering of perceptions, the transfer of knowledge, and the maintenance of inter-state relations, a great deal of valuable work has already been done, even if most of the research on exchange programmes to date has been focused on the US and Europe as initiators of exchange programmes and host nations for participants coming from the rest of the world. Imperial networks, decolonisation, and the Cold War have ensured that the West maintained a dominant position in educational exchange throughout the 20th century. A greater interest in socialist internationalism has broadened the scope from the West to the North (Applebaum, 2015; Katsakioris, 2019). Efforts to provide all-encompassing overviews of exchanges as a global phenomenon have also moved exchanges out of the margins of historical enquiry and into mainstream thinking on transnationalism, internationalism, and global connectivity (Perraton, 2020; Tournès & Scott-Smith, 2017).

For future research, two principal lines of enquiry can be identified. First, more attention for the diversity of actors involved. The role of non-state actors in facilitating exchanges globally needs to be brought more into focus, in terms of their own agendas and outlook. Philanthropic initiatives such as the exchange activities of major US foundations like Ford and Rockefeller[1] (with some attention also being given to German counterparts) has opened up this field, but the interests of corporate actors in sponsoring exchanges remains under-researched (Scott-Smith, 2011, 2019). Smaller-scale operations such as the Esalen Foundation and its focus on promoting US–Soviet understanding in the 1980s have also been kept beyond detailed scrutiny due to a lack of accessible sources (Clines, 1989). Researching private entities is in this sense also problematic, there being nothing beyond moral obligation to provide transparency.

Second, there is a need to devote more attention to the influence of organised exchange in the context of *all* inter-regional relations, to look beyond the power relations of the global North. Brazilian involvement in exchanges has been studied, as has the JET programme of Japan (Ferreira de Lima, 2017; McConnell, 1996), and some work has been done on the role of exchanges in generating regional identity, such as in Latin America (Smith, 2017). China's Confucius Institutes have received attention, although not in terms of detailed analysis of exchange participants themselves (Wang et al., 2021). Australia's

---

[1] See the Heralds of Globalization project led by Ludovic Tournès that traces the career development of Rockefeller Foundation fellows from the 1920s to the 1970s: https://heraldsofglobalization.net (accessed 2 May 2022).

Colombo Plan for regional interchange across South and South-East Asia in the 1950s and 1960s deserves more attention, especially since its revival in the mid-1990s (Auletta, 2000). India's Technical and Economic Cooperation Program has been running since 1964 and has been of major importance for India to function as a development node – both sending and receiving – with South–South relations, yet it has so far received very little scholarly attention.[2] Likewise, educational exchanges within the Islamic world centred on Cairo or Riyadh are also absent from most accounts.

Conclusion

As the above research clearly indicates, organised exchanges have occupied a unique place within public diplomacy and have undoubtedly been a significant contributor to the passage of international and transnational relations since the late 19th century. While PD has adapted to advances in technology, exchanges continue to operate according to their original logic: that direct personal experience of another culture holds an intrinsic and unique value. This contribution encompasses diverse effects, from the general (increase in national income, projection of soft power, generation of positive perceptions) to the specific (instrumental vectors for knowledge circulation, transfer, and institutional consolidation). Measuring those effects is generally agreed to be important, but the methods used are often too narrow in purpose due to policy requirements.

In contrast, since historians and political scientists began to take exchanges seriously as an object of research, it has opened up as a multi-disciplinary field of enquiry: psychologists have concentrated on the behaviour patterns of the individual, communication scientists on the transfer of information, geographers on the power relations held in the spatial dynamics of knowledge production. Future research on the theory and practice of exchanges can be enriched by cross-disciplinary awareness of these different perspectives.

---

[2]   See the Indian Ministry for External Affairs website: https://www.itecgoi.in/index # (accessed 11 February 2022).

References

Abdel-Malek, K. (2000). The America I have seen: In the scale of human values. In K. Abdel-Malek (Ed.), *America in an Arab mirror* (pp. 9–27). Palgrave Macmillan.

Ackers, L. (2005). Moving people and knowledge: Scientific mobility in the European Union. *International Migration, 43*(5), 99–131.

Applebaum, R. (2015). The friendship project: Socialist internationalism in the Soviet Union and Czechoslovakia in the 1950s and 1960s. *Slavic Review, 74*(3), 484–507.

Atkinson, C. (2010). Does soft power matter? A comparative analysis of student exchange programs 1980–2006. *Foreign Policy Analysis, 6*(1), 1–22.

Auletta, A. (2000). A retrospective view of the Colombo Plan: Government policy, departmental administration and overseas students. *Journal of Higher Education Policy and Management, 22*(1), 47–58.

Banks, R. (2011). *A resource guide to public diplomacy evaluation.* Figueroa Press.

Bettie, M. (2015). Ambassadors unaware: The Fulbright Program and American public diplomacy. *Journal of Transatlantic Studies, 13*(4), 358–72.

Bevis, T. B. (2014). *A history of higher education exchange: China and America.* Routledge.

Brewster Smith, M. (1955). Evaluation of exchange of persons. *International Social Science Bulletin, 7*(3), 387–97.

Brooks, C. (2015). The ignorance of the uneducated: Ford Foundation philanthropy, the IIE, and the geographies of educational exchange. *Journal of Historical Geography, 48*, 36–46. https://daneshyari.com/article/preview/1038966.pdf.

Clines, F. (1989, September 19). Yeltsin in US: Pravda's ugly profile. *New York Times,* 14.

Cresswell, T. (2010). Towards a politics of mobility. *Environment and Planning, 28*(1), 159–71.

Cull, N. (2008a). *The Cold War and the United States Information Agency: American propaganda and public diplomacy, 1945–1989.* Cambridge University Press.

Cull, N. (2008b). Public diplomacy: Taxonomies and histories. *Annals of the American Academy of Political and Social Science, 616*(1), 31–54.

Ellis, H., & Müller, S. (2016). Educational networks, educational identities: Connecting national and global perspectives. *Journal of Global History, 11*, 313–19.

Ferreira de Lima, A. (2017). The role of international educational exchanges sponsored by the Brazilian government in the perception of the external image of Brazil. Paper given at the 58th Convention of the International Studies Association, Baltimore.

Ferreira-Pereira, L. C., & Pinto, J. (2021). Soft power in the European Union's strategic partnership diplomacy: The Erasmus Plus Programme. In L. C. Ferreira-Pereira & M. Smith (Eds.), *The European Union's strategic partnerships* (pp. 69–74). Palgrave Macmillan.

Fett, A. (2021). US people-to-people programs: Cold War cultural diplomacy to conflict resolution. *Diplomatic History, 45*(4), 714–42.

Fisher, Y. (2010). Measuring success: Evaluating educational programs. *US–China Education Review, 7*, 1–15.

Fu, M., & Zhao, X. (2017). Utilizing the effects of the Fulbright Program in contemporary China: Motivational elements in Chinese scholars' post-Fulbright life. *Cambridge Journal of China Studies, 12*(3), 1–26.

Garner, A., & Kirby, D. (2018). *Academic ambassadors, Pacific allies: Australia, America and the Fulbright Program.* Manchester University Press.

Goebel, M. (2015). *Anti-Imperial metropolis: Interwar Paris and the seeds of Third World nationalism.* Cambridge University Press.

Hargreaves, J. (1987). *Sport, power and culture: A social and historical analysis of popular sports in Britain.* Polity.

Heffernan, M., & Jöns, H. (2013). Research travel and disciplinary identities in the University of Cambridge, 1885–1955. *British Journal for the History of Science, 46*(2), 255–86.

Holloway, S., & Jöns, H. (2012). Geographies of education and learning. *Transactions of the Institute of British Geographers, 37*(4), 482-8.

Hunt, M. (1972). The American remission of the Boxer Indemnity: A reappraisal. *Journal of Asian Studies, 31*(3), 539–59.

Institute for International Education (2019). *Open Doors Report on International Educational Exchange.* https:// www .iie .org/ Research -and -Insights/ Publications/ Open-Doors-2019.

Johnson, W., & Colligan, F. (1965). *The Fulbright Program: A history.* University of Chicago Press.

Jones, C. (2014). Exploring the microfoundations of international community: Toward a theory of enlightened nationalism. *International Studies Quarterly, 58*(4), 682–705.

Jöns, H. (2009). Brain circulation and transnational knowledge networks: Studying long-term effects of academic mobility to Germany, 1954–2000. *Global Networks, 9*(3), 315–38.

Jöns, H. (2011). Centre of calculation. In J. Agnew & D. Livingstone (Eds.), *SAGE handbook of geographical knowledge* (pp. 158–70). Sage.

Jöns, H., Heffernan, M., & Meusburger, P. (Eds.) (2017). *Mobilities of knowledge.* Springer.

Katsakioris, C. (2019). The Lumumba University in Moscow: Higher education for a Soviet–Third World alliance, 1960–91. *Journal of Global History, 14*(2), 281–300.

Klineberg, O. (1976). *International educational exchange: An assessment of its nature and its prospects.* Mouton.

Krotz, U. (2002). Ties that bind? The parapublic underpinnings of Franco–German relations as construction of international value. Working Paper 02.4, Program for the Study of Germany and Europe, Harvard University. https:// ces .fas .harvard .edu/ publications/ 000075 -ties -that -bind -the -parapublic -underpinnings -of -franco -german -relations -as -construction -of -international -value (accessed 2 May 2022).

Kuhn, T. (2012). Why educational exchange programmes miss their mark: Cross-border mobility, education and European identity. *Journal of Common Market Studies, 50*(6), 994–1010.

Laqua, D. (Ed.) (2011). *Internationalism reconfigured: Transnational ideas and movements between the World Wars.* I.B. Tauris.

Latour, B. (1987). *Science in action: How to follow scientists and engineers through society.* Harvard University Press.

Lebovic, S. (2013). From war junk to educational exchange: The World War II origins of the Fulbright program and the foundations of American cultural globalism, 1945–1950. *Diplomatic History, 37,* 280–312.

McConnell, D. (1996). Education for global integration in Japan: A case study of the JET Program. *Human Organization, 55*(4), 446–57.

Marrou, H. L. (1956). *A history of higher education in antiquity.* Sheed and Ward.

Mathews-Aydinli, J. (2017). *International education exchanges and intercultural understanding: Promoting peace and global relations.* Palgrave Macmillan.

Matwiczak, K. (2010). Public diplomacy model for the assessment of performance. Research Report 170, Lyndon B. Johnson School of Public Affairs, University of Texas at Austin. https://repositories.lib.utexas.edu/handle/2152/17688.

Medalis, C. (2012). The strength of soft power: American cultural diplomacy and the Fulbright Program during the 1989–1991 transition period in Hungary. *International Journal of Higher Education and Democracy, 3,* 144–63.

Messer, D., & Wolter, S. (2007). Are student exchange programs worth it? *Higher Education, 54,* 647–63.

Ninkovich, F. (2008). *US information policy and cultural diplomacy.* Foreign Policy Association. https://eric.ed.gov/?id=ED460891.

Oborune, K. (2013). Becoming more European after Erasmus? The impact of the Erasmus Programme on political and cultural identity. *Epiphany: Journal of Transdisciplinary Studies, 6*(1), 182–202.

Padover, S. (1951). Psychological warfare. *Foreign Policy Association Headline Series, 86,* 3–56.

Perraton, H. (2020). *International students 1860–2010: Policy and practice round the world.* Palgrave Macmillan.

Pietsch, T. (2013). *Empire of scholars: Universities, networks and the British academic world 1850–1939.* Manchester University Press.

Pietsch, T., & Chou, M.-H. (2018). The politics of scholarly exchange: Taking the long view on the Rhodes Scholarships. In L. Tournès & G. Scott-Smith (Eds.), *Global exchanges: Exchange programs, scholarships and transnational circulations in the modern world* (pp. 33–49). Berghahn.

Riegel, O. (1953). Residual effects of exchange-of-persons. *Public Opinion Quarterly, 17,* 319–27.

Schaeper, T., & Schaeper, K. (2010). *Rhodes scholars, Oxford, and the creation of an American elite.* Berghahn.

Scott-Smith, G. (2006). Searching for the successor generation: Public diplomacy, the US embassy's international visitor program and the Labour Party in the 1980s. *British Journal of Politics and International Relations, 8*(2), 214–37.

Scott-Smith, G. (2007). The ties that bind: Dutch–American relations, US public diplomacy and the promotion of American studies in the Netherlands since the Second World War. *The Hague Journal of Diplomacy, 2*(3), 283–305.

Scott-Smith, G. (2008a). *Networks of empire: The US State Department's Foreign Leader Program in the Netherlands, France and Britain 1950–1970.* Peter Lang.

Scott-Smith, G. (2008b). Mapping the undefinable: Some thoughts on the relevance of exchange programs within international relations theory. *Annals of the American Academy of Political and Social Sciences, 616*(1), 173–95.

Scott-Smith, G. (2011). Cultural exchange and the corporate sector: Moving beyond statist public diplomacy? *Austrian Journal of Political Science, 3,* 301–13.

Scott-Smith, G. (2015). The Fulbright Program in the Netherlands: An Example of science diplomacy. In J. V. Dongen (Ed.), *Cold War science and the transatlantic circulation of knowledge* (pp. 128–53). Brill.

Scott-Smith, G. (2019). Transatlantic cultural relations, soft power, and the role of US cultural diplomacy in Europe. *European Foreign Affairs Review, 24*(2), 21–41.

Scott-Smith, G. (2020). Exchange programs and public diplomacy. In N. Snow & N. Cull (Eds.), *Routledge handbook of public diplomacy* (pp. 38–49). Routledge.

Scott-Smith, G. (2023). Sites of exchange: Locating mobility in Cold War internationalisms. In D. Matasci & R. R. Coutaz (Eds.), *Educational internationalisms in the global Cold War* (pp. 258–74). Routledge.

Sevin, E. (2017). A multilayered approach to public diplomacy evaluation: Pathways of connection. *Politics & Policy, 45*(5), 879–901.

Smith, R. C. (2017). *Improvised continent: Pan-Americanism and cultural exchange.* University of Pennsylvania Press.

Synnestvedt, S. B. (2017). Rejecting America's Cold War: Sayyid Qutb's nationalist-Islamist agenda and the failure of US efforts to win over Egyptian Muslims following World War II. PhD dissertation, Georgetown University.

Tournès, L., & Scott-Smith, G. (Eds.) (2017). *Global exchanges: Scholarships and transnational circulations in the modern world.* Berghahn.

Trilokekar, R. D., & Rasmi, S. (2011). Student perceptions of international education and study abroad: A pilot study at York University, Canada. *Intercultural Education, 22*(6), 495–511.

US Department of State (2017). Program and project design, monitoring and evaluation policy. https://www.state.gov/wp-content/uploads/2018/12/Department-of-State-Program-and-Project-Design-Monitoring-and-Evaluation-Policy.pdf (accessed 1 May 2022).

Vaughn-Williams, N. (2009). *Border politics: The limits of sovereign power.* Edinburgh University Press.

Vion, A. (2002). Europe from the bottom up: Town twinning in France during the Cold War. *Contemporary European History, 11*(4), 623–40.

Wang, J., & Nisbet, E. (2018, June 25). Reimagining exchanges: The local impact of cultural exchanges. CPD Blog. https://uscpublicdiplomacy.org/blog/reimagining-exchange-local-impact-cultural-exchanges (accessed 1 May 2022).

Wang, Y. et al. (2021). The path, value and limits of the Confucius Institute in carrying out public diplomacy. *Economic and Political Studies, 9*(2), 217–29.

Welch, A. (1997). The peripatetic professor: The internationalisation of the academic profession. *Higher Education, 34*(3), 323–45.

Werner, A. (2013). *The transatlantic world of higher education: Americans at German universities, 1776–1914.* Berghahn.

Wilson, E., & Bonilla, F. (1955). Evaluating exchange of persons programs. *Public Opinion Quarterly, 19*(1), 20–30.

Wilson, I. (2011). What should we expect of "Erasmus Generations"? *Journal of Common Market Studies, 49*(5), 1113–40.

Wilson, I. (2015). Ends changed, means retained: Scholarship programs, political influence, and drifting goals. *British Journal of Politics and International Relations, 17*(1), 130–51.

Xu, G. (1999). The ideological and political impact of US Fulbright on Chinese students: 1979–1989. *Asian Affairs, 26*(3), 139–57.

17   Digital public diplomacy

Ilan Manor

Introduction

On February 19, 2022, the Russian Embassy to the United Kingdom (UK) tweeted a statement by Russian ambassador, Andrei Kelin. Though diplomats often employ ambiguous terminology and settle for vague statements, the Ambassador's could not be clearer saying "When Joe Biden says that Russia is about to invade Ukraine, he is absolutely wrong." Five days later, Russian troops were marching on Kiev. The Russia–Ukraine war of 2022 is demonstrative of the digitalization of public diplomacy (PD). By digitalization this chapter refers to a long-term process in which digital technologies impact the norms, values and working routines of diplomats and their institutions.

The war in Ukraine was not marked by the use of innovative technologies in PD activities but, rather, by the innovative use of existing technologies. Throughout the war, besieged Ukrainian President Volodymyr Zelenskyy used social media to share short videos vowing to resist Russia's invasion. These videos became viral sensations with Zelenskyy coming to personify Ukrainian courage while rallying online publics to Ukraine's cause. The president also used Zoom to address mass protests across Europe and deliver virtual speeches to several Parliaments. The importance of these speeches lies not in their content but in the fact that as long as Zelenskyy tweeted, and spoke to global publics, Ukraine remained unconquered, and Russia could not declare victory.

The Ukrainian Minister for Digital Transformation used social media to demand that global tech companies boycott Russia. Throughout the war, the Minister tweeted letters he had sent to the CEOs of PayPal, Apple, Facebook and more. These letters, which were re-tweeted thousands of times, galvanized global publics and resulted in these companies' decision to limit their services in Russia. Additionally, Ukrainian embassies across the world shared bank details of the Ukrainian armed forces and effectively crowdfunded Ukraine's war, raising more than $100 million; the Ukrainian government established a global "IT" army which coordinated cyber-attacks on Russia while military units uploaded videos of successful raids on Russian tanks and armored vehicles.

Of course, Ukraine's government was not the only one to rely on digital technologies during the war. EU and NATO leaders met using Zoom in order to rapidly impose financial sanctions on Russia following its invasion. While China did not officially support Russia, its state broadcaster shared Russian propaganda and conspiracy theories on social media. Pro-Ukrainian activists used Facebook ads in order to target Russian internet users and share accurate information on the war. Later, activists created websites used to send emails to Russians that rebuked Russian state narratives. Finally, both the BBC and the *New York Times* joined the DarkWeb. This digital realm, normally the last refuge of criminals and terrorists, was now used to reach Russians as the country isolated itself from the outside world.

These examples all demonstrate that digital technologies have been imbedded into the very DNA of PD as states, activists and media institutions use digital technologies to shape global beliefs and perceptions. This is true in times of war and times of peace. And though scholars have spent the past decade researching diplomats' use of digital technologies, crucial questions have remained unanswered. This chapter identifies these questions and lays out a research agenda for the digitalization of PD. To do so, it first reflects on the current research corpus.

Mind the gaps

Scholars seem to agree that the digitalization of PD started circa 2008 when nations, such as Sweden, launched digital embassies in the virtual world of Second Life. These global embassies, accessible to anyone with an internet connection, were mainly used to promote nations' cultural achievements. The Swedish embassy, for example, hosted film festivals, meetings with Swedish artists and even gallery exhibits. By 2012, scholars began to investigate diplomats' use of digital technologies (Metzgar, 2012; Pamment, 2013). Since the early 2010s, this research corpus has grown substantially and can be grouped into four clusters.

The first cluster analyzed diplomats' use of digital technologies to overcome the limitations of traditional diplomacy. Such was the case with America's virtual embassy to Iran which was meant to substitute a physical embassy (Metzgar, 2012), the State Department's Digital Outreach Team which sought to engage with Muslim internet users during the Obama presidency (Khatib, Dutton & Thelwall, 2012) and Palestine's Facebook embassy to Israel which overcomes the lack of Palestinian diplomatic presence in Israel (Manor & Holmes, 2018). Studies have also examined whether peripheral states (e.g., Kosovo) may use social media to become central to online networks of diplomatic institutions (e.g., UN Missions) thus influencing diplomats' agenda and overcoming the limitation of a small number of physical embassies (Manor & Segev, 2020). Finally, studies have examined how diplomats and foreign ministries use digital technologies to counter the online recruitment efforts of extremist organizations such as al-Qaeda or Daesh (Hallams, 2010). More recent studies have investigated how diplomatic institutions used Zoom during the Covid-19 pandemic to continue time-sensitive negotiations or perform routine functions in multilateral settings (Danielson & Hedling, 2021; Eggeling & Adler-Nissen, 2021).

The second cluster includes studies that have sought to define and conceptualize engagement between diplomats and digital publics. Most of the digitalization research corpus is dedicated to this issue given that social media sites are based on two-way exchanges of information and facilitate the creation of relationships between diplomats and foreign publics (Bortree & Seltzer, 2009; Lee & Kwak, 2012). Moreover, engagement is a central dimension of the "New" public diplomacy which emerged following the 9/11 terror attacks (Cull, 2008; Melissen, 2005; Pamment, 2013). Scholars have used a host of approaches to measure engagement including big data analysis, longitudinal analysis, and network and semantic analysis (Collins, DeWitt & LeFebvre, 2019; Enverga III, 2021; Kampf, Manor & Segev, 2015; Khan et al., 2021; Mazumdar, 2021; Spry, 2018; Spry & Lockyer, 2022; Yarchi, Samuel-Azran & Bar-David, 2017). In these studies, the focus is often on measuring engagement parameters (e.g., likes, re-tweets) or diplomats' online reach. Studies have also evaluated the sentiment of comments posted by digital publics in response to diplomats' messages (Sevin, Ayhan & Ingenhoff, 2021; Manor, 2019).

The third cluster examined diplomats' use of digital technologies to manage their nation's image (Gilboa, 2016). These studies have examined the digital activities of Chile, China, Ethiopia, India, Rwanda, Sweden, the UAE, the US and more (Antwi-Boateng & Al Mazrouei, 2021; Danziger & Schreiber, 2021; Ittefaq & Kamboh, 2022; Garud-Patkar, 2021; Huang & Wang, 2021). Scholars have argued that states use digital technologies to create a positive online persona which reflects on a state's offline reputation or exemplify how norms and values shape states' foreign policies (Manor & Segev, 2015). Several studies have focused on nations' use of online humor, or memes, to strengthen their brand (Manor, 2021; Chenobrov, 2021).

Finally, studies have examined diplomats' use of digital technologies to manage crises. Seib (2012) noted early on that digitalization had led to a form of real-time diplomacy in which diplomats narrate global events and crises in near-real time. Scholars have examined the digital activities of the Global Coalition Against Daesh (Manor & Crilley, 2018), the trade war between China and the US (Huang & Wang, 2021), NATO's use of social media during the war in Afghanistan (Wright, 2019), Turkey's use of digital tools following the 2016 coup attempt (Sevin, 2018) and Israel's use of digital communications during the Gaza wars (Manor & Crilley, 2018). Special attention has been paid to digital disinformation and propaganda (Bjola & Pamment, 2018; Fjällhed, 2021).

The aforementioned studies have all offered valuable insight into the process of digitalization. Studies have demonstrated that diplomats' adoption of digital technologies is indeed a long-term process which may be impacted by many variables ranging from Ministries of Foreign Affairs' (MFAs) institutional mentality to the affordance of digital technologies, whole-of-government approaches to digitalization, the digital enthusiasm of senior policymakers and even the logic of digital platforms (Al-Muftah et al., 2018; Kļaviņš, 2021). Such is the case with diplomats' strategic use of humor to create a unique online persona that may attract social media users or diplomats' newfound commitment to transparency which is demanded of all social media users (Bauman & Lyon, 2013).

While the digitalization of PD is increasingly studied by scholars, there are important gaps in the current research corpus that must be addressed. This chapter identifies three gaps and, in so doing, lays out a research agenda for studying the practice of PD in the digital age. The first gap stems from scholars' focus on social media sites even though diplomats have embraced a host of digital technologies including big data analysis, smartphone applications and algorithms. The second gap arises from the modest number of studies examining the role of diasporas. In the digital and globalized age, diasporas are important actors who may facilitate bi-lateral relations or harm a nation's reputation (Gilboa, 2022). The third and perhaps most important gap is the lack of attention to the impact that social media feeds have on diplomats' online activities. In the following section, each gap is elaborated upon while possible studies are outlined.

Scholars' day-long obsession

Impressionist painter Claude Monet famously stated that "color is my day-long obsession, joy and torment." The same is true of PD scholars. Like impressionist painters they too have grown obsessed, not with color but with social media sites. The majority of PD studies published between 2008 and 2022 examined diplomats' embrace of social media sites including Twitter, Facebook, Instagram, TikTok, Weibo and Snapchat. This obsession has prevented scholars from examining the diversity of digital technologies employed by diplomats and researching how each technology is leveraged toward different ends.

One important area of research is the development of smartphone applications by MFAs. In recent years, several MFAs including Poland, Canada and India have launched such applications. While the Polish and Canadian applications offer citizens consular services including travel warnings and means of communicating with nearby embassies, India's application is far more comprehensive enabling users to track visa applications, accompany Prime Minister Modi on state visits, review bi-lateral accords signed by India and foreign states and access press briefings (Manor, 2019).

These smartphone applications warrant investigation as they may represent two shifts in the practice of PD. The first is MFAs' use of digital technologies to practice domestic PD, as evident in consular applications. Indeed, scholars have asserted that in a global and digital world numerous government ministries collaborate with their foreign peers. As such, MFAs have lost their monopoly on managing a state's foreign affairs. Faced with narrowing remits within governments, MFAs now seek to cultivate a domestic constituency (Bjola & Manor, 2018; Hocking & Melissen, 2015; Huang & Wang, 2021). One way of doing so is providing services to national citizens, including consular services (Melissen & Caesar-Gordon, 2016). India's smartphone application may demonstrate a second shift – the growing demand for transparency in diplomacy. As some have argued, in the digital age everything once done in private must be done in public and for public consumption (Bauman & Lyon, 2013). Subsequently, digital publics now demand greater transparency from their diplomats. The question that follows is whether smartphone applications such as India's do promote a more transparent form of diplomacy or whether they offer the mere veneer of transparency by publishing press briefings and accords that could be accessible by the public through a simple internet search.

A second digital technology that warrants academic attention is WhatsApp groups which have become an important diplomatic tool. This was especially true during the Covid-19 pandemic. As diplomats practiced social distancing, and embassies were forced to shut their doors, WhatsApp groups were used to coordinate embassy responses to the pandemic, respond to media queries, manage engagement with digital publics and conduct routine embassy functions (Ullenhag, 2022). WhatsApp groups are also used regularly by ambassadors to the UN in Geneva to coordinate votes in UN forums, strengthen social ties between ambassadors and negotiate the texts of UN resolutions (Manor, 2018).

Ambassadors' use of WhatsApp groups may be used to examine two broader processes in PD. The first is the practicing of real-time diplomacy. Through WhatsApp groups, ambassadors can quickly respond to crises, or negotiate alterations to a UN resolution thus securing a majority of votes. Second, WhatsApp groups may indicate that the digitalization of PD evolves differently in different diplomatic venues. Geneva is an important multilateral hub in which ambassadors are accredited to many institutions including the ITU, WHO, ILO and the Human Rights Council. Thus, at any given time, Geneva ambassadors are in different parts of the city. WhatsApp groups enable ambassadors to coordinate action and ensure that members of a group all assemble in one venue when a crucial vote is taking place (Cornut, Manor & Blu, 2022). Yet it is possible that WhatsApp groups are not used by ambassadors to the UN in New York as most activities occur in the same building. Thus, it is incumbent on scholars to examine how digitalization evolves in different niche venues.

Equally important is an analysis of diplomats' use of big data in PD. In the wake of Brexit and Russia's disinformation campaign, the UK Foreign Office launched a big data unit tasked with monitoring and disabling fake social media accounts. Other MFAs, such as Lithuania, use big data analysis to identify Russian digital narratives that seek to undermine Lithuania's image (Manor, 2019). The growing use of big data brings to the fore another important research question – has the public become a problem in PD (Manor, Jiménez-Martínez & Dolea, 2021)?

In many MFAs, digital publics are now viewed as naïve at best, and gullible at worst. This is because publics are supposedly easily swayed by disinformation. The public then becomes a problem as it must be protected from disinformation and propaganda. Yet viewing the public as a problem, rather than a stakeholder, may lead to monumental shifts in PD activities as diplomats no longer seek to foster relationships with publics but manage publics' access to information. It is possible that the view of the public as a problem, may ultimately undo two decades of PD initiatives in which diplomats have tried to prioritize relationship building.

Finally, scholars must pay closer attention to diplomats' development of in-house algorithms. The Israeli MFA, for one, developed an algorithm that automatically reported hate speech on Facebook. This was part of an MFA-wide attempt to stem the flow of anti-Semitism on social media, which often includes calls for violence against Jews (Ratson, 2019). The British Foreign Office has created an open-source intelligence unit that uses algorithms to analyze swarms of online data and gather intelligence that can inform the activity of diplomats (Manor, 2019). In both instances, MFAs have developed digital skills and capabilities that require the recruitment of professionals including computer programmers and code writers.

This could represent another shift in PD as MFAs' digital units increasingly become inhabited by technological experts, rather than diplomats. While experts may offer data analysis, it is diplomats who can best determine what information would be of value to the MFA. It may also lead to a gap whereby diplomats no longer understand the technologies used to inform their work or grasp what information could be availed to them. Such a digital divide within an MFA would signal a new stage in the digitalization of PD, one marked by decreased digital agency as diplomats become wholly dependent on tech experts.

Diasporas: from traitors to saviors

Bernal (2014) has argued that in the digital age, national borders can expand and contract. When nations use digital technologies to engage with diasporas, the borders of the state expand digitally, and they come to include diasporas (Gilboa, 2022). However, when diasporas become critical of their origin country, states may seek to distance themselves from diasporas and so national borders contract. The digitalization research corpus has yet to investigate how diasporas leverage digital technologies to interact with either their host or origin country. Likewise, only a few studies to date have evaluated if, and when diplomats interact with diasporas. This represents a major gap for three reasons.

First, in many developing countries there has been a renewed emphasis on diaspora engagement. Although they were once viewed as traitors, who abandoned their origin countries during years of hardship, diasporas are increasingly viewed as saviors that can contribute to the financial prosperity of their origin country. This is especially true of African states that are heavily reliant on remittances sent by diasporas to family members left behind. The view of diasporas as saviors has led many countries to develop diaspora engagement strategies and these tend to focus heavily on the use of digital technologies. Countries such as Ethiopia, India, Kenya, Mexico and Rwanda have turned to social media to establish ties with diasporas (Manor & Adiku, 2021).

Second, diasporas may be viewed as boundary spanners. For instance, the children of diasporas, born in a host country, are viewed as digital assets as they sit at the intersection of several online networks. As such, they can help diplomats reach larger audiences. The "Know India" program, for instance, offers the children of diasporas the opportunity to visit India and learn about its rich culture and traditions. These youngsters are expected to share their experiences on social media thus offering their "friends" and peers a new perspective on India. It is therefore through diasporas that the "Know India" program can reach audiences across the globe. The program also nurtures an emotional bond between participants and their origin country, a bond that is central to the diasporic experience (Rana, 2013).

However, the aforementioned activities raise an important, ethical question and that is whether diplomats seek to create relationships with diasporas, or merely leverage diasporas toward increasing their digital reach. This question relates to the very core of the "New" PD and the use of digital technologies in PD. The "New" PD offered a vision of mutually beneficial relationships between states and digital publics, relations rooted in shared interests and goals (Cowan & Arsenault, 2008). It was the "New" PD that emphasized the term public over audiences. When using the word "publics," scholars and diplomats ascribed importance to their online contacts as publics have needs that must be addressed and a voice that must be listened to. So, while the term "public" denotes a dialogic approach to PD, the term audience relates to a broadcast approach in which diplomats speak while audiences listen and "share" information.

By researching diplomats' use of digital technologies in diaspora diplomacy, scholars may be able to discern if the promise of the "New" PD has been realized. Scholars may find that while diasporas are viewed as strategic partners that can strengthen bi-lateral ties, they are not equal partners in the communicative process. This would suggest that digitalization has not led to a "New" PD but has merely provided new tools for practicing traditional PD as diplomats speak at, not with, diasporas.

The digitalization of diaspora diplomacy should also be studied as it may offer insight into the role that emotions play in digitalized PD (Duncombe, 2019). A current review of the digital activities of MFAs and diplomats reveals that nostalgia is a common feature. Indeed, Russian digital diplomacy seeks to associate present-day Russia with the scientific achievements of the USSR, the British Foreign Office draws on World War II to narrate its post-Brexit foreign policies (Manor & Pamment, 2022) while Western diplomats now argue that a digital "iron curtain" is falling on Russia.

Nostalgia is a common feature in digital diplomacy given that digitalization leads to the creation of multiple and conflicting realities. When using digital technologies to narrate global events, states often fracture reality. For instance, according to some state websites, the city of Aleppo is finally rid of terrorists while residents are flocking back to rebuild their homes. According to other websites, the city of Aleppo has been reduced to rubble. Similarly, according to some sites, there is now a place known as the Republic of Crimea. It has borders, a parliament, and an MFA. According to other sites there is no such place. It does not exist. A world in which cities are simultaneously liberated and reduced to rubble, in which republics both exist and do not exist, is a world that cannot be fathomed by its inhabitants. In this way, states' use of websites, blogs and social media to narrate reality has fractured reality leading to high levels of uncertainty. To contend with uncertainty, diplomats use nostalgic tropes and summon the past to make sense of the present (Surowiec & Manor, 2021).

This is evident when diplomats use the term "Cold War" to describe US–China relations, when Russian diplomats speak of "spheres of influence" or when the UK promises to rebuild its once glorious British Navy. Of course, nostalgia is not the only emotion employed in digitalized PD. Humor and satire are also commonly employed by diplomats online as is fear spread through conspiracy theories (Chernobrov, 2021). Given that diasporas are characterized by an emotional link to their origin country, studying digital diaspora diplomacy may offer insight into the greater role that emotions now play in PD. Studies may examine how diplomats use digital technologies to nurture and cement an emotional bond with diasporas or how diasporas express this emotional bond through digital activities.

A hollow crown

It is a melancholy fact that on social media sites, one's worldview is shaped by who s/he follows. Sites such as Twitter or Facebook are not the utopian realization of a new town square but a dystopian reality in which information is carefully filtered through algorithms. These create walled gardens in which like-minded individuals can discuss topics ranging from international politics to the musings of Kanye West. Information is presented to social media users in the form of a feed, or a scroll of posts and tweets. Although PD studies have paid great attention to diplomats' use of social media, none have sought to research the impact that feeds have on users' engagement with PD content. This is a substantive gap given that social media sites are rich with emotional and cognitive stimuli that can impact users' willingness to interact with such content.

At the most basic level, feeds may mitigate a tweet's ability to shape users' beliefs and worldviews. This is because PD content is always part of a scroll of information, and tweets that precede diplomatic content may shape how diplomatic content is perceived. For instance, a Twitter user may enter his feed and view a video of a cat playing the piano, a tweet by President Donald Trump warning North Korea that he has a red nuclear button on his desk and, finally, a tweet celebrating a friend's workplace promotion. This user would assume that s/he was in the midst of an ordinary day under Trump. Another user may enter his feed and view a tweet by CNN warning of tensions between the two Koreas, Trump's nuclear tweet and a tweet with images from a North Korean military parade. This user would assume that war in the Korean peninsula is imminent. In this way, information that precedes and follows PD content may shape the importance ascribed to diplomatic tweets.

Moreover, language and images may have a priming effect. Written content and images that appear in a feed may impact a user's emotional and cognitive state. For instance, violent images or images of war and destruction may elicit negative emotions reducing social media users' willingness to interact with diplomats' messages. Conversely, inspirational images or images of celebrations may elicit a positive emotional state increasing users' willingness to stop scrolling through their feed and read a diplomat's message.

The same is true of certain topics. Tweets that deal with contentious issues such as police violence, or tweets bearing ill news such as Covid-19 updates, may trigger a negative emotional state leading users to log off Twitter before even reaching diplomats' tweets. Such topics may also elicit certain cognitive processes leading users to "skim" through their feed thus ignoring diplomats' content. However, information on major world events, such as geopolitical crises or war, may increase users' desire to engage with diplomats' content as users seek to make sense of the world around them.

The location of PD messages within a feed, the images that precede a diplomat's message and even topics discussed in a feed may thus all limit diplomats' ability to use social media sites toward relationship building and influence. Notably, the impact of social media feeds may be relevant to all PD actors ranging from MFAs and diplomats to cultural institutes, multilateral organizations, military alliances, activist groups, and civil society organizations. Addressing this important gap may require that PD scholars follow in the footsteps of social physiologists and media scholars who have researched the impact of priming for several decades. Rather than measure diplomats' reach, scholars may need to build simulated Twitter feeds and test the impact of priming through an experimental design that includes a study and control group. In such experiments, users would be exposed to the same tweet located in different feeds. For instance, a study group may encounter MFA tweets after viewing positive and negative images while the control group would encounter the same tweet at random. Scholars may then examine if feeds elicit specific online behaviors. For example, do positive images impact users' willingness to stop scrolling, read an MFAs' tweet and engage with that tweet through re-tweets or commenting?

Simulated feeds may be used to explore differences between PD actors. It is possible that feeds have a greater impact on users' willingness to engage with MFAs' message than with one tweeted by the UN. It is also possible that feeds impact users' willingness to engage with MFA tweets but not with diplomats' messages. This is because MFAs are associated with a nation state and its policies, while diplomats are viewed as peacemakers tasked with ensuring the tranquillity of international relations (Ish-Shalom, 2015). Given that social media feeds are rich with cognitive, visual and emotional stimuli, it is incumbent on PD scholars to turn their attention to the impact of feeds on digitalized PD. Although diplomats and scholars tend to view social media as the epitome of the "New" PD, social media sites may be adorned by a hollow crown.

Conclusions

The digitalization of PD will continue in coming years with diplomats seeking to leverage new technologies including virtual reality, augmented reality and immersive environments. However, scholars have yet to adequately investigate the current use of digital technologies in PD. Three major global events of recent years: the climate change conference in Glasgow, the Covid-19 pandemic and the Russian war in the Ukraine provide a wide range of potential case studies for future research. This chapter outlines three existing gaps, while demonstrating the insight to be gained by addressing each gap. As such, the chapter lays out a new research agenda for digitalized PD.

References

Al-Muftah, H., Weerakkody, V., Rana, N. P., Sivarajah, U., & Irani, Z. (2018). Factors influencing e-diplomacy implementation: Exploring causal relationships using interpretive structural modelling. *Government Information Quarterly, 35*(3), 502–14.

Antwi-Boateng, O., & Al Mazrouei, K. A. M. (2021). The challenges of digital diplomacy in the era of globalization: The case of the United Arab Emirates. *International Journal of Communication, 15*, 4577–97.

Bauman, Z., & Lyon, D. (2013). *Liquid surveillance: A conversation.* John Wiley & Sons.

Bernal, V. (2014). *Nation as network.* University of Chicago Press.

Bjola, C., & Manor, I. (2018). Revisiting Putnam's two-level game theory in the digital age: Domestic digital diplomacy and the Iran nuclear deal. *Cambridge Review of International Affairs, 31*(1), 3–32.

Bjola, C., & Pamment, J. (Eds.) (2018). *Countering online propaganda and extremism: The dark side of digital diplomacy.* Routledge.

Bortree, D. S., & Seltzer, T. (2009). Dialogic strategies and outcomes: An analysis of environmental advocacy groups' Facebook profiles. *Public Relations Review, 35*(3), 317–19.

Chernobrov, D. (2021). Strategic humor: Public diplomacy and comic framing of foreign policy issues. *The British Journal of Politics and International Relations, 24*(2), 277–96.

Collins, S. D., DeWitt, J. R., & LeFebvre, R. K. (2019). Hashtag diplomacy: Twitter as a tool for engaging in public diplomacy and promoting US foreign policy. *Place Branding and Public Diplomacy, 15*(2), 78–96.

Cornut, J., Manor, I., & Blu, C. (2022). WhatsApp with diplomatic practices in Geneva? Diplomats, digital technologies, and adaptation in practice. *International Studies Review.* https://doi.org/10.1093/isr/viac047.

Cowan, G., & Arsenault, A. (2008). Moving from monologue to dialogue to collaboration: The three layers of public diplomacy. *The Annals of the American Academy of Political and Social Science, 616*(1), 10–30.

Cull, N. J. (2008). Public diplomacy: Taxonomies and histories. *The Annals of the American Academy of Political and Social Science, 616*(1), 31–54.

Danielson, A., & Hedling, E. (2021). Visual diplomacy in virtual summitry: Status signalling during the Coronavirus crisis. *Review of International Studies, 48*(2), 243–61.

Danziger, R., & Schreiber, M. (2021). Digital diplomacy: Face management in MFA Twitter accounts. *Policy & Internet, 13*(4), 586–605.

Duncombe, C. (2019). The politics of Twitter: Emotions and the power of social media. *International Political Sociology, 13*(4), 409–29.

Eggeling, K. A., & Adler-Nissen, R. (2021). The synthetic situation in diplomacy: Scopic media and the digital mediation of estrangement. *Global Studies Quarterly, 1*, 1–14. https://doi.org/10.1093/isagsq/ksab005.

Enverga III, M. (2021). Helpful partner or infringing interloper? Examining discursive contestation in the engagements on the EU delegation in the Philippines' Facebook page. *Place Branding and Public Diplomacy,* 1–12. https://doi.org/10.1057/s41254-021-00216-4.

Fjällhed, A. (2021). Managing disinformation through public diplomacy. In P. Surowiec & I. Manor (Eds.), *Public diplomacy and the politics of uncertainty* (pp. 227–54). Palgrave Macmillan.

Garud-Patkar, N. (2021). An examination of factors influencing national reputation of India among south Asians on social media. *International Journal of Communication, 15*, 2442–61.

Gilboa, E. (2016). Digital diplomacy. In C. Constantinou, P. Sharp, & P. Kerr (Eds.), *Sage handbook of diplomacy* (pp. 540–51). Sage.

Gilboa, E. (2022). Theorizing diaspora diplomacy. In L. Kennedy (Ed.), *The Routledge international handbook of diaspora diplomacy* (pp. 379–92). Routledge.

Hallams, E. (2010). Digital diplomacy: The internet, the battle for ideas & US foreign policy. *CEU Political Science Journal, 4*, 538–74.

Hocking, B., & Melissen, J. (2015). *Diplomacy in the digital age*. Netherlands Institute of International Relations Clingendael.

Huang, Z. A., & Wang, R. (2021). Exploring China's digitalization of public diplomacy on Weibo and Twitter: A case study of the US–China trade war. *International Journal of Communication, 15*, 1912–39.

Ish-Shalom, P. (2015). King diplomacy for perpetual crisis. *The Hague Journal of Diplomacy, 10*(1), 10–14.

Ittefaq, M., & Kamboh, S. A. (2022). COVID-19 and national images: The case of #ResignModi. *Place Branding and Public Diplomacy, 18*(1), 15–17.

Kampf, R., Manor, I., & Segev, E. (2015). Digital diplomacy 2.0? A cross-national comparison of public engagement in Facebook and Twitter. *The Hague Journal of Diplomacy, 10*(4), 331–62.

Khan, M. L., Ittefaq, M., Pantoja, Y. I. M., Raziq, M. M., & Malik, A. (2021). Public engagement model to analyze digital diplomacy on twitter: A social media analytics framework. *International Journal of Communication, 15*, 1741–69.

Khatib, L., Dutton, W., & Thelwall, M. (2012). Public Diplomacy 2.0: A case study of the US digital outreach team. *The Middle East Journal, 66*(3), 453–72.

Kļaviņš, D. (2021). Mapping innovation diplomacy in Denmark and Sweden. *The Hague Journal of Diplomacy, 16*(4), 565–96.

Lee, G., & Kwak, Y. H. (2012). An open government maturity model for social media-based public engagement. *Government Information Quarterly, 29*(4), 492–503.

Manor, I. (2018, February 20). The evolution of WhatsApp as a diplomatic tool. exploring digital diplomacy. Retrieved from https://digdipblog.com/2018/02/20/the-evolution-of-whatsapp-as-a-diplomatic-tool/

Manor, I. (2019). *The digitalization of public diplomacy*. Springer.

Manor, I. (2021). The Russians are laughing! The Russians are laughing! How Russian diplomats employ humor in online public diplomacy. *Global Society, 35*(1), 61–83.

Manor, I., & Adiku, G. A. (2021). From "traitors" to "saviours": A longitudinal analysis of Ethiopian, Kenyan and Rwandan embassies' practice of digital diaspora diplomacy. *South African Journal of International Affairs, 28*(3), 403–27.

Manor, I., & Crilley, R. (2018). The aesthetics of violent extremist and counter-violent extremist communication. In C. Bjola and J. Pamment (Eds.), *Countering online propaganda and extremism: The dark side of digital diplomacy* (pp. 121–39). Routledge.

Manor, I., & Holmes, M. (2018). Palestine in Hebrew: Overcoming the limitations of traditional diplomacy. *Mexican Journal of Foreign Policy, 113*, 1–17.

Manor, I., Jiménez-Martínez, C., & Dolea, A. (2021, November 16). An asset or a hassle? The public as a problem for public diplomats. *The Hague Journal of Diplomacy Blog*. Retrieved from https://www.universiteitleiden.nl/hjd/news/2021/blog-post---an-asset-or-a-hassle-the-public-as-a-problem-for-public-diplomats.

Manor, I., & Pamment, J. (2022). From Gagarin to Sputnik: The role of nostalgia in Russian public diplomacy. *Place Branding and Public Diplomacy, 18*, 44–8. https://doi.org/10.1057/s41254-021-00233-3.

Manor, I., & Segev, E. (2015). America's selfie: How the US portrays itself on its social media accounts. In C. Bjola & M. Holmes (Eds.), *Digital diplomacy theory and practice* (pp. 89–108). Routledge.

Manor, I., & Segev, E. (2020). Social media mobility: Leveraging Twitter networks in online diplomacy. *Global Policy, 11*(2), 233–44.

Mazumdar, B. T. (2021). Digital diplomacy: Internet-based public diplomacy activities or novel forms of public engagement? *Place Branding and Public Diplomacy*, 1–20. https://doi.org/10.1057/S41254-021-00208-4.

Melissen, J. (Ed.) (2005). *The new public diplomacy*. Palgrave Macmillan.

Melissen, J., & Caesar-Gordon, M. (2016). "Digital diplomacy" and the securing of nationals in a citizen-centric world. *Global Affairs, 2*(3), 321–30.

Metzgar, E. T. (2012). Is it the medium or the message? Social media, American public relations & Iran. *Global Media Journal*, 1–16. http://bit.ly/2y9NWof.

Pamment, J. (2013). *New public diplomacy in the 21st century*. Routledge.

Rana, K. S. (2013). Diaspora diplomacy and public diplomacy. In R. S. Zaharna, A. Arsenault, & A. Fisher (Eds.), *Relational, networked and collaborative approaches to public diplomacy: The connective mindshift* (pp. 70–85). Routledge.

Ratson, E. (2019). Understanding Israeli algorithmic diplomacy [in person].

Seib, P. (2012). *Real-time diplomacy: Politics and power in the social media era*. Palgrave Macmillan.

Sevin, E. (2018). Digital diplomacy as crisis communication: Turkish digital outreach after July 15. *Mexican Journal of Foreign Policy, 113*, 185–207.

Sevin, E., Ayhan, K. J., & Ingenhoff, D. (2021). Capturing country images: A methodological approach. *The Journal of International Communication, 27*(2), 237–57.

Spry, D. (2018). Facebook diplomacy: A data-driven, user-focused approach to Facebook use by diplomatic missions. *Media International Australia, 168*(1), 62–80.

Spry, D., & Lockyer, K. (2022). Large data and small stories: A triangulation approach to evaluating digital diplomacy. *Place Branding and Public Diplomacy, 18*(2), 243–61.

Surowiec, P., & Manor, I. (Eds.) (2021). *Public diplomacy and the politics of uncertainty*. Palgrave Macmillan.

Ullenhag, E. (2022). Using digital diplomacy during the pandemic [in person].

Wright, K. A. (2019). Telling NATO's story of Afghanistan: Gender and the alliance's digital diplomacy. *Media, War & Conflict, 12*(1), 87–101.

Yarchi, M., Samuel-Azran, T., & Bar-David, L. (2017). Facebook users' engagement with Israel's public diplomacy messages during the 2012 and 2014 military operations in Gaza. *Place Branding and Public Diplomacy, 13*, 360–75.

18 Hybrid communication

Jian Wang and Jack Lipei Tang

Introduction

The outbreak of Covid-19 will be remembered as a singular global crisis moment. While the pandemic does not alter the fundamental dynamics already underway, it is accelerating the change concerning our thinking and practice in public diplomacy (PD). One aspect of the change is a hybrid future, where the various tools and platforms of PD are to be re-evaluated and re-adjusted to develop a spectrum of experiences through integrating both in-person and digital elements. This chapter seeks to explore the conceptual foundations for hybrid communication in PD and to identify research areas that will help us better understand the evolving practice.

The impact and implications of the pandemic have been examined as a striking communication phenomenon. Indeed, it provides a critical discourse moment that reveals societal tensions and dynamics. As expected, much research attention is directed at public health and crisis communication. For instance, the journal *Health Communication* convened a special research forum "Public Health Communication in an Age of COVID-19" in 2020 to explore the role of communication in shaping perceptions and behaviours in the context of the pandemic. Topics ranged from norms formation, identity and political ideology, and communicating uncertainty, to messaging in an evolving social media environment, visual communication, and community-level health promotion. The pandemic has sharpened research focus on the rapidly unfolding conduct and consequences of misinformation and disinformation (Brennen et al., 2020; Enders et al., 2020). In the consumer marketplace, for example, retailing is undergoing dramatic transformation as a result of advances in digital technology and changing purchasing behaviour resulting from the pandemic (Grewal et al., 2021). The pandemic has also changed the tone and tenor of corporate communication, against the backdrop of growing brand activism and a greater public awareness of safety and lifestyle balance (Ward, 2021).

Closer to the field of PD, the National Intelligence Council's Global Trends 2040 report noted, "the ongoing Covid-19 pandemic marks the most significant, singular global disruption since World War II, with health, economic, political and security implications that will ripple for years to come." Kissinger (2020) declared that the pandemic "will forever alter the world order". Others are more sceptical of the pandemic's transformative effects on global affairs, as Drezner (2020) argued in the article he published in *International Organization*'s special issue on Covid-19 and international relations. Nonetheless it does seem clear that the pandemic has further exposed the fault lines between national and cultural communities and exacerbated the existing tensions in globalization as manifested in the mobility of goods, information and people.

As Brooks (2020) observed in his *New York Times* column, if history is any guide, unlike natural disasters such as hurricanes and earthquakes, pandemics generally drive people apart rather than bring them together. The pandemic is a key element in diplomacy as it shapes a nation's reputation and soft power as well as international relationships. It also serves as a catalyst for technological adoption to expand the reach and impact of diplomacy. The pandemic has renewed attention to health diplomacy in bilateral, regional and global contexts (Fazal, 2020; Kolker, 2020). Zaharna (2021) argued that the pandemic heightens the need for a humanity-centred PD rather than a state-centric approach to realize collaborative problem solving for the global good. The experiences of virtual diplomacy during the height of the pandemic have laid the groundwork for hybrid diplomacy in the years to come. As noted in a report by *The Economist* (1 May 2021, p. 55), "Covid-19 has hastened the arrival of hybrid diplomacy, a blend of the physical and digital."

In this chapter, we address the concept of hybridity in PD. There is a vast interdisciplinary literature on hybridity. Our goal is to provide some conceptual grounding for analysing hybridity in PD practices through a review of relevant research. The scope of the review is modest, as we focus on how hybridity, as a technological arrangement, has been conceptualized and discussed in studying communicative practices. For the purpose of this chapter, we view PD as a nation's engagement with foreign publics, through the toolkit of informational, educational and cultural programmes, to advance policies and actions. Our illustrative focus will be on educational and cultural programming rather than information advocacy, the other mainstay of PD, which requires a different set of analytical paradigms and frames of references.

We start with a discussion of the fundamental shifts in PD in the context of the pandemic. The next section examines the concept of hybridity in a range of disciplines and discusses their relevance and implications for the study and design of hybrid communication through combining in-person and virtual communication in PD. We then put forth key issues and opportunities in understanding hybridity for future PD research.

Public diplomacy goes hybrid

The upheaval wrought by the Covid-19 pandemic is unmistakable. The pandemic has changed the way we work, shop and play; and that has taken place across geographies and nations as we are all at risk. Digital adoption has experienced exponential growth in the aftermath, surpassing pre-pandemic levels. As the pandemic simmers down, digital growth has begun to plateau (Hajro et al., 2021). Given the erratic nature of the virus and the uncertainty it continues to engender, the post-pandemic focus is increasingly on the "Phygital" – the intertwining of the physical and digital worlds, a phenomenon that began before this pandemic but is now taking on new significance and prominence.

The pandemic is likewise poised to change some of the fundamental practices and processes of PD. Wang and Yang (2019, p. 294) outlined the overarching disruptive, interwoven trends on the global scene along every key aspect of communication, including context, audience, platform, player, and issue concern. The pandemic has only accelerated these changes and adjustments already underway in global affairs and communication. The context and environment for PD is becoming more volatile and competitive.

For instance, the field of cultural and educational exchanges sees a steady increase of programmes and offerings by major and middle power nations (see Chapters 13 and 16 in this volume). Furthermore, our age of information abundance creates an "attention economy" – the poverty of attention necessitates the competition for attention. As a result, the rapidly evolving information eco-system is exacerbating distrust and division (e.g. Settle, 2018). Compounding this communication challenge are the rising geopolitical tensions, which include political realignments currently unfolding in various parts of the world. Although it is still premature to ascertain what the contours of the practice might look like beyond the pandemic, as in other sectors, some pandemic-induced behaviours will stay, while others will be replaced by new ways of doing things.

Much of PD is grounded in the value of direct face-to-face interaction in enabling real and genuine human engagement. This is especially the case in the long-standing practices of cultural programmes and exchanges, with the general aim of nurturing mutual understanding as a bedrock of international relationships. Such engagement through physical co-presence is believed to be essential to illuminating commonalities between peoples and societies across national boundaries. Moreover, intergroup contact theory suggests that interactions and contacts may help reduce prejudice and conflict between groups (e.g. Pettigrew et al., 2011). Cultural and educational programmes are a modest avenue for developing capacity for international and cross-cultural understanding and cooperative behaviour. These programmes rely on the "last three feet" effect, which represents an elemental form of human communication.

Even before the pandemic, our digital life started to interact ever more with the physical realm. On the one hand, digital access through connected devices is having a growing influence on one's perceptions and behaviours surrounding their world. On the other hand, in a growingly tech-infused world, there seems to be a craving for a sense of conviviality that in-person engagement provides. Physical presence remains fundamental as a transcultural human condition. This has been made particularly poignant, as national and individual isolation and confinement during the pandemic have accentuated the need to recover our senses of space and place.

As pointed out in the *Socially Distanced Diplomacy* report,

> While much of the world remains frozen in a socially distanced stasis and international travel remains nearly impossible, the need for meaningful global engagement, higher levels of trust between allies and international partners, and effective cross-border collaboration has only intensified. The role of soft power and PD in delivering on these fronts remains paramount" (McClory, 2021).

The Covid-19 pandemic makes it apparent to us that, despite the ease of communication through digital tools, something fundamental is missing when we are removed from our physical environment.

From a practical standpoint, there is general agreement that in-person engagement is most effective for building relationships and creating trust, especially when dealing with complex and challenging issues. Meanwhile, our pandemic experience has shown that "digital platforms have opened up opportunities for new conversations, new participants, and new ideas" (McClory, 2021). For instance, virtual exchange programmes during the pandemic have demonstrated the benefit of being more inclusive by being able to engage a much broader array of participants. The absence of regular international travel has reduced carbon footprint, making exchange programmes more climate friendly. Moreover, online engagement makes exchange programmes more open-ended by expanding interaction opportunities both before and after the exchange experience.

Admittedly, much of PD engagement is hybrid to start with. The current endeavour is about reconfiguring engagement and experience through an optimized mix of virtual and face-to-face interactions. As digital technology provides a key capacity for PD to grow and expand, it is crucial to figure out what is worth doing in-person vis-à-vis remotely by leveraging the efficiency and convenience afforded by digital capability. The question then becomes how we integrate the need for creating a distinct digital presence in PD programmes and that for maintaining human touch through direct person-to-person contact. This is no different from the wider discussion surrounding the notion of "Phygital" in consumer marketing – "the combination of physical and digital for enhanced experience" (Prior, 2021). And for PD, hybrid engagement is the question of how the online and offline worlds complement each other in creating and maintaining relationships. We next review various frameworks and approaches to hybridity in a range of literature to make sense of the general conceptual grounding and to explore implications for PD research and practice.

Hybridity: a conceptual overview

Hybridity refers to the process whereby separate social structures or practices mix to produce new elements. Derived from biology, the concept and discourse of hybridity quickly expands to literary theories, cultural research and social sciences (García-Canclini, 2001). The theoretical connotations of hybridity usually vary across disciplines. For example, hybridity is used by post-colonial scholars to allow cross-boundary experiences when discussing the politics of difference and diaspora. The previous social and conceptual demarcation is drawn between us and them or between one race and another, which is obfuscated by globalization (Ang, 2003; Drichel, 2008). Hybridity confronts and problematizes boundaries and always implies an unsettling of identities. In a broader sense, as Paz (1999, pp. 80–81) wrote, "the great creations, be they collective or individual, are the result of the fusion of different, event opposing elements. Culture is hybridity." By extension, Kraidy (2002) called for addressing hybridity in international communication scholarship.

The concept of hybridity has been applied in the analysis of various forms of organizations, including regimes, government bureaucracies, corporations and civil society groups (Rantanen, 2021). In media studies, hybridity refers to the ambivalence of genres of media products and suggests a new form of audience engagement of such media works (Bore, 2009). Or as Chadwick (2013, p. xi) has noted, this mixed genre represents "systemic hybridity in flow – in information consumption and production patterns". Economic hybridity of media content, on the other hand, refers to a media franchise that represents both public interest and private profit-driving goals (Patterson, 2016).

Communication scholars describe the current media landscape as a hybrid media system such that different audiences are targeted through a variety of media channels (Chadwick, 2013). Political campaigns with hybrid competence would be more influential than a singular form of media engagement (Karlsen & Enjolras, 2016). In these contexts, the fluidity of hybridity allows scholars to describe the state of mixing and fusing boundaries across various social and cultural conditions and offers new opportunities to think about the consequences of such a mixture.

Hybrid communication

The emergence of information and communication technologies (ICTs) transforms the human communication process. In this chapter, we are particularly interested in the sociotechnical construction of hybrid communication, a mode of communication that breaks the boundary between the online and offline, mixes experiences of the in-person and the virtual, and generates unprecedented communication practices and consequences.

Researchers from the fields of interpersonal communication and computer-mediated communication (CMC) have devoted much effort to understanding how online communication supplements, suppresses or mixes with face-to-face communication. For instance, compared with face-to-face communicators, people who are making conversations through computer-mediated channels express more affection and relaxation (Walther, 1995). People already integrate CMCs into their daily lives, which has proven to be a valuable tool for many to initiate, develop and maintain relationships (Rabby & Walther, 2003). Vergeer and Pelzer (2009) found that online network capital augments offline network capital. The network capital was measured in terms of network size and time spent on the network.

While communication is just one aspect of socializing activities, the results of studies like this one imply that online communication could strengthen offline communication in both communication network size and the time people spend in that communication network. A longitudinal study conducted in Germany (Dienlin et al., 2017) found that social network site (SNS) communication increased both face-to-face communication and instant message (IM) communication six months later.

Likewise, offline interaction can affect the characteristics of online interaction. Matzat (2010) found that a mixture of virtual and real-life interaction, in contrast to purely virtual interaction, among members of knowledge-sharing online communities reduces the problems of sociability, namely, lack of trust and free-riding behaviours. By reducing the problems of sociability, offline networks facilitate online knowledge sharing, while in other settings, the internet is mainly used as a tool to obtain information, and it is the social ties formed in the computer club that facilitate social interactions among a group of older Americans (Xie, 2007). Zuo et al. (2012) revealed that more than half of the online interactions are included in the offline interaction network in a conference. The results show that physical contact in a social proximity-based system can lead to more online interaction.

Previous literature has also documented the benefits of hybrid communication in practice. For example, blended care, a combination of online and face-to-face therapy, is being applied in mental health care to obtain optimal health outcomes (Wentzel et al., 2016); blended learning, the convergence of online and face-to-face education, could support academic success and engage students more effectively (Watson, 2008).

The application of hybrid communication reshapes the experiences of events visitors. Digital arts communities can utilize both cyberspace and physical gatherings to allow social interaction and knowledge creation. Online discussion and offline participation in major arts festivals can formulate the hybrid community (Marletta, 2010). Another study examining hybrid event communities identifies three virtual practices: connection, recruitment and creation. The everlasting online social interaction supplements the events with limited time and space (Simons, 2019). Yet, it is worth noting that most of the event organizers agree that the success of the event is based on the offline experience, especially the offline interaction quality (Lu, 2019).

The integration of digital technologies in public engagement

ICTs have reshaped the human communication process and, as the last section demonstrated, hybrid communication has emerged as a new communication modality that combines the advantages of both online and offline interaction.

Specifically, a wide range of cutting-edge technologies has been integrated into the communication process especially in the setting where the public is engaged, such as exhibitions, museums and urban communities. The introduction of these interactive technologies into public engagement has completely transformed the relationship among the environment, the media and the people.

Since the 2000s, hybrid spaces and networked communities of place have emerged. Offline communities are being suffused with digital layers and social networks that were also taking place online which further facilitates community participation in educational, cultural, health care, and other venues (Fernback, 2005). The urban community can benefit from hybrid forms of community engagement that are enacted through a constant back and forth between online and face-to-face interactions (Mosconi et al., 2017). To cite an example, the hybrid forms of community engagement combine online interactions in a closed Facebook group with face-to-face meetings and engage the public in accomplishing certain immediate or ongoing needs (Mosconi et al., 2017). By presenting the exciting new possibilities for engagement and communication across boundaries, the hybrid cyber- and physical-space nurture inclusion and diversity that are core values in the democratic process of community building (Fernback, 2005).

The introduction of virtual technology to exhibitions and museums quickly draws scholarly attention to understand the best practices of the arrangement and the effects of such technological reform. In the museum setting, technological affordances (such as live chat, 3D navigation, customization) can enhance perceived reciprocity, social presence, reality and usability (Sundar et al., 2015), which later translate into an overall more positive visiting experience. The presence of augmented reality (AR) and virtual reality (VR) objects are found to be correlated with the enjoyment of visitors in a virtual museum (Sylaiou et al., 2010). Compared with an immersive 360-degree VR video and physical visit, the 2D video tour significantly lowers participants' spatial presence and emotional engagement with the tour. The 360-degree video tourism can be a good analogue to a real-world experience (Wagler & Hanus, 2018). Immersion and interaction are the two most important dimensions to understand how AR and VR technologies become potential means of communication for cultural experiences (Carrozzino & Bergamasco, 2010).

In addition to enhancing the visitors' experience and engagement with the cultural artefacts, the technologies (e.g. AR, VR) can protect the cultural artefacts, and multimedia information can be easily stored and retrieved. However, images produced by the advanced graphic system can be too realistic. Also, computer reconstructions are often based on partial evidence, which might be biased towards historical objects (Styliani et al., 2009).

The power of digital technologies can be maximized when the optimal environment design (e.g. physical layout and accessibility) is present (Kim, 2018). This study argued that compared with dynamic visual cues, dynamic verbal cues lead to visitors' higher levels of willingness to pay more, and the effects are strengthened when environmental augmentation provides a high level of virtual presence. Appropriate installation of technologies with the aid of environment design seems to generate the most desirable outcomes.

In concerts and sports games, the effect of using digital technologies on liveness and satisfaction is more complicated. It is common to see the audience waving their smartphone recording, uploading, and sharing the performance of musicians or the exciting moments of a game. The boundaries of these live events are extended to the online audience who are remotely located. The audience who are physically present collects and preserves the moments but also tries to remain engaged in the events (Bennett, 2016). In addition, the use of smartphones such as texting, taking pictures, and recording a clip can be seen as a distraction by other audiences. Therefore, many stadiums and arenas prohibit the use of smartphones by spectators during events (Hutchins, 2016). Taking photos at exhibitions may also lower the chance of revisiting by visitors as the experience has been remembered by the machine (Lee et al., 2021). These tensions question the use of technologies by acknowledging the sense of being there together and liveness. However, with proper guidance, the use of mobile communication devices can increase the time visitors spend at exhibitions and the levels of mindfulness and perceived learning (Hughes & Moscardo, 2017).

Further research

The general concept of hybridity underscores "complexity, interdependence and transition" (Chadwick, 2013, p. 10). About digital technology and its transformational impact, hybridity needs to be conceptualized as relational, rather than binary as in the simple dichotomy of online versus offline. In this respect, practices of hybridity provide a spectrum of experiences across the physical and virtual worlds. There are tensions and opportunities in this dynamic relationship between online and offline spheres. Our thinking of their interaction and integration began with, if not first rooted in, the physical world. From there and with the adoption of digital technology, we consider the extent to which technology enhances or inhibits, replaces or supplements physical experience.

As digital technology further expands into our daily lives, our attention turns to the question of how the physical might in fact shape and structure the digital. There is also the possibility of juxtaposing the physical and the digital experiences as parallel, separate spaces all together. The next generation of the internet "the metaverse", a form of "3-D internet" that spans the physical and virtual worlds, is gaining growing momentum. As noted in a McKinsey & Company (Hazan et al., 2022) report, the metaverse is here to stay, given ongoing technological advances, wider applications of the metaverse, and major investments in its infrastructure. As brands start to explore marketing opportunities in the metaverse, venture capitalist Matthew Ball wrote in the *Wall Street Journal* (2022, p. C4) that metaverse-related applications have moved "beyond consumer leisure into infrastructure, healthcare and warfare". A related development is that of "Web3", an internet platform that builds upon blockchain technologies. While still at their early stages, these technologies and platforms, as they evolve, are poised to significantly impact the hybridity of PD.

As the prospects of hybrid PD take shape, a core research question becomes how in-person and virtual interactions influence each other based on their respective qualities. How do they reconcile tensions and structure PD outputs and shape outcomes? Specifically, in the realm of cultural programming and exchanges, we may raise several key questions for research. One set of questions is to develop better understanding of the general practices of online and offline engagement in the aftermath of the pandemic. How do online and offline practices interact with and affect each other in programme design, its implementation and participant experience? How are AR and VR tools deployed in PD, and how do they impact PD audiences? Are there patterns of processes and practices that are germane to hybridity of communication in general, and are there features and characteristics specific to the PD realm? What are the factors and mechanisms underlying the structuring of a hybrid experience?

Another set of issues addresses the expectations of programme participants in the ways of combining different modes of engagement. This arises from the need for appreciation of variations across countries and locations, due to regulations, politics and user behaviours, which all are highly pertinent to PD work. How to arrive at a right balance of in-person and virtual engagement practices first and foremost depends on participant needs, preferences and constraints. Does PD continue to embody "places-based" approaches? Are there geographic patterns in hybrid PD?

The other potential research path is to look at how the hybrid mode of communication in PD affects community and network building as PD outcomes. While virtual communication might accelerate the tie formation among different sectors such as government organizations and business communities (Wang, 2006), it remains a puzzle how strong such ties are compared with conventional face-to-face communications in building cross-border relationships. Hybrid communication can also create hybrid ties and how such hybrid ties might create cohesion and clustering in the community could be highly useful for practitioners. Lastly, it is essential to understand how hybrid communication influences community building at different levels (i.e. national, regional and global) as various forms and tools of diplomacy are required to meet the multilevel network building process (Goff, 2015).

This chapter has explored the concept and literature of hybridity and discusses the implications for PD research from the perspective of hybridity as a technological arrangement. The paths and patterns of integrating in-person and virtual engagements provide new opportunities to make sense of the benefits and limits of PD in a digitally enabled environment. The applications of theories and concepts of hybridity in the PD realm will add to our general understanding of hybrid communication.

References

Ang, I. (2003). Together-in-difference: Beyond diaspora, into hybridity. *Asian Studies Review, 27*(2), 141–54. https://doi.org/10.1080/10357820308713372.
Ball, M. (2022, August 13–14). What the metaverse will mean. *Wall Street Journal*, p. C4.
Bennett, L. (2016). Fandom, liveness and technology at Tori Amos music concerts: Examining the movement of meaning within social media use. In M. Reason & A. M. Lindelof (Eds.), *Experiencing liveness in contemporary performance* (pp. 48–59). Routledge.
Bore, I.-L. K. (2009). Negotiating generic hybridity: Audience engagement with *The Office. Continuum, 23*(1), 33–42. https://doi.org/10.1080/10304310802570882.
Brennen, J. S., Simon, F. M., Howard, P. N., & Nielsen, R. K. (2020). *Types, sources, and claims of COVID-19 misinformation*. Reuters Institute for the Study of Journalism, University of Oxford. https://www.hsdl.org/?abstract&did=836968.
Brooks, D. (2020, March 12). Pandemics kill compassion, too. *The New York Times*. https://www.nytimes.com/2020/03/12/opinion/pandemic-coronavirus-compassion.html.

Carrozzino, M., & Bergamasco, M. (2010). Beyond virtual museums: Experiencing immersive virtual reality in real museums. *Journal of Cultural Heritage, 11*(4), 452–8. https://doi.org/10.1016/j.culher.2010.04.001.

Chadwick, A. (2013). *The hybrid media system: Politics and power.* Oxford University Press.

Dienlin, T., Masur, P. K., & Trepte, S. (2017). Reinforcement or displacement? The reciprocity of FtF, IM, and SNS communication and their effects on loneliness and life satisfaction. *Journal of Computer-Mediated Communication, 22*(2), 71–87. https://doi .org/10.1111/jcc4.12183.

Drezner, D. W. (2020). The song remains the same: International relations after COVID-19. *International Organization, 74*(supplement), E18–E35.

Drichel, S. (2008). The time of hybridity. *Philosophy & Social Criticism, 34*(6), 587–615. https://doi.org/10.1177/0191453708090330.

Enders, A. M., Uscinski, J. E., Klofstad, C., & Stoler, J. (2020). The different forms of COVID-19 misinformation and their consequences. *The Harvard Kennedy School (HKS) Misinformation Review, 1*(8). https://misinforeview.hks.harvard.edu/article/the -different-forms-of-covid-19-misinformation-and-their-consequences/.

Fazal, T. M. (2020). Health diplomacy in pandemic times. *International Organization, 74*(supplement), E78–E97.

Fernback, J. (2005). Information technology, networks and community voices. *Information, Communication & Society, 8*(4), 482–502. https:// doi .org/ 10 .1080/ 13691180500418402.

García-Canclini, N. (2001). Hybridity. In *International encyclopedia of the social & behavioral sciences* (pp. 7095–8). Elsevier. https://doi.org/10.1016/B0-08-043076-7/00890-1.

Goff, P. M. (2015). Public diplomacy at the global level: The Alliance of Civilizations as a community of practice. *Cooperation and Conflict, 50*(3), 402–17. https://doi.org/10 .1177/0010836715574915.

Grewal, D., Gauri, D. K., Roggeveen, A. L., & Sethuraman, R. (2021). Strategizing retailing in the new technology era. *Journal of Retailing, 97*(1), 6–12.

Hajro, N., Hjartar, K., Jenkins, P., & Vierira, B. (2021, May 23). What's next for digital consumers. McKinsey Digital. https:// www .mckinsey .com/ capabilities/ mckinsey -digital/our-insights/whats-next-for-digital-consumers.

Hazan, E. et al. (2022). Marketing in the metaverse: An opportunity for innovation and experimentation. *The McKinsey Quarterly.* https:// www .mckinsey .com/ capabilities/ growth -marketing -and -sales/ our -insights/ marketing -in -the -metaverse -an-opportunity-for-innovation-and-experimentation.

Hughes, K., & Moscardo, G. (2017). Connecting with new audiences: Exploring the impact of mobile communication devices on the experiences of young adults in museums. *Visitor Studies, 20*(1), 33–55. https://doi.org/10.1080/10645578.2017.1297128.

Hutchins, B. (2016). We don't need no stinking smartphones! Live stadium sports events, mediatization, and the non-use of mobile media. *Media, Culture & Society, 38*(3), 420–36. https://doi.org/10.1177/0163443716635862.

Karlsen, R., & Enjolras, B. (2016). Styles of social media campaigning and influence in a hybrid political communication system: Linking candidate survey data with Twitter data. *The International Journal of Press/Politics, 21*(3), 338–57. https://doi.org/10.1177/ 1940161216645335.

Kim, S. (2018). Virtual exhibitions and communication factors. *Museum Management and Curatorship, 33*(3), 243–60. https://doi.org/10.1080/09647775.2018.1466190.

Kissinger, H. (2020, April 3). The Coronavirus pandemic will forever alter the world order. *Wall Street Journal*. https://www.wsj.com/articles/the-coronavirus-pandemic-will-forever-alter-the-world-order-11585953005.

Kolker, J. (2020). COVID-19 and global health governance. *The Foreign Service Journal* (July/August). https://afsa.org/covid-19-and-global-health-governance.

Kraidy, M. M. (2002). Hybridity in cultural globalization. *Communication Theory, 12*(3), 316–39.

Lee, J. C., Cui, Y. (Gina), Kim, J., Seo, Y., & Chon, H. (2021). Photo taking paradox: Contrasting effects of photo taking on travel satisfaction and revisit intention. *Journal of Travel Research, 60*(4), 833–45. https://doi.org/10.1177/0047287520912334.

Lu, D. (2019). Connecting online and offline worlds: The impact of cross-boundary artifact on hybrid communities. PhD dissertation, University of Pittsburgh. http://d-scholarship.pitt.edu/id/eprint/37965.

Marletta, D. (2010). Hybrid communities to digital arts festivals: From online discussions to offline gatherings. In D. Riha & A. Maj (Eds.), *Emerging practices in cyberculture and social networking* (pp. 83–96). Rodopi.

Matzat, U. (2010). Reducing problems of sociability in online communities: Integrating online communication with offline interaction. *American Behavioral Scientist, 53*(8), 1170–93. https://doi.org/10.1177/0002764209356249.

McClory, J. (2021). *Socially distanced diplomacy: The future of soft power and public diplomacy in a fragile world*. Sanctuary Counsel and USC Center on Public Diplomacy. https://uscpublicdiplomacy.org/sites/default/files/Sanctuary%2BCounsel%2BCPD_Socially%2BDistanced%2BDiplomacy%2BReport_May%2B2021.pdf.

Mosconi, G., Korn, M., Reuter, C., Tolmie, P., Teli, M., & Pipek, V. (2017). From Facebook to the neighbourhood: Infrastructuring of hybrid community engagement. *Computer Supported Cooperative Work, 26*(4–6), 959–1003. https://doi.org/10.1007/s10606-017-9291-z.

Patterson, E. (2016). This American franchise: This American Life, public radio franchising and the cultural work of legitimating economic hybridity. *Media, Culture & Society, 38*(3), 450–61. https://doi.org/10.1177/0163443716631287.

Paz, O. (1999). *Itinerary: An intellectual journey*. Harcourt.

Pettigrew, T. F., Tropp, L. R., Wagner, U., & Christ, O. (2011). Recent advances in intergroup contact theory. *International Journal of Intercultural Relations, 35*, 271–80.

Prior, P. (2021, June 30). Phygital – what is it and why should I care. *Forbes*. https://www.forbes.com/sites/forbesbusinesscouncil/2021/06/30/phygital---what-is-it-and-why-should-i-care/?sh=53b43e68587a.

Rabby, M. K., & Walther, J. B. (2003). Computer-mediated communication effects on relationship formation and maintenance. In D. J. Canary & M. Dainton (Eds.), *Maintaining relationships through communication* (pp. 141–62). Routledge.

Rantanen, T. (2021). Toward hybridity? Nationality, ownership, and governance of news agencies in Europe. *Journalism & Mass Communication Quarterly, 98*(1), 263–82. https://doi.org/10.1177/1077699020923605.

Settle, J. E. (2018). *Frenemies: How social media polarizes America*. Cambridge University Press.

Simons, I. (2019). Events and online interaction: The construction of hybrid event communities. *Leisure Studies, 38*(2), 145–59. https://doi.org/10.1080/02614367.2018.1553994.

Styliani, S., Fotis, L., Kostas, K., & Petros, P. (2009). Virtual museums, a survey and some issues for consideration. *Journal of Cultural Heritage, 10*(4), 520–28. https://doi.org/10.1016/j.culher.2009.03.003.

Sundar, S. S., Go, E., Kim, H.-S., & Zhang, B. (2015). Communicating art, virtually! Psychological effects of technological affordances in a virtual museum. *International Journal of Human–Computer Interaction*, 31(6), 385–401. https:// doi.org/ 10 .1080/ 10447318.2015.1033912.

Sylaiou, S., Mania, K., Karoulis, A., & White, M. (2010). Exploring the relationship between presence and enjoyment in a virtual museum. *International Journal of Human–Computer Studies*, 68(5), 243–53. https://doi.org/10.1016/j.ijhcs.2009.11.002.

Vergeer, M., & Pelzer, B. (2009). Consequences of media and Internet use for offline and online network capital and well-being: A causal model approach. *Journal of Computer-Mediated Communication*, 15(1), 189–210. https://doi.org/10.1111/j.1083 -6101.2009.01499.x.

Wagler, A., & Hanus, M. D. (2018). Comparing virtual reality tourism to real-life experience: Effects of presence and engagement on attitude and enjoyment. *Communication Research Reports*, 35(5), 456–64. https://doi.org/10.1080/08824096.2018.1525350.

Walther, J. B. (1995). Relational aspects of computer-mediated communication: Experimental observations over time. *Organization Science*, 6(2), 186–203.

Wang, J. (2006). Public diplomacy and global business. *Journal of Business Strategy*, 27(3), 41–9. https://doi.org/10.1108/02756660610663826.

Wang, J., & Yang, A. M. (2019). Public relations and public diplomacy at a crossroads: In search of a social network perspective. In J. Strömbäck & S. Kiousis (Eds.), *Political public relations: Principles and applications*, 2nd edn (pp. 287–307). Routledge.

Ward, D. (2021, September 2). *How COVID-19 is changing how companies communicate*. Association of Equipment Manufactures. https://www.aem.org/news/how-covid19-is -changing-how-companies-communicate.

Watson, J. (2008). Blended learning: The convergence of online and face-to-face education. Promising practices in online learning. In *North American Council for Online Learning*. North American Council for Online Learning. http:// eric .ed .gov/ ?id = ED509636.

Wentzel, J., Vaart, R. van der, Bohlmeijer, E. T., & Gemert-Pijnen, J. E. W. C. van (2016). Mixing online and face-to-face therapy: How to benefit from blended care in mental health care. *JMIR Mental Health*, 3(1), e4534. https://doi.org/10.2196/mental.4534.

Xie, B. (2007). Using the internet for offline relationship formation. *Social Science Computer Review*, 25(3), 396–404. https://doi.org/10.1177/0894439307297622.

Zaharna, R. S. (2021). *Boundary spanners of humanity: Three logics of communications and public diplomacy for global collaboration*. Oxford University Press.

Zuo, X., Chin, A., Fan, X., Xu, B., Hong, D., Wang, Y., & Wang, X. (2012). Connecting people at a conference: A study of influence between offline and online using a mobile social application. *2012 IEEE International Conference on Green Computing and Communications*, pp. 277–84. https://doi.org/10.1109/GreenCom.2012.52.

Index